AGRARIAN SOCIALISM

SEYMOUR MARTIN LIPSET is professor of government and sociology and a member of the Center for International Affairs at Harvard University. He has been professor of sociology and director of the Institute of International Studies at the University of California, Berkeley, and Henry Ford Visiting Research Professor of Political Science and Sociology at Yale. He has also been visiting professor at the University of Warsaw and the Free University of Berlin. He is author of, among other books, POLITICAL MAN (A330) and THE FIRST NEW NATION (A597); co-author of UNION DEMOCRACY (A296); and co-editor of THE BERKELEY STUDENT REVOLT (A486).

AGRARIAN SOCIALISM

THE COOPERATIVE COMMONWEALTH
FEDERATION IN SASKATCHEWAN

A Study in Political Sociology

S. M. LIPSET

Anchor Books

DOUBLEDAY & COMPANY, INC.
GARDEN CITY, NEW YORK

Agrarian Socialism was originally published by the University of California Press in 1950. The Anchor Books edition has been revised by the author and is published by arrangement with the University of California Press.

Anchor Books edition: 1968

TO THE MEMORY OF MY FATHER

MAX LIPSET

WHO HAD THE SAME DREAMS

AS THE FARMERS OF SASKATCHEWAN

CONTENTS

INTRODUCTION TO THE ANCHOR EDITION

To RETURN intellectually to a book one wrote two decades ago is a peculiar experience. On one hand, the fact that some people think well enough of the book to be interested in publishing a new paperback edition is flattering. On the other hand, in rereading the book, I feel chagrined about parts of it that strike me as weak, and that I would do differently if I were beginning the research with my present knowledge.

Agrarian Socialism is a reworking of my doctoral thesis in sociology at Columbia University. My reasons for selecting the topic at the time were at least as much political as scholarly. As a young socialist, I was interested in learning why an avowedly socialist party, the Cooperative Commonwealth Federation, was winning elections in Canada, when comparable efforts had brought no such success in the United States. At the time, the CCF had won a majority in Saskatchewan, was the second largest party and the official opposition in Ontario and British Columbia, and had considerable strength in Manitoba.

From my then limited knowledge of Canada, it seemed that many of the social conditions that various commentators had cited to explain "why there is no socialism in the United States" were also present in Canada. Yet, there was socialism in Canada. The conditions precluding it most often mentioned for the United States included the effects of an open land frontier and the absence of a feudal past, with a characteristic high rate of social mobility (supposedly endemic in an expanding frontier society) and a low level of status differentiation, compared to European nations. Two other factors suggested to explain the absence of socialism, which seem to be present both in Canada and the United States, are a high per capita income and an early history, prior to the emergence of a mass working class, of a democratic society based on two strong major parties and universal manhood suffrage. From outward appearances the success of a socialist party in Canada indicated that these explanations were either wrong or limited in character. That is, they did not include some pertinent factors. One purpose of the study, then, was to try and specify what was present in the Canadian situation that made it easier for a mass socialist party to emerge there than in the United States.

A second, somewhat different interest was my concern with the forces at work that checked the power of socialist parties to produce democratic reforms once they assumed office. Long before beginning graduate work, I became particularly impressed, as I have written before, with the analysis of oligarchy and bureaucracy within socialist parties contained in Robert Michels' *Political Parties*. Michels argued that oligarchy was ever present, an inevitable product of the organization, within mass parties, and that the heads of such parties, in or out of office, were primarily concerned with organizational stability and not with democratic or egalitarian social reform. In different ways, the history of Communism and Social Democracy in office in various parts of Europe validated Michels' propositions. A close study of a new socialist government and its relations with its party seemed to offer an opportunity to shed further light on these problems.

Much of the book is addressed to understanding why the CCF came to power in Saskatchewan, and for that reason an emphasis was put on the special conditions of the wheat-belt social structure and the Saskatchewan polity that encouraged farmers to form and support a radical third party. Included in these conditions were the tensions fostered in a prairie economy by unstable wheat prices and frequent droughts, and the one-class social structure in which wheat farmers in roughly similar social and economic conditions formed and staffed a large variety of non-governmental institutions.

The original edition of *Agrarian Socialism* dwelt at length on how the farmers developed and formed a political leadership elite from among themselves. At the time of the study I saw a partial explanation of this in the existence of a condition unique to western Canada—the rural municipality, which did not include any urban communities no matter how small. Except for this difference between a county system in the United States that includes both rural and urban communities, and a system that separates them, the social and economic conditions of the province seemed like those in the states south of the border. For instance, as my reading and fieldwork went on, I became increasingly impressed with the great similarity between the economic and political behavior in Saskatchewan and in North Dakota. The Non-Partisan League, formed by American socialists, with a program not unlike that of the CCF, had in fact held power for many years in North Dakota. It, however, eschewed the word socialism and operated as a faction within the state Republican Party.

These findings suggest that the big difference between the United States and Canada, in their relative propensities to throw up third parties, lies in their varying electoral systems. The U.S. system with its concentration on elections of Presidents and governors reduces the significance of constituency strength and makes it much harder to create third parties. In the United States the effective constituency in national elections is really the entire country; in the state it is the entire state. This has prevented American third parties from building up local constituencies such as labor, agrarian, religious, or ethnic parties have done in some single constituency systems. The primary system of nominations also encouraged factions to remain within their original party rather than to form new ones. By permitting different factions within the party to compete in state-conducted, intraparty contests to determine party candidates and officials, the interests and values of different groups—which would give rise to third parties elsewhere—are given a chance to be expressed within the major parties. Hence the Canadian electoral system of constituency elections and the absence of primaries has been a major differentiating element.

While this explanation is hinted at in *Agrarian Socialism,* it is not really developed in any sense, and I must confess that, while I was aware of its importance, I did not then see it as a major factor. Subsequent consideration of the variations between Canada and the United States did bring me to suggest that comparative evidence indicates that constitutional provisions determining electoral systems and ways of choosing executives are probably as important as any of the broad sociological factors that are adduced to explain why the United States has a two-party system. It seems clear that the comparative question between the United States and Canadian electoral systems is not why there is a successful socialist party in Canada and not in the United States, but rather why Canada has supported a large number of third parties—socialist, Social Credit, Progressives, and assorted French Canadian ones in Quebec.

In subsequent writings on Canadian politics, I concluded that with a constituency parliamentary system, the United States would probably have a multi-party system, one of which would be a labor party.[1] This analysis was later elaborated beyond consideration of the United States and Canada into a detailed comparison of the relationship between social structure and party systems and the ways in which they are affected by electoral systems.[2]

A basic weakness of the original study, then, was my failure to consider the rise of the CCF in Saskatchewan in its larger Canadian framework. I did not ask what elements in Canadian economic and social structure may have contributed to the specific form politics took in the country as a whole and in Saskatchewan in particular. Since then, further research on differences between Canada and the United States has suggested two broad categories of relevant factors, one economic and the other sociohistorical.

The economic relates to the relative role of exports in the economics of the two great North American democracies. While the United States had become a major industrial society in which primary production and exports constituted a small proportion of the gross national product, the Canadian economy of the 1930's continued in some ways to resemble that of the late nineteenth-century United States. The export of primary products—agricultural, furs, minerals—constituted a major segment of the economy. This meant that while the United States could establish domestic prices for wheat and other agricultural products that were above the world market price, and could guarantee farmers a constant profitable price level, Canada could not do so. Thus Canadian wheat farmers received a much lower and more variable price for their product than the farmers south of the border. In a sense, prairie Canada remained in a situation comparable to that of the prairie United States in the late nineteenth and early twentieth centuries.

These periods in the United States saw the rise of the Populist Party and later of the Non-Partisan League, agrarian movements that fostered programs in the wheat belt quite similar to that advocated by the CCF decades later. Agrarian radicalism in the United States wheat belt declined sharply with the emergence of federal price-support programs. But it remained a viable force in Canada for at least another generation, because it took the rapid industrialization and urbanization of the 1940's and 1950's, together with a heavy demand for Canadian wheat from the Communist and emerging nations, to create comparable conditions for Canadian agriculture.

The political consequences of these changes in Canada have been obvious. Since the 1958 elections, Saskatchewan and other parts of the prairies have opted for a predominant Conservative representation in the Federal House of Commons. The Conservative Party, in office during the period 1957 to 1962, was credited with the economic improvements, and as a result there was a heavy shift in its direction. In the 1958 elections, the CCF lost seats that it had controlled since the formation of the party, including Rosetown-Biggar, the constituency long held by its national leader, M. J. Coldwell. And it has not succeeded in winning a federal constituency in Saskatchewan since that time. A recent study of Canadian elections, based on survey data, reports that in the 1958 election, held after the Conservatives had been in office for slightly over a year, 22 per cent of the prairie electorate who had voted CCF in the previous election opted for the party of Prime Minister Diefenbaker. Four years later, almost a fifth of those plains residents who had remained loyal to the CCF in 1958 also turned to back the incumbent Conservatives.[3] Thus, by 1962 about one third of those western Canadians who backed the CCF before John Diefenbaker, the prairie "radical" leader of the Conservatives, took office in 1957, had shifted to his party. Clearly, in western Canada, as in the United States, the achievement of the agrarian goal of guaranteed wheat prices has sharply reduced the support for agrarian radicalism. It has not ended it, of course, since the CCF still secures a substantial vote in federal elections and has remained one of the two major provincial parties.

On the more broadly sociological level, my earlier analysis of Saskatchewan politics erred in not seeing that Canada and the United States did vary in highly significant ways that have affected their political life. As S. D. Clark and Frank Underhill have pointed out, Canada has been a much more conservative, traditional, and hierarchical-elitist society than the United States. These differences stem from the varying histories of the two nations. The United States is a result of a victorious revolution against British rule; Canada is an outgrowth of the triumph of the counterrevolution. The disparate results of the revolution meant the creation of two very different national ethos. One took pride in being the result of a revolution, and emphasized egalitarian and populist elements in its self-image. Canada justified itself in not being like the United States; it long took pride in its ties with Britain, its monarchical institutions, its elitist character. Following the American Revolution, Tories migrated north of the new border, supporters of the revolution moved south. The established Anglican Church was strengthened in the north; the Congregational Church was reinforced by the migration of its ministers south.[4]

These initial differences tended to inform later events in both countries. American political parties following the rise of Jacksonian democracy justified themselves as popular parties. In Canada, the democratic populist forces tended to lose their struggles through most of the nineteenth century. To protect itself against a constant tendency of the Canadian frontier to identify with the United States, the Canadian government emphasized centrally controlled structures. If in the United States sheriffs and marshals responsive to local sentiment dominated the law-enforcement scene, in Canada it was the National Northwest Mounted Police who kept law and order on the frontier and in the mining camps. A tradition of respect for authority and for law and order far stronger than that in the United States has remained down to the present. Crime rates in Canada remain considerably lower than in the United States.

The very strength of hierarchical status, traditional religion, and governmental authority in Canada has meant that in a variety of ways, which I have documented elsewhere, Canadian values fall somewhere between those of Britain and the United States, rather than being almost identical with those of the United States, as I had assumed when working on *Agrarian Socialism*. One consequence of the relative conservatism of Canadian society has been that greater emphasis is placed on particularist group identifications, especially ethnic and regional but also, to some limited degree, class and status. Canadian education has remained more elitist and less widespread than education in the United States. Seemingly, one result of a Canadian society more particularistic, more European than the United States, is this greater potential for third parties, a European characteristic.

And if one assumes that this set of comparative generalizations about Canada and the United States is valid, then as Canada becomes more modern, more "American," more urban, many of the social and political differences separating the two nations will decline. It still remains true, however, that the differences between the two countries that are exhibited in the Canadian propensity to give greater support to particularist third parties reflect the greater conservatism of the larger Canadian society, rather than its greater liberalism. Clearly, a detailed study of Canada's parties in this context would produce somewhat different results than my original one. It suggests that agrarian socialism in Saskatchewan, reflecting the effects of economic forces discussed earlier, was a consequence of anachronistic forces within the society, rather than a wave of the future.

Another weakness of the work, to which some Saskatchewan reviewers called attention after the book appeared, was its lack of appreciation of the limits placed on the Saskatchewan CCF as party and government by the fact that it was operating within a provincial polity that was a relatively small segment of a large federal union and national party. The limitations on the local party were less significant during the 1930's and early 1940's than later, since the Saskatchewan party was by far the strongest unit within the national CCF. The Saskatchewan CCF supplied the national leader, M. J. Coldwell, and for at least two parliaments furnished half or more of the M. P.'s elected under the party's banner throughout Canada.

The limitations placed on the provincial government were more significant. Like the other less populous and industrialized provinces, Saskatchewan has limited taxation revenues. The CCF government, together with the governments of these other provinces, called for a national taxation program in which the federal government would collect all income taxes and then redistribute these to the provinces. Such a system would enable the rural provinces to share in the taxable wealth of richer provinces such as Ontario, Quebec, and British Columbia. Without increased federal support, any efforts drastically to enlarge the welfare program of the province would require increased provincial taxation in the form of direct, highly visible taxes, the only ones that the Canadian constitution permits a province to levy. Rightly or wrongly, the CCF in Saskatchewan felt that such tax increases would be highly unpopular with its rural constituency. Hence, the absence of a sympathetic government in Ottawa placed sharp limits on the freedom of action of the Saskatchewan CCF. One of the reasons that the Saskatchewan government held back in implementing its early commitment to a system of socialized medicine was the hope that the federal government would ultimately provide a major part of the additional revenues such a system would require. The provincial government was even more limited in what it could do to improve the economic conditions of the farmers, since matters affecting farm prices were exclusively in the hands of the federal government. Its efforts in this regard were largely reduced to acting as a pressure group on the federal government, and to seeking new markets abroad.

In dealing with urban labor and trade unions, the CCF had the majority in the provincial legislature to pass progressive labor legislation, raise minimum wages, and other similar measures, and as I documented in the book, it did so. However, these policies had basic limits as well, since Saskatchewan could hardly afford to get far out of line with comparable policies in the rest of the country and still hope to attract industry. Finally, the opposition parties in the province were, of course, only too willing to point out that increased salaries for provincial government employees, or for employees of the distributing institutions, were ultimately paid for by the farmers in the form of higher taxes or prices.

The position of the Saskatchewan party within the national party has become more delicate with the gradual change in the national electoral base. The creation of federal government policies that deal more adequately with prairie agriculture's demand for constant prices; federal aid in securing irrigation; and crop insurance sharply weakened the voting strength of the CCF, not only in Saskatchewan but in rural Manitoba and Alberta as well. But while the party declined in these areas, it retained or increased its federal base in urban centers, particularly in British Columbia, Manitoba (Winnipeg), and Ontario.

The unified Canadian labor movement, formed as a result of joining the Canadian Congress of Labour (CIO) and the Trades and Labour Congress (AFL) into the Canadian Labour Congress (AFL-CIO), created a trade-union polity with a CCF majority. This came about because the CIO unions had always been overwhelmingly friendly to the CCF, while within the AFL the CCF had been backed by a sizable minority. The CCF supporters within the trade-union leadership decided to reconstruct the national party under a new label, the New Democratic Party. From a public standpoint, the new party formed in 1961 was largely a merger of the old CCF with the trade-union movement, and it is now viewed by many as a Canadian labor party. This growth in trade-union influence within the national party may have contributed to the relative weakness of the CCF in rural areas of the west. In Saskatchewan, as the essay in this volume by Sanford Silverstein documents, the party is now much stronger among urban labor than among the farm population. It may be that a trade-union-oriented, left party has inherent difficulties in securing support of farmers. It is certainly true that many in the Saskatchewan party opposed seeing the CCF absorbed in the New Democratic Party even though the national leader is T. C. Douglas, the former premier of Saskatchewan. The Saskatchewan party has resisted the name change, voting in convention to call itself the Cooperative Commonwealth Federation, Saskatchewan Section of the New Democratic Party. An analysis of Canadian voting patterns also suggests the effort to create a new party image with a large trade-union component has contributed to the CCF-NDP weakness in the 1960's. The study quotes as typical the statement of a fifty-two-year-old farmer from Rosetown-Biggar, who had voted CCF all his life but had shifted to support Diefenbaker, saying: "That party [the CCF] has done more for the common man than any other—but they are a labour party now."[5]

A major theme of *Agrarian Socialism* is the analysis of the way the high level of agrarian community and occupational organization among the farmers contributed to their political activity and to democracy within the CCF. I attempted to show that party conferences did function as realistic means of communication between sentiment at the rural grass roots and the party summits. I argued that the Saskatchewan CCF has been more democratic in this sense than urban-based parties in Canada and other countries. The Saskatchewan movement indicated limitations on Michels' iron law of oligarchy. At the same time I also pointed out that the factors in the Saskatchewan social structure that made for a high level of rural political activity were declining with the improvement in communications and transportation facilities. Cars and good roads meant the breakdown of the significance to the rural community of the network of political and social communications that once were so necessary, and the increased domination of the growing urban centers over the cultural and political life of the farm areas. In a real sense, Saskatchewan over the past two decades has become more like Manitoba, with which I contrasted it in the book. If rural participation in Manitoba was weaker than in Saskatchewan thirty years ago because Winnipeg dominated the life of the province in ways that Saskatchewan cities did not, this difference between the two provinces is now much smaller. Regina and Saskatoon and other cities have grown considerably, while the farm population has declined sharply. One would expect, if the analysis presented in the book is correct, that grass roots involvement in the formation of party policy would have been weakened, and the essay in this edition by John Richards indicates that this is correct.

Any renewed interest in Saskatchewan must, of course, consider the impact of twenty years of power upon a reform party. Since I have not done any recent fieldwork in the province, I do not want to comment in precise terms on this problem. Clearly, a detailed study of what happened to the party over this period is in order. Not the least source of change is the fact that those who joined or moved up in the party hierarchy or government since 1944 were joining a party in power. One is hardly engaged in radical activity in adhering to such a movement. The limitations placed on provincial action, discussed earlier, have meant that with some important exceptions, among which the medicare proposals are the most important, the party exhausted most of the innovations within its power within a few years after taking office. From then on, it would seem, its main claim to electoral backing was the ability to administer the province better than its opponents. And as it became clear that the party was not gaining electoral strength, it necessarily became more cautious in fostering new policies.

Perhaps the most intriguing question, then, in the history of the Saskatchewan CCF as a government, is why it decided after eighteen years in office to bring in the highly controversial medicare program. To some degree, this innovation can also be related to its gradual loss of strength. Party leaders felt the need to find an issue around which they could rally their increasingly apathetic supporters, one that had also been historically popular among the farm population. There is some indication that this strategy did not work. The fight over medicare seemed to revolve around those who opposed it—largely the middle class—much more than it stirred those who traditionally supported the CCF. But it permitted the CCF to go out of office in a blaze of glory, and gave the party a national issue with which the more deprived segments of the Canadian population could identify.

The enactment of a comprehensive system of medicare that covered all residents of the population bears witness to the significance of ideology on the actions of the party leaders. The party and Saskatchewan farmers may not be "socialists" as Bennett and Krueger argue in their essay in the second half of this book, but the Saskatchewan CCF certainly remains one of the most progressive large parties in Canada or the United States. Some more detailed analysis of the social change effected in different areas of the polity by ideological commitments that have been institutionalized in party form would certainly be worth investigating. Perhaps the best way to do this is to compare the activities of the conservative Social Credit government in Alberta with those of the Saskatchewan CCF. Both parties and governments are products of a major depression, which stimulated agrarian radicalism. One moved in a sharply conservative direction, the other reduced its reformist zeal but remained committed to an image of a cooperative commonwealth, or a more egalitarian society, in which the state uses communal resources to upgrade the poor, to reduce the hazards inherent in economic changes. There has not yet been an adequate explanation, or even a detailed descriptive account of the factors involved that resulted in such different reactions from two quite similar social units. Really to understand agrarian socialism, one must also understand agrarian reaction. It is a weakness of my work that it did not try to deal with this problem in depth.

The political potential of rural population has become of critical importance in recent years, particularly in the economically less developed areas of the world. The Chinese Communists have explicitly identified the peasantry and landless rural labor as the key source of mass support for revolutionary parties. Lin Piao, Mao's designated successor, has described the revolutionary process as one in which the countryside surrounds and overwhelms the city.[6] A Latin American Marxist sociologist has recently attempted to demonstrate that the peasantry in his area fulfill Marx's conditions for a class to play a self-conscious revolutionary role.[7] On the other hand, there is abundant evidence from various European countries that peasants have furnished a large part of the social base of fascist and reactionary movements, such as the Nazis in Germany in the 1930's and the Poujadist movement in France in the 1950's. In the United States, the North Dakota wheat farmers who strongly backed the left-wing, radical Non-Partisan League in the years just before and after World

War I also constituted a major portion of the support for the Union Party led by Father Charles Coughlin in the 1936 Presidential elections. Common to most forms of agrarian protest movements, whether of the left or right, has been antagonism to symbols of urban power, often in the form of banks, middlemen, and big business, but sometimes also trade unions.

It is clear that farmers may be recruited for sharply different types of politics: left, right, and center, democratic and authoritarian. Some of the differences are a function of variations in major social conditions, i.e., relative wealth—whether landowners, tenants, or farm laborers; stability or instability of crop yields and prices; relations with urban areas; links to other institutions such as churches; proportion of the population in national, or in local rural polities; electoral systems; degrees of group organization; and many others. What this listing of variables points to, of course, is that one can no more talk of the politics of the "rural population" than of "urban people." Each must be differentiated among categories that can react quite differently politically.

What makes rural politics somewhat confusing, however, is that in many countries, it is dependent politics. That part of the farm population that can be mobilized politically is often won by various different urban groups. Or, as the case of the North Dakota wheat farmers illustrates, the same farm strata may at different times, or within different political units, identify with sharply variant urban ideologies. When farmers are faced with major social problems, such as those faced by the prairie farmers, protest movements, any one of which can promise guaranteed farm prices and reduction of the power of that part of the urban economy the farmers deal with, may win support. Thus rural politics, far from being steady and traditional, often seems to be highly volatile. Some of the same people who voted for the CCF have also backed Social Credit and the Conservatives in Saskatchewan. We need more detailed knowledge than has been gathered in this book or others, on what party identification means to farmers.

Although agrarian socialism may no longer be important in Canadian politics, the national movement it fostered is currently (Fall 1967) stronger than ever. In the 1967 provincial elections, it gained considerably in percentage of popular vote in Saskatchewan (45) and Ontario (26). The labor-based NDP appears to have a good chance to become the second largest party in Canada. If it does, it may very well reclaim a considerable proportion of the prairie wheat-belt electorate. But whether it succeeds or not, the fact remains that the credit for introducing dynamic reformist politics into Canadian politics in the twentieth century must go to the embattled wheat farmers of Saskatchewan. Changes in the social and economic situation have undermined their potential to continue as the political vanguard of the country. But no one will be able to understand the reasons for changes in Canadian party structure without seeing how the strains and social organization inherent in the wheat belt fostered a maximum degree of self-conscious, self-interested politics.

When plans were first broached for an Anchor paperback edition of *Agrarian Socialism* some years ago, I thought of returning to Saskatchewan for a few months in order to do a small follow-up survey. Because of other commitments, it proved difficult to find the time, and I was very pleased, therefore, to learn that in the Department of Sociology and Anthropology of Washington University at St. Louis some members of the faculty and graduate students had been engaged in research on different aspects of Saskatchewan. The University had, in a sense, developed a center of Saskatchewan studies. This seemed to offer the opportunity to have the follow-up written by others, who could bring the advantages of new insights and detailed research on the issues I had dealt with earlier. I invited a number of the people engaged in such research to write essays for this book. The results of this work are reported in the second part of this book in the essays written by Bennett, Krueger, Gouldner, Richards, and Silverstein. Unfortunately, this section does not have the comprehensive coverage I had hoped for, since some of the people who had planned to write for it found they could not do so. I do feel, however, that the essays that were completed add considerably to the value of this volume, particularly since a subject that is treated comprehensively, the medicare program and the doctors' strike, is clearly the most important event in the recent history of the province.

These essays, of course, do not try to evaluate the efforts of the CCF government and party in any detailed way. This subject remains to be treated, and it is my hope that this new edition of *Agrarian Socialism* may stimulate such an effort. There have been few political units, relatively small in population, as interesting as the province of Saskatchewan. Over the past two decades its people have been actively engaged in a series of efforts to modify social institutions. Theirs is not the story of a failure, but of an experiment still in progress.

This enlarged version of *Agrarian Socialism* has been made possible by support provided by the Center for International Affairs of Harvard University. I would also like to express my appreciation to all those at Washington University who have written for this volume. And I would like to repeat again my gratitude to Robert S. Lynd, without whose encouragement and help the original study would never have been completed. To Lynd, the opportunity to study the early stages of a radical government was the kind of chance that comes once in a lifetime. And he convinced me I could do it. I still feel a little awed, even at this distance in time and space, that a young man from New York City, who had literally not been more than a few miles west of the Hudson, could think of heading off to the Canadian prairies to study the political behavior of wheat farmers. That the effort turned out reasonably well, I owe also to the patience of the many hundreds of Saskatchewan residents who were willing to try to teach me. I recommend to other social scientists further efforts to learn from the people of Saskatchewan.

SEYMOUR MARTIN LIPSET

Cambridge, Massachusetts
January 1967

NOTES

1. S. M. Lipset, "Democracy in Alberta," *The Canadian Forum*, 406 and 407 (1954), pp. 175–77, 196–98.

2. S. M. Lipset, "Party Systems and the Representation of Social Groups," *European Journal of Sociology*, 1 (1960), pp. 50–85.

3. Peter Regenstreif, *Parties and Voting in Canada. The Diefenbaker Interlude* (Toronto: Longmans, Green & Co., 1965), pp. 137–39. See also John C. Courtney and David E. Smith, "Voting in a Provincial General Election and A Federal By-Election: A Constituency Study of Saskatoon City," *Canadian Journal of Economics and Political Science* 32 (1966), pp. 338–53 for further evidence of the interchangeability of CCF and Conservative support.

4. I have brought together much of the material bearing on the interpretation of the United States as the product of the revolution, and Canada of the counterrevolution, in S. M. Lipset, "Revolution and Counter-Revolution—The United States and Canada," *The Revolutionary Theme in Contemporary America* ed. Thomas Ford (Lexington: University of Kentucky Press, 1965), pp. 21–64.

5. Regenstreif, *op. cit.*, p. 142.

6. Lin Piao, "Long Live the Victory of the People's War!", *Peking Review*, 8 (Sept. 3, 1965), pp. 9–30.

7. Anibal Quijano, "Contemporary Peasant Movements," *Elites in Latin America* ed. S. M. Lipset and Aldo E. Solari (New York: Oxford University Press, 1967), pp. 301–40.

Part I
AGRARIAN SOCIALISM

FOREWORD

No PHENOMENON is more urgently in need of study today than the conditions under which new social movements may emerge in our society. Man's fate in societies living by big technology, urbanization, and division of labor is from now on a collective one. But social atomism has deeply corrupted our capacity to live together; and both personally and collectively our helplessness grows as democracy wanes. The recovery of democracy, if indeed it can occur, can happen only through men thinking together of what it is they want and organizing to move together. As a study at first hand of such a contemporary people's movement on our continent, Professor Lipset's deeply perceptive study is of first-rate importance.

We people on the North American continent have been bemused by our favored circumstances. We came to a new continent rich in resources coincidentally with the upsurge of the machine age. Protected by continental isolation, we have been able to take ourselves and our institutions for granted while we spread out westward in the pursuit of wealth. The abundance of our good fortune relative to older, crowded nations abroad has encouraged in us a pragmatic, unspeculative temper; and as a result today we watch with skepticism and not a little impatience the innovations of nations across the world that have forsaken liberal go-as-you-please and are attempting to discover new and more effective ways of living together.

History will probably look back on the twentieth century as one of the great eras of institutional change, comparable in magnitude to the shifts from feudalism to capitalism and the age of power-driven machinery. Industrial society is being forced toward one or another form of collective organization because the effort to operate modern technology under rules appropriate to the eighteenth century is wracking society to pieces.

As liberal society resists this change, it is taking on more and more the form of what in Europe is called "mass society." This does not mean "big" in the numerical sense, but the attrition of strong, spontaneous ties among men and the resulting loss of durable, autonomous standards of thinking and feeling and acting. Men in mass society become social atoms suspended in insignificance, acted upon but incapable of initiative save in the narrowest personal sense. Hitler deliberately exploited and speeded up this movement in German industrial society, as a necessary condition for the imposition of Nazi controls, by seeking to capture, neutralize, or destroy vocational and recreational organizations, the churches, and even the autonomy of the family.

Among us, the tendency to mass society accompanies the growth in the business world of bigness and power without responsibility, of urban propinquity careless of social belonging, and the resulting depersonalizing of all social processes. So much of decision making has ceased to go forward at the level of a man's eye and subject to local relevance and control that democracy is becoming a form increasingly devoid of feeling tone and is denied in action. As persons we are blurred; as citizens we become helpless participants in actions we do not understand. It is difficult to sustain the personal tensions of such living as social irrelevants in the midst of large issues that dominate our lives. So, as our public lives become more helpless, we seek escape and the sense of personal recovery through turning away from the issues themselves. We give over to others the search for solutions to our social dilemmas, while we concentrate on means to momentary self-identity, seeking a sense of personal idiom through such specious spontaneities as rivalrous consumer spending.

In such circumstances, those solicitous for the welfare of democracy search the horizons for signs of genuine democratic organization. And it is precisely such a movement that Professor Lipset here analyzes. That a regathering of the forces of democracy should appear on the agricultural periphery of industrial society is significant. Farmers, especially those in the one-crop economy of the Great Plains, embody in an extreme form the modern anachronism of the independent enterpriser bereft of control over his market, a stranger in the ruling institutional world of organized urban big business. And yet the farmer retains, better than the urban man, sources of resistance to the mass tendency: he produces a product that men indubitably need, and he accordingly respects his crop, the land that produces it, and his own labor. He and his family, especially in regions remote from large cities, know the value of cooperative social living, and they are relatively less distracted by the impersonal substitute activities that accompany competitive urban getting and spending. Here is a stance from which a man may still believe in the democratic right to stand and fight.

And yet even this show of independence may be a passing phase. The farmer owns or aspires to own land, and Hitler found massive support among German farmers by exploiting this desire. Our own world of industrial controls has discovered the political power of crop subsidies, and, presumably, the party of big business will not again overlook, as did the Republican Party in 1948, the clamor of farmers for storage facilities for their crops. In the present era, in which progress may no longer be taken for granted as a built-in feature of liberal democracy, and in which the volume and finesse of controls from the top of a class-stratified social system are rapidly increasing, it becomes more than ever important to study the conditions under which men can and will cease to "grin and bear it" and can and will organize to make their wants politically effective.

The urban middle class may not be looked to for democratic leadership. They have, it seems probable, learned far less than both the upper class and labor about the meaning of events since the First World War. Their nostalgia for a vanishing way of life is deep and genuine, whereas the upper class of big business uses these now primitive symbols only as convenient political weapons.

Today, democratic leadership can come, if it comes at all, only from labor, if possible in collaboration with farmers. And the growth of organized labor in the United States in the past decade and a half would seem to suggest, as does the

Labor government in Britain, that labor is on the offensive.
But labor itself has become big business in the managerial
struggle of business unionism for a widening share of the
capitalist "take"; and it remains to be seen whether big profit-
oriented labor, operating under narrow bureaucracies habitu-
ated to managing the rank and file, will or can become more
than a junior partner within a limited welfare capitalism.
Those who view the fountain of progressive social legislation
as inexhaustible should bear in mind the historic "ransom"
character of such legislation, and the prospect that capitalism
may reach the point where it neither can nor will continue to
grant such concessions. Perhaps only then will labor on this
abundant continent recognize its true class position and prepare to fight. But in this extremity, if the lessons of fascism
have been learned, it may be too late.

Can the fire spread from the prairies? I do not know how
far Professor Lipset would go in agreement with my appraisal
of the position in which we appear now to find ourselves. But
I have read and reread his close analysis for clues as to the
larger potentialities of this "provincial socialist beachhead
within capitalism." Here exists as clear and clean a democratic
base as yet remains on this continent: a pervasive web of
organization and participation. In wheat pools and other cooperatives and local services there is one elective position for
every two or three farmers in Saskatchewan. After nearly
fifty years of agrarian organization, "The CCF has succeeded
in involving more people in direct political activities than any
other party in American and Canadian history, with the possible exception of certain similar farmers' parties." In 1945, 8
per cent of the electorate belonged to the party.

Here indeed is healthy democratic tissue, democracy living
as it has largely ceased to live among urban men. But the
apparent singleness of the pressure on the farmer living by a
one-crop economy deceives him even as it unites him; for, as
Professor Lipset so well shows, it fails to equip him for the
bold extension of his somewhat parochial version of democracy to other elements in a wider population living predominantly by urban industry and trade. As the cooperating farmer's ideology meets the factory worker and the middle-class
businessman, it wavers, blurs, and recedes. An agrarian social-

ist party becomes a liberal agrarian protest movement, and programs for the socialization of industry falter. Truly, he who sets out to make significant reforms should never hesitate or compromise!

As this is written, the Cooperative Commonwealth Federation as a national party in Canada has been thrown into retreat. In June, 1948, its systematic work at the level of municipal politics, in addition to its provincial and national campaigning and trade-union support in urban areas, was bearing fruit; and observers were speaking openly of the prospect of its superseding the Conservative Party as the official opposition to the Liberals in Ottawa. But the national election in June, 1949, brought crushing defeat. The CCF captured only 13 seats in the national Parliament, a scant 3 more than the Social Credit Party, while the Liberals won 190 seats and the Conservatives 42. Even in Saskatchewan, where a CCF government had been in power for five years, the Liberals won 14 of the 20 seats in the national Parliament. There was evidence that many voters throughout Canada voted in a "Stop Socialism" mood. How much the election reflected Canadian reaction to the Labor government in Britain and to anti-left propaganda from the United States it is difficult to say.

Likewise, it is hard to estimate the impact of the new mineral and industrial prosperity that has come to the Prairie Provinces since the war. They now realize the advantages of diversifying their economic base by inviting new industry. Coal and natural gas abound in Alberta, next door to Saskatchewan, and since 1947 Imperial Oil (a Standard Oil subsidiary) has found oil in abundance in Alberta and to a somewhat lesser extent in Saskatchewan. This casts a dangerous light on socialism in Saskatchewan and is likely to invite serious pressures upon the CCF.

It is difficult for one who has lived among men engaged in a noble and hopeful movement and shared their hopes and frustrations to reveal to them in cold print the full measure of one's sober conclusions. Am I mistaken in sensing in Professor Lipset's concluding chapter more disappointment with the prospects of the Cooperative Commonwealth Federation than he explicitly states? I hope I am. It may be that we are reduced to taking comfort from the reflection that, as he says,

"As long as there are social organizations that produce men who do not accept the *status quo,* who see 'the inhumanity of man to man' as a crime, there will be hope in the human race."

I, too, am confident of the long future. And that future will gain immeasurably from the candid realism of this truly sophisticated study. But for the immediate future, our lifetime and that of our children, I fear it is later than we and the men of Saskatchewan think. We on this side of the Atlantic Ocean live in an angry world dominated by power committed to reaction. And we too, despite our knowledge and resources, perhaps shall only learn at long last, and the hard way.

                                        ROBERT S. LYND

Columbia University
January, 1950

AUTHOR'S PREFACE

IT IS OBVIOUS that research studies are not a simple reporting of all the facts, or the relationships that exist within the area analyzed. A study can deal only with the questions which the researcher raises, and it is possible to ask an almost infinite number of questions about any sociological problem. Some sociologists unfortunately do not recognize this, and present their research reports as definitive and "correct" studies of class, race relations, the family, and so on.

The theoretical framework within which one operates determines in large measure the results obtained. This does not mean that it is impossible to be objective because all the variables in a situation are not studied. Within the context of a given theoretical system and set of research questions it is possible to measure objectively the relationship among the variables that seem significant. One can, for example, study class structure by raising the question, as W. Lloyd Warner has done, of the relation between the status structure and the customs and institutions of society. It is equally possible to study the implications of a hierarchical societal structure in terms of its organized power and influence, as the Lynds did in their *Middletown* studies.

I personally believe that the problems raised by the Lynds are more important for an understanding of the way in which our society operates; but, regardless of how different sociologists look at the problem of class structure, each can make an "objective" study. This does not suggest that one conceptual scheme is as good as any other, but it does mean that many of them are not mutually exclusive and that there is room for different approaches to the analysis of the same phenomena. It is necessary, therefore, that the sociologist make clear the

nature of the theoretical system he uses in research, that is,
through which set of theoretical spectacles he views a
problem.

My own theoretical framework is derived largely from the
sociologists who have been concerned with problems of
power, influence, class, organization, social change, and functional analysis. In terms of the "classical" sociologists, I have
been most influenced by Karl Marx, Max Weber, and Emil
Durkheim, and by Robert S. Lynd and Robert K. Merton
among contemporary sociologists. I have not integrated the
various theoretical systems into one system. The task of developing and integrating a systematic sociology is one which
the entire discipline faces and which few persons pretend to
have resolved. I have deliberately avoided explicit discussions
of sociological theory in this study, though I believe that the
reader will recognize the conceptual schemes used.

Intellectual honesty impels me to make explicit the political
assumptions underlying this study of a socialist movement. I
am a supporter of the democratic socialist movement of which
the CCF is a part, but I have been concerned with the wide
discrepancy between the ideology and behavior of most
present-day democratic socialist governments. As the Western
world moves increasingly in a collectivist or statist direction,
whether it is called "a fair deal," socialism, communism, or
fascism, I believe that the social scientists operating in the
relatively free atmosphere of Western democratic society
must increasingly turn to the analysis of the operation and
development of such systems. Our lack of knowledge of the
social forces determining the actions of governments means
that the people called upon to do the planning in present-day
society are often engaged in logically contradictory behavior
—planning without knowledge.

A gradually increasing body of sociological literature is developing in studies of organizations, political and private.
Much of this research is, however, conducted in the context
of the theory of organization, that is, using the concept of
bureaucracy as the key analytical variable, and analyzing the
behavior of different groups as related to the needs of the
bureaucratic structure. I believe that such research is extremely valuable and fruitful but that it tends to oversimplify

and overdetermine the process of social change. The needs of the organization and the individuals inhabiting the bureaucratic structure are only part of the cluster of factors that determine organizational action. It is impossible, as I see it, to understand the activities of a government political party without relating them to the structure of the community within which the movement arose, the opposition and support it received at different stages, the nature of the bureaucratic structure which the party develops, the ideological framework of the party, the climate of opinion within which it operates, the nature of the governmental bureaucratic structure which it is called upon to administer, and the immediate socioeconomic problems it faces when taking office. Behavior and institutional patterns should be discussed in functional terms, that is, related to the specific needs of specific groups and structures; but no one structure, like the party or governmental bureaucracy, can be singled out as the principal variable to which other behavior is functional. This study, therefore, was begun with the conscious decision not to use this approach, though I recognize the important contributions which men using it have made to the understanding of bureaucracy.

The preface of a book is traditionally used to express the indebtedness of the writer to those who aided him in obtaining and assembling the data. To do so for this study would be a herculean and almost impossible task. I spent almost fourteen months in Saskatchewan, and during that time was assisted by thousands of people in and out of the CCF.

Saskatchewan is a unique and rewarding place for a social scientist to do research, for the province contains a larger proportion of lay social scientists than any other area I have visited. The farmers are interested in their society and its relations to the rest of the world. Winter after winter, when the wheat crop is in, thousands of meetings are held throughout the province by political parties, churches, farmers' educational associations, and cooperatives. There are informal gatherings, also, in which farmers discuss economic and political problems. Not hedged in by the necessity of punching a time clock daily, these farmers, who have come from every part of Europe and North America, have frequent sessions in which they consider the ideas of Adam Smith, Karl Marx,

William Morris, Henry George, James Keir Hardie, William Jennings Bryan, Thorstein Veblen, and others.

Almost every English-speaking farmer subscribes to three or four farm weeklies, which are veritable storehouses of economic and political debate. In their correspondence columns the more literate and vociferous farmers argue the merits of religion, systems of government, the Soviet Union, socialism, socialized medicine, Social Credit, and schemes for marketing wheat. In traveling about the province I soon learned not to be surprised when a farmer whom I was interviewing would open a book by Morris, Henry George, Veblen, Major C. H. Douglas, or some technical social scientist.

The role of the social scientist was, therefore, a definable one to the leaders of organized rural activity in the province, as well as to many farmers. They knew, at least, that people made studies of economic and social problems. I was someone who was trying to discover why Saskatchewan alone among the major governmental units of the United States and Canada had elected a socialist party to office, and who was interested in finding out what that party was now doing. I think I can safely say that this activity was not regarded as "queer." Obviously, those whom I met in the course of the study defined it in different ways, but all were extremely cooperative.

A one-man study of a large social movement is necessarily limited in scope, but its limitations were overcome, in part at least, by the large measure of cooperation freely granted by leaders and members of the CCF and other Saskatchewan groups. Questionnaires were distributed by the CCF and two other Saskatchewan farm organizations to their leaders. Permission to use documentary materials was easily obtainable. Leaders and members of the three major political parties— the CCF, the Progressive Conservatives, and the Liberals,— trade-unions, cooperatives, and farm organizations were generous indeed with both time and information. Members of the government, cabinet members, members of the legislature, and civil servants were equally helpful.

There are certain persons, however, whose aid must be individually acknowledged. These include Premier T. C. Douglas and the entire membership of his cabinet; Dr. Morris C.

Shumiatcher and Thomas McLeod of the Premier's staff; Professor Carlyle King, president of the CCF, Saskatchewan Section; Gladys Strum, Dr. Cecil Sheps, Dr. Mindel Sheps, M. F. Allore, Gertrude Telford, Frank Hanson, Mr. and Mrs. Charles Pfeiffer, "Em" Allore, and Marion Bryden. I am especially indebted to Mrs. Austin Bothwell, Legislative Librarian, who made possible much of the documentary research.

It is impossible to end this preface without acknowledging the great debt I owe to my friend and teacher, Robert S. Lynd. His insight into the problem of class and political power was of great assistance in the organizing of my work. I should also like to thank Robert K. Merton for his invaluable help. Whatever methodological acumen and statistical background this study possesses can be attributed primarily to Paul Lazarsfeld. I am indebted also to my former colleagues at the University of Toronto, Professor S. D. Clark and Dr. Jean Burnet, who know more about western Canada than I can ever hope to learn, and who gave me the benefit of their knowledge.

I am especially indebted to the Social Science Research Council of the United States for making this study possible through the award of a predoctoral research fellowship, and to the Canadian Social Science Research Council for a grant-in-aid for statistical analysis of election data.

The major acknowledgment has been left to the end. Elsie Braun Lipset collaborated in every stage of this study. It would never have assumed its present form without her participation.

SEYMOUR MARTIN LIPSET

Berkeley, California
October, 1949

I

THE BACKGROUND OF
AGRARIAN RADICALISM

RADICAL POLITICAL movements are assuming a dominant position in the world today. England, France, Norway, Israel, Russia, China, Hungary, Poland, are but some of the countries in which political parties whose avowed goal is a "socialist" society control or form part of the government. In many other countries in Europe, South America, and Asia, democratic leftist or totalitarian communist parties are major political forces.[1]

The United States and Canada are the foremost exceptions to the growing collectivist trend. Capitalist democracy, which attained its greatest heights on this continent, has not been challenged by a significant nation-wide socialist movement. The immense material wealth of North America, which has given workers and farmers a higher living standard than in any other place on earth, has apparently prevented any organized threat to the capitalist system.

Various attempts have been made to explain why there is no socialism in the United States or Canada. For the most part, these have tried to answer the question by comparing the social and economic structures of North America and of Europe. Among the factors differentiating the American scene from that of Europe, the following have been suggested:

1. The absence of a feudal tradition prevented fixed social strata and explicit institutionalization of class lines.[2]

2. A richly endowed and sparsely settled continent encouraged an economically expanding capitalist society in which many could rise in the economic and social structure after this became impossible in Europe.[3]

3. The emergence of the United States as a nation co-

incidently with the Industrial Revolution has meant that the institutions of this new, sprawling, loosely structured population have been associated in the popular mind as the cause of the country's prosperity. So long as the level of living rose, there seemed no reason to make radical changes in "the American way."[4]

4. The open frontier absorbed malcontents and acted as a safety valve to prevent organized radicalism.[5]

5. The steady influx of foreign-born constituted the labor floor and distracted the attention of American-born labor from the fact that it was part of the "lower class." This also resulted in cleavages along national, racial, and religious lines rather than along class lines.[6]

6. The conflicting interests and different rates of development of the various regions channeled internal conflicts along geographical lines and made most of the social protest movements regional rather than national.[7]

7. The political system typical of the United States concentrated power in a popularly elected executive and made third parties much more difficult to launch in America than in parliamentary countries.

These factors have probably been important, but both radicals and conservatives have accepted too automatically the assumption that North American political radicalism must develop under conditions similar to those in Europe. The tactics of radicals and the theoretical approach of social scientists have both been biased by an implicit assumption that American radicalism, when and if it developed, would be a simple repetition of European working-class movements. Few have focused on the forces in North American culture that might create native patterns of organized discontent.

There have, in fact, been large and significant class movements for social and economic change in the United States which have attempted to challenge the business control of society. It is in order, then, to analyze the problem of American radicalism by studying the conditions under which class-conscious protest movements have arisen, as well as the factors that account for their success or failure. Such studies would be more fruitful for an understanding of why North America has no significant socialist movement than would general discussions of differences between American and European social structures.

If American social and political history is examined from this point of view, a significant pattern emerges. The history of American political class consciousness has been primarily a story of agrarian upheavals. From Shay's Rebellion through the Jeffersonian and Jacksonian movements in the United States and the "Clear Grits" in Canada, American farmers have been in the forefront of the battle against the control of society by business. The agrarian revolt became significant as part of the world-wide movements for economic collectivism after the Civil War, when western wheat-belt farmers had to resort to various collectivist schemes to alleviate the coercions of a growing monopoly capitalism.

It is significant that the first electorally successful North American socialist movement, the Cooperative Commonwealth Federation (CCF), came to power in the almost completely rural province of Saskatchewan in 1944. It is impossible to understand why an avowedly socialist party should have won a majority vote among supposedly conservative farmers unless one recognizes how often the social and economic position of the American wheat-belt farmer, in the United States as in Canada, has made him the American radical.

Agrarian radicalism after the Civil War developed with the extension of the railroad west of the Mississippi. The western frontier continued to advance as the railroads supplied a steady horde of new settlers from the East and from Europe. A new population striving for freedom and security pushed west with the railroads, only to find themselves bound hand and foot to the coercions of the new transportation in attempting to market their crops. Once settled on their raw new farms and deeply in debt to the bankers for equipment, the farmers' whole existence rested precariously on the weather and the world price of wheat. "The farmers were as a class *a priori* unprotected, the victims of a system of free trade selling and protected purchasing—in their economic relation as consumers paying heavy prices for high tariff goods, and as producers most of them selling against the competition of the world's markets."[8]

To the frontier farmer the business tactics of the local banker seemed erratic and ruthless. When times were good the farmer was urged to expand his use of bank credit, but in periods of depression he found himself caught helplessly in a vise. He faced chronic high freight rates and a grain-elevator monopoly. He was forced to sell his wheat to the local grain elevator and to accept the prices and grades arbitrarily set by the elevator agent.

As John D. Hicks, a historian of American Populism, pointed out, farmers "suffered from the railroads, from the trusts and the middlemen, from the money lenders and the bankers, and from the muddled currency. . . . Hence arose the veritable chorus of denunciation directed against those individuals and those corporations who considered only their own advantage without regard to the effect their actions might have upon the farmer and his interests."[9]

Organized rural protest took three forms: educational organization, such as the Patrons of Husbandry and the Farmers' Alliance, to put pressure on government to aid farmers; cooperative organization to eliminate the profits of middlemen; and, after these two methods failed, political parties seeking control of the state in the interest of organized agriculture.

The first major agrarian upheaval after the Civil War developed during the great depression of 1873–78. The price of wheat fell 49 per cent between 1868 and 1878. Capital became scarce in the West, while the costs of distribution and of the goods which the farmers bought remained relatively high. The gradualist solution of cooperation and political pressure that had been practiced by the Patrons of Husbandry, then the dominant educational group among farmers, seemed futile, and the various state organizations of the Patrons began to organize local political parties to obtain direct control of state governments.[10]

The Independent (or Reform) parties concentrated on controlling the railroads and the middlemen; later came the Greenback parties, which focused on monetary reform. These parties expressed the frustrations of the frontier farmers who had seen their years of toil come to nought while railroads and businessmen continued to make profits. From the start, therefore, the programs and propaganda of the agrarians were explicitly opposed to big business.

The Independents, who organized in 1873, demanded "the subjection of corporations, and especially of the railroad corporations, to the control of the state."[11] They also called for reductions in tariffs that aided eastern manufacturers, and the elimination of the middleman's profits. "Cooperation" and "Down with Monopolies" were their popular slogans.[12] In some areas, especially in the more radical northwestern wheat belt, government ownership of railroads was advocated. In order to break the power of the middleman, cooperatives were formed, including

local, county, and state agencies for the purchase of implements and supplies and the sale of farm products, local grain elevators, and cooperative stores, the manufacture of farm machinery, banking, insurance, and even organizations for bringing direct trade between the American producer and the European consumer. . . . [The farmers] believed it possible to regain their economic independence by themselves assuming the management of those industries which touched them most closely.[13]

Such collectivist agrarian programs recurred in the American Northwest until the explicit formulation of socialism as a goal in the CCF program of the 1930's.

The Independent parties were extremely short-lived. Most of them disappeared within two or three years, before the presidential election of 1876. Their major proposal—government regulation of railroads—proved a failure, as the laws passed in various states to control the railroads were invalidated in the courts. Their disappearance, however, was not a result of a decline in agrarian protest. The continuing and deepening depression of the 1870's led many farm leaders to the conviction that a more fundamental change in economic structure was needed; and accordingly they turned to monetary reform as a solution.

The frontier settlers, who carried a heavy load of debt, believed that an increase in the circulation of money, with consequent higher farm prices, would enable them to get rid of their debts. To do this required a frontal attack on the banks and their power to issue credit. This took the organized form of Greenback parties, demanding that the federal government should issue all money and regulate its value, and that "there be an adequate supply of money fixing a minimum amount per capita of the population."[14]

Continuing rural antagonism to large-scale wealth was expressed in the demand that government bonds be taxed and that "a graduated income tax should be levied for the support of the government and the payment of its debts." The Greenbackers felt that the adoption of their program "would muster out of service the vast army of idlers who, under the existing system, grow rich upon the earnings of others, that every man and woman may by their own efforts secure a competency, so that overgrown fortunes and extreme poverty will seldom be found within the limits of our republic."[15]

The Greenback movement represented a significant advance in the thinking of agrarian leaders. The failures of local Independent parties had taught them that economic evils could not be controlled by influencing local state governments. They thought that they had located the nucleus of the problem in the operations of the banking system; but it would be impossible to reform the national banking system without control of the federal government. So the Greenbackers soon realized that they needed urban allies. An alliance with eastern business groups was obviously impossible, in view of the program of the movement; therefore they sought an alliance with various radical labor groups in the East, and renamed their organization the Greenback Labor Party. The common antagonism of rural and urban radicals to the power of big business and their need for mutual support to win electoral majorities led both groups to overlook temporarily any divergences of outlook or interest. This effort by agrarian leaders to find labor allies who would support the demands of the farmers in return for rural support of labor's program is characteristic of American agrarianism.

In the congressional elections of 1878 the Greenback Party received 1,000,065 votes. This was the high point of the movement. In 1880, the next presidential election year, their strength declined to 308,578 votes. The main support of the movement came from the western agrarian states.[16]

The return of prosperity, with consequent higher prices for wheat and other farm goods, increased the circulation of money. "As prosperity returned, the strength of the Greenback Party waned."[17] Its rapid decline indicated the lack of any fundamental desire for basic social and economic change on the part of the farmers. The Party leaders had concentrated on the need for cheap money, which, they argued, required control of the bankers. But when prosperity gave the farmers what the Party advocated, the latter lost interest in monetary reform. This transitory character of organized rural protest was to prove characteristic of subsequent agrarian movements.

The next upswing in the cycle of agrarian protest followed the economic crisis of 1887. Credit had again become very difficult to obtain in the West. The old cry of the Greenbackers for monetary reform revived.

In the rural portions of the central regions, where farmers stayed and struggled with failing crops and low prices, with unyielding debts and relentless taxes, where they fought a battle, now successful, now unavailing, to retain the land they had bought and to redeem the high hopes with which they had come to the West—in this region unrest and discontent prevailed . . . finally to break forth in a program of open revolt.[18]

A new economic and educational organization, the National Farmers' Alliance, grew up in the old Independent Party states. Simultaneously, the Southern Alliance emerged in the South. The programs of both called for "financial reform of an inflationist nature, . . . and asked that the government take over and operate all means of transportation and communication."[19] It was not until 1890, when crop prices again began to fall drastically, that various state Alliances organized independent political parties, called People's parties. Kansas started a new party in June, 1890. Nebraska and the middle border joined the movement. North and South Dakota, Colorado, and even Michigan and Indiana nominated state tickets. In the South, the Southern Alliance operated through Democratic Party primaries. Much of the propaganda of these groups was directed at Wall Street, the banks, the railroads, and big business.[20]

Like the Greenbackers before them, the supporters of Populism attempted to obtain the backing of the labor movement. The Knights of Labor agreed to work with the organized farm movement, but the growing American Federation of Labor refused, because the Alliances were "composed of employing farmers."[21] In spite of opposition from A. F. of L. leaders who were under Socialist influence, the Northern Alliance stated its sympathy for "the just demands of labor of every grade"; and it recognized "that many of the evils from which the farming community suffers oppress universal labor, and that therefore producers should unite in a demand for the reform of unjust systems and the repeal of laws that bear unequally upon the people."[22] The Northern Alliance called for farmer-labor unity to gain control of the government.

The political Populist movement became a loose coalition of three separate groups: Rocky Mountain Populism, which was interested primarily in the free coinage of silver and was neither agrarian nor radical; southern Populism, which could not make a radical break because of the necessity of upholding "white supremacy"; and wheat-belt Populism, which was the agrarian radical wing of the movement.[23]

The Populists won a number of important local victories in 1890, but when the price of wheat declined further, they realized that they needed a national victory.[24] In 1892 the party nominated James B. Weaver as its presidential candidate and adopted a platform designed to appeal to farmers, workers, and the silver interests of the mountain states:

Wealth belongs to him who creates it and every dollar taken from industry without an equivalent is robbery. If any will not work, neither shall he eat. The interests of rural and civil labor are the same, their enemies are identical. . . .

. . . The time has come when the railroad corporations will either own the people or the people will own the railroads . . . the telegraphs and the telephones . . . should be owned and operated by the government in the interests of the people. . . .

[We demand:] (1) free and unlimited coinage of silver at the present legal ratio of 16 to 1; (2) the amount of circulating medium be speedily increased to not less than $50 per capita; (3) . . . a graduated income tax.[25]

The most important agrarian part of the platform, however, was the so-called subtreasury plan to require the federal government to store nonperishable farm products and to advance money up to 80 per cent of their market value at 1 or 2 per cent interest. "The farmers believed that through this subtreasury plan the volume of money would become adequate and elastic enough at harvest time and the rates of interest low enough to permit of their moving their crops at a good profit."[26]

Weaver succeeded in polling over a million votes, and he actually carried Colorado, Idaho, and Kansas. In the congressional elections of 1894 the Populists won 1,500,000 votes, which virtually eliminated the Democrats as a major party in the West and the Northwest. In 1896 the Democratic Party saved itself from possible extinction by taking over that part of the Populist program which advocated free coinage of silver, and succeeded in getting the majority of the Populist Party to fuse with it behind the candidacy of William Jennings Bryan.[27]

The wheat-belt agrarians had resisted the merger of the Populists with the Democrats, but they lost control of the party to the free silverites, who were not interested in the radical economic phases of the Populist platform. Many of the radicals were bitter at this "betrayal" of their earlier hopes of building a new radical party that would destroy the growing power of eastern monopoly; but their original compromise in joining with the nonradical mining interests had destroyed the force of their criticism. As prosperity returned in the late 'nineties, even the wheat-belt farmers lost interest in building a new party, and all efforts to revive the movement on a purely agrarian basis failed.

The lack of a long-term program for social change accounted, in part, for the failure of Populism to become a permanent radical protest movement. The farmers struck out at random at the most visible economic evils that affected them. They opposed the banks, the railroads, the wheat-elevator companies, and the shortage of money, but they saw each evil as an evil in itself, not as part of the total economic system. They accepted without question the support of any group that would join them. By focusing on specific transitory evils, the agrarian leaders failed to lay the educational base for a new radical movement, and they were unable to hold their followers in line when the manifestations of these evils disappeared during the upswings of the business cycle.

The weakness of elected Populist officials contributed also to the downfall of the Party, as John D. Hicks has pointed out.

Populist legislation was all too frequently found defective and unconstitutional. In administrative affairs the Populists were even less successful. Evidently their genius lay in protest rather than in performance. The third party men who took office were often inexperienced as administrators and it is not surprising that they were baffled by the difficulties that confronted them, difficulties that, incidentally, were made just as baffling as the opponents of Populism knew how to make them. . . . From the men they elected to office the Populists expected more than was humanly possible; and when the millennium failed to arrive they turned promptly from ardent supporters to disappointed critics.[28]

An examination of the electoral support of these agrarian movements reveals a consistent pattern. It was the economic and climatically vulnerable wheat belt that formed the backbone of all the protest movements, from the Independent parties of the 1870's down to the contemporary CCF in Canada.

The Independent parties had their main source of strength in the Northwest of the 1870's, in Illinois, Iowa, Wisconsin, and Minnesota. In the order named, these were the greatest wheat-producing states in the Union at that time: they produced more than one-third of all the wheat raised in the United States.[29] Similarly, Oregon and California, the two western states that joined the movement, were largely grain-growing states in the 1870's. All these areas were following a one-crop type of agriculture, with very little mixed farming, and therefore were almost completely exposed to the fluctuations of the world wheat market.

The same conditions were associated with the rise of the Independent and Greenback movements. In Iowa and Wisconsin, "the year of the poorest yield per acre of wheat in the history of both states was the year of the organization of the Greenback Party . . . [and] the years of the lowest prices and the greatest agricultural depression were also the years of the greatest strength of the Greenback Party."[30] A comparison of election returns by counties with the census data on agricultural production reveals distinct differences between rural supporters and opponents of the Greenbackers. The dairy and mixed farmers of both states "paid but little attention to the Greenback movement."[31] In the leading Greenback counties, however, "there was little stress upon . . . diversified farming and dairy, and marked concentration upon grain farming."[32]

Agrarian Populism also arose in the wheat belt.

The driving force for a new party came from the wheatbelt, although many other forces were eventually rallied around the idea and the organization. Populist expression was strongest and clearest in the wheat states. The degree of Populist strength in other sections can be gauged with amazing accuracy by an examination of the type of farming. The stresses inherent in the economy of cotton were not less severe than those in wheat, but the organizational and political expression of southern agriculture was poisoned by the vestiges of feudalism. The agriculture of the middle and eastern states was diversified in character, a fact which cushioned the shock of the clash with monopoly and thwarted clear-cut expression of the farmers' needs.[33]

An analysis of the Populist vote reveals clearly the role of the grain growers as the backbone of the Populist revolt.[34] During the Populist agitation there were three farming sections in the upper Mississippi Valley: "corn-livestock farming in a wide belt stretching from Ohio westward through Iowa and gradually pushing into eastern Kansas and Nebraska; dairy farming, found principally in Wisconsin and southeastern Minnesota; and grain farming, predominantly wheat, which had pushed out into a broad crescent sweeping from Kansas, through Nebraska, the Dakotas, and western Minnesota."[35] It was the latter area that backed the Populists.

In Minnesota the wheat areas supplied the greater part of

the Populist vote. ". . . there was throughout the farmer agitation of the period a distinct cleavage between that part of the state where dairying had developed and the western counties which were predominantly given over to wheat production."[36] The Populist strength in Kansas was in the central part of the state, which was predominantly a wheat region; the older, settled portion had changed over in part to the corn-livestock system and remained solidly conservative Republican.[37] Similar conditions prevailed in Nebraska. ". . . the western counties, which were still cattle country, and the eastern counties, where the corn-livestock system had gained a foothold, were least affected, while the center of Populist power was in the central part . . . where grain farming was still the dominant system."[38] The same tendency existed in Iowa, for the chief strength of the Populists was in the north-western grain-growing section, where "the Populists made important gains over the Greenback vote of 1880."[39] Other sections of Iowa, which had earlier supported the Greenbackers but had changed in the intervening decade from wheat to hogs and cattle, were uninfluenced by the new agrarianism.[40]

It is apparent, therefore, that agrarianism remained essentially the same throughout the latter half of the nineteenth century. The wheat-growing and frontier areas were most vulnerable economically, and had the newest and least-integrated social structure. These areas formed the basic core of all the movements.

The Socialist Party, which was the major third-party movement in the United States from 1900 to the First World War, was the sole major radical political movement that did not follow the pattern of agrarian revolt. The organizers of the Party were almost entirely urban workers or intellectuals, and its platform and leaders made their major appeal to the urban working class. But the major strength of the Socialist Party vote at its high point in 1912, when it received 5.9 per cent of the national vote for president, was not in the manufacturing centers but in the western states.

As the *New Republic* commented at the time:

In certain agricultural states, where there are few wage earners, and where farm-owners and tenants who wish to become farm-owners do not know what wage slavery is, the Socialist vote is comparatively strong. In Kansas, in Minnesota, in Texas, in several other preponderately agricultural states, the proportionate Socialist vote is much larger than in New York, Pennsylvania, New Jersey, and other industrial states.[41]

Robert F. Hoxie, who made a study of Socialist Party electoral victories in 1911, found a pattern of Socialist success

based on Socialist organization and agitation, but occurring for the large part in small agricultural or semiagricultural communities. Victories of this kind are pretty generally diffused, but their special habitat seems to be in the old stronghold of Populism. The brand of socialism which they represent tends to be in outer seeming of the ultra-theoretical blood-and-thunder variety; but an examination of the party membership in these areas often discloses a surprisingly high proportion of farmers.[42]

The Socialist Party was strongest in Oklahoma, which was then a wheat state. "At the height of the movement, the Socialist Party commanded close to one-third of the total vote of Oklahoma, elected six members of the state legislature, and a number of county officers."[43] Virtually all this vote came from the wheat-growing regions. Substantial support for the Socialist Party was obtained from farmers, in spite of the fact that a large section of the Party opposed such recruiting. At the first convention of the Party in 1900, the delegates were unable to decide whether they should even make an appeal to farmers. As Job Harrison, a Party leader, stated, "We are building in this convention a working-class platform; the farmers do not belong to the working class, because the farmers own the farms."[44] In 1910, after a bitter fight, the Party reversed itself on the land question. The program adopted, however, advocated that existing government lands should be used for "model state farms and various forms of collective agricultural enterprise."[45]

In view of the antagonism felt by a large section of the Socialists toward the farmers as a class, one may wonder how much more rural support the Party might have gained if it had really attempted to present a farm program designed to protect the farmer on his land and aimed at the elimination of the middleman and the socialization of monopolies, as earlier agrarian parties had advocated. In North Dakota, the heart of the wheat belt, A. C. Townley, who subsequently founded the Non-Partisan League, recruited hundreds of farmers to the Socialist Party, but he was forced to break with the Party in 1914 when its doctrinaire leaders opposed the mass recruitment of farmers. "[The orthodox Socialists] feared—and apparently with good reason—that it wasn't dyed-in-the-wool Socialism that Townley was spreading among the farmers. They were inclined to believe that his converts weren't really Socialist at all. This man Townley, with his talk of a 'state program,' evidently was only an opportunist, a 'yellow-belly,' a hated 'reformer.' "[46]

The destruction of the Socialist Party during and after the First World War by a combination of government persecution and Communist splits prevented the development of an American agrarian socialism. If the Party had not been destroyed by the war, the wheat farmers of Oklahoma or North Dakota might have taken the lead in establishing a strong socialist movement on this continent. The Saskatchewan Co-operative Commonwealth Federation, as we shall see later, follows directly in this tradition of North American socialism.

The most important radical agrarian movement after the First World War was the Non-Partisan League, which attained great influence in the western Great Plains region of the United States from 1916 to 1922. The League was organized in the wheat state of North Dakota in 1915 by A. C. Townley and a small group of socialist farmers. They attacked existing political parties as "useless for the farmers' purpose" and called for a farmers' alliance "to grapple with organized 'big business' greed."[47]

Many wheat farmers had again become convinced that the system of marketing grain was unfair to the producers. They believed that "bankers, merchants, and professional politicians were in league with the millers to exploit them."[48] In 1911 farmers in North Dakota organized a marketing cooperative designed to eliminate the profits of elevator companies, grain traders, and speculators in futures on the Grain Exchange;

but business struck back by refusing trading rights on the Minneapolis Exchange to this farmers' Equity Cooperative Exchange.[49] Farm organizations thereupon demanded in 1913 that North Dakota build a state-owned "terminal elevator, which it was hoped would be able to store enough wheat to create the independent market so earnestly desired."[50] But the Republican-controlled legislature refused. This action by the dominant political party in the state gave impetus to the Non-Partisan League drive to build a radical class-conscious agrarian movement.

The program of the League, drawn up by socialists, dealt in the main with proposals for government ownership and control of various enterprises:

1. State ownership of terminal elevators, flour mills, packing houses, and cold-storage plants.
2. State inspection of grain and grain dockage.
3. Exemption of farm improvements from taxation.
4. State hail insurance on the acreage tax basis.
5. Rural credit banks operated at cost.[51]

The strategy of the League was to attempt to capture the North Dakota Republican Party by entering a League slate in the primaries rather than by starting a new party. In 1916, the first election contested by the League, it elected the governor and all the other state officials. After winning control of both houses of the legislature in 1918, it enacted a large part of its program into law: a state bank; a Home Building Association to lend money at low rates of interest; a graduated state income tax distinguishing between earned and unearned income; a state hail-insurance fund; a workmen's compensation act that assessed employers for its support; the eight-hour day for working women; and regulation of working conditions in the mines.[52]

Such forthright action in North Dakota alerted many members of the national Socialist Party, for they felt that the agrarian organization was carrying out the Socialist program. Many members of the Socialist Party were accordingly brought in from outside the state to assist the League's work. This move was openly defended in the Socialist Party's na-

tional organ by Arthur LeSeur, Townley's legal adviser, and
himself a Socialist. "While the Non-Partisan League in North
Dakota is composed exclusively of farmers, the Labor unions
of the state have stood as one man with the League . . . [and]
its program is composed of precisely the points included in
the Socialist Party platform for the last six years."[53]

In 1917 the League began to organize in neighboring states,
and eventually enrolled more than 200,000 members.[54] Almost all its support, however, was in the wheat area tributary
to Minneapolis and St. Paul. It never completely captured any
other state than North Dakota, though the old Republican
machine in South Dakota adopted much of its program and
set up a "state rural credits system, a state-owned coal mine,
and a state cement plant," and promised that if the North
Dakota flour mill and packing plant were successful, South
Dakota would adopt them also.[55]

The agricultural depression of 1920 damaged the League,
as the decline in the price of wheat reduced the state's finances and embarrassed the state-owned industries and the
state bank. The state attempted to raise funds by selling state
bonds; but private bankers seized this opportunity to bring
the agrarian reformers to their knees. A report of a committee of the North Dakota Bankers' Association to the general
body makes this clear:

It was urged by your committee that the construction and
operation of mills, elevators, and banks by the State was an
experiment, was theoretical, was without precedent, and its
success far from assured; that investors now proposing to buy
the State's bonds were naturally cautious; that if these industries should prove gross failures, and the people of the future
feel aggrieved, the ultimate payment of these bonds might be
questioned, and therefore they would not pay the bonds, unless some assurance is given that no large similar indebtedness is to be created until it is determined whether or not
these ventures are a success; in short, that $3,000,000 was
enough with which to experiment.

Your committee is reminded that there is no law by which
a state can be compelled to pay its indebtedness. If coming
generations, when the bonds mature, should have found that
these experiments were unsound and these millions wasted,

it is not inconceivable that they might hesitate to pay an enormous debt for which they never received any value. If the experiments proved successful the contrary would be the case. It would take at least two or three years to determine the question by actual experience.[56]

The bankers' committee demanded that the state "Provide some assurance to the public that the so-called farmers' industrial program will be confined to the Grand Forks mill and elevator, to the Drake mill, and the Bank of North Dakota."[57] The Non-Partisan State Industrial Commission refused to accept the bankers' terms.

The proposition . . . cannot honorably be considered by the Commission for the reason that it is a plain attempt on the part of the financial interests, presumably Wall Street financiers, to dictate the political, financial and industrial policies of the State of North Dakota, and requiring a surrender of the sovereign powers of the State. The time has not yet arrived when any group, no matter how powerful financially, can dictate to this State how to manage its own affairs. Every State in the Union is guaranteed a republican form of government under our constitution. The officers of the State, even though elected by the people, have no authority to surrender its sovereignty. . . . We are satisfied that any group of men that would exact such a surrender and arrogate to themselves the prerogative of making the laws for the people of the State would rule with a tyrannical hand.[58]

North Dakota then tried to get out-of-state bankers to handle the bonds, "but the financial houses of Minneapolis and Chicago were unwilling to undertake the sale of the state's bonds."[59] An investigation of the state bank in 1921 revealed its insolvency. The conservative opposition to the League thereupon initiated a recall election. The League officials were defeated by a small majority, though in the same election a majority of the voters cast their ballots in favor of maintaining the state industries.[60]

The failure of the Non-Partisan League indicates one of the crucial difficulties facing all agrarian protest movements that attempt to solve the farmers' ills on a local or regional level. The economic and financial system of a nation involves a single web of power, and any part severs itself from the whole at its own peril. This was especially true in the unbalanced single-crop wheat economy of North Dakota. Like the Independents of the 1870's, the Non-Partisans were attacking giants with a slingshot.

An analysis of the voting strength of the Non-Partisan League reveals the same geographical pattern of agrarian radicalism that was exhibited by earlier farm parties: the one-crop wheat-growing regions gave the movement its greatest support. In Minnesota the League candidates "received heavy support from northwestern wheat counties and very light support from the southern and corn-growing counties."[61] The Non-Partisan vote in South Dakota in 1920 "was determined by sectional differences associated with crop-producing areas,"[62] the main support coming from wheat-producing areas. The greatest vote of the Non-Partisan League was received, of course, in North Dakota, which is the second most highly rural state in the Union and raises only wheat.

The hard-times, "grudge" character of agrarian movements within the prevailing North American optimism was borne out by the sharp decline of the Non-Partisan League in the prosperous 1920's.[63] After 1929 the League revived and returned to power in North Dakota in 1932. An offshoot of the League, the Minnesota Farmer-Labor Party, also succeeded in electing state officials and United States senators in the 'thirties. The revived protest movement did not, however, succeed in permanently rebuilding a strong national movement, though there seemed to be popular sentiment for it in the early 'thirties. The New Deal program, setting a floor under agricultural prices and providing crop insurance and extensive federal government aid projects, gave farmers what they wanted and destroyed the embryonic radicalism. Had Roosevelt not headed off the potential radical revolt by making sharp concessions to the farmers, North Dakota and its neighbors might again have challenged the two-party system. It should be noted that North Dakota lies directly south of Saskatchewan and is the state most comparable to it, both geographically and economically.

Farmers are customarily considered a slow-moving group,

long on stability and short on innovation. Both conservatives
and radicals have agreed that the farmer is too individualistic
to be a natural "joiner" and too "set in his ways" to become
a sustained radical. As Veblen remarked of the farmer,

. . . he is, on the whole, an obstinately loyal supporter of
the system of law and custom which so makes the conditions
of life for him.

His unwavering loyalty to the system is in part a holdover
from that obsolete past when he was the Independent Farmer
of the poets; but in part it is also due to the still surviving
persuasion that he is on the way, by hard work and shrewd
management, to acquire a "competence"; such as will enable
him some day to take his due place among the absentee owners of the land and so come in for an easy livelihood at the
cost of the rest of the community; and in part it is also due to
the persistent though fantastic opinion that his own present
interest is tied up with the system of absentee ownership, in
that he is himself an absentee owner by so much as he owns
land and equipment which he works with hired help,—always
presuming that he is such an owner in effect or in prospect.[64]

The role of revolutionary catalyst, which might eventually
lead to an overthrow of existing capitalist society, has commonly been assigned to the working classes. In the United
States and Canada, however, workers as a group have never
fulfilled either the hopes of Marxists or the fears of conservatives. On the contrary, certain groups of farmers have been
more wont to seek redress for their economic grievances
through class-conscious political action.

Agrarian radicalism, although it rarely is explicitly socialist,
has directed its attack against big-business domination. In certain economic areas farmers have openly challenged private
ownership and control of industry. American agrarians have
attempted, either through government or cooperative ownership, to eliminate private control of banking, insurance, transportation, natural resources, public utilities, manufacture of
farm implements, wholesale and retail distribution of consumers' goods, and food commodity exchanges. The large measure of "socialism without doctrine" that can be found in the
programs of agrarian political and economic organizations is

in many respects more socialistic than the nationalization policies of some explicitly socialist parties.

Agrarian radicalism has developed within the same American cultural framework that has proved so great a stumbling block to the organization of working-class radicalism. The farmers, like the workers, have been exposed to the material benefits of American society, to ethnic heterogeneity, to the American creed of opportunity and classlessness, and to similar social pressures. This suggests that some of the explanations cited earlier for the failure of American socialism may be oversimplified in that they neglect significant variables that may cause a lower economic class to turn against the *status quo*.

In Saskatchewan a new agrarian social movement, the Cooperative Commonwealth Federation, which is avowedly socialist, has won majority power in an almost completely rural area. It is highly significant that the first electorally successful socialist party in the United States or Canada should have developed in the same Great Plains wheat belt that earlier produced the Greenbackers, the Populists, the Non-Partisans, and other agrarian upheavals. The existence of a socialist government in rural Saskatchewan confounds those who would perpetuate the myth of the conservative farmer.

The success of the CCF to date presents us with a dynamic experiment-in-process in the development of radical class consciousness. It offers a significant opportunity for a detailed study of the factors in North American society that are conducive to the development of organized radicalism. It should be possible from its study to cast light on the relationship between economic pressures and organized class action. To recognize that depressions result in agrarian protest in the wheat belt tells little of the process by which economic reverses produce class action; for many rural and urban groups have been exposed to depressions without forming any large protest movement. Obviously, some important variables must intervene between the economic factor and organized social action.

NOTES

1. Harry W. Laidler, *Social-Economic Movements* (New York, Thomas Y. Crowell Co., 1949).

2. "[The Americans] are born conservatives—just because America is so purely bourgeois, so entirely without a feudal past." Karl Marx and Friedrich Engels, Letter 209, "Engels to Sorge," *Correspondence, 1846–1895* (New York, International Publishers, 1936), p. 467.

3. Gunnar Myrdal, *An American Dilemma* (New York, Harper and Brothers, 1944), p. 714.

4. "[The weakness of Marxism in America] is not a function of some immaterial national spirit, but a product of material conditions. A nation rapidly growing rich has sufficient reserves for conciliation between hostile classes and parties. . . . America was free of . . . [Marxism] only because it had a plethora of virgin areas, inexhaustible reserves of national wealth and, it would seem, limitless opportunities for enrichment." Leon Trotsky, *The Living Thoughts of Karl Marx* (New York, Longmans, Green and Co., 1939), p. 34.

5. Myrdal, *op. cit.*, p. 714.

6. "The huge immigration through the decades has constantly held the lower classes in a state of cultural fragmentation. They have been split in national, linguistic and religious sub-groups, which has hampered class solidarity and prevented effective mass organization." *Ibid.*, p. 713.

7. Frederick J. Turner, *The Significance of Sections in American History* (New York, Henry Holt and Co., 1932).

8. "The Voice of the Farmer," *The Nation,* Vol. 50, p. 329, quoted in John D. Hicks, *The Populist Revolt* (University of Minnesota Press, 1931), p. 80.

9. *Ibid.*, p. 95.

10. S. J. Buck, "Independent Parties in the Western States, 1873–1876," in *Essays in American History Dedicated to Frederick Jackson Turner* (ed. by Guy Stanton Ford; New York, Henry Holt and Co., 1910), pp. 137–64.

11. Buck, *The Granger Movement* (Harvard University Press, 1913), p. 100.

12. *Ibid.*, p. 53.

13. *Ibid.*, pp. 238–39.

14. Fred E. Haynes, *Third Party Movements since the Civil War* (State Historical Society of Iowa, Iowa City, 1916), p. 123.

15. *Ibid.*

16. *Ibid.*, pp. 124, 142.

17. C. O. Ruggles, "The Economic Basis of the Greenback Movement in Iowa and Wisconsin," Mississippi Valley Historical Society, *Proceedings,* Vol. 5, p. 160.

18. Hicks, *op. cit.,* p. 35.

19. *Ibid.,* p. 124.

20. *Ibid.,* pp. 155–58.

21. *Ibid.,* p. 115.

22. *Ibid.,* p. 125.

23. Harlen P. Crippen, "Conflicting Trends in the Populist Movement," *Science and Society,* Vol. 6 (1942), p. 134.

24. In "1888–1891, the farm price of wheat was 82 cents a bushel; for 1892–1895 it had declined thirty-three per cent and was 55 cents a bushel. The average aggregate farm value of wheat crops in the two periods showed a decline of thirty-one per cent; from 393 million to 249 million dollars." Nathan Fine, *Labor and Farmer Parties in the United States* (Rand School of Social Science, New York, 1928), p. 73.

25. *Ibid.,* pp. 77–78.

26. *Ibid.,* p. 76.

27. Hicks, *op. cit.,* pp. 321–79.

28. *Ibid.,* pp. 299–300.

29. Haynes, *op. cit.,* p. 51.

30. Ruggles, *op. cit.,* p. 160.

31. *Ibid.,* p. 157.

32. *Ibid.,* p. 165.

33. Crippen, *op. cit.,* p. 142.

34. *Ibid.,* p. 134.

35. Benton H. Wilcox, "An Historical Definition of North-Western Radicalism," *Mississippi Valley Historical Review,* December, 1939, p. 381.

36. *Ibid.,* p. 386.

37. Raymond C. Miller, "The Economic Basis of Populism in Kansas," *Mississippi Valley Historical Review,* Vol. 11 (1925), p. 481.

38. Wilcox, *op. cit.,* p. 386.

39. Walter E. Nydegger, "The Election of 1892 in Iowa," *Iowa Journal of History and Politics,* Vol. 25 (1927), p. 466.

40. Herman C. Nixon, "The Populist Movement in Iowa," *Iowa Journal of History and Politics,* Vol. 24 (1926), pp. 103–4.

41. Editorial, December 12, 1914, p. 11.

42. Robert F. Hoxie, "The Rising Tide of Socialism: A Study," *Journal of Political Economy,* Vol. 19, p. 625.

43. Oscar Ameringer, *If You Don't Weaken* (New York, Henry Holt and Co., 1940), p. 269.

44. Fine, *op. cit.,* p. 210.

45. *Ibid.,* p. 272.

46. Herbert G. Gaston, *The Non-Partisan League* (New York, Harcourt, Brace and Co., 1920), p. 54.

47. *Ibid.,* p. 59.

48. W. B. Bizzell, *The Green Rising* (New York, Macmillan Co., 1926), p. 180.

49. Paul Fossum, *The Agrarian Movement in North Dakota* (Baltimore, Johns Hopkins Press, 1925), pp. 85–86.

50. Andrew A. Bruce, *The Non-Partisan League* (New York, Macmillan Co., 1921), p. 56.

51. Fred E. Haynes, *Social Politics in the United States* (New York, Houghton Mifflin Co., 1924), p. 309.

52. Gaston, *op. cit.*, pp. 285–87.

53. Arthur LeSeur, in *The Call,* March 2, 1917, quoted in Bruce, *op. cit.,* p. 141.

54. Gaston, *op. cit.,* pp. 237–38.

55. Wilcox, *op. cit.,* p. 391.

56. Quoted in S. Roy Weaver, *The Non-Partisan League in North Dakota* (Canadian Reconstruction Association, Toronto, 1921), p. 44.

57. *Ibid.,* p. 43.

58. *Ibid.,* p. 45.

59. *Ibid.*

60. Fossum, *op. cit.,* p. 124.

61. Stuart A. Rice, *Farmers and Workers in American Politics* (New York, Longmans, Green and Co., 1924), p. 162; see also Wilcox, *op. cit.,* p. 372.

62. Rice, *op. cit.,* p. 174.

63. The presidential elections of 1924 in the United States witnessed the most successful third-party movement since the Civil War. Robert M. La Follette, running as an independent candidate for president, succeeded in polling over five million votes.

La Follette's candidacy, however, was not the result of a genuine new-party movement. It was organized by a coalition of the A. F. of L., the Railroad Brotherhoods, the Socialist Party, and the agrarian reformers who had supported the Non-Partisan League. The trade-unions supported La Follette because of repeated legislative rebuffs by both of the old parties and their nomination of conservative presidential candidates. The Socialists and agrarians backed La Follette in the hope of building the new national party which they had long wanted.

The La Follette candidacy did not create an organized new party. The campaign was conducted around the personality of La Follette, and no attempt was made to set up a permanent party organization. "The progressive campaign concentrated upon attaining success for the national ticket to the exclusion of state and local contests. La Follette supporters for local offices were encouraged to seek places on the Democratic or Republican tickets." William B. Heseltine, "Third Parties: The Progressives of 1924," *The Progressive,* August 25, 1947, p. 4.

Soon after the election, La Follette and the trade-unions withdrew from attempts to establish a new party. This left the agrarians and Socialists to continue the fight alone. The prosperity of the 'twenties made the effort impossible, and the movement soon disappeared.

Heseltine, *The Rise and Fall of Third Parties* (Washington, D.C., Public Affairs Press, 1948), pp. 28–33.

64. Thorstein Veblen, *Absentee Ownership* (New York, Viking Press, 1945), p. 130.

2

THE SOCIAL AND ECONOMIC SETTING

THE GREAT PLAINS region of Canada is the last settled agricultural frontier on the North American continent. Lying directly north of the wheat belt of Dakota and Montana, it is in every major respect similar to those regions in geographic appearance and economic structure.

Until 1870 the area that now comprises Alberta and Saskatchewan was governed as the private property of the Hudson's Bay Company. Its population consisted of Indian tribes and small groups of whites and half-breeds who worked for "the Company." In 1869 the newly formed Dominion of Canada purchased the rights to this gigantic territory, including what is now the province of Manitoba.

The land was thrown open to agricultural development after 1870. Settlement was encouraged on a homestead basis similar to the manner in which the western United States was occupied. Despite the fertility of the land, however, settlement lagged. By 1891 only 251,473 people lived in the entire region, while the much smaller Territory of Dakota, directly south, had a population of 510,000. The major reason for the failure to attract settlers was the existence of free homestead land south of the border. The United States had a greater appeal to European immigrants than did the unknown Canada, and it also had a larger population in the East to draw upon for western settlement.[1]

The turn of the century, however, witnessed the beginnings of a flood of immigration into the Canadian North-West Territories. Free fertile lands in the United States were becoming exhausted, and the world wheat price had begun a gradual but steady rise. These economic factors, combined with the aggressive immigration policy fostered by the Laurier administration, brought immigrants from England, Europe, eastern Canada, and the United States. Expansion was continuous and rapid. Most of this new settlement occurred between 1900 and 1914. "An area larger than Vermont was 'entered' in free homesteads in 1909; twice the area of Connecticut in 1910; more than Delaware and New Hampshire in 1911; nearly the area of Maryland in 1912; more than Massachusetts in 1913; and more than the area of Wales in 1914."[2] The First World War slowed the rate of expansion, but in less than a decade almost the whole "last best West" was occupied.

More than 1,000,000 people settled on the Canadian prairies between 1896 and 1913, and the population constituted 20 per cent of the total population of Canada in 1913, as over against only 7 per cent in 1896. Occupied land rose from 10,000,000 to 70,000,000 acres. Wheat production increased from 20,000,000 to 209,000,000 bushels. In the three Prairie Provinces the total value of agricultural production amounted to between $300,000,000 and $400,000,000 annually by the end of this period.[3] Settlers came from every part of Europe and America and soon destroyed the ethnic homogeneity of Canada as a British and French nation. Saskatchewan in 1911 had about 275,000 immigrants from parts of Europe other than Britain and France.

In 1905 the North-West Territories were divided into the provinces of Alberta and Saskatchewan.[4] The relative recency of their frontier period is an important factor in the contemporary social and political history of the two provinces. Much of rural western Canada is still in the semifrontier stage from which the Great Plains agrarian states of the United States emerged at the end of the nineteenth century. Thus Saskatchewan and Alberta today are comparable to the frontier areas of Kansas and Nebraska in the late nineteenth century when these states were strongholds of Greenbackism and Populism. The Canadian West still lacks a static social structure, and in this respect it is characteristic of frontier areas.

Along with this open social system before the depression of the 1930's went unlimited optimism. Those who moved to the Western Provinces were attracted by the hope of bettering their lot. Subsequent failure to attain their original goals

TABLE 1

OCCUPATIONAL BACKGROUNDS OF FARM OPERATORS IN
SAMPLE AREAS, 1930–31

District	Total farm operators	FARMING EXPERIENCE ONLY		NONAGRICULTURAL EXPERIENCE	
		Number	Per cent	Number	Per cent
Saskatchewan:					
Davidson	136	71	52.2	64	47.1
Kindersley	204	84	41.2	114	55.9
Turtleford	174	78	44.8	94	54.0
Alberta:					
Medicine Hat	290	143	49.3	139	48.0
Olds	125	53	42.4	72	57.7
Peace River	332	94	28.3	238	71.7
Totals	1,261	523	41.5	721	57.2

SOURCE: Canadian Pioneer Problems Committee Surveys, quoted in C. A. Dawson and Eva A. Younge, *Pioneering in the Prairie Provinces* (Toronto, 1940), p. 318.

and the absence of strong, settled ties to a traditional pattern of economic, political, and social behavior have made the frontier farmers of Canada, like the frontier farmers of the United States before them, receptive to new ideas, to panaceas that promise the opportunities they seek. First-generation frontier settlers still form a large proportion of the farm heads of the province. Many of the men who came to Saskatchewan before the First World War are still vigorous and influential in the life of the province. One still senses in Saskatchewan today the meaning of frontier restlessness, the desire of these farmers for change, and the gropings for new horizons.

The readiness to improvise and adopt new ideas has not been limited to political behavior. In the 1920's many local rural governments in Saskatchewan developed an indigenous system of socialized medicine. The movement for Protestant church unity, which resulted in the formation of the United Church of Canada from a merger of Methodist, Presbyterian, and Congregational churches, was largely a movement of the Canadian West. The sparsely settled frontier regions could not support competing Protestant sects, and the farmers insisted

TABLE 2

Nonagricultural Occupations Previously Engaged in by Farm Operators, 1930–31

District	Farm operators who had nonagricultural occupations	Total number of nonagricultural occupations	PERCENTAGE DISTRIBUTION				
			Professional men	Business proprietors	Clerical and service workers	Skilled workers	Semiskilled and unskilled workers
Saskatchewan:							
Davidson	64	102	5	18	16	15	46
Kindersley	114	163	4	3	20	24	49
Turtleford	94	133	3	9	26	26	36
Alberta:							
Medicine Hat	139	206	3	7	16	17	57
Olds	72	111	6	11	11	13	59
Peace River	238	365	5	8	31	13	43

SOURCE: Canadian Pioneer Problems Committee Surveys, quoted in C. A. Dawson and Eva R. Younge, *Pioneering in the Prairie Provinces* (Toronto, 1940), p. 123.

that theological differences be sacrificed to the needs of the people.[5]

There is one significant difference, however, between frontier settlement in the United States in the nineteenth century and that of Saskatchewan in the early twentieth century. Saskatchewan was settled in part by working-class immigrants during a period of rising trade-unionism, a growing world socialist movement, and an active cooperative movement in England, Germany, and Scandinavia. Tables 1 and 2 indicate, for a sample of Saskatchewan and Alberta farm heads in 1930–31, the class origins of frontier farmers. Of the farmers in the sample, 37 per cent had been laborers—skilled, semi-skilled, or unskilled—before going to the frontier. Some had been trade-union members and even socialists at home. Fred Green, the secretary of the Saskatchewan Grain Growers' Association (S.G.G.A.), the first large agrarian movement before the First World War, and George Langley, one of its major leaders, had both been members of the British Labor Party.[6] Langley had been one of the first members of the Fabian Society.[7] The two most important permanent officials of the United Farmers of Canada (Saskatchewan Section), the present-day successor to the S.G.G.A., were members of the Independent Labor Party of England and the Socialist Party of the United States, respectively.[8]

The role of an open frontier as a safety valve preventing the growth of a large organized radical movement in the United States and Canada has often been stressed. Unfortunately, no statistical data are available on the political backgrounds of the pioneers. One gains the impression in Saskatchewan that at least one aspect of this hypothesis is correct—namely, that a considerable number of those whose discontent with social and economic conditions at home had led them to join radical parties were attracted to the new world of the frontier. In virtually every area visited in the course of this study, one or more old-country socialists were encountered. This was true not only for the farmers who came from Europe but for many of the American and eastern Canadian settlers as well. Three of the CCF members of the 1944–48 legislature, previously residents in the United States, had voted for Eugene V. Debs for president of the United States.

One had been a supporter of the I.W.W. The reverses suffered by the socialist movements back home helped create the environmental basis for Saskatchewan's socialist movement in the 1930's.[9]

The frontier character alone would not have created or maintained the conditions for rapid social change. Most North American frontier areas that were once centers of agrarian radicalism became strongholds of political and economic conservatism within a few decades after their original settlement as economic conditions became more stable. A clue, therefore, to understanding the continued unrest on the Canadian prairies lies in the perpetuation of an extremely unstable agricultural economy.

Like the neighboring state of North Dakota, the stronghold of American agrarianism, the life of the Prairie Provinces of Canada still depends on the frontier crop, wheat. Saskatchewan has never been able to develop a mature, stable economy, either industrially or agriculturally.

To an unique extent, the economic history of Saskatchewan is that of wheat. No other governmental unit in the world attempting to maintain a modern civilization is so completely dependent on the production and marketing of one commodity —a commodity which under even normal conditions is subject to wide variations in production and price. *On the average, about 85 per cent of the value of all net production in Saskatchewan is supplied by the agricultural industry, and about 80 per cent of the cash income of the agricultural industry is derived from wheat.*[10]

As in frontier days, almost every person in the province today is in agriculture or in an occupation servicing farmers. The occupational structure of the region reveals this fact clearly. As table 3 shows, only 3 per cent of the total working force was engaged in manufacturing in 1936, when the CCF emerged as a large socialist party.

The lack of important secondary industries means that any change in the fortunes of wheat necessarily affects almost everyone in the province. The implications of this fact for the continuation of organized unrest can easily be seen from table 4, which presents the fluctuations in yield and price of wheat from year to year. These variations are caused by three factors: weather variations in wheat yield, price fluctuations, and variations in grade of wheat. In Saskatchewan all three factors are extremely variable.

Year after year, Saskatchewan wheat farmers have perforce lived the life of gamblers. They invest their money and labor on the same plot of land in an enterprise that may arbitrarily leave them either poverty-stricken or comparatively well to do at the end of the harvest. Actually, the wheat yields of Saskatchewan are more variable "than those of the Argen-

TABLE 3

OCCUPATIONS OF SASKATCHEWAN RESIDENTS FOURTEEN YEARS
OF AGE AND OVER

Group	1936		1941	
	Number	Percentage	Number	Percentage
Agriculture	217,315	62.7	197,009	58.3
Service	46,960	13.5	48,371	14.3
Trade and finance	21,084	6.1	24,249	7.2
Transport	15,649	4.5	15,868	4.7
Manufacturing	11,116	3.2	16,184	4.8
Clerical	10,625	3.1	13,233	3.9
Laborers	9,310	2.7	9,424	2.8
Other occupations	8,759	2.5	11,267	3.3
All occupations	346,604	100.0	337,881	100.0

SOURCE: Dominion Bureau of Statistics, *Census of Saskatchewan, 1936*, pp. 518–27; *Eighth Census of Canada, 1941*, Vol. 7, pp. 316–17.

tine, Australia, the United States, . . . India, . . . and Canada as a whole."[11] The wheat lands of the province are part of the dust bowl of North America, and thus are subject to recurrent droughts. The absence of rain or the coming of insect pests spells financial ruin for the entire year. Even in years of sufficient average rainfall in the province as a whole, many farms suffer crop failure. "In the period 1918 to 1935, there were only three years, 1922, 1923, and 1928, when the average yield of wheat did not fall to 5 bushels per acre or less in any one [rural] municipality of the province, and even in those years . . . crop failure was experienced on a considerable number of individual farms."[12]

As table 4 indicates, a good crop is no guaranty of a decent income for the wheat farmer. Wheat prices are even more variable than crop yields. Canadian wheat is primarily an export crop. Since more wheat per capita of total population is grown in Canada than in any of the other major exporting countries—Argentina, Australia, and the United States —the price received by the Canadian farmer is more closely determined by world market conditions. Twice within a decade, in 1921 and in 1930, the price of Canadian wheat fell to

TABLE 4

YIELD AND PRICE OF WHEAT IN SASKATCHEWAN BY YEARS

Year	Av. yield (bu. per acre)	Price per bu.	Year	Av. yield (bu. per acre)	Price per bu.
1900	8.8	....	1927	19.5	0.97
1905	23.1	....	1928	23.3	0.77
1906	....	....	1929	11.1	1.03
1908	14.5	....	1930	14.0	0.47
1909	23.1	....	1931	8.8	0.38
1910	15.8	0.69	1932	13.6	0.35
1911	20.8	0.58	1933	8.7	0.47
1912	19.2	0.56	1934	8.6	0.61
1913	21.3	0.64	1935	10.8	0.60
1914	13.7	1.48	1936	7.5	0.92
1915	25.1	0.91	1937	2.7	1.05
1916	16.3	1.28	1938	10.0	0.58
1917	14.3	1.95	1939	19.1	0.54
1918	10.0	1.99	1940	17.1	0.53
1919	8.5	2.32	1941	12.0	0.53
1920	11.3	1.55	1942	24.7	0.69
1921	13.8	0.76	1943	15.2	1.02
1922	20.3	0.85	1944	18.9	1.06
1923	21.3	0.65	1945	12.4	1.16
1924	10.2	1.21	1946	14.6	1.14
1925	18.8	1.25	1947	12.2	1.15
1926	16.2	1.08			

SOURCE: Records of Secretary of Statistics, Department of Agriculture, Regina.

less than half of the previous year's price. No other nongrain crop varies so much in price.[13]

Variations in grade of wheat are not so important as price and yield in affecting income. There are, nevertheless, wide fluctuations in the grade of wheat from year to year because of changing weather conditions, and these variations directly affect the price received.

More than any other rural group, the wheat farmer is economically naked, completely exposed to the vagaries of the price system. There is no doubt that many farmers in other parts of Canada and the world are in a worse financial position, but few experience the chronic alternation between wealth and poverty of the farmers of Saskatchewan. It is possible to adjust to a continuously low income and standard of living, as do many farmers in the Maritime Provinces; for one can plan one's life ahead, make provision for future expenditures, and adjust community institutions to the economic possibilities of an area. The pattern of life of the mixed-crop farmer may be upset by severe depression, but food, clothing, and shelter are secure, and price fluctuations are not so great as in the wheat belt. But it is the "boom and bust" character of wheat production that unhinges life's plans.

The oscillating character of the Saskatchewan economy went far toward preventing the emergence of an integrated, conservative rural society. The farmers continued to be a marginal frontier group in relation to the total society, and developed attitudes characteristic of outcast groups, believing that they did not receive their just or "parity" share of the national wealth and culture. The cleavage that developed early in the history of the province between the economically dominant urban world and the insecure rural areas was sharpened by the fluctuations of the business cycle; and this encouraged conflict between the urban middle class and the farmers.

Farm owners have traditionally been lumped by many sociologists with the middle class, along with urban business and professional groups. This broad concept of the middle class not only blurs significant class differences in urban areas; it also disguises the most significant social cleavage in the Great Plains farming region—that between the farm world and the world of the towns and cities linked to urban eastern business. Farmers and middle-class businessmen in western Canada are groups apart, with different patterns of life, and they are in many ways hostile to each other.[14]

Economic class differences tend to be played down in the local community, though every farmer is aware that some of his neighbors are big and powerful, and others are small and weak. Actually, some farmers have life chances that in prosperous periods are typical of the middle class, whereas others will remain as helpless economically as the urban working class. Economic classes, therefore, do exist among Saskatchewan farmers, though the pressure of outside circumstances on the grain market makes farmers stand together. The conflict between urban and agricultural worlds involves first, the grip of the eastern urban world of grain trading, distribution, and credit on *all* grain farmers, and second, the traditional immediate exploitative relation of the town to its rural hinterland, which Veblen has pointed out:

The country town is an organization of business concerns engaged in buying things from the farmers in order to sell at an advance to the central markets, and in buying from the central markets in order to sell at an advance to the farmers. The country town is an organization of "middlemen" and it is out of this difference between the buying price and the selling price that the entire town gets its living. . . .
. . . it is to be admitted without argument or hesitation that these country-town merchants, bankers, and buyers are by law and custom entitled to all the profits which they can get, and as long as they can get them. . . . It is the time-honored customary right of the townsman to turn an honest penny at the cost of the countrymen.[15]

External business controls tend to make farmers hostile— the degree of hostility varying with the price of wheat—to the entire urban world, including the cities and towns of Saskatchewan. Some big farmers, of course, are treated with deference in the banks of Regina, for here the urban group and middle-class farmers meet as members of a common class. Both farmers and townspeople in Saskatchewan belong to the same economic class, if class position is determined by the amount of property owned and the chance of getting ahead. But economic class consciousness is prevented from developing by the fact that the obvious power of the absentee eastern grain brokers, bankers, and railroad companies over the lives of western farmers encourages strategic solidarity among Saskatchewan farmers vis-à-vis an urban world in which all business and some urban labor are lumped together.

This cleavage between farmers and the urban middle class is accentuated by the fact that the organized community life of the rural population is carried on independently of social activities in the neighboring towns and cities. There are very few institutions which bind farmers and townspeople together in a common enterprise.[16] The farmers have their own economic organizations and their own marketing and consumers' cooperatives. The cooperative movement, which today includes the majority of Saskatchewan farmers, is an indication of the desire to stabilize rural economy by eliminating the middleman.[17] This movement is also a cause of increased tension between the urban middle class and the farmers.

Very little intermingling occurs between the cliques of the towns and those of the countryside; each has an independent social life. A recent study of town-country relations in a district in Alberta comparable to Saskatchewan reports that townspeople and country people shop at different times, patronize different restaurants and hotels, and do not belong to the same churches or organizations. Few of the townspeople reported personal acquaintances among the neighboring farmers.[18]

Saskatchewan has few cities, and no large urban center dominates the life of the province. There are only four widely scattered cities: Regina, the provincial capital, with a population of 58,000; Moose Jaw, forty miles west of Regina, with 20,000; Saskatoon, the site of the provincial university, with 43,000; and Prince Albert, in northern Saskatchewan, with 13,000. Only 16 per cent of the population of the province lives in these urban centers, with another 10 per cent living in towns or villages of more than 1,000 population.[19]

The cities are only larger versions of the country towns; they are primarily trading centers serving rural areas. Transportation and wholesale and retail trade employ most of the urban population.[20] Little economic or political power is concentrated in the cities. The urban upper class, to the extent that such a class exists at all, is composed of branch managers of national banks and corporations or heads of small local manufacturing or trading organizations. The visitor is struck by the number of banks bearing such names as the Royal Bank of Canada, the Bank of Montreal, the Bank of Toronto. The large department stores and mail-order houses are owned by national chains: Eaton's, Simpson's, the Hudson's Bay Company. These signify the extent to which the local commercial life is a branch of the urban world "back East." To the farmer they symbolize the world of eastern business that controls his fate.

Unlike the situation of farmers in Michigan or Ontario, there is little in Saskatchewan to array farmers psychologically against labor. Well under 5 per cent of the population is industrial labor, excluding railroad workers, as against 58 per cent in agriculture. Urban labor is, then, a negligible factor in the life of the province. Most of its workers are employed in retail stores or small shops. Until the 1940's the organized labor movement was limited to the Railroad Brotherhoods and small locals of skilled craftsmen, such as printers and carpenters.

The lack of powerful urban centers means that the basically rural character of the province dominates its social and political life. The provincial government, the newspapers, and the university must all be oriented toward the farmer. This has made it difficult for professional politicians and urban newspapers to eliminate the group consciousness of the farmer.

The development of agrarian group consciousness over against the urban world has been further strengthened by the social structure created by the wheat economy. It is difficult to apply class terminology to these farmers. The sparsity of population, because of the large size of wheat farms, means that most of the farm communities contain not more than a hundred families.

Mechanization has reduced the importance of the traditional lower class, the farm laborer. "Technological advance in farm machinery has, within a generation, hurried the plains region farmer from ox-drawn plough to four-horse binder, . . . to today's rubber-tired power combine and one-way seeder with which one man can farm a section [640 acres] of grain land."[21] Two-thirds of the farmers of Saskatchewan did not employ anyone outside their own families in 1941. This stands in interesting contrast to mixed farming in Ontario, where almost half of the farms had hired help.[22] A large part of Saskatchewan farm labor is hired only for August and September, when additional help, composed primarily of students, is required for the harvest.

Within the farm operators' group, variations in size of farm and income usually reflect class differences. Sharp variations exist in Saskatchewan as a whole; but they exist mainly *between* areas rather than *within* individual rural communities. Farmers in districts of good soil are generally more well to do than those in poor regions. Large farms of 640 acres to double that size are to be found on the rich Regina plains and and in the Rosetown district west of Saskatoon, while small farms of 160 to 320 acres are clustered in the poor-soil regions of northern Saskatchewan. Within the province the average assessment per acre of land varies from an index of 9 for the poorest rural municipality to 76 for the wealthiest.[23] Within any one community, however, variations in the value of land are necessarily small, for with few exceptions farms have the same conditions of soil and rainfall. Differences in income do exist within individual rural communities, but they are not large enough to result in the emergence of distinct social classes.

Although tenancy was a growing phenomenon in Saskatchewan before the Second World War, it does not constitute a predominant class difference as it does in many other agricultural regions on this continent. This is due to the fact that poor land yields a cash return so low that tenancy is unprofitable, and when an owner dies or is foreclosed the property is resold at any price it will bring. On the other hand, when land falls vacant in regions of highly productive soil, the owner of

TABLE 5

DISTRIBUTION OF SASKATCHEWAN TENANTS BY AGE, 1943
(Percentages)

Under 20	21–30	31–40	41–50	51–60	61–70	71–80	Total
1.1	32.8	31.0	18.2	12.2	4.2	0.5	100.0

SOURCE: Provincial Mediation Board, *A Survey of Agricultural Land Debt and of Ownership and Tenancy in Saskatchewan, as at December 31, 1943* (1944), p. 31.

an adjoining farm usually rents or buys it, or an energetic young farmer occupies it as a tenant. Tenant farmers, therefore, are often among the more well-to-do members of the farming population in the province as a whole. Second, and more important, is the following fact:

Tenancy in this Province is not a permanent factor . . . but is rather a part of the progress pattern of Ownership— young farmers with a limited capital renting land until they are able to purchase land through Agreement of Sale, or by the acceptance of a Mortgage for the unpaid balance, achieving titled ownership at higher ages, depending on the speed made possible by favourable, or unfavourable, economic conditions.[24]

A comparison of a large random sample of owners and tenants revealed that the average age of farm owners in Saskatchewan in 1943 was 51 years, while that of tenants was 39. The median age of tenants was 36.5 years, and, as table 5 shows, 64 per cent of them were under 41 years of age. Tenancy, therefore, would appear to be largely an age rather than a class difference, a transitional phase in a farmer's career.

Cleavages in ethnic background and religion have been more important than economic class divisions in separating agrarians into distinct social groups. Ethnically, the three Prairie Provinces of Canada are more comparable to the heterogeneity found in many areas south of the border than to the rest of Canada. As table 6 shows, only 41.9 per cent of the population of rural Saskatchewan is of English, Scotch, and Irish origin. Much of this settlement has been in distinct ethnic enclaves. Saskatchewan has many Ukrainian, German, French, and Polish settlements. Dwelling together, settlers from non-English-speaking countries have not participated as much in rural community organizations as have English-speaking farmers. There is considerable prejudice against non-Anglo-Saxon groups, especially those from central and eastern Europe.

Ethnic differences are accompanied by religious cleavages. Most of the central European groups, Ukrainian, Russian, Pol-

TABLE 6

TOTAL POPULATION OF SASKATCHEWAN BY
ETHNIC ORIGINS, 1941

Ethnic origin	Number	Percentage
British	397,905	44.9
English	205,519	23.2
Irish	104,072	11.7
Scottish	108,919	12.3
Others	2,995	0.4
French	50,530	5.7
Austrian	10,655	1.2
German	130,258	14.7
Hungarian	14,578	1.6
Dutch	35,894	4.1
Polish	27,902	3.1
Russian	25,933	2.9
Scandinavian	68,806	7.8
Ukrainian	79,777	9.0
Others	26,962	3.0
Asiatic	3,420	0.4
Indian and Eskimo	13,388	1.5

SOURCE: Dominion Bureau of Statistics, *Eighth
Census of Canada, 1941,* Bulletin B-7, p. 3.

ish, German, and Hungarian, as well as the French Canadians,
are Roman Catholics. A small minority are Greek Orthodox.
The majority of the Saskatchewan citizens, however, belong
to one of the Protestant denominations, as shown in table 7.
Religious differences have at times created serious conflicts,
especially between Protestants and Roman Catholics. The
strength of this feeling was evident in the late 1920's, when
the Ku Klux Klan entered the province and gained support
for its anti-Catholic program.

We have seen that the similarity of climate, crops, markets,
and agricultural technology has provided the wheat farmers
of Saskatchewan with the structural basis for collective action.
"Though these men and women are of varied national and
racial backgrounds, and many religious beliefs, their common,
day-to-day problems, their persistent economic struggle for
'better price for wheat,' 'lower freight rates,' 'parity prices for
farm crops,' have, within one generation, brought about a
unity of purpose that seems a perpetual source of surprise to

TABLE 7

TOTAL POPULATION OF SASKATCHEWAN
BY RELIGIOUS AFFILIATIONS, 1941

Religion	Number	Percentage
United Church	230,495	25.7
Roman Catholic	243,734	27.2
Anglican	117,674	13.1
Lutheran	104,717	11.7
Presbyterian	54,856	6.1
Mennonite	32,511	3.6
Greek Orthodox	37,699	4.2
Baptist	19,460	2.2
Others	54,846	6.1
Totals	895,992	100.0

SOURCE: Dominion Bureau of Statistics, *Eighth Census of Canada, 1941*, Bulletin A-5, pp. 2–3.

the residents of older provinces wherein there is much greater diversification of industrial and financial activity, readier access to markets—and more rain."[25]

The recent frontier background has meant that agrarians were comparatively free to adopt new and seemingly radical solutions for social and economic problems. There have been few tradition-bound patterns of political and economic action. In the last three decades two predominantly agrarian political parties, the Progressives in the 1920's and the CCF in the 1930's and 1940's, have won sweeping support.

The sparse settlement and lack of large urban centers, which made various community and social services economically unprofitable, have also increased local cooperative endeavors. Farmers have been forced to unite cooperatively to obtain telephone service, local roads, medical and hospital facilities, and other social services. Today 125,000 farmers hold almost 500,000 cooperative memberships; that is, on the average a farmer belongs to four or five cooperatives. Through cooperative and political action, grain growers have attempted to resist the coercions of a fluctuating market economy. The resulting widespread community participation has facilitated the rapid development and acceptance of new community institutions as events demonstrated the need for them. In succeeding chapters an attempt will be made to show how a radical agrarianism emerged as a direct and logical expression of the problems of the Saskatchewan wheat economy.

NOTES

1. Arthur S. Morton, *History of Prairie Settlement* (Toronto, Macmillan Co. of Canada, Ltd., 1938); Chester Martin, *"Dominion Lands" Policy* (Toronto, Macmillan Co. of Canada, Ltd., 1938); C. A. Dawson and Eva A. Younge, *Pioneering in the Prairie Provinces* (Toronto, Macmillan Co. of Canada, Ltd., 1940); *Report of the Saskatchewan Royal Commission on Immigration and Settlement, 1930* (Regina, 1930).

2. Martin, *op. cit.*, p. 519.

3. *Report of the Royal Commission on Dominion-Provincial Relations: Canada, 1867–1939* (Ottawa, 1940), Book I, p. 68.

4. Charles Cecil Lingard, *The Autonomy Question in the Canadian North-West* (University of Chicago Press, 1942).

5. Claris Edwin Silcox, *Church Union in Canada* (New York, Institute of Social and Religious Research, 1933); Dawson and Younge, *op. cit.*, pp. 237–41.

6. Interviews with former members of the S.G.G.A.

7. Hopkins Moorhouse, *Deep Furrows* (Toronto, George J. McLeod, Ltd., 1918), pp. 231–32.

8. Interviews with leaders of the U.F.C.

9. Frontier Oklahoma, which had the strongest Socialist Party before the First World War, also had been settled by many former working-class radicals. See Oscar Ameringer, *If You Don't Weaken* (New York, Henry Holt and Co., 1940), p. 260.

10. Bank of Canada, *Report of the Financial Position of the Province of Saskatchewan* (Ottawa, 1937), p. 2. (Italics mine.)

"The composition of freight loaded on cars in Saskatchewan in 1936 was: agricultural products, 79.5 per cent; mineral products, 8.8 per cent; forest products, 5.1 per cent; manufacturing and miscellaneous, 6.6 per cent." G. E. Britnell, *The Wheat Economy* (University of Toronto Press, 1939), p. 33.

11. R. E. Motherwell, "A Study of Crop Insurance," *Report of the Saskatchewan Reconstruction Council* (Regina, 1944), p. 30.

12. Wilmer J. Hansen, "Economic Aspects of Crop (Yield) Insurance with Reference to the Province of Saskatchewan," Ninth Annual Meeting, Canadian Agricultural Economic Society, *Proceedings*, 1937, p. 49.

13. Dominion Bureau of Statistics, *Canada Year Book, 1922–1923*, pp. 282, 283; *ibid.*, *1932*, p. 1061.

14. Jean Burnet, "Town-Country Relations and the Problem of

Rural Leadership," *Canadian Journal of Economics and Political Science*, August, 1947, pp. 395–97.

15. Thorstein Veblen, *Essays in Our Changing Order* (New York, Viking Press, 1934), pp. 286–93.

16. Burnet, *op. cit.,* pp. 404–5.

17. Province of Saskatchewan, Department of Cooperation and Cooperative Development, *Third Annual Report* (Regina, 1948).

18. Burnet, *op. cit.,* pp. 405–7.

19. Dominion Bureau of Statistics, *Eighth Census of Canada, 1941*, Bulletin A-6, p. 6.

20. Britnell, *op. cit.,* p. 23.

21. Jim Wright, "Saskatchewan," *Canadian Geographic Magazine,* March, 1947, p. 120.

22. *Farms and Farmers in Canada: Facts from the Census, 1941 and 1931* (Sanford Evans Statistical Service, Winnipeg, 1944), p. 8.

23. The provincial government assesses the relative worth of parcels of land and assigns to each an index number that is used as the basis for computing the tax rate.

24. Provincial Mediation Board, *A Survey of Agriculture Land Debt and of Ownership and Tenancy in Saskatchewan, as at December 31, 1943* (Regina, 1944), p. 31.

25. Wright, *op. cit.,* pp. 117–20.

3

THE EMERGENCE OF AGRARIAN
CLASS CONSCIOUSNESS

ECONOMIC and political class consciousness obviously does not emerge as a simple reaction to the position of a group in the economic and social structure. The transformation of a group from a large mass of individuals, who do not recognize the existence of a basic, common class interest, to a self-conscious class occurs through the intervening factor of organized group action. Max Weber has well described the conditions that give rise to this development.

. . . the factor that creates "class" is unambiguously economic interest, and indeed only those interests involved in the existence of the "market". . . .

The degree in which "communal action" and possibly "societal action," emerges from the "mass actions" of the members of a class is linked to . . . the extent of the [economic] contrasts that have already evolved, and is especially linked to the *transparency* of the connections between the causes and the consequences of the "class situation." For however different [economic] life chances may be, this fact in itself . . . by no means gives birth to "class action". . . . The fact of being conditioned must be distinctly recognizable. For only then the contrasts of life chances can be felt . . . as a resultant from either (1) the given distribution of property, or (2) the structure of the concrete economic order. It is only then that people may react against the class structure not only through acts of an intermittent and irrational protest, but in form of rational association.[1]

The development of economic class consciousness on the Canadian prairies dates from the first large-scale settlement at the turn of the century. Tens of thousands of farmers were scattered throughout the immense prairie region. They grew wheat which they sold at various railroad points to the representatives of the grain companies. This situation placed them at the mercy of these large companies and the railroads, which dictated the conditions of sale.

The Canadian Pacific Railway (C.P.R.), then the only line in western Canada, gave monopolies to individual trading companies at various railroad stops in order to encourage them to build grain elevators. In 1897 the C.P.R. ruled that no grain would be received for shipment except through the trading companies' elevators. This monopoly prevented farmers from selling to small individual buyers who did not have an elevator, or from shipping directly to the market in Winnipeg without having to store their wheat in a grain elevator.[2]

By the year 1900, almost three-quarters of the grain elevators in western Canada were owned by five companies. Monopoly control of elevator and grain companies was further strengthened by the formation of the Manitoba and North-West Grain Dealers' Association, which included most of the grain dealers and "soon had command of the situation from the buyers' standpoint."[3]

The monopoly eliminated competitive bidding for the farmers' wheat and permitted the trading companies to set the conditions of sale. As a result of the uneven distribution of bargaining power, many farmers maintained that the private companies were making exorbitant profits and could force them to accept less than the market price. The grain growers also asserted that the elevator agents undergraded wheat and thereby made additional unearned profits for the companies. Other common complaints were that the elevator agents deducted unnecessarily for unclean wheat and that they short-weighted the grain.

The trade practices of the railroads and grain companies aroused bitter resentment in the farmers.

After all, they were the men who provided the golden stream out of which others were dipping repeatedly and making fortunes. It was all very well to pay for services rendered, but farmers complained that they were paying entirely too much. The townsmen were fleecing them, was their bitter reflection as they sweated in the prairie heat. Whether entirely justified or not, in those years a hostility toward middlemen was born that has never since expired.[4]

As long as the scattered farmers suffered one by one, with the sense that nothing could be done about their plight, they had no effective basis for action. They could only vote their individual protests at the next election. How did organization among them come about?

The year 1901 witnessed a major economic crisis in the West which resulted in the formation of the first powerful farmers' movement in western Canada. In that year the prairies produced 60,000,000 bushels of wheat—almost twice as much as had ever before been harvested. The railroads were unprepared to handle a crop of that size, and almost half of it was lost because there were not enough freight cars to move it before winter. The farmers complained bitterly that the railroads gave preference to the elevator companies in allotting cars. Spontaneous meetings of protest were held in many places. The temper of the times is described in the following statement by W. R. Motherwell, a subsequent leader of Saskatchewan farmers:

There was incipient rebellion when we organized. It's too late for organization; it's bullets we want, men were saying. But we really didn't know what we wanted; we were in despair. It was not a question of growing crops but of marketing them. In the fall when the elevator opened, you would see a rush of wagons, wheel to wheel, to see who would get there first. . . .

Well, we grew the wheat, which was valueless unless marketed. Wheat was regarded as gold by Easterners, but it had no value for us unless shipped out of the country. . . . Such conditions engendered bitterness and the country was ready for anything.[5]

A group of farmers around the town of Indian Head in the southwestern part of what is now Saskatchewan, where the wheat blockade had caused a loss of three-quarters of the crop, decided to form a farmers' organization to protect their rights. The Indian Head district was one of the oldest and richest in the then North-West Territories, as it was on the main line of the C.P.R. close to the Manitoba border. On December 18, 1901, these farmers formed the Territorial Grain Growers' Association (T.G.G.A.), called the Saskatchewan Grain Growers' Association (S.G.G.A.) after 1905. This was the first permanent agrarian organization in what is now Saskatchewan and Alberta.[6]

The idea of an organized farmers' movement caught on quickly, and within two months the Association was able to hold its first convention. Delegates were present from sixteen local organizations with a total of 500 members. The delegates established a permanent organization and passed resolutions condemning the C.P.R. for its failure to supply railroad cars and its refusal to load wheat directly from farmers' wagons instead of from grain elevators. The convention also attacked the elevator companies for depressing the price of wheat through their monopoly control. The assembled agrarians hoped to bring pressure on Parliament to change railroad regulations.[7]

The convention also decided on a major plan which was to prove crucial in the later development of the movement: the inauguration of regular meetings of Association members in every locality for discussion of common problems. Here was the beginning of an activity fundamental to the continued vitality and growth of any movement. By 1916, fifteen years after its founding, the S.G.G.A. had 1,300 locals and a membership of 28,000.[8] The locals met once or twice a month to discuss rural, national, and world problems. They sent delegates to annual conventions of the Association where political problems were thrashed out in heated debate. These meetings came to be known as the "Farmers' Parliament"; and the provincial and federal governments not only recognized them as an authentic expression of rural opinion but adopted many of their proposals.

Soon after the first T.G.G.A. convention, the farmers seemed to have tangible evidence of the power of organization. The federal government passed remedial legislation requiring railway shipping agents to assign freight cars in the order in which they were applied for, regardless of whether the applicant was a farmer or an elevator company.[9] But this victory proved short-lived, for in the fall of 1902 a new wheat blockade developed as a result of another record-breaking crop. Instead of abiding by the new federal legislation, the railroad continued to cooperate with the private elevator companies by giving them most of the available freight cars. At the 1902 convention of the T.G.G.A., the president, W. R. Motherwell, asserted, "The plain provisions of the car distribution clause are disregarded at every shipping point. . . . Of sixty-seven spotted cars at Sintaluta only seven have been assigned to farmers."[10] This monopoly enabled the elevator agents again to buy wheat on their own terms. The farmers maintained that local elevator prices were ten cents a bushel beneath the price they could receive after paying the freight to ship direct to the open market in Winnipeg.[11]

The T.G.G.A. now brought suit against the railroad, although many members were skeptical about the possibility of taming the mighty C.P.R. The Association charged one of the agents of the company with breaking the federal law by making preferential assignment of freight cars to the elevator companies. The T.G.G.A. not only won its suit in court, but, as a result, the railroad dropped its efforts to bolster the monopoly position of the grain companies.[12]

The victory of the T.G.G.A. over the railroad gave tremendous prestige to the farmers' organization. The Association began to form new locals in the more densely settled parts of what were then the North-West Territories, and a Manitoba Association was organized in 1903. The influence of the new organization was strongest in areas that had been settled for ten years or more, for the older pioneers were the ones who had lost their illusions about the West and accepted the necessity for group organization.[13]

The victory over the railroad did not end the farmers' suspicions that the elevator monopoly was still cheating them. The grain buyers continued to classify into different grades wheat that the farmers believed to be identical, and the day-to-day fluctuations on the Grain Exchange looked to the farmers more like the results of gambling in wheat than the orderly operation of a market. In 1905 the T.G.G.A. sent E. A. Partridge, one of its leaders, to Winnipeg to investigate the activities of the trading companies and of the Grain Exchange. His report to the Association was typical of agrarian feeling at the time.

. . . the North West Grain Dealers Association [of Winnipeg], which sets "street prices," [reduces] charges wherever a farmers' elevator or an independent dealer operates. The object of the elevator companies was to give the farmer the lowest price possible and get the largest amount of wheat through the elevators. More powerful than the line elevators, however, were the exporters and millers. The large amount of capital and credit required, the difficulties of establishing trade connections . . . put limitations on competition, and the "wheat business is thus practically in the hands of three milling companies and five exporting firms." The Grain Exchange itself [is] "a combine" with a "gambling hell thrown in."[14]

Farmers were rapidly learning the advantages of group action. Partridge now set out to organize a farmer-owned cooperative grain company with its own elevators and flour mills, which would eventually eliminate middlemen in the grain trade. The top officials of the Grain Growers' Associations opposed the suggestion at first, because, as they said, they feared that the farmers would not support such a company and that its failure would endanger the existence of the Associations. This opposition by the executive of the Grain Growers was the first of many attempts by the elected leaders of prairie farm organizations to block the formation of new institutions to meet agrarian needs. But, in the end, antagonism to the private grain companies overrode the bureaucratic conservatism of the leaders; and Partridge was able to secure enough money from a large number of well-to-do farmers to start a farmers' company.[15]

This new venture, the Grain Growers' Grain Company, Ltd. (G.G.G.C.), was set up in 1906 as a cooperatively owned grain agency to receive grain from members and sell it directly on the Grain Exchange. To insure democratic control, no farmer was permitted to buy more than four of the $25 shares or to cast more than one vote at meetings. Six weeks after the G.G.G.C. started to operate, the Winnipeg Grain

Exchange suspended the right of the new company to trade on the Exchange on the ground that the company had issued pamphlets "offending against the honour and dignity of the Exchange and reflecting on the methods adopted by certain members of the trade."[16] The farmers' company was charged also with paying patronage dividends to its clients, which violated the rules of the Exchange.

This open attack by the hated Grain Exchange spurred farmers to take another step in the direction of class-conscious action. It was evident that cooperative economic action was not enough to control the power of the grain monopoly. Only government intervention against the Exchange could save the company. In Manitoba, where the Exchange was incorporated, the Manitoba Grain Growers' Association threatened to take political action against the provincial government unless it forced the Exchange to readmit the company. The provincial cabinet attempted to dodge responsibility on the issue, but, with an election approaching, it finally prevailed upon the Exchange to take the company back.[17] The Exchange agreed to do so if the company would drop its plans for cooperative distribution of profits and would elect a new president in place of E. A. Partridge, who had been particularly violent in his attacks on the grain companies.[18]

The heads of the Grain Exchange recognized in Partridge a permanent and dangerous menace to their security. From the time of his arrival in the West from Ontario in 1883, as a young man of twenty-one, to his death in 1931, Partridge had the reputation of being a radical and a visionary. In an older, more stable society such a man would have been simply another "crackpot" agitator. In the newly settled, loosely structured society of the West, with its numerous unsolved economic and social problems, a man with ideas could command a hearing, and Partridge did so from the formation of the Grain Growers' Grain Company to his speeches urging socialism, in 1930 and 1931. "More ideas . . . originated with him affecting the farmers' social and economic welfare than with any other dweller in the grain country."[19]

From the very first, Partridge saw the emerging farmers' movement as part of a world-wide conflict between capital and labor. The reforms that he advocated were part of a conscious, long-range program to get the agrarians to accept Ruskinian socialism, as he once made clear in an interview: "Cooperation provided a temporary remedy for the existing abuses of the grain trade. It would provide out of its revenues a great educational fund which would finance a newspaper and a campaign which would culminate in the domination of the legislature by the common man, and in the introduction of state ownership of public utilities and natural resources. Then would come true cooperation based on the ethics of Ruskin."[20]

The G.G.G.C. refused the demand of the Grain Exchange for Partridge's removal as president of the company. In 1907, however, when a permanent organization of the company was established, Partridge refused to run again for the presidency. Essentially, he was an agitator who had to engage in new battles, but who withdrew from the administrative scene as soon as the fight was won.[21] The replacement of the aggressive fighting leader by a more conservative bureaucratic type is characteristic in organizations such as trade-unions, political movements, and cooperatives.[22] Partridge's career was peculiar only in the fact that he consciously recognized the pressure for such change and stepped down willingly. This left him free to take on new battles.[23]

The attack by the Exchange on the young farmers' company was as important for it as the earlier victory of the Territorial Grain Growers' Association over the C.P.R. had been for that organization. The Exchange had explicitly recognized that the Grain Growers' Grain Company was a menace to its power. The economic enemy of the agrarians was becoming clearly identified. Publicity and interest were easier to obtain on a concrete issue than through abstract propaganda against the private companies and the Exchange. T. A. Crerar, who had succeeded Partridge as president of the G.G.G.C., "expressed the view that the company might never have survived had it not been for the publicity it was given by expulsion from the Exchange."[24]

The financial stability of the company enabled its directors to take another step in organizing and unifying agrarian opinion. In 1908 they decided to issue their own weekly newspaper. This paper, the *Grain Growers' Guide*, was supported also by the interprovincial council of the three Grain Growers' associations in Alberta, Saskatchewan, and Manitoba. Partridge, the foremost exponent of education in the movement, was chosen as its first editor. He hoped to make the paper the joint organ of the organized farmer and labor movements in the battle against organized capital, but the rest of the officials objected. Again the "agitator" dropped out of responsibility to resume his gadfly role, declaring, "I'm too irritable to get along with anybody in an office."[25] Partridge left behind him, however, a new means of solidifying rural opinion and action. The movement now had a newspaper to point out to the farmers the evils of the commercial system, advocating cooperation and, later, government ownership as the solution.[26]

But the stability of the G.G.G.C. was short-lived, as could have been expected in a contest with an institution so powerfully entrenched as the Grain Exchange. The company was growing steadily. Despite its inexperience and the lack of grain elevators of its own, it handled 3 per cent of the total grain crop in its first year of operation, 1907. This rose to 8 per cent by 1909.[27] These percentages may appear small, but it must be remembered that the company was not yet able to do business at most country points, and many farmers preferred to sell directly to elevator companies who paid immediately upon delivery rather than to wait until the G.G.G.C. sold their crop.

In 1909–10 the private companies struck back at the economic taproot of the farmers' company. The Exchange abolished its rule that a one-cent commission must be paid to companies handling wheat. This did not greatly affect the private elevator companies, as most of their profits were secured from storage charges and trading grain on the market. The farmers' company was, however, completely dependent on the commission to pay all its expenses.[28] The company organized a campaign among the farmers, pointing out that unless they agreed to continue paying the one-cent commission which underwrote its operating costs, the elevator combine would be able to destroy the company, and again have a complete monopoly. The *Grain Growers' Guide* rallied the farmers to the support of the company through arguments such as the following:

As we have often pointed out . . . the Exchange is being used by the Elevator Interests that seem to dominate it, to further their own particular ends with the result that the nefarious methods of the Elevator Trust bring suspicion and condemnation upon the Exchange and its members.

The pooling of receipts at country points is not forgotten by the farmers; heavy dockage and unfair grading and low prices paid when the farmers were compelled to sell and could not help themselves, are also not forgotten.

Every injustice and disturbance in the trade that has taken place since grain commenced to be marketed in Manitoba, can be traced to the Elevator Monopoly.

The farmers in this country owe nothing to the Elevator Trust and we have confidence in them to believe that they will not be bought over by them now.[29]

When the question of the farmers assuming the cost of the G.G.G.C. was put to the test in a shareholders' referendum, 98 per cent backed the company.[30] Thousands of letters poured into the head office, many of them expressing willingness to pay more than one cent a bushel rather than sell to the monopolies.[31] The aroused farmers voted with their wheat that fall, sending 16,332,645 bushels to the company, more than twice the amount in the year before.[32] This figure actually represented only 15 per cent of the total wheat marketed in western Canada that year, for the coverage of the G.G.G.C. was still spotty. But 16,000,000 bushels constituted a powerful symbol.

This conflict and partial victory convinced the more militant of the organized farmers that their economic position would not be secure until they had successfully eliminated the middlemen all along the line. Although E. A. Partridge had refused to continue as a full-time officer, he had remained on the board of directors of the company; and he now began agitating for government ownership of all grain elevators to prevent a recurrence of attacks on the farmers by the elevator companies. Through the *Grain Growers' Guide* and the annual conventions of the provincial associations he was able to reach the farmers. Between 1907 and 1908, all three associations adopted the Partridge Plan for government ownership.[33] The *Guide* argued that "the large elevator interests, supported by many strong financial interests and working in harmony with large milling interests, were becoming dangerously strong. . . . they can steadily undersell competitors [such as the G.G.G.C.] having no storage facilities until such competitors are out of business."[34]

The Liberal governments of the three Prairie Provinces attempted to circumvent the suggestions of the farmers by proposing increased government regulation of the elevators, arguing that it would be unconstitutional for them to operate an elevator monopoly.[35] These arguments were ridiculed by the Grain Growers, who inaugurated a public campaign which obtained tens of thousands of petitions demanding government action. A conference of the reeves (heads) of the Manitoba rural municipalities also supported government ownership.[36] Faced by this challenge, the governments began to retreat. Saskatchewan appointed a Royal Commission to make a "searching inquiry into proposals looking to the creation and operation of a system of elevators to effect the objects outlined by the Grain Growers' Association,"[37] while the Manitoba government, facing an early election, agreed, in December, 1909, to set up a line of elevators as a public utility.[38]

Unfortunately for the success of the scheme, the provincial governments were making only superficial concessions to appease the electorate. The Manitoba cabinet refused to implement the plan, which called for an independent elevator commission named by the Grain Growers, and for the purchase of private elevators at their replacement cost. The Manitoba Elevator Act, which placed the elevators under the supervision of a government-appointed commission, required "A petition signed by sixty per cent of the farmers contributory to a proposed elevator . . . before it could be purchased," and subjected the purchase price of elevators to arbitration.[39]

As the Grain Growers' leaders had predicted, the Manitoba experiment in government ownership ended in complete failure. The elevators lost money and in 1912 the government decided to go out of the elevator business. The *Grain Growers' Guide* charged that "the 'elevator fiasco' was due to the government's lack of sympathy for the scheme; seemingly it had been intended that the enterprise should fail. The elevators purchased . . . were worth only one-half the sum that had been paid for them."[40] The G.G.G.C. thereupon took over the elevators and operated them as a farmer-owned chain.

In Saskatchewan the government also disappointed the farmers who had believed that the appointment of a Royal Commission was the first step toward obtaining government-owned elevators. The Commission, however, recommended a farmer-owned cooperative system.[41] After a long debate at its 1911 convention, the S.G.G.A. approved the Commission's plan, stating that it would rather have a "cooperative system within the reach of their hand than one publicly-owned over which they had no influence."[42] The Saskatchewan Cooperative Elevator Company was organized in that year. By 1913 it owned 133 elevators and was supported by 13,156 members from among a total of 95,013 farmers in the province.[43]

It must be remembered that the agrarian organizations involved only a minority of the farmers. These organizations developed during the period of the greatest migration to the West. The tens of thousands of new settlers were interested in establishing farms, not in political or economic protest. Except for the convinced radicals, disillusion with existing economic practices probably came only as a result of personal misfortune. The S.G.G.A. and the Cooperative Elevator Company, for example, received most of their support from the earliest settled regions, where farmers had gradually learned the lessons of monopoly control of the grain trade. It is significant that the two most important centers of organized action in this early period were Indian Head and Sintaluta, in the southern part of the province on the first rail line that entered Saskatchewan. These areas had been settled as early as the 1880's.

A second influence negating the rapid growth of the agrarian movement was the presence of large numbers of immigrants from non-English-speaking countries. These farmers usually settled in ethnic enclaves and had little to do with the English-speaking settlers.

A third factor accounting for the spotty support of cooperatives was the fact that their organization required financial investment by members. Money was difficult to obtain in the newly settled districts, where farmers were usually in debt. The fact that the farmer-owned companies were handling 20 per cent of all wheat grown on the prairies by the outbreak of the First World War is, therefore, more significant than it first appears.

The first twelve years of the century had witnessed a growing awareness by western farmers of the nature of their economic problem. They had fought for government regulation of the grain trade, cooperative marketing of wheat, and government ownership of elevators. They had succeeded in building the largest cooperative elevator system in the world, which both bought and sold grain. In the process, farmers were developing an increasingly critical attitude toward all middlemen in the distribution process. A common economic class situation was resulting in heightened consciousness and sharpened class attitudes. Out of economic conflict, agrarian class unity was emerging.

The collectivist ideas, which were to mature in the CCF in the 1930's, were based directly on the farmers' day-to-day experiences. The experiences of two of the foremost leaders of the movement were typical of many western farmers.

He [Crerar] could not forget his own early experiences in marketing grain when the elevators offered him fifty-nine cents per bushel, nineteen cents under the price at the terminal at the time. The freight rate of his No. 1 Northern wheat he knew to be only nine cents per bushel and when he was docked a bushel and a half to a load of fifty bushels on top of it he had been aroused to protest.

. . . But when . . . he had pointed out the injustice of the price offered and the dockage taken—the elevator man, quite calmly, had told him to go to the devil!

"There's no use going to the other elevators, for you're all alike," said young Crerar hotly.

"Then take your damned grain home again!" grinned the elevator operator insolently.

So the young farmer was compelled to sell his first wheat for what he could get. He was prepared to pay three cents per bushel on the spread, that being a reasonable charge; but although plenty of cars were available at the time, the spread cost him ten cents, a direct loss of seven cents per bushel.[44]

Roderick McKenzie, who succeeded Partridge as editor of the *Guide*, had similar experiences.

He disposed of two loads of wheat at one of the elevators in Brandon one day and was given a grade and a price which he considered fair enough. When he came in with two more loads of the same kind of wheat next day, however, the elevator man told him that he had sent a sample to Winnipeg and found out that it was not grading the grade he had given him the day before.

"The train service wouldn't allow of such fast work, sir," said Roderick McKenzie. "I suppose you sent it by wire. . . . That five cents a bushel you want me to give you looks just as good in my pocket as in yours."

So he drove up town where the other buyers were and three of them looked at the wheat but refused to give a price for it. One of them was a son of the first elevator man to whom he had gone and, said he, "The Old Man gave you a knockdown for it, didn't he?"

"Yes, but—!"

"Well, we're not going to bid against him and if you want to sell it at all, haul it back to him."[45]

Long before most of them had ever heard of socialism, western farmers believed that they were economically oppressed and exploited by the large commercial organizations. The report of the Saskatchewan Royal Commission, set up in 1910 to investigate the elevator situation, summarized the opinions of hundreds of rural leaders who had testified before it as follows:

Against the Initial Elevators.

1. Weights. That they give lower weights than the farmer is entitled to.

2. Dockage. That they take too large a percentage as against claiming the grain to grade. . . .

3. Grades. That in buying the grain they give lower grades than the grain is entitled to.

4. Prices. That they give too low prices even for the grades allowed. . . .

7. Substituting grain. That they often give the farmer inferior grain, taking his superior lot instead. . . .

Against the Banks.

1. That by restricting or refusing credit to many farmers, they force these to put their grain upon the market as soon as it is threshed, depriving them of the opportunity to hold it for a raise in price and compelling them to sell when the market is glutted and the price tends to be lowest. . . .

2. That in giving lines of credit for moving the crops they favor the larger companies and at times favor a few such companies. Thus giving these a virtual monopoly of bank credit, and assisting them in monopolizing the grain business.

Against the Railway Companies.

2. That they construct loading platforms as if the object was to render the use of them by the farmers as difficult as possible.

3. That in the past they helped to create elevator monopolies and assisted them, and that at present they favor the large milling and elevator companies wherever they can. . . .

Against the Terminal Elevator.

1. That they take too much dockage as against the shrinkage of the grain in handling. . . .

2. That they mix the different grades of grain, selling grain of the lower grade at the price of the higher grade, and that, the grain being dirty and lowered in grade by mixing, export prices are lowered and the prices paid to the farmers are also lowered. . . .

Against the Grading System.

1. That the grades do not represent the different values of the grain for milling purposes. . . .

Against the large Western Milling Companies.

4. That besides lowering the prices by lowering the grades, they artificially depress prices.

(a) By spreading false reports about crops.

(b) By juggling in options and especially by selling below market value early in the season in the Liverpool market quantities of grain for future delivery.

Against the Winnipeg Grain Exchange.

The large milling and elevator companies . . . exercise a controlling influence in the Exchange. . . . If the dominating interests maintain several elevators and buyers at any shipping point, and if they tolerate in the Exchange a number of apparently independent and competing commission men and exporters, it is only to deceive the public into believing that there is real competition in the trade.

And the dominating companies can make full use of the

speculative market of trading in futures, of hedging . . . of profiting by the rise and fall of the price in their own market, and of dealing in spreads when they occur between prices in different markets. Most important of all, they can complete the work of fixing the prices paid to the farmer.[46]

To this list of rural grievances against the big interests can be added the protests against the protective tariff, which, farmers felt, aided the manufacturing corporations of the East.

The highly visible character of economic constraints on the wheat farmers was an effective teacher. It was just one short step from wheat to the rest of the business system. An early history of the western farmers' movement described the reaction of a typical farmer of the time to the middleman.

The fellow who made that stove paid a profit to the Iron an' Steel Trust who supplied the raw iron ore. Then, he turned around and added a profit of his own before he let the whole-saler have it. Then the wholesaler chalked up more profit before he shipped it along to Joe Green over in town an' Joe just naturally had to soak me something before I got her aboard for home. That's profits on the profits! It's a hot proposition and it's my money that goes up the flue![47]

The conventions of the Grain Growers' Association gave recurrent expression to the deep-rooted antagonism of organized farmers to profits. They kept hitting out, almost at random, at the sore spots in the economy, and began saying, "There ought to be a law" to alleviate one or another evil. As yet there was no realization of the fact that they were actually challenging the fundamental economic base of the society, that this was a power fight between organized agrarians and organized business.

The 1907 convention passed a resolution "That the time has arrived for the installation of a provincial telephone system owned and operated by the government."[48] That same convention suggested that "oil fields and coal lands not at present exploited should be owned and controlled in the interests of the people."[49] It became very clear that the delegates were motivated by the desire to lower prices through eliminating profits. As one delegate put it, "We pay considerably too much for our fuel and if the government controlled the mines, it could control the price as well. . . . We discussed this question at our local meeting and there is a growing sentiment in this country for government ownership of the railroads."[50]

In 1909 the S.G.G.A. convention extended advocacy of government ownership to "timber, coal, oil or other mines," which should be operated so that "the profits and benefits be shared by all alike."[51] Public utilities, transportation, and banking were added to the list by the 1913 convention.[52] The receptivity of the provincial Liberal government to the farmers' demands is evidence of the strength of the farmers' movement. The province initiated government ownership of the telephones and of a coal mine. The coal mine proved unsuccessful and was later dropped, but the telephone lines continued under provincial ownership.

While agitating for increased government ownership, the organized farmers continued to push their cooperative elevators and other cooperative ventures. The *Grain Growers' Guide* turned its fire against the Retail Merchants' Association of Canada, which "is determined to keep the farmers and laboring classes subservient. They wish to keep all business in their own hands and thus take from the pockets of producers and consumers every cent."[53] In 1916 the S.G.G.A. organized a department to handle the wholesale purchase of supplies to be sold by the locals.[54]

By the time of the First World War the more militant farmers of Saskatchewan were organized as a fighting bloc. The S.G.G.A. continued to grow in size as well as in economic achievements. By 1916 it had over 1,300 separate locals, and 28,000 members, out of a possible 104,000 farmers.[55] This meant that there was an organized local of the S.G.G.A. with an average membership of twenty each in almost every farm community in the province. The fact that only one of every four farmers belonged to the organization did not mean that it was opposed by the majority of the rural community. The active members of the S.G.G.A. were leaders in the farming community. The officials of the rural municipalities, local school boards, and cooperative committees were members of the farmers' organization.

The same factors that led the farmers of Saskatchewan and western Canada to organize as a class for economic reform led to early support of direct political action. Many of the farmers' needs could be secured only with the aid of friendly governments, for, unlike the urban workers, the agrarians had no direct economic weapon such as the strike.

The first political movement in the West developed in the 1890's when the Patrons of Husbandry, with substantial support in Manitoba and the North-West Territories, elected a few independent farmers' candidates. The movement did not last, however, as it was based mainly on opposition to the high protective tariff and had, therefore, little to distinguish it from the low-tariff Liberals.[56]

In Saskatchewan the Grain Growers' Association first began to consider political action during the agitation for government-owned elevators. In 1909, when the Saskatchewan Liberal government hesitated to accede to the farmers' demands, Partridge, the principal advocate of government ownership, urged that

every man get busy and, working within the party of his choice, make that party the instrument of his will . . . it is not necessary that a single man now occupying a seat in the local legislature who is opposed to Government ownership should be a member of the next legislature. The farmers are a majority of both parties. Let them go en masse to the councils of their respective parties and force the acceptance of this principle on both.[57]

The Liberal government appointed the Royal Commission to investigate government ownership of elevators.[58] This attempt to circumvent the desires of the farmers would have failed were it not for the fiasco of government-owned elevators in Manitoba. The S.G.G.A., therefore, accepted the suggestion that it start cooperative elevators rather than follow up Partridge's proposal for political action.

Interest in politics was strengthened from 1906 on by the desires of farmers to reduce the high protective tariff. Grain growers had to lower the costs of production as well as of marketing, after 1909 particularly, when "the world price of wheat began a downward trend, and the rising costs of transportation and of manufactured goods rose in conjunction to wipe out and reverse that favourable differential between the two on which the wheat boom of the early years of the century had been based."[59]

Farm organizations repeatedly petitioned the Ottawa government to reduce the tariffs on manufactured goods. The Liberal Party, the traditional low-tariff party, held power during this period, but like its Conservative protectionist predecessors, did little to reduce the tariff load on farmers. Opposition to the tariff reinforced the hostility of farmers to big business and the manufacturing interests. Resolutions of farmers' conventions and articles in the *Grain Growers' Guide* repeatedly denounced "the manufacturing interests [who] are continually using their influence with our legislators to maintain, secure or increase their privilege to charge more for their products than the cost of production warrants through the instrumentality of the protective tariff."[60]

Growing discontent with agrarian dependence on favors from the traditional parties was evidenced from 1909 onward. The *Guide* editorialized against the two-party system. "[The big interests] realize that so long as the people are willing to endorse either of the old parties they are safe, but that if they send down to Ottawa insurgents or Progressives, then Special Privilege will not be able to plunder the people as in the past."[61] Letters to the editor urging political action appeared regularly after 1909.[62]

These murmurings of discontent did not receive much popular support. Farmers had not yet reached the point of recognizing a need for direct control of the government. The price of wheat held up and, with the exception of 1910, crops were good. Discontent with the tariff and the monopolistic distribution system was not great enough to create the basis for political action. Except for convinced radicals like Partridge, these evils were viewed not as the consequences of a total system, but rather as isolated problems that could be solved in time by cooperatives and remedial legislation. Farm leaders were still fumbling politically. They would strike out at visible economic evils, but did not yet realize that fundamental economic or political problems existed.

In 1913, however, a sharp drop in the price of wheat

brought a demand for independent political action. Two resolutions were introduced at the S.G.G.A. convention of that year suggesting an "Independent party representing Agriculture and Labor similar to the [British] Labor Party."[63] The discussion of the resolutions revealed substantial support for the third-party idea. Many delegates objected to the low price of wheat, which they said was caused by high freight rates, and they urged a farmers' party that would nationalize the transportation system and thus increase the price of wheat. The resolutions favoring a third party were defeated only after C. C. Dunning, a leader in the S.G.G.A. and subsequently a Liberal Premier of the province, proposed in a substitute motion that "Direct legislation, the initiative and referendum and recall will more effectively bring about government of the people, by the people, for the people than any third party . . . [and therefore] this convention does not favor the establishment of a political third party."[64]

Proposals for a third party recurred at conventions during the war years, but were not adopted.[65] The debates indicated, however, that farmers in S.G.G.A. locals were discussing the need for a new party that would represent them. In 1915 the Non-Partisan League, which was then organizing just south of the border in North Dakota, made its way into Saskatchewan and received rural support. By 1917 it was publishing two weekly papers and had over 3,000 members in the province. The League's program in Saskatchewan was the same as the semisocialist one it was furthering in the United States.[66]

The new political movement encountered the carefully cultivated tie between S.G.G.A. leaders and the provincial Liberal Party. At conventions of the farm organization, Liberal leaders were careful to appear to be supporting farmers' demands. Several leaders of the S.G.G.A., W. R. Motherwell, the first president, J. A. Maharg, the second president, and George Langley and Charles Dunning, members of the board of directors of the S.G.G.A., became members of Liberal cabinets. The Grain Growers' leaders, who entered the provincial government, retained their membership and sometimes their official position in the organization. They appeared regularly as delegates to S.G.G.A. provincial conventions. The Liberals were therefore able to retain influence in the movement and to defeat any move toward class-conscious political action. Liberal leaders continually referred to the Liberal government as the farmers' government, and stressed the fact that a new political movement was not needed, as the agrarians controlled the existing government.[67] Premier Martin told the S.G.G.A. convention in 1919, "There are questions now coming before you affecting the welfare of the entire community of the province. It is the policy of the present government and will continue to be the policy of the present government to carry out these suggestions."[68]

On the whole, the claims of the provincial Liberals appear to be valid. They did implement most of the proposals of the S.G.G.A. which came under provincial jurisdiction. The Grain Growers were too strongly organized to be ignored by any government that hoped to retain power in a rural province. The conflict over government-owned elevators was the only significant point of difference between government and farmers. Unfortunately for the provincial Liberals, however, they were part of a national party, in which the influence of eastern business had more weight than did the western farmers. Many farmers believed that the federal Liberals in office had shown little more willingness than the Conservatives to yield to the farmers on issues such as the tariff and reduced distribution costs.[69] This fact helped to negate the efforts of Saskatchewan Liberals to prevent the emergence of an independent farmers' party.

Agrarian discontent continued during the First World War, a period of sharp increase in the cost of goods and services that farmers used. Farm leaders believed that high prices were a result of the protective tariff designed to strengthen the position of eastern manufacturing companies. In 1917 the S.G.G.A. adopted, as its political program, the "Farmers' Platform" of the Canadian Council of Agriculture, which called for elimination of virtually all tariffs on the grounds that they were fleecing agriculture and "making the rich richer and the poor poorer." The continued rural antagonism to private industry and profits was clearly revealed in the proposals for sharply graduated taxes on incomes over $4,000, heavily graduated inheritance taxes on large estates, and graduated profits taxes on large corporations. The convention of that year asked also for nationalization of railroads, telegraphs, and express companies, and opposed the alienation by the government of any of its natural resources.[70]

The end of the First World War coincided with a sharp drop in farm income as a result of declining wheat prices and a drought, while the prices of manufactured goods remained at wartime levels. To farm leaders this appeared to be another example of big interests profiting at the expense of farmers. The Non-Partisan League and other advocates of independent agrarian political action, such as E. A. Partridge, began to win increasing support among western grain growers. In March, 1919, the S.G.G.A. leaders finally yielded to the pressure for a new party and began to organize for federal political action on the basis of the "Farmers' Platform."[71] A federal by-election held in October, 1919, in the Assinaboia constituency of southern Saskatchewan, gave concrete evidence that the farmers wanted a new party. Oliver Gould, a farmers' candidate, defeated W. R. Motherwell, the former president of the S.G.G.A. and now the Liberal nominee, by 5,224 votes.[72]

At the same time that Saskatchewan was forming a new farmers' party, agrarians in the other Prairie Provinces and in Ontario began organizing. Their candidates swept the polls in the provincial election in Ontario just one week before Gould's election in Saskatchewan.[73] Ontario farmers were more conservative than those on the prairies, and their political action was largely a protest against the conscription of farmers' sons in the last months of the war, but the phenomenon of a farmers' government in conservative Ontario strengthened the hands of the advocates of political action in the West. The leaders of the farm organization in Alberta and Manitoba, facing the same rank-and-file pressures as the heads of the S.G.G.A., joined in the growing movement for a new party.[74]

On January 6, 1920, the National Progressive Party was formed under the leadership of T. A. Crerar, who had succeeded Partridge as head of the G.G.G.C. and who had been in the wartime union cabinet as the Grain Growers' representative.[75] This choice was to prove unfortunate for the young political movement, for Crerar, like most of the Grain

Growers' leaders, had not been a supporter of agrarian political action until mass sentiment for it developed.[76] The presence of a large number of political opportunists in its top leadership prevented the Progressives from making a clean break with the old parties, especially with the Liberals.

The time was ripe for a new party in western Canada. The price the Saskatchewan farmer received for his wheat fell from $1.50 a bushel in 1920 to 76 cents a bushel in 1921. The disparity between the price of wheat and the price the farmer paid for other goods squeezed him hard. Between 1919 and 1920 the wholesale price index increased 16.3 per cent, while the price of wheat fell 31.7 per cent. In 1921 wheat fell exactly 50 per cent in price, and wholesale prices declined 29.5 per cent.[77]

The Progressives and the farmers' organizations were therefore able to win a tremendous response from the rural population on a program opposing business profiteering and the tariff. The western Progressives were insistent also on the reëstablishment of government marketing of wheat and the closing of the Grain Exchange. The farmers believed that if they could abolish gambling on the Exchange and eliminate private trading companies the price of wheat would go up.

In the federal election of 1921 the Progressives elected 65 members of Parliament out of a total of 245 in the House of Commons. Of these, 39 were from the prairie wheat belt, 15 of them from Saskatchewan. The only seat that was lost by the Progressives in Saskatchewan was the urban seat of Regina. The Party succeeded in polling 62.6 per cent of the total vote in the 13 predominantly rural seats of Saskatchewan.[78] Its actual farm vote was probably higher, as the figures include the vote in towns and small villages, which were strongholds of the old parties.

This great victory of a party that was little more than a year old is an indication of the tightly organized nature of the Saskatchewan farming community. The S.G.G.A. had grown to a total of 36,000 members in 1919, which meant that almost one farmer in every three in the province belonged to the organization.[79] The Progressive victory was possible because of the educational and organizational work of the previous two decades. It was comparatively easy to create

a new party in the grain belt, in a community that had had
the experience of fighting for economic rights. The history
of independent political action in Canada and the United
States has shown the extent to which unified action to achieve
economic goals can be quickly mobilized in the wheat belt.
The absence of serious economic cleavages within the rural
society and the common economic experiences of grain growers made this possible.

In the face of this agrarian success, the Liberal Party did
what liberal parties on this continent tried to do in the past
under similar circumstances: its new Prime Minister, W. L.
Mackenzie King, sought to win back the agrarian radicals by
offering them representation in the federal cabinet and promising to reduce the tariff. Unfortunately for the hopes of
those who would build a permanent new party, many of
the leaders had never been converted to the necessity for a
class party. They had gone along with the tide until they
thought that they could control it. Many Progressive members
of Parliament, including T. A. Crerar, the national leader,
had close ties with the Liberal machines in their areas, and
favored accepting King's offer from the outset. The attempt
to reach such unity after the elections in 1921 failed; there
were too many newly elected agrarian members of Parliament
who regarded such a proposal as a betrayal of their followers.
Crerar was successful, however, in getting the Progressives to
decline their rightful place as the official opposition to the
Conservatives, who had fewer seats than the agrarians.[80]

Within two years the Progressive group in the House found
themselves gradually led back into the Liberal fold by Crerar
and others. They continually supported the government on
controversial issues against the Conservatives, although they
were able to gain few concessions from the Liberals on the
tariff and the government marketing of wheat. In 1924 a
few of the more radical members from Alberta and Saskatchewan broke with the Progressive Party because it was too
closely allied with the Liberals.[81]

The results of the Progressive experiment taught many Saskatchewan farmers a needed lesson. A new movement requires
leaders who believe in it; if they are forced to act radically,
they will revert to their original conservatism at the first op-

portunity. In interviewing members of the Saskatchewan CCF who were active in the Progressive movement, I was struck by the number of old farmers who expressed the view that "you can't trust any politician, even those on our side," and then described the Progressive "betrayal."

In Saskatchewan the Liberal Party was even more success-ful in killing the agrarian threat. Recognizing that the farmers were behind the Progressives, Premier Martin announced that his provincial government was neutral in federal politics.[82] Early in 1921 he appointed J. A. Maharg, the president of the S.G.G.A., to the provincial cabinet, and called an election before the farmers' organization could decide whether to enter provincial politics.[83] These tactics succeeded in returning the Liberals to power. Twelve out of the thirteen independent farmers' candidates, who contested the election without any party or formal Grain Growers' support, were elected and formed the second largest group in the provincial House.[84] Had Premier Martin not called this "snap" election with the assistance of the Grain Growers' leaders, he would have been defeated, in all probability, as were the less politically astute old-party governments of Alberta and Manitoba. The lack of reality in the division between federal and provincial Liberals was made clear a few months later, when Martin dropped his neutrality on federal issues and backed the Liberals against the Progressives. Here was still another lesson for the Grain Growers to absorb.

A few Progressives continued to be elected federally and provincially in Saskatchewan until the 'thirties. The federal members joined with a similar farmers' group from Alberta and two socialist members from Winnipeg to form a small, independent left-wing group in the House of Commons op-posed to the two old parties. This small "Ginger Group" was to keep alive the idea of a third party after the larger or-ganization had collapsed, and was to help form the socialist CCF of the 1930's.

It is difficult to explain why the Progressives hung on in a few constituencies, while disappearing almost completely in the rest. The constituency of Rosetown, which elected a Progressive until 1930, is one of the richest areas in Saskatch-ewan, while Mackenzie, which had a similar political record, is one of the poorest. One of the main factors seems to have been the political courage of the Progressive member of Parliament in a district. Where elected Progressives remained loyal to the third-party ideal and retained their ties with the local farm organizations, they could maintain strong electoral support, but where members of Parliament supported the Liberals, the Progressive movement died away.

The Progressive movement failed principally because it was more a product of immediate discontent than of long-term crisis. It was not the expression of a self-conscious class demanding deep-rooted changes. The farmers turned to independent political action because of the threat to their way of life posed by the postwar crisis. Once the conditions which produced the protest disappeared, the mass movement died.

Though unsuccessful in building a permanent agrarian party, the Progressive movement left deep roots in the Saskatchewan scene. It was the first important step in alienating farmers from their old party loyalties. Many who were active in the farmers' party never again supported the old parties, but continued to work for a new party. The success of the movement had proved that a third party could be built successfully within a short time.

The history of protest movements suggests that they have two elements: one is the formal organization; the other is the hard core of scattered adherents whose allegiance expresses a deep conviction of the need for change. The former tends to fall apart and disappear when protest is at the sporadic stage; the tougher supporters simply resume their earlier quest for a means of expressing their protest. The western frontier in the United States and Canada had a disproportionate share of such agitators. The protests of the Partridges of Saskatchewan arose not from a specific grievance but from the desire for a fundamental change in the social order. Movements rise and fall or grow conservative, but a nucleus of social innovators may hang on, waiting for the next opportunity to introduce change. They are the ones who attempt to learn from defeat. The Progressive experience did not permanently discourage the more politically militant of the Saskatchewan farmers, but rather taught them that political action was a possibility. As we shall see later, when discussing the background of the CCF leaders of the 'thirties, more than 30 per cent of them were active in the Progressive Party. The CCF arose as a direct descendant of the earlier political movement.

Two forms of class action run through the agrarian movement: cooperative self-help in the strictly economic sphere through such devices as cooperatively run grain elevators; and, political action as an indirect device for achieving economic ends. At various periods one appears to be stressed more than the other. This has been as true in most of the Great Plains region as in Saskatchewan. Political action usually arises in a depression or during a major social crisis such as war, whereas cooperation occurs more frequently in periods of prosperity.

The reasons for this difference are twofold. Cooperation is a more gradualist approach to the problems of economic reform than political action. In a depression, farmers are less likely to accept gradualism when immediate action is called for. The problems of low prices, government relief, mortgage foreclosures, and credit become urgent, and only government action can remedy these conditions. A second reason for cooperation being weak in a depression is that the investment and share capital required to form a cooperative enterprise is not available during depressions. The depression effectively cancels out the alternative of cooperation and leaves political action as a weapon.

The same tendency of alternating class action can be seen in the organizational behavior of urban workers. Concentration on politics is most evident during a crisis, whereas trade-unionism is stressed in prosperous periods. In Europe, where the working class organized fairly early into trade-unions and political parties, the gradualist ideology of stressing trade-union gains tended to submerge the revolutionary aims of political parties during the periods of prosperity before and after the First World War. This was especially true in Germany. There has been, of course, a long-term secular trend in favor of class-conscious political action, in that workers or farmers who organize politically during one crisis rarely go back completely to the economic pressure-group stage. Basically, however, workers' and farmers' movements tend to drop objectives of far-reaching economic and political change if the *status quo* becomes stabilized over a period of years.

In Saskatchewan the postwar depression precipitated the tremendous sweep of the Progressive Party in 1921. Saskatchewan farmers hoped that the rural protest would compel the new government to restore government marketing of wheat through the Canadian Wheat Board, for wheat had reached its highest price level when the Board marketed the entire crop. The failure of both Conservative and Liberal governments to do anything about government marketing of wheat led many farmers to turn to the support of a proposal for a farmers' Wheat Pool, which would receive the grain from the farmers and market it cooperatively on the world market in a fashion similar to the work of the government board. The proposals for government and cooperative marketing of wheat renewed the perennial conflict between the agitators in the movement and heads of the farm organizations.

Many leaders of farm organizations feared that the idea of farmers taking complete control of their own crop was too radical, and would meet with such opposition from private elevator companies that it would fail. The officials of the farmers' companies, the Saskatchewan Cooperative Elevator Company, and the Grain Growers' Grain Company sought to delay the creation of a marketing pool for fear that it "would gradually encroach on the activities of the two companies."[85]

The bureaucratic conservatism of the leaders of the established farm organizations resulted finally in a split from the Saskatchewan Grain Growers' Association. In 1921 a small group of militant farmers, some of whom had had earlier experience in the trade-union movement, formed the Farmers' Union "with the object in view of supporting and affiliating with farmers' organizations in all the large producing countries to obtain control of all main farm produce, to regulate and obtain reasonable prices above cost of production, and also to protect the farmers' interests by the support and strength of their own organization!"[86] The new, more radical organization began a vigorous drive for a Wheat Pool.

The campaign of the Farmers' Union succeeded and the older S.G.G.A. agreed to work with the Union to build the Pool. Both organizations campaigned throughout the province, urging farmers to sign contracts agreeing to turn all their wheat over to the Wheat Pool for five years and thus completely eliminate the influence of middlemen. Thousands of volunteer organizers traveled from farmhouse to farmhouse throughout the province.

The new drive faced powerful opposition. The private grain companies vigorously propagandized against it. The daily press tried to convince the farmers that the Pool could not work. This resulted only in convincing the organized agrarians that they needed a paper of their own. The newspapers had earlier opposed the efforts of farmers to build an independent political movement. All four major papers, the Regina *Post*, the Regina *Leader*, the Saskatoon *Star*, and the Saskatoon *Phoenix*, were owned in 1923 by the Sifton Publishing Company, which was closely allied to the Liberal Party. The opposition of this one-company monopoly led many organized farmers to identify the daily press with the other "vested" business interests which they were fighting. This was a major step in the development of class consciousness and political sophistication. It was part of the emerging suspicion of one after another of the institutions of capitalism. "The farmers of the province were in no mood for anything that savoured of opposition. Considerable feeling was aroused and ere long the suspicion found expression . . . in the allegation that the *Morning Leader* was being financed by the grain trade."[87]

The 1923 convention of the S.G.G.A. instructed its executive to start a farmers' newspaper. The *Progressive*, later known as the *Western Producer*, began publication as a weekly on August 27, 1923, and has continued as the voice of the organized educational and cooperative movement of Saskatchewan.[88]

The resistance of the daily press and the grain trade to the Wheat Pool failed. The personal farm-to-farm canvass of Saskatchewan by members of the Farmers' Union and the S.G.G.A. enabled the Pool's supporters to overcome the superior economic power of their opponents. The organized agrarians were determined to take complete control of the marketing of their crops. Within one year, 45,000 farmers had signed contracts agreeing to sell all their wheat through the Pool for a period of five years, in spite of the fact that this

meant an immediate financial sacrifice for many of them, as
the private grain companies raised the price which they would
pay above the Pool's price.[89]

The Wheat Pool campaign, like the earlier battles of the
western farmers, must not be viewed as a conscious plan of
radical leaders. Though there were hundreds of convinced
socialists, monetary reformers, and cooperators among the
leaders of the farm organizations, the overwhelming majority
of farmers were never oriented to any long-term goal of
major social change. The active farm leaders learned from one
fight to the next. In attempting to gain economic security, in
fighting for concrete objectives as solutions to particular
problems, the farmers gradually came to believe that they
were fighting a total system, that the railroads, the Grain Exchange, the newspapers, all were pitted against them.

Following the successful Pool drive, the militant elements
in the Farmers' Union initiated a campaign to merge the old
Saskatchewan Cooperative Elevator Company with the Wheat
Pool. The efforts to organize the Wheat Pool had been obstructed by the board of directors of the Elevator Company,
who had rightly feared that the marketing cooperative would
eventually attempt to absorb their organization. Local farm
leaders, especially those in the Farmers' Union, felt that the
Cooperative Elevator officials, many of them leaders in both
the S.G.G.A. and the Liberal Party, had become profit-
minded and preferred to hold their positions of power rather
than involve their organization in the building of an experimental marketing pool.[90] The Union's drive against the old
leaders succeeded when, in 1925, the majority of the shareholders of the Elevator Company voted to sell out to the
Pool.[91] This victory was part of the recurrent struggle in the
farm movement between the more militant, unpaid local
leaders and the top officials.

It is difficult to overestimate the importance of the campaign for the Wheat Pool in the organization of farmers into
a self-conscious class. The almost evangelical appeal for
farmers finally to destroy the middlemen in the grain trade
and control their own economic destiny activated more farmers than ever before in Saskatchewan history. More than half
of the wheat growers of the province joined the new co-

operative within two years after it was organized. As one observer of the prairie scene in the middle 'twenties commented, "The new cooperation has indeed become a veritable religion among the farmers."[92] The impetus for the development of the Wheat Pool resulted in the growth of cooperative marketing pools for livestock, dairies, and eggs. Consumers' cooperatives and purchasing associations made significant gains.

Another important step in the development of organized class consciousness was the great increase in educational activities. The cooperative and other agrarian organizations had been engaged in an extensive educational program almost from the start of the cooperative movement. Partridge had helped launch the *Grain Growers' Guide* as a means of educating the farmers in regard to their economic problems. The cooperatives hired full-time men to travel around the province holding educational meetings and helping new local cooperatives to get started. These field men were usually hardworking enthusiasts, who left their farms to help further their economic ideals. The creation of the Wheat Pool meant that an educational program reached more farmers than ever before in the history of the farmers' movement.

Since the Pool had continually to face the effective opposition of the grain trade, which had a local representative in the person of the elevator agent in every Saskatchewan community, and since private grain companies continued to offer financial rewards of higher immediate prices to farmers who would not deal with the Pool, the Pool set up elected committees of about ten members each at every shipping point. These committees met from six to twelve times a year to discuss local Pool problems. In order to further the rural antagonism toward the private interests, the provincial office of the Pool sent study outlines to the committees on subjects such as the operation of the Grain Exchange, the effects of tariffs on agriculture, the profit structure of industries that affected farmers, and current legislation.[93]

The Pool organization became an effective educational agency. The most influential farmers were usually elected to the Pool committees. Through them, rural leaders were made aware of significant agricultural problems. To facilitate this work, the province was divided by the Pool into 16 large districts and 165 subdistricts. In each large district a full-time field man visited the committees and helped their work. Each of the subdistricts elected a delegate to the annual provincial convention. The delegates, who had to be farmers, were paid by the Pool to visit the Pool committees within their subdistrict during slack seasons.[94] This meant that there was one delegate for every eighty Pool committeemen, who in turn were responsible to about four hundred members.

The *Western Producer,* the weekly organ of the Pool, which went out to most of the farmhouses in the province, helped to maintain a unified agrarian opinion. It was edited by men who were hostile to many of the institutions of private capitalism. Farmers were encouraged to write for the paper on agrarian and political questions. An "Open Forum" carried discussions of political affairs, socialism, currency reform, and problems of the cooperative movement.[95] Interviews with many local farm leaders indicate that it is still widely read.

Educational work was carried on also by the United Farmers of Canada (Saskatchewan Section) (U.F.C.), which had been formed in 1926 as a result of a merger of the S.G.G.A. and the Farmers' Union. The U.F.C. had about 20,000 members from the time it was founded until the depression. The leaders of the unified organization conceived of their association as a vanguard movement that would lead the farmers to new conquests. The educational movement had organized the cooperatives and the Progressive Party, and the leaders now saw their role as one of preventing conservatism in the cooperative movement. The vanguard conception is clearly indicated in the first pamphlet published by the U.F.C.:

Our leaders must always be in advance of the thought of the rank and file. . . . There is nothing to fear from the most radical ideas expressed on the platform, because . . . the body can move only as fast as the majority of the members are willing to go . . . [but] there must ever be leaders pointing out new paths to follow, stimulating the organizations with new hope and new conquests or rust and decay and rottenness will soon undermine its power.[96]

The new U.F.C. hoped to be in a better position to play this vanguard role by erecting constitutional barriers against multiple officeholding. Its constitution barred officers from holding executive positions in any other farm organization, or political office.[97] Many of the more conservative leaders in the farm movement who had retained their positions in the S.G.G.A. while becoming Liberal Party leaders or officers of the cooperatives had to resign. As a result, the Wheat Pool leaders were predominantly former members of the S.G.G.A., while the U.F.C. was controlled at the top by old Farmers' Union people.

At the grass-roots level there was considerable overlapping of the active members of the U.F.C. and of the Wheat Pool and other cooperatives. In general, however, the difference between the sections of the farm movement was the same as in the top leadership. The more radical participants devoted more time to educational activities than to the cooperatives. The agitators like Partridge, who was made the honorary president of the U.F.C., believed that cooperation was only a steppingstone in the long-term fight against "vested interests." This emphasis can be seen in a pamphlet issued by the U.F.C. after unification.

First then we need a United Economic Farmers' Organization. This organization will supplement the efforts of the Wheat Pool and inspire it with courage and determination to win. But this is not the end, it is the beginning. . . .

When we farmers have organized our forces we shall have completed the organization of society on the individual basis. The next task will then be to work for the breakdown of all the conflicting forces by advocating the Cooperative Commonwealth. . . .

The private ownership of the machinery of production and the private control of currency and credit are the two great forces which prevent a cooperative society.[98]

Nineteenth-century liberal society accustomed men to constant change and to the expectation that change meant progress despite the industrial business cycles or the shifting price of wheat. The crisis in liberal democracy developed around growing doubts whether political democracy founded on capitalism could, in fact, continue to result in progress. These doubts led to restlessness under the old parties, efforts to dominate the latter by farmers electing their own men to the provincial legislature, sporadic new party movements, and self-help through direct interference in economic institutions through the setting up of farmers' grain elevators, a Wheat Pool, and an educational movement—all looking vaguely but with increasing self-confidence toward a cooperative commonwealth.

The factors that generated doubt in the old system and its institutions and prompted action were, first, the sense of helplessness of farmers before a remote business system of private grain elevators, middlemen, the Grain Exchange, the national banks, and the powerful railway system—all of which habitually dictated to farmers according to rules of their own; second, the recurrence of violent fluctuations in wheat prices and crop yield, the sole basis of the wheat farmers' standard of life; and third, the inability to get help fast enough and regularly enough from the reigning political parties.

This combination of old institutions and new doubts matured into a crisis. Because of the clarity of the relation between wheat prices and total welfare, the need for organized self-help was recognized earlier in the wheat area. In the more varied economy of eastern Canada, industry, business, and finance were less simply related to welfare, and division of labor meant that different men had different perceptions of their relations to their institutions. Under such circumstances they worked along in the increasing complexity of industrial society with no clear sense of what and who were responsible for their fluctuating fate. Some drifted hopefully West to try their luck. But in the prairie frontier there was no place else to go. The issue could not be evaded. Men's fate narrowed to a single element—wheat. The crisis matured, therefore, in a simplified setting; the enemy was identified, and men began to think and act radically.

Conservative economists, Royal Commissions, and representatives of the institutions disliked by farmers have criticized the ideas and organized action of the agrarians on the ground that they were based on erroneous economic assumptions. Repeated attempts have been made to convince farmers that the handling of commodities involves intermediate steps, and that the middlemen are receiving only a fair return for necessary services. These logical arguments, however, ignore the fact that many of the charges of farmers are nonlogical. They have their basis not in the specific ills that farmers criticize, but in the totality of social and economic relations that bind the wheat grower to the railroads, the Grain Exchange, and the banks. The farmer saw the middlemen and said, "Let's abolish them." He was hitting out at the things he could see, not realizing that the problem was not these middling processes but the total system that determines how and by whom and for what they shall be operated.

The western farmer is in much the same position as the worker in large-scale industry. The price which each receives for his labor is determined by a complex of powerful factors of which only the part immediately impinging upon his life is visible.

It is not the rentier, the shareholder, and the banker who suffer the ill will of the workers, but almost exclusively the manufacturer and the business executive who are the direct opponents of workers in price wars. This is so in spite of the fact that it is precisely the cash boxes of the rentier, the shareholder, and the banker into which the more or less "unearned" gains flow, rather than into the pockets of the manufacturers or business executives.[99]

The situation in which all power is concentrated on one side can only lead to suspicion and conflict from the other side in a society with democratic values. Workers and farmers are forced to accept the rules laid down by the possessors of economic power. Living in a society dominated by competitive pecuniary values, they come to believe that those with power are using it to exploit them.

The workers' reactions to this feeling of exploitation can be observed in their restriction of output.[100] Max Weber has called attention to the universality of this phenomenon: "the 'murmuring' of the workers known in ancient oriental ethics: the moral disapproval of the work-master's conduct, which in its practical significance was probably equivalent to an increasingly typical phenomenon of precisely the latest industrial development, namely, the 'slow down' of laborers by virtue of tacit agreement." The extent to which organized class action emerges "is especially linked to the *transparency* of the connections between the causes and the consequences of the 'class situation.' "[101] Among industrial workers, increasing recognition of the causes of their inferior, exploited situation leads to the organization of trade-unions and eventually class political parties seeking to acquire power from the business classes.

Similarly, farmers organize to cut down or eliminate, through government or cooperative action, the profits and power of those with whom they deal, either as producers or consumers. The more the farmer is involved as a small cog in a complex, fluctuating market economy, the more likely is he to become class-conscious and radical in his economic and political ideas. All over North America, the wheat farmers who are least involved in a subsistence rural economy, and are the most commercially oriented of the farmers, have been radical, while the poorer subsistence farmers, who are less subject to direct economic relations with big business organizations, have remained conservative.

Organized self-help was spurred on by the presence in western Canada of many settlers who had been active in socialist and cooperative movements in the old country. The instability of the frontier wheat economy offered these radicals a continuous forum in which to present their ideas. The records of farm organizations reveal a preoccupation with problems of debt, currency reform, tariff, railroad rates, and profits of manufacturers and distributors. This gave the comparatively small group of economic and political radicals an influence far out of proportion to their numbers.

The tendency toward radical change because of the economic crisis was counterbalanced by the institutionalization of the once-militant organizations. The bureaucratic summits of each new movement developed a vested interest in preserving the stability of its organization. The officials feared that support of new and untried ideas might lead to the complete collapse of the old institutions. Their positions as leaders, often full-time urban-dwelling officials of farmers' organizations, gave them a feeling of security and status which led them to depreciate the urgency of the problems of those still on the farm. Many of the early farm leaders were taken into the leadership of the Liberal Party and acquired an interest in preserving the political *status quo*.

The bureaucratic conservatism of the top officialdom was reflected in almost every advance of the farmers' movement. The S.G.G.A. first opposed Partridge's idea of a farmers' marketing company because of the fear that the failure of such a company would destroy the Association. Later, the leaders of the same organization fought against independent political action by farmers and had to be forced into it by rank-and-file pressure. The cleavage between the Farmers' Union and the S.G.G.A. was in part a result of the difference in attitude between the radicals who were ready to take on the job of organizing a Pool, and the overlapping officials of the S.G.G.A. and the Saskatchewan Cooperative Elevator Company who feared to endanger their organizations by new ventures.

This bureaucratization and growing conservatism of reform movements as they gain acceptance is found in every area of society. Trade-unions, cooperatives, and left-wing political parties have repeatedly become bulwarks of the *status quo*. In Saskatchewan, where continual adjustments to economic pressures and changes were necessary, the bureaucratic conservatism of top leaders resulted in agrarian distrust of all officialdom. Restrictions were placed on officials: they could not hold more than one position at a time or for longer than a certain term. Farm leaders were not to take part in politics while holding office in the cooperative or educational movement. The need for annual secret elections in the cooperative movement was recognized. Saskatchewan farmers repeatedly express their fear that farm leaders may be corrupted by the city and its influences. The "city" is the farmers' functional equivalent for bureaucracy.

To sum up, the first three decades of the twentieth century witnessed the creation of a powerful, organized, class-conscious agrarian movement in Saskatchewan. The wheat farmer, who was situated at the producing start and the consuming end of a highly organized and often monopolistic distribution system, became convinced that he, as the primary producer of wealth, was being exploited by "vested interests." He developed hostile class attitudes to big business, to the newspapers, which he believed served the "interests," and to merchants. As a result, a large proportion of the farming population supported an agrarian socialistic program designed to eliminate private profits by governmental or cooperative action before an explicitly socialist party appeared upon the scene.

NOTES

1. Max Weber, *Essays in Sociology* (ed. by H. H. Gerth and C. W. Mills; New York, Oxford University Press, 1946), pp. 183–84.

2. Harold S. Patton, *Grain Growers' Cooperation in Western Canada* (Harvard University Press, 1928), p. 14; Hugh Boyd, *New Breaking: An Outline of Cooperation among the Farmers of Western Canada* (Toronto, J. M. Dent and Sons, Ltd., 1938), pp. 19–20; W. A. Mackintosh, *Agricultural Cooperation in Western Canada* (Toronto, Ryerson Press, 1924), p. 8; Hopkins Moorhouse, *Deep Furrows* (Toronto, George J. McLeod, Ltd., 1918), pp. 37–38.

3. L. A. Wood, *Farmers' Movements in Canada* (Toronto, Ryerson Press, 1924), p. 170. See also Boyd, *op. cit.*, pp. 24–25; Moorhouse, *op. cit.*, p. 45; Patton, *op. cit.*, p. 31.

4. Boyd, *op. cit.*, p. 21.

5. *Ibid.*, pp. 30–31.

6. Moorhouse, *op. cit.*, pp. 29–52; Boyd, *op. cit.*, pp. 26–29; Patton, *op. cit.*, pp. 32–34.

7. Patton, *op. cit.*, p. 34; Boyd, *op. cit.*, pp. 29–30; Wood, *op. cit.*, pp. 174–75.

8. Moorhouse, *op. cit.*, p. 230.

9. "The government was impressed, and the Grain Growers' resolutions were incorporated in almost the very language of the petitioners [the Territorial Grain Growers' Associations] in amendments to the shipping clauses of the Manitoba Grain Act." Patton, *op. cit.*, p. 35.

10. *Ibid.*

11. *Ibid.*, p. 33.

12. *Ibid.*, pp. 35–36; Moorhouse, *op. cit.*, pp. 55–58; Wood, *op. cit.*, p. 180; Mackintosh, *op. cit.*, p. 15.

13. Patton, *op. cit.*, p. 37; Boyd, *op. cit.*, p. 36.

14. Mackintosh, *op. cit.*, p. 19.

15. Boyd, *op. cit.*, pp. 41–47.

16. Letter of Grain Growers' Grain Company to Premier R. P. Robbin, December 20, 1906, quoted in Mackintosh, *op. cit.*, p. 23.

17. *Ibid.*, pp. 25–26; Moorhouse, *op. cit.*, pp. 119–21; Patton, *op. cit.*, pp. 53–58.

18. See Manitoba *Free Press*, December, 1906, to April, 1907.

19. Wood, *op. cit.*, p. 183.

20. Quoted in Mackintosh, *op. cit.*, p. 34.

21. Moorhouse, *op. cit.*, pp. 61–72, 85–92, 133.

22. A. J. Muste, "Factional Fights in Trade Unions," and J. B. S. Hardman, "Problems of a Labor Union Somewhere in the U. S.," *American Labor Dynamics* (ed. by J. B. S. Hardman; New York, Harcourt, Brace and Co., 1928).

23. See E. A. Partridge, *A War on Poverty* (Winnipeg, Wallingford Press, Ltd., 1926), for a statement of his long-range views.

24. Mackintosh, *op. cit.*, p. 27.

25. Moorhouse, *op. cit.*, p. 133.

26. *Grain Growers' Guide*, June, 1908, and *passim*.

27. Mackintosh, *op. cit.*, p. 157.

28. Patton, *op. cit.*, pp. 73–74.

29. Editorial quoted in Moorhouse, *op. cit.*, p. 60.

30. United Grain Farmers, Ltd., *Farmers in Business for Ten Successful Years, 1906–1916*, p. 6.

31. Moorhouse, *op. cit.*, pp. 155–56.

32. Patton, *op. cit.*, p. 75.

33. Mackintosh, *op. cit.*, p. 34.

34. Pamphlet of Manitoba Grain Growers' Association, cited in *Grain Growers' Guide*, June, 1908, p. 6. (This issue was edited by E. A. Partridge.)

35. Patton, *op. cit.*, p. 82–83.

36. Moorhouse, *op. cit.*, pp. 169–70.

37. Wood, *op. cit.*, p. 211.

38. A Grain Growers' candidate had contested a provincial by-election on the issue of government ownership of elevators and won it not long before the Manitoba government agreed to support government ownership.

39. Wood, *op. cit.*, p. 212; Patton, *op. cit.*, pp. 86–87; Boyd, *op. cit.*, p. 58.

40. Wood, *op. cit.*, p. 220.

41. *Report of the Elevator Commission of the Province of Saskatchewan* (Regina, 1910). "This [Saskatchewan Royal] commission was headed by Robert Magill, Professor of Political Economy at Dalhousie. The scholarly reasoning by means of which he demonstrated in his report that public ownership of elevators would not work suggests strongly that he was opposed to public ownership in principle, and an inference hard to escape is that the Saskatchewan government was aware of that opposition before he was appointed." V. C. Fowke, "Royal Commissions and

Canadian Agricultural Policy," *Canadian Journal of Economics and Political Science*, May, 1948, p. 171.

42. Wood, *op. cit.*, p. 214.

43. Patton, *op. cit.*, pp. 110–11.

44. Moorhouse, *op. cit.*, pp. 110–11.

45. *Ibid.*, pp. 134–35.

46. *Report of the Elevator Commission of the Province of Saskatchewan*, pp. 19–22.

47. Moorhouse, *op. cit.*, p. 209.

48. Minutes of the 1907 S.G.G.A. Convention, pp. 60–61.

49. *Ibid.*, p. 23.

50. *Ibid.*, p. 19.

51. Minutes of the 1909 S.G.G.A. Convention, p. 13.

52. Minutes of the 1913 S.G.G.A. Convention, p. 34.

53. *Grain Growers' Guide*, March 2, 1910, p. 8.

54. "The Central [S.G.G.A.] is handling a full line of staple groceries and is about to greatly extend this field of operation. . . . It is a well known fact that the west is outrageously overloaded with retailers, so that coupled with poor service, the rural consumer has to pay in many cases exorbitant prices for inferior goods, and by purchasing in wholesale quantities it is obvious that the farmers can effect and are effecting material savings." *Prairie Farms and Homes*, April 12, 1916, p. 2.

55. Moorhouse, *op. cit.*, p. 230.

56. Wood, *op. cit.*, pp. 125–28; Morton, *op. cit.*, pp. 115–16.

57. Minutes of the 1909 S.G.G.A. Convention, pp. 21–22.

58. Fowke, *op. cit.*, pp. 170–71.

59. W. L. Morton, an unpublished study of the Progressive Party.

60. Minutes of the 1909 S.G.G.A. Convention, pp. 29–30.

61. *Grain Growers' Guide*, July 12, 1911, p. 5.

62. See letter by "Marieta," *ibid.*, August 7, 1909, p. 11. "I am pretty sure if they [the farmers] had a party in the [legislative] houses of Alberta, Saskatchewan and Manitoba, the Premier's reply respecting the elevator question would be entirely different and until the farmers have their representatives in the different parliaments of the provinces and at Ottawa, legislation in their favor will move very slowly indeed."

63. Minutes of the 1913 S.G.G.A. Convention, pp. 25–28.

64. *Ibid.*, p. 31.

65. Minutes of the 1914 S.G.G.A. Convention, pp. 20–26.

66. See Minutes of the S.G.G.A. Board of Directors, 1916, p. 100, for discussion and report on the N.P.L.; Wood, *op. cit.*, p. 340.

67. Minutes of the S.G.G.A. Board of Directors, October 7, 1916, pp. 108–9; November 24, 1916, pp. 55–56.

68. Minutes of the 1919 S.G.G.A. Convention, p. 4.

69. Wood, *op. cit.*, p. 348.

70. Minutes of the 1917 S.G.G.A. Convention, pp. 46–48.

71. Minutes of the S.G.G.A. Executive Board, March 26, 1919, p. 105; May 21, 1919, p. 111.

72. *Canadian Parliamentary Guide, 1921* (ed. by E. J. Chambers; Ottawa, Mortimer Co., Ltd.), p. 279; Wood, *op. cit.*, pp. 349–50.

73. Wood, *op. cit.*, pp. 329–31.

74. *Ibid.*, pp. 339, 341–43.

75. *Ibid.*, pp. 351–55.

76. *Ibid.*, p. 358; interviews.

77. *Canada Year Book, 1941*, p. 181; *ibid., 1945*, pp. 52, 235.

78. *Canadian Parliamentary Guide, 1922*, pp. 204–90.

79. Wood, *op. cit.*, pp. 293–94.

80. *Ibid.*, pp. 357–60; interviews with former Progressive leaders.

81. *Ibid.*, p. 364.

82. The Provincial Treasurer, Charles Dunning, told the convention that "as a government, the Saskatchewan government does not support the party led by Mackenzie King [Liberals] or T. A. Crerar [Progressives] or Meighen [Conservatives]. As an aggregation of individuals there may be one or two who support King. I am dead sure there are some who will support Crerar, but I do not know one who will support Meighen." Minutes of the 1921 S.G.G.A. Convention.

83. Wood, *op. cit.*, pp. 340–41.

84. *Canadian Parliamentary Guide, 1922*, pp. 547–50.

85. S. W. Yates, *The Saskatchewan Wheat Pool*, U.F.C. (Saskatchewan Section) (Saskatoon, 1947), pp. 32–36.

86. *Ibid.*, p. 57. "The new movement [the Farmers' Union] had its roots in the post-war agricultural depression and in a growing reaction against the alleged domination of the conventions and policies of the Saskatchewan Grain Growers' Association by a group who also variously shared office in the Saskatchewan Co-operative Elevator Company and the Saskatchewan government." Patton, *op. cit.*, pp. 213–14.

87. Yates, *op. cit.*, p. 89.

88. *Ibid.*, p. 90.

89. Saskatchewan Cooperative Wheat Producers, Ltd., *Handbook* No. 2 (Regina, 1927).

90. See "Open Forum," *Western Producer*, 1924, for repeated criticisms of Cooperative Elevator officials by local farm leaders.

91. Yates, *op. cit.*, pp. 116–28; Patton, *op. cit.*, p. 233.

92. Patton, *op. cit.*, p. 405.

93. Saskatchewan Cooperative Wheat Producers, Ltd., *Annual Report* (Regina), 1925–48.

94. Saskatchewan Cooperative Producers, Ltd., *Handbook* No. 1 (Regina, 1944).

95. "Open Forum," *Western Producer*, 1924–48.

96. George F. Stirling, "Mind Your Own Business," U.F.C.

(Saskatchewan Section), *Pamphlet* No. 1 (Saskatoon, n.d.), pp. 12–13.

97. U.F.C. (Saskatchewan Section), *Constitution and By-Laws.*

98. Stirling, *op. cit.,* p. 13.

99. Weber, *op. cit.,* p. 186.

100. Stanley B. Mathewson, *Restriction of Output among Unorganized Workers* (New York, Viking Press, 1931).

101. Weber, *op. cit.,* pp. 183–84.

4

THE FARMERS' MOVEMENT
GOES SOCIALIST

THE SPLIT of the Farmers' Union from the S.G.G.A. in 1921 gave temporary formal recognition to a cleavage that had existed between radical and conservative members of the agrarian movement for a number of years. The successful joint struggle of the two rival educational organizations to build the Wheat Pool led to organizational unity in the United Farmers of Canada (Saskatchewan Section) in 1926, but it did not end the fundamental differences between those who saw the agrarian movement as a gradualist liberal development designed to solve specific problems, and the more class-conscious radicals who felt that the farmers would never be secure until the power of their economic enemies was broken. These radicals continued their fight in both the U.F.C. and the Wheat Pool during the prosperous 'twenties, when the combination of high prices and a Wheat Pool, which marketed the wheat of more than two-thirds of the farmers of the province, led the majority of farmers to lose interest in further reform.

A not inconsiderable sprinkling of pioneer settlers in the West had been active radicals in their earlier homes. In present-day Saskatchewan the influence of these early socialists, many of them immigrants from England, is still apparent. In discussing with older members of the CCF the causes of the development of socialism in the province, one may hear comments like the following:

Like a great many others, I absorbed my socialist ideas and ideals from Robert Blatchford and his associates in the United Kingdom. On coming to Canada in 1902, I looked around

for men of my understanding and found them in the old
Grain Growers' Association. . . . From then on, through trial
and error, we reached the Farmers' Union, the first lodge of
which was organized at Ituna, my home town. . . . I was
[then] in the delegate body of the Wheat Pool for sixteen
years, from 1924 to 1942, with only two breaks in my term
of office. In the early days a sprinkling of the delegates were
socialist and near socialist in some of their statements. I saw
the socialist sentiment grow from year to year in the organization, and many like myself who could hold the confidence
of the farmers in our subdistrict were able to carry on socialist
education at our meetings. This was a double-barreled gun,
as we were paid for looking after the business of the Co-op
and could through the meeting propogate the idea of a Cooperative Commonwealth.[1]

Similar work had been going on earlier. The first secretary
of the S.G.G.A., Fred W. Green, had been a socialist in
Lancashire, England. He often used his regular column in
the *Grain Growers' Guide* to disseminate ideas on socialism
without explicitly mentioning the word.[2] Under his secretary-
ship the S.G.G.A. distributed thousands of copies of Edward
Bellamy's socialist classics, *Looking Backward* and *Equality*.
Many CCF farmers cite these books as their first contact with
socialist ideas.

The left-wingers stressed the existence of a basic cleavage
between the producers of wealth—the farmers and workers—
and the "vested interests." In the *Western Producer,* the
weekly organ of the Wheat Pool, which went to most of the
farm homes in the province, the radicals repeatedly presented
an extreme ideology of class conflict.

The laboring people should unite and protect themselves
against all idlers. You can divide mankind into two classes,
the laborers and the idlers, the supporters and the supported,
the honest and the dishonest. Every man is dishonest who
lives on the unpaid labor of others no matter if he occupies
a throne.[3]

The workers know that capitalism is the cause of poverty,
of unemployment, of mortgages and debts—and that the farmers will find no solution to their problem within the framework of the capitalist society. Something more do we know

and it is this: that the ending of capitalist exploitation is the task of the industrial and agrarian workers.[4]

Politically, the leftists supported the activities in the House of Commons of J. S. Woodsworth, a Methodist minister, who was to become the first national leader of the CCF. Woodsworth was elected to Parliament continuously from 1921 as an Independent Labor Party member from the city of Winnipeg. He felt that the cooperative farmers of the West were a promising group for socialist propaganda and cultivated them.[5] The Farmers' Union convention of 1924 adopted a resolution endorsing Woodsworth's efforts to nationalize the banking system and calling upon "every citizen to vote only for those federal nominees who pledge themselves to support . . . the principles embodied in the Woodsworth motion [to nationalize the banks]."[6] From 1927 to 1929 the United Farmers of Canada also supported Woodsworth and sent him on frequent speaking tours throughout Saskatchewan to preach his socialist message.[7]

Having helped build the Wheat Pool, the left-wingers now began to argue that it was not enough. Partridge, now an elderly man, sounded a new battle cry. In 1926, noting the failure of "the great Raisin Growers' Cooperative Association of California [which] went broke a short time ago" as a result of opposition from "vested interests," he drove its moral home as an argument for an all-out cooperative commonwealth as the only safeguard for farmers.

Vocational cooperation is not the cure, as many think, for ills due to selfishness and to great inequality of wealth and opportunity from which we are suffering today. Canada is full of vocational cooperation. A trust, a merger, a manufacturer's association, a trade union, a grain-grower's selling or buying agency, a retail merchant's association, are all cooperatives for vocational advantage. When we have been convinced by actual trial that these partial cooperatives are weak and temporary remedies—just a replacing of the competitive struggles of individuals by the competitive struggles of groups—and not a cure of our ills, we will then seek in national cooperation an ending of the costly war of clashing vocational interests and the establishment of a single basic interest—the ample supplying of our physical needs. . . .

Take it or leave it—we must speedily establish a system of production for *Use* instead of for *Profit* or our present so-called civilization will perish.[8]

During the late 'twenties the left-wingers, consciously thinking of themselves as such, attempted to involve the organized farmers' movement in new struggles. In 1927 the left wing undertook a campaign that was to have significant results for the eventual emergence of the CCF. Seeking to extend economic cooperation, they proposed that the Wheat Pool secure 100 per cent control of wheat marketing in Canada instead of the 60 per cent control it then had. They urged that unless the Pool controlled the entire crop it would not be strong enough to resist a decline in the price of wheat; for as long as a minority of farmers stayed outside the Pool, it would be in a weak bargaining position on the world market. They suggested, therefore, that the Pool ask the provincial government to enact legislation requiring that all grain grown in Saskatchewan be marketed through one Pool, subject to the approval of two-thirds of the farmers in a special referendum.[9]

The more conservative leaders of the Wheat Pool, led by A. J. McPhail, its president, opposed the plan: first, because they thought that it was not necessary and would give the government control over the Pool; second, because it had undesirable features of compulsion that were contrary to co-operative principles.[10] The prosperity of the 'twenties, the fact that for the first time the price of Canadian wheat was "frequently higher by several cents a bushel than the corresponding price across the International Boundary,"[11] negated the pessimistic predictions of the radicals, and the 1929 convention of the Wheat Pool rejected a compulsory pool by a substantial majority. The U.F.C., which was a smaller organization composed of the more class-conscious farmers, passed a resolution favoring the 100 per cent pool in its 1928 convention.[12]

As a result of the controversy, George Williams, one of the left-wingers in the U.F.C., was elected president of that organization in 1928. A year later the left wing repeated its presidential victory, and for the first time won a clear majority of the executive board as well. The rift between the two groups became so bitter that the right-wing minority on the executive board and the entire administrative staff of the organization resigned, charging that the agitation for a 100 per cent pool was "destroying the foundation of the whole cooperative movement."[13]

The dispute may seem far removed from the emergent socialist ideology, but actually it contained the nucleus of all that was to follow. The right-wing officials of the cooperative movement were opposed to any reliance of the movement on the state, believing in gradual education and recruitment. The left-wingers feared that education would take too long and that the cooperative farmers, who were a majority of the total farming population, had to use the state to prevent the minority from weakening the movement. The U.F.C. convention of 1929 clearly indicated the long-range motives of the left wing when it established as a basic principle of the U.F.C. that "the farmers are in favor of the abolition of the present system of capitalistic robbery and the establishment of a real cooperative social system controlled by the producers."[14]

The year 1929 was decisive. Everywhere in the province the rift between the left and right wings over the plan for a 100 per cent pool continued in both the local committees of the Wheat Pool and the lodges of the U.F.C., with the U.F.C. pushing forward and consolidating its position favoring radical action and the Wheat Pool hanging back. Times were good and this played into the hands of the conservatives, who were able to retain the support of the majority of the 80,000 Pool members. Then came the financial crash in the autumn of 1929. Had this not happened, the Saskatchewan farmers probably would have oriented ideologically in a stable, conservative direction. The intruding variable of the world business depression gave a positive and final decision to the leftist side, for the economic collapse bankrupted the gigantic Canadian Wheat Pool.

In the fall of 1929 the Wheat Pool made an initial payment to the farmers of $1.00 a bushel. World prices at that time were about $1.50 a bushel, and there was ample reason to expect that the Pool would eventually add substantially to the original payment. The October stock-market crash brought prices down on the Grain Exchange as well. By the end of the crop year, July 31, 1930, the price of wheat on the Winnipeg Grain Exchange had fallen below the initial payment of $1.00 a bushel. The Pool was threatened by bankruptcy and the governments of the three Prairie Provinces agreed to guarantee the banks' advances in order to save the Pool. Conditions grew even worse in 1930, whereupon the Pool lowered its initial payment on No. 1 Northern wheat to 50 cents.[15]

In these two catastrophic years the wheat pools of the West lost about $25,000,000 because of overpayments to farmers. They were forced to give up their sidestepping of the Grain Exchange and to deal again on the Exchange.[16] Wheat prices had become too precarious to continue the system of initial payments, with final payments being made when the total crop was sold. By December, 1932, No. 1 Northern wheat had dropped further, to 38 cents a bushel.[17] At this point the pools were forced to stop their marketing operations and become primarily farmers' elevator companies.[18]

The alarmist prophecies of Partridge and other left-wingers had come true. The wheat pools, the pride of western agriculture, had collapsed. One can scarcely overemphasize the effect of this breakdown on the farmers of Saskatchewan. The left-wingers and socialists, who had made little headway in gaining the support of the Wheat Pool members for more radical measures before 1929, now saw the opposition to their proposals virtually disappear.

The convention of the Saskatchewan Wheat Pool in June, 1930, reversed its previous opposition to the 100 per cent pool. A referendum revealed 34,621 members voting in favor of a compulsory pool and 13,621 voting against it. Of the 48,000 farmers who voted, 71.3 per cent favored the left-wing proposal.[19] The provincial legislature passed the enabling legislation after a delegation of 1,500 farmers, the largest in the history of the province, descended on Regina to demand its passage.[20] The legislation, however, never went into effect, for the courts declared it unconstitutional.

The Saskatchewan farmers' movement had reached a turning point in its history. In their desire for security the farmers had tried various expedients of political and cooperative action, but each remedy in turn had failed to eliminate the hazards of the fluctuating wheat economy. After thirty years of hard work, individually and collectively, western farmers saw the fruits of all their labor destroyed. The depression forced the price of wheat down to its lowest level, increased the volume of farm debt to a new high, and destroyed the equity of thousands of farmers in their land. Because of the drought that began in 1930, many farmers could not even maintain a bare subsistence. (See chap. 5.)

The left-wing leaders who dominated the U.F.C. decided that the time was ripe for an avowed socialist movement among the farmers. George Williams, left-wing president of the U.F.C., had attempted without success, in the middle 'twenties, to organize a radical farmers' party. Efforts had been made at every convention from its founding one in 1926 to get the U.F.C. to support independent political action. But these were defeated in view of the apparent success of pure cooperation.[21]

The convention in February, 1930, met a few months after the disastrous fall in the price of wheat. Williams and his followers seized the strategic time to channel the U.F.C. in a socialist direction. E. A. Partridge, now honorary president of the U.F.C., told the delegates that "true cooperation has its final goal in socialism, which is the continual observance of the Golden Rule." In the discussion on the resolution in favor of political action, various delegates argued in the same vein. "It is a fight to the finish between capitalism and cooperation, and how can we support cooperation better than by putting farmer members in our Provincial and Federal Legislatures?"[22]

The majority of the delegates, 306, favored political action; 165 opposed it. But the resolution was defeated, because two-thirds of the votes (314) were needed for a constitutional amendment.[23] The depression was only five months old, and the effort to secure the 100 per cent pool had not yet been outlawed by the courts, so the opponents of political action could still argue that cooperative self-help had not failed.

At the convention of 1930 the left wing accepted a compromise resolution suggesting that "the farmers should set up an organization outside the United Farmers of Canada for the purpose of more directly selecting and electing representatives to the Legislature and the House of Commons pledged to support the demands of organized agriculture."[24] The U.F.C., accordingly, adopted a farmers' program that was recommended to all candidates who wanted farmers' support. Its principal planks were:

1. Abolition of the competitive system and substitution of a cooperative system of manufacturing, transportation, and distribution;
2. 100 per cent marketing pool by legislation;
3. Abolition of military training and removal of all war incentives from school books and moving pictures. Teaching of cooperative principles in public schools, colleges, and university;
4. State medicine and health insurance;
5. Free trade with the mother country.[25]

The convention also called for the nationalization of the Canadian Pacific Railway, public utilities, and natural resources.

A few months after the U.F.C. convention, the Farmers' Political Association (F.P.A.) was formed by the political activists of the farmers' movement to contest the Dominion election of 1930. The leaders of the new organization were active members of the U.F.C., though officials of the U.F.C. were forbidden by the constitution to participate. The new party called for the encouragement of "all cooperative enterprises as steps leading to the establishment of a cooperative commonwealth . . . public ownership of our public resources and lower tariffs."[26] It was backed by the remnants of the old Progressive Party, which had continued in a few constituencies, and by the newly formed urban Independent Labor Party.

The propaganda of the F.P.A. stressed the need for workers' and farmers' class representation in Parliament because "powerful capitalists by campaign fund contributions had made the political parties responsible to them instead of to the people."[27] Though the party did not mention socialism in speeches or printed propaganda, it stressed the need for a new system of production for use in a cooperative commonwealth. The basic rural bias against urban domination can be seen in the demand that "the country school house should be the basis of [political] organization, rather than city hall."[28]

In the Dominion election of that year the new farmers' organization succeeded in obtaining 40,000 votes.[29] Only thirteen constituencies out of a total of twenty-one in the province had farmers' candidates, as the organization had been initiated only a few months before the election. The party won 23.1 per cent of the vote in these thirteen predominantly rural constituencies. Actually, its rural vote was higher than the figure indicates, as the party had virtually no organization or support in the small urban centers. This seemed to be a significant indication of the desire of the agrarians for a new political movement, for the F.P.A. was able to get this vote with scanty funds and in spite of the fact that it was a small local party fighting in a national election.

The election was important from another point of view as well, for it resulted in a partial shift in Saskatchewan from its traditional Liberal allegiance to the Conservative Party. The latter, as the official opposition and the only other national political party, received the votes of many who blamed the depression on the incumbent Liberals. The Tories, while sweeping the rest of Canada, gained nine of the twenty-one seats in Saskatchewan, whereas in the previous election they had not captured a single constituency. To vote Conservative represented a major shift in the electoral traditions of Saskatchewan, since the farmers had always favored a low tariff, associated with the Liberal or Progressive parties. Despite the growing radical declarations of farm leaders when meeting as an embattled bloc in conventions, the majority of the farmers were still careful men and, when faced with an election, tended to choose the lesser of two evils. They were learning—but the hard and slow way.

In the economic confusion and political fumbling of the first years of the depression, revolt was taking shape among the farmers. In the autumn of 1930 there was a movement for the secession of the Western Provinces. If the farmers could not live with the financial and industrial East, they would try living without it. The new movement believed that if the

Western Provinces could secede from Canada they would cease subsidizing eastern manufacturers through high tariffs, and could establish a barter trade agreement with England, sending wheat in return for manufactured goods. The movement was backed by many prominent farm leaders, including A. J. Macauley, president of the U.F.C., and John Wesson, director and later president of the Wheat Pool.[30] This may seem a far cry from the emerging socialist movement, but in the minds of many radical farmers it was tied up with their traditional fight against the national economic structure controlled in Montreal and Toronto. As early as 1926, at the height of prosperity, E. A. Partridge had suggested that the progressive provinces of the West secede from the hopelessly reactionary and business-dominated provinces of the East and form a western cooperative commonwealth.[31]

Throughout the winter of 1930-31, large meetings demanded secession. The reforms that were expected to result from secession included nationalization of banks, reduced interest rates, lower cost of farm implements, free tariff, and a moratorium on all debts. Newspapermen reported that the movement was most popular with the grain farmers, but was not popular with those who produced livestock.[32] As always, it was grain farmers who were most disastrously affected by the decline in prices.

Secession may now seem a wild idea, but the fact that it was seriously considered indicates the desperate condition of the grain growers. Their livelihood was being destroyed by forces beyond their control. Meanwhile, the politically sophisticated leaders of the U.F.C., who in 1930 had persuaded that body to go on record in favor of independent political action, had not been idle. Some had gone along with the secession movement, but not as an alternative to forthright political action. There were rumblings of radical discontent in eastern centers like Toronto, and the extreme step of seceding did not seem the only choice.

In February, 1931, while the secession movement was still strong, the U.F.C. board of directors, composed of socialists, both old and newly converted, received overwhelming convention support for an economic and political program that stated an ultimate socialist objective: "That in the opinion of this convention the present economic crisis is due to the inherent unsoundness of the capitalistic control of production and distribution and involves the payment of rent, interest and profit, we recognize that social ownership and cooperative production for use is the only sound economic system."[33] The farmers were in a mood for desperate remedies. Delegates told of the intolerable nightmare of succeeding evictions in their neighborhoods, and demanded action: "We can fight against evictions, against foreclosures, directly, or we can fight through our legislatures, but if we urge the legislatures to fight the creditors, they fight the creditors with creditors, for the legislators are of the creditor class. We may get concessions for a short time if the farmers appear militant. The only way is to do the fighting ourselves."[34]

The provincial economic program adopted by the convention accordingly demanded a moratorium on "foreclosures, evictions or seizures, and exemption of the farmers home quarter-section [160 acres] from seizure, crop insurance, adjustment of farm debts," and that "no more homesteads be granted on farm lands sold," but that *"use leases [on all farms] be instituted and that all land and resources now privately owned be nationalized as rapidly as opportunity will permit."*[35] The federal part of the program demanded a fixed price for grain above the costs of production, fixed prices for the goods farmers consumed, nationalization of railroads and lower freight rates, government control of currency and credit, the 100 per cent Wheat Pool, and the abolition of the Grain Exchange.

The opposition to radical proposals which had existed at earlier conventions had all but died out at this one. After two years of depression, the Wheat Pool was bankrupt. The temper of the delegates can be seen from the fact that the only amendments to the program recommended by the executive were in a more radical direction. The proposal for land nationalization came from the floor of the convention. It was introduced by delegates who had been influenced by the British Labor Party, which had a similar rural program. During the depression the lessening of the sense of security on the part of landholding farmers taught many of them that the ownership of property was not the crucial factor; rather, it was the use of that property. They proposed to let the Commonwealth hold title and modify the risks of fluctuating values, provided the farmers could farm the land and concentrate on their proper business as wheat growers.

After agreement was reached on the economic policy, the leaders of the U.F.C. brought in a resolution on political action: "Should the Federal or Provincial Governments or either of them fail to accede to these demands . . . the U.F.C. [should] take political action as an organization which should seek the cooperation of all citizens in electing candidates pledged to these principles."[36] The provisional form of the resolution was adopted because the leaders sought to put the onus of responsibility on the governments of the day, stating that farmers would take political action only if their demands were refused. This time there was little opposition, and the resolution was overwhelmingly approved. Delegate after delegate demanded that the farmers take over the government themselves in statements such as the following:

You have been passing legislation here in your interests. We have done it for years at conventions similar to this, and after we did that, practically all the influence we had was to send a delegation to some political leader whether it be a provincial or federal one, and ask him, "Please, Mister, will you give us this?"[37]

We are fighting the capitalist party. Why is it that these members of two different political parties are really fighting for one group? The reason is that the majority of the members are engaged in callings that depend on profit, and are those who exploit the farmers.[38]

While the Saskatchewan farmers' movement was tending in a socialist direction, an urban socialist movement emerged in the cities of the province. In 1929 a small group of trade-unionists and teachers under the leadership of M. J. Coldwell, a former member of the English Fabians, who was then a school principal in Regina, decided to form the Independent Labor Party (I.L.P.) of Saskatchewan. Most of the members were Englishmen who had belonged to, or had supported, the labor movement in the United Kingdom.[39] They had been inspired to organize by the success of the I.L.P. of Manitoba, which had elected a mayor, two members of Parliament, and several provincial legislators from Winnipeg. J. S. Woodsworth, then an I.L.P. member of Parliament for Winnipeg, and the recognized leader of the Ginger Group of left-wing farmer and labor members of Parliament, was instrumental in organizing the Saskatchewan group.

The depression began soon after the Saskatchewan I.L.P. was organized, and unemployment developed in the urban areas. The socialist I.L.P. spread until it had branches in all the cities and many of the larger towns of the province. It never, however, had more than 500 members.[40] The Party advocated increased relief to the unemployed. It also contested municipal election campaigns and succeeded in electing a few aldermen.

Realizing that it could not hope to become a major group without the support of the farmers in overwhelmingly rural Saskatchewan, the I.L.P. attempted to cooperate with the growing left-wing political-action movement among the farmers. In 1930 the Party supported the short-lived Farmers' Political Association in their election campaign. One year later, when the U.F.C. decided to enter politics on a socialist basis, the leaders of the U.F.C. and the I.L.P. agreed to work together to create a large farmer-labor party with a socialist program.

The leaders of the two organizations followed the tactics which had been mapped out by the U.F.C. leaders at their convention. Instead of launching a political movement at once, the executive of the U.F.C. organized a series of district conventions, ostensibly for the purpose of putting pressure on the provincial government to accede to the demands of organized farmers and workers. Large meetings were held to introduce a program of action designed to protect workers and farmers against creditors. Delegates were elected from each of the district conventions to go to Regina, the provincial capital, to ask the government to implement their demands. If the government failed to do so, the U.F.C. was authorized to enter political action.

The strategy worked well. The delegates met in Regina on June 26, 1931, with representatives of the I.L.P. led by Coldwell.[41] As was expected, the Conservative government rejected their demands. The delegates were especially infuriated by the statement of Mr. Buckle, the Minister of Agriculture, that "the most hopeful development he had noted was the successful launching of a Colonization Company by an aggregation of Land and Mortgage Companies."[42] This approval by a cabinet minister of the growth of tenant farming under the ownership of the mortgage companies was anathema to the farmers. It provided further justification for the U.F.C. proposal that every farmer be given a use-lease title to his land instead of a private title that could be lost to a mortgage company.

The answer of the joint conference of U.F.C. and I.L.P. delegates to this rebuff was a decision to work together to "establish a cooperative commonwealth, and that in the event of an approaching election, municipal, provincial or federal, we will constitute ourselves as a committee . . . with the view of gaining individual support for candidates pledged to our principles."[43]

The two organizations threw themselves into the work of building the new political movement. The U.F.C. had nominally over 20,000 members, though less than 10 per cent had been able to pay dues because of the depression.[44] The difficulty of organizing a new movement in a poverty-stricken province was tremendous. Tens of thousands were completely dependent on relief for food, clothing, and seed grain. The attitude of many of the impoverished farmers was similar to that of unemployed workers—apathetic rather than protesting.

Many in my district oppose the government but are afraid to attend, for this is an 100 per cent relief district and they are all afraid to compromise themselves until they know how their relief applications will be treated.[45]

I received a letter from the Chairman of the —— Constituency in which he states that in his opinion, the constituency is not organized properly for an election and the farmers would support a Government candidate because they are all on relief and will be looking for assistance.[46]

In spite of the severity of the depression and drought and the consequent lack of finances, U.F.C. and I.L.P. organizers toured the province speaking to large meetings of farmers and workers. They were aided by the fact that the U.F.C., as the educational organization of farmers, received free space every week in the *Western Producer,* the organ of the Wheat Pool, which went to the majority of farm homes in Saskatchewan.[47] The farmers' movement had started on a new path the end of which was now a socialist society rather than a series of immediate reforms. This was the beginning of a movement which within the next decade and a half was to sweep Saskatchewan and become a major threat to the old parties in most of the provinces of Canada.

Meanwhile, similar developments were occurring elsewhere in Canada. A national movement, the Cooperative Commonwealth Federation, was being born. The United Farmers' organizations in Alberta and Manitoba followed Saskatchewan in endorsing "the establishment of the cooperative commonwealth state."[48] In British Columbia the Socialist Party, which had existed in that province since the turn of the century, succeeded in electing its first member of Parliament from the city of Vancouver in 1930.[49]

Intellectual and religious Canada also began to stir in a socialist direction. In 1931 a large group of university professors and other intellectuals formed the League for Social Reconstruction, modeled on the English Fabian Society, to do educational and research work for Canadian socialism.[50] The Toronto conference of the United Church, Canada's leading Protestant group, unequivocally stated:

First of all, it is our belief that the application of the principles of Jesus Christ to economic conditions would mean the end of the capitalist system. (By the capitalist system we mean that order of things under which capital, which is a vital factor in the economic field and represents the part of the economic product used as a means to further production, is owned and administered by individuals and special groups with a view to their own profits. Our contention is that capital, especially in those large-scale forms that are essential to the life of the whole people, should be owned and operated instead, not for private gain, but in the services of the general good.)[51]

As the Conservatives revealed their inability to cope with the deepening depression, which had started under the Liberals, socialists made headway in converting the Canadian people. It became clear that Canada was ready for a new radical third party. The direct impetus for organizing such a party came from Saskatchewan, where the socialist faction had complete control of a mass organization. The U.F.C. suggested to Woodsworth and other left-wing members of Parliament that a national conference be held. All groups who believed that capitalism should be overthrown, and that a new social order based on production for use and not for profit was needed, were invited to Calgary, Alberta, in August, 1932. The conference was attended by the Ginger Group of members of Parliament, the representatives of the United Farmers' organizations of Manitoba, Alberta, and Saskatchewan, and delegates from the Labor and Socialist parties of the three Prairie Provinces and British Columbia.

The conference brought together, for the first time in Canadian history, Marxian socialists from British Columbia, men raised in the traditions of the British labor movement, and the agrarian radicals. The delegates decided to form a new national political party to be known as the Cooperative Commonwealth Federation (CCF). Its first national convention, meeting in Regina in July, 1933, drew up a lengthy program that was a compromise between the Marxian socialists and the much more conservative farmers' representatives from eastern Canada.[52] Each provincial section of the party, however, was left free to interpret the program as it saw fit and to draw up its own provincial program.

The Regina convention marked a turning point in the history of the Saskatchewan farmers' movement as well as in the socialist movement across Canada. For the first time the agrarians had become part of a national radical movement allied with urban labor. Instead of attacking only the aspects of the economy that could be controlled by cooperative action within the province, the farmers were now engaged in a frontal attack on the total economic structure. The organized class consciousness that had developed to defend the farmers' economic position now assumed the offensive.

NOTES

1. From a letter to the author by a former Wheat Pool leader.

2. "They tell us the larger the institution the more economically it can be managed, and by the amalgamation of capital a concern similar to our Canadian Pacific Railway can be better managed and give better service and be more profitable to its shareholders because of its magnitude. If this be so, is it not possible for such an institution to be managed in a similar manner for all the people; and to an even much greater advantage when the principle of self-help and cooperation had been planted in the heart of every workman in the system; and when those who perform the labor are receiving an equitable share in the proceeds. If such a gigantic institution can be so successfully worked for a corporate few, what might we not hope for from it when all the workers have an equitable share in the wealth they create." *Grain Growers' Guide,* May 4, 1910, p. 9.

3. "Farmers' Union Page," *Western Producer,* September 25, 1924, p. 8.

4. *Ibid.,* October 9, 1924, p. 8.

5. J. S. Woodsworth, "Labor in the Canadian Parliament," in H. W. Laidler and Norman Thomas (eds.), *The Socialism of Our Times* (New York, Vanguard Press, 1929), pp. 134–43.

6. Minutes of the 1924 Farmers' Union Convention, p. 5.

7. Minutes of the U.F.C. Board of Directors, March, 1928, p. 10.

8. E. A. Partridge, *A War on Poverty* (Winnipeg, Wallingford Press, Ltd., 1926), p. 80.

9. S. W. Yates, *The Saskatchewan Wheat Pool,* U.F.C. (Saskatchewan Section) (Saskatoon, 1947), pp. 137–45.

10. H. A. Innis (ed.), *The Diary of Alexander James McPhail* (University of Toronto Press, 1940), pp. 185–89.

11. *Saskatchewan Cooperative Wheat Producers, Ltd.: Its Aims, Origins, Operations and Progress, June, 1924–January, 1928* (Regina, 1928), p. 7.

12. *Western Producer,* February 21, 1928, p. 13.

13. Minutes of the U.F.C. Board of Directors, March 5–13, 1929.

14. *Summary of Resolutions Passed at the 1929 Convention of the U.F.C.,* p. 10.

15. Paul F. Bredt, *Submission on Behalf of the Pool Organization of Alberta, Saskatchewan and Manitoba to Royal Grain Inquiry Commission, 1937,* p. 27.

16. Saskatchewan Cooperative Producers, Ltd., *The Wheat Pool and Its Accomplishments to 1946* (Regina, 1946), p. 10.

17. Saskatchewan Cooperative Producers, Ltd., *Submission of Saskatchewan Cooperative Producers Limited and Its Subsidiaries to Commission on Taxation of Cooperatives* (Regina, 1945), p. 9.

18. *The Wheat Pool and Its Accomplishments to 1946,* p. 9.

19. *Western Producer,* July 31, 1930, p. 9.

20. *Ibid.,* February 26, 1931, pp. 2–3.

21. Minutes of the U.F.C. Convention, 1926–29.

22. Minutes of the 1930 U.F.C. Convention, p. 19.

23. *Ibid.,* p. 231.

24. *U.F.C. Official Record of Resolutions, 1930 Convention,* p. 2.

25. Regina *Leader-Post,* May 23, 1930, pp. 1, 12.

26. *Ibid.,* July 12, 1930, p. 12.

27. *Ibid.,* July 7, 1930, p. 1.

28. *Ibid.*

29. *Canadian Parliamentary Guide, 1930,* pp. 215–314.

30. Regina *Leader-Post,* January 24, 1931, p. 1.

31. Partridge, *op. cit.,* pp. 197–202.

32. Regina *Leader-Post,* February 7, 1931, p. 2.

33. Minutes of the 1931 U.F.C. Convention, p. 211.

34. *Ibid.,* p. 168.

35. *Ibid.,* pp. 124, 210. (Italics mine.)

36. *Ibid.,* p. 312.

37. *Ibid.,* pp. 328–29.

38. *Ibid.,* p. 360.

39. Interviews with founders of the I.L.P.

40. Interviews with founders of the I.L.P.

41. Minutes of the Joint Conference of U.F.C. and I.L.P. Delegates in Regina, June 26–27, 1931.

42. U.F.C. (Saskatchewan Section), *Another Explanation of Clause No. 8 of the Provincial Economic Policy* (Saskatoon, 1932), p. 1.

43. Minutes of the Joint Conference of U.F.C. and I.L.P. Delegates in Regina, June 26–27, 1931, p. 9.

44. Interviews with leaders of the U.F.C.

45. Letter from a U.F.C. supporter to a U.F.C. official, Mrs. Louise Lucas, 1931.

46. Letter from Frank Eliason to Mrs. Louise Lucas, April 1, 1932.

47. "United Farmers' Page," *Western Producer,* 1931–32.

48. Regina *Leader-Post,* January 25, 1932, p. 12. See also *ibid.,* December 2, 1932, p. 2. The more conservative United Farmers of Ontario also voted late in 1932 to support the socialists.

49. *Canadian Parliamentary Guide, 1933,* p. 302.

50. League for Social Reconstruction, *Social Planning for Canada* (Toronto, Thomas Nelson and Sons, Ltd., 1935).

51. J. King Gordon, "Socialism and Christianity," *Saskatchewan CCF Research Review,* May, 1934, pp. 4–9.

52. F. R. Scott, "The CCF Convention," *Canadian Forum,* September, 1933, pp. 447–49.

5

THE ECONOMIC CONSEQUENCES
OF THE DEPRESSION

ONLY BY KEEPING in mind the background of the "terrible 'thirties" can one understand the rapid growth of the CCF in Saskatchewan and the continued existence of protest movements in the West. Saskatchewan, a community that had enjoyed year after year of prosperity, was struck without warning by a misfortune that lasted for nine years and wiped out the source of income of well to do and poor alike—a combined catastrophe of drought and low prices. At the same time, a great economic depression hit the whole world, distracting outside attention from the crisis in Saskatchewan.

Before the depression this province was one of the most prosperous farming communities on the North American continent. Serious differences of income and size of farms had not yet developed. The rich soil produced a crop that was in great demand in the industrial nations of Europe.

In the four years 1925 to 1928, Saskatchewan agriculture flourished. Wheat crops averaging 260 million bushels sold at an average price of $1 at country delivery points during this period, and the returns were on the whole well distributed. Gross agricultural income was about $400 millions a year. . . . On the whole, the net cash income of the average citizen in Saskatchewan during this period probably exceeded that in any other economy in the world of about equal population, with the exception of certain areas in the middle west of the United States.[1]

From 1930, the farmers of Saskatchewan were destitute. They were affected not only by the decline in the price of wheat, which at one point reached a low of 19 cents a bushel, but by the longest and severest drought in the history of western settlement. Table 4 (p. 46) shows that the yield per acre fell as low as 2.7 bushels, while the average annual price fell as low as 35 cents. Conditions grew steadily worse. If the crops were good one year in certain parts of the province, the price of wheat was too low to enable farmers to make a profit or to build up reserves. Except for the poor-soil areas in the extreme north, almost every farm was completely dried out during some years. Many did not yield a decent crop for six or seven years. It is impossible to exaggerate the extent to which the social, economic, and political life of the province was affected by the depression in the 'thirties.

The blunt, dry language of economists who recorded the catastrophe tells the financial side of the story.

Gross cash income (the average for 1928–30 compared with the average for 1930–37) fell from 100 to 32, while cash operating expenses fell from 100 to 67. The result was that the net cash income fell from 198 million dollars to 20 million dollars, while in the year 1932 there was not sufficient net income to pay the mortgage interest and nothing for living expenses which had to be met out of borrowing, past savings, consumption of capital and government relief.[2]

The year-by-year reports of the University of Saskatchewan show clearly what crop failures and low prices meant to the farmers:

To pay interest on the present [1934] farm debt of Saskatchewan would have required about 4/5 of all wheat available for sale from the 1933 crop, and for payment of farm taxes two-thirds of this wheat.[3]

To pay interest on the present farm debt [1935] of Saskatchewan would have required about two-thirds of all the wheat available from the 1934 crop . . . , to pay the current [tax] levies would have required at least one fifth of the wheat for sale.[4]

It would require more than one half of all the wheat available for sale from the 1935 crop . . . to pay the interest on the present farm debt, and to meet the current tax levies at least one-sixth of the revenue would have been demanded.[5]

The disaster of the 1937 crop year is the worst of the series.

. . . Since 1930 the average values of the wheat crops have been about one-quarter of those from 1924–28, with that of 1937 being only one-eighth of the amount. The absence of receipts from other sources, the loss of feed crops, and the partial or complete failures of pastures and grazing areas accentuated the difficulties. . . . Only about 14 million bushels of wheat were available for sale from this crop, which is scarcely one tenth of the average for this ten year period.[6]

The 1938 crop year proved to be a very disappointing one for Saskatchewan farmers. The spring and early summer gave promise of a good harvest, but rust and grasshoppers, with scattered drought, seriously reduced yields and grades of all crops over most of the province. Added to this depressing production situation, prices for grain on the open market declined to very low levels.[7]

The 1939 crop proved to be one of the best in the history of the province. . . . From 1930 to 1938 the average gross value per acre of wheat for Saskatchewan was about $5.10; the extreme range was from $6.60 per acre in 1936 to $2.73 in 1937. In light of the facts 1939 may be considered a comparatively good year as the average gross value per acre of wheat is $9.00, the best since 1930. [The Dominion government regards a crop of less than $6.00 an acre as a crop failure.]

For the first time in 10 years, the average Saskatchewan farmer has been able to meet farm cash operating and living costs. However, a still higher income will be necessary to allow satisfactory servicing of the present indebtedness.[8]

The effects of the drought and depression were felt by every group in the rural population. In the early years of the decade, the larger, well-to-do farmers actually suffered more in straight monetary terms than the smaller farmers, as they required large amounts of working capital and did not earn enough to meet the year's expenses. They therefore went deeper into debt.

In the first period, 1929–31, the small farms had a small Net Cash Income but increases in size of the farm were accompanied by a declining income until at 500 acres no Net Cash Income was obtained. Farms larger than 500 acres experienced operating losses. For the period of the severe depression, 1932–34, the smallest sized farms had practically no

Net Cash Income and increasingly larger operating losses resulted for larger farms.[9]

Table 8 makes clear the relation between the size of farms and the loss of farm income.

TABLE 8

RELATION OF SIZE OF FARM TO FARM INCOME, 1932–34

Cultivated acres	Net cash income	Net farm income	Cash family living	Farm surplus
	YIELD OF 0–4 BUSHELS PER ACRE			
0–249	$ 28	–$ 102	$ 270	–$ 372
250–399	–150	– 552	360	– 912
400–549	–280	– 862	450	–1,312
550–699	–430	–1,220	552	–1,772
700–849	–530	–1,705	690	–2,395
	YIELD OF 5–8 BUSHELS PER ACRE			
0–249	$ 138	–$42	$ 283	–$ 325
250–399	138	–255	415	– 670
400–549	138	–405	522	– 927
550–699	123	–577	660	–1,237
700–849	149	–825	837	–1,662
	YIELD OF 9–12 BUSHELS PER ACRE			
0–249	$ 216	$ 35	$ 307	–$ 272
250–399	365	– 27	457	– 484
400–549	480	– 77	577	– 654
550–699	568	–130	722	– 852
700–849	725	–207	905	–1,112
	YIELD OF 13–16 BUSHELS PER ACRE			
0–249	$ 245	$ 80	$ 315	–$ 235
250–399	615	180	497	– 317
400–549	860	260	642	– 382
550–699	1,082	355	817	– 462
700–849	1,370	470	1,025	– 555
	YIELD OF 17–20 BUSHELS PER ACRE			
0–249	$ 408	$ 200	$ 330	–$ 130
250–399	858	410	565	– 155
400–549	1,202	590	715	– 125
550–699	1,532	785	917	– 132
700–849	1,928	1,020	1,170	– 150

SOURCE: University of Saskatchewan, College of Agriculture, "Changes in Farm Income and Indebtedness in Saskatchewan during the Period 1929 to 1940," Agricultural Extension *Bulletin* 105 (1940), p. 13.

No other province in Canada—and, for that matter, few other places in the entire world—suffered so sharp a decline in income and required so much government assistance in order to survive. Every available economic index points to this fact. The decline in provincial per capita income was greatest in Saskatchewan, as table 9 indicates. It is worth noting that Alberta, the only province that is comparable to Saskatchewan, is the home of the successful Social Credit protest movement and, like Saskatchewan, is a wheat province.

A comparison of the relative economic decline by industries reveals similar results. Agriculture in the Prairie Provinces declined in monetary income by 92 per cent from 1928

TABLE 9

DECLINE IN PROVINCIAL INCOMES

Province	1928–29 average per capita	1933 average per capita	Percentage decrease
Saskatchewan	$478	$135	72
Alberta	548	212	61
Manitoba	466	240	49
Canada, national average	471	247	48
British Columbia	594	314	47
Prince Edward Island	278	154	45
Ontario	549	310	44
Quebec	391	220	44
New Brunswick	292	180	39
Nova Scotia	322	207	36

SOURCE: *Report of the Royal Commission on Dominion-Provincial Relations: Canada, 1867–1939* (1940), Book I, p. 150.

to 1932. In the rest of Canada the agricultural decline was 68 per cent, while the loss in salaries and wages was appreciably less.

Table 10 helps in part to explain the reasons for the varying reactions of different classes and communities to the depression. Only the wheat farmers of the West and the rural community of Saskatchewan were adversely and uniformly affected by the economic decline. Some working-class groups improved their economic position in terms of their share of the national income. The nonagricultural middle and upper classes likewise increased their proportionate share.

The extent of the depression in Saskatchewan forced hundreds of thousands of farmers and workers to go on government relief rolls. The drought, and the fact that many grain growers did not raise livestock, meant that government relief foodstuffs had to be brought into one of the most rural areas

TABLE 10

DEPRESSION DECREASES IN NET MONEY INCOME
BY SOURCE OF INCOME

Source of income	Percentage change 1932–33 average income from 1928–29 average income
Agriculture, Prairie Provinces	−94
Fisheries	−72
Salaries and wages in construction	−68
Agriculture, other provinces	−64
Salaries and wages in exporting industries	−50
Total national income	−41
Dividends received by stockholders	−40
Salaries and wages in protected manufacturing industries	−37
Income of small businessmen and professionals	−36
Salaries and wages in sheltered occupations	−30
Miscellaneous income	−18
Bond interest, property income from life insurance, and interest on farm mortgages received by individuals	+13

SOURCE: *Report of the Royal Commission on Dominion-Provincial Relations: Canada, 1867–1939* (1940), Book I, p. 150.

in the world in order to prevent starvation. In 1937 "the completeness of crop failure . . . had placed two-thirds of the rural population on the relief rolls, and 290 of the 302 rural municipalities of the province had sought assistance from the government."[10] Thousands of carloads of vegetables, fruits, clothing, and coal were brought in by voluntary relief agencies and the Red Cross. The total cost of relief from 1930 to 1937 amounted to almost two-thirds of the total local and provincial government revenues in the province.[11] The proportionate amount of government relief in Saskatchewan was far greater than that of any other province in Canada, as table 11 indicates.

The excessive costs of relief in Saskatchewan were not a result of any extravagance in the scale of allotments. The Saskatchewan Relief Commission in 1933–34 set a maximum monthly food allowance for a family of five at $10 plus one 98-pound bag of flour. The Bureau of Public Welfare, which took over the relief work, set monthly relief limits for the same size of family at $13.15 in 1935, $16.50 in 1936, and $20.20 in 1937, with no separate allowance for flour. "If the

TABLE 11

DISPARITIES IN RELIEF BURDEN OF VARIOUS PROVINCES, 1930–37

| | RATIO OF TOTAL RELIEF COSTS TO TOTAL PROVINCIAL INCOME | |
| | Relative severity of burden; index of ratios, national average = 100 | Percentage of total relief expenditures to total provincial income |
Province		
Saskatchewan	367	13.3
Manitoba	115	4.2
British Columbia	100	3.6
Alberta	100	3.6
Canada, national average	100	3.6
Quebec	90	3.2
Prince Edward Island	76	2.8
Ontario	76	2.7
Nova Scotia	70	2.5
New Brunswick	67	2.4

SOURCE: *Report of the Royal Commission on Dominion-Provincial Relations: Canada, 1867–1939* (1940), Book I, p. 164.

applicant had meat, 10 per cent was to be deducted from the allowance; if dairy products, a further 10 per cent; if potatoes, 5 per cent; where it is practicable for the relief recipient to have wheat gristed, no order for flour [was] issued."[12]

The Relief Commission permitted no purchases of fruit, and no vegetables except potatoes and dried beans. It is not surprising, therefore, that the federal Minister of Agriculture, James G. Gardiner, who had been Premier of Saskatchewan in 1935–36, reported, in 1937, "There have been reports from prairie medical men that they have seen signs of scurvy for the first time. It is not on a widespread scale and the number of cases is not available. It is apparent, however, that there has been a shortage of vegetables and fruit in the diet of people on relief."[13]

A further index of the effect of the decline in income on living standards can be seen in the decline of the volume of retail trade in Saskatchewan compared to the rest of Canada. As table 12 indicates, no other province came close to Saskatchewan in this respect. Between 1930 and 1933, retail sales in the province fell more than 45 per cent.

The economic statistics give the objective picture of the effect of depression and drought on the economy, but leave out the complete destruction of the way of life, the hopes and aspirations, of hundreds of thousands of people. The depth of their misery and defeat is suggested by accounts of contemporary journalists:

There is virtually nothing in the rolling hills and valleys at Buffalo Gap and Big Beaver, which is near the U. S. border due south of Bengough. Gardens were a failure. Potatoes will have to be brought in. Clothes are worn thin. . . . One man told of children whom he knew, who had not tasted any other vegetables than potatoes for over two years. Meat, bread and potatoes form the diet of the majority, it was stated, but this year it was feared that the meat will often be lacking and the potatoes as well. Such is the progressive effect of years of drought.[14]

Many of the social necessities of rural life had to be discarded by Saskatchewan farmers. "Clothing has been reduced to a minimum and bed clothes are reported as a great necessity, being but a remnant of what they once were and worn thin with age. . . . One farmer described the situation as 'patching up old clothes with clothes already patched only to discover that the garment had given way somewhere else.' "[15]

The rural telephone system, which had been built up by the government and local farmers' companies, reached a total of

TABLE 12

RETAIL MERCHANDISE TRADE BY PROVINCES

Province	TOTAL NET SALES 1930	INDEX OF RETAIL SALES (1930 = 100)						
		1931	1932	1933	1934	1935	1936	1937
Prince Edward Island	$ 13,733,700	83.8	67.4	64.7	70.3	71.9	82.4	85.3
Nova Scotia	99,519,900	90.3	75.1	69.2	77.2	81.6	88.7	99.8
New Brunswick	84,371,900	85.0	67.6	62.1	69.1	73.1	79.4	90.9
Quebec	651,138,500	86.4	71.5	64.9	69.0	71.3	76.5	86.9
Ontario	1,099,990,200	86.6	71.8	67.4	74.9	78.0	83.0	92.9
Manitoba	189,243,900	81.3	69.6	64.5	69.4	73.4	78.5	85.2
Saskatchewan	189,181,100	70.8	59.2	54.5	59.4	63.2	69.2	68.3
Alberta	176,537,100	76.1	65.6	61.8	69.0	74.0	78.7	86.3
British Columbia	248,597,500	83.7	65.9	62.6	69.6	75.8	84.0	93.6
Canada, totals	$2,755,569,900	82.2	69.8	64.8	74.1	74.6	80.1	89.0

SOURCE: *Retail Merchandise Trade in Canada, 1937* (1938), quoted in G. E. Britnell, *The Wheat Economy* (1939), p. 198.

71,616 telephones in 1930. It declined to 39,488 by 1934.[16] One woman living in rural Saskatchewan commented on the significance of this fact.

Consider a farmer's financial straits when for $10.50 a year he will do without a telephone. Perhaps he is 10 or 15 miles from town, perhaps a mile from his nearest neighbor, yet for the sake of that paltry sum, he will face the hazards, the isolation, the social inconvenience of doing without his telephone. I think this more than anything else shows our western financial position.[17]

The automobile, which during the 'twenties replaced the horse and buggy on most Saskatchewan farms, also began to vanish. The number of cars registered in the province fell from 108,630 in 1929 to 69,040 in 1933. This represented a drop of 36 per cent, while for Canada as a whole cars declined only 13 per cent in the same period.[18] As the number of cars in operation decreased, the use made of the remaining ones declined; the average number of gallons of gasoline for each registered motor vehicle dropped from 366 in 1929 to 256 in 1933 in Saskatchewan, while the decline for Canada as a whole was from 404 to 395 gallons.[19]

Educational standards fell sharply. Schools shortened their academic year, and teachers' salaries were so small that many had to apply for relief. In 1930 the average salary of a male rural teacher with a first-class certificate was $1,159; in 1935 it was $523. Salaries of women teachers fell from $1,142 to $443.[20] Many local school boards could not pay even these small sums, and teachers were often forced to accept interest-bearing notes instead of salary. "Information was given of cases where one girl wore the 'dress' to school one day while a sister stayed at home. Next day they alternated, one staying home and one going to school."[21] The provincial government was forced to waive, temporarily, the requirement that school children pay $2 to take the annual provincial examinations, as many parents could not afford this petty sum.

The Ford car has become a horse-drawn vehicle. The rural telephone system is breaking down with the staggering losses in the number of subscribers every year. Farm products (where there have been crops) supply an ever larger part of the farm diet. Farm clothing constitutes a problem of the first magnitude; it has been estimated recently that it would take $30,000,000 to restore the clothing of the rural population of Saskatchewan to pre-depression standards. The unrepaired houses aggravate a fuel problem which has always been acute on the prairie plains where no wood is available. . . . The total arrears in rural taxes at the end of 1932 was almost equal to two years taxes on every acre of farm land in Saskatchewan. . . . Less than 40 per cent of rural schools were open for the full year in 1932. . . . A considerable number of rural schools close for some months during the winter because (*a*) the school district can not afford to buy coal; (*b*) children have not sufficient clothes to go to school.[22]

One Saskatchewan farm youth depicts the effects of the torturous drought years.

The first calamity which we suffered was drought. It was a long torturous summer. Our grain, grass, fruit trees, and garden were all burned to the ground, leaving no feed for the horses, cows, and hogs, plus the fact that it left no fruit or vegetables to provide us for the long winter. We managed somehow for the first year, since it was the first time we'd ever had such an experience. We mended our old clothes, and resoled our shoes. We managed to buy food for ourselves and the stock and to pay the doctor and the dentist and the veterinary bill. It meant going without anything that wasn't absolutely necessary, and the first year we felt like experts. We never doubted for a minute that when next year came things would be better.

The following spring promised to be a good year, and optimists and gamblers that all farmers must be, they got seed on credit, and everyone worked hard and planted his crops. Things seemed to be working out again for all of us. People became a little more dependent on each other, using one plough because each couldn't afford repairs. Peoples became closer because they had common experiences. Again the summer months became intensely hot and people were fearing what might happen. Then about noon one day everything became black. At first we couldn't imagine what was happening. Dust was sifting through the open doors and windows. Our priceless seeds were gradually being blown from the soil. I shall never forget that night as we sat silently eating our supper. It was happening to us again! Soon we would have no garden left. By this time we really had no money. Our only thread of life was our cows. There was enough grass and pasture that they could eat, and we sold cream for almost nothing, and had those wonderful cream checks. . . .

We got through that winter somehow. We had to be on relief. I guess lots of city people thought that we were a shiftless lot. . . .

In the spring the people again renewed their hope. We thought there could never, never be another winter like that. Again the spring seemed a bewitching promise. It was after this one that I came to loathe the springs. They were so deceptive, and I became a realist about the seasons; preferring the harvest to all because then you knew if it was good or bad, and whether or not you were going to eat and be warm and have enough clothes to go to school.[23]

The complete breakdown of the provincial economy forced a migration from the drought-devastated areas. Farms in southern and central Saskatchewan were abandoned. Many families moved to the northern fringe of the province where unbroken bushland was available for homesteads. The soil was much poorer than in the south, but at least it rained in the north. Between 1930 and 1938 over 45,000 persons moved to this northern frontier.[24] They had given up their farms to move to a land where they had to clear much of the forest and build new homes, roads, hospitals, and schools. Until the war prosperity of the 'forties, many of the settlers were dependent on government relief, for it took years to clear the land and raise a paying crop.

The hardships they faced can be seen from the following extracts from the diary of the Rev. A. M. Nicholson, then a United Church minister in the north:

Thursday, March 28, 1935
Drove from Carragana to Bell's Hill. R—— offered to send one of the family to a neighbor's and let us have the bed. . . . They had no hay or oats for our team. . . . They apologized for their food—moose meat, white bread, tea without sugar or milk. They had no fruit, butter or potatoes.

Friday, March 29

. . . They had gone to the neighbors for additional food supplies and we had potatoes, butter and a pie as "extras" for breakfast. . . . Supper with S—— M——. Bread, butter, tea (cream and sugar); no meat, fruit or syrup. It is hard for bachelors to get adequate relief, he complained. . . . We went to J—— R——'s for the night. J—— and the man who is "batching" with him slept on the floor while F—— and I had the only bed in the shack. They had a cup of tea and bread without butter before we went to bed.

Saturday, March 30

. . . J—— had hot cakes for us for breakfast with syrup he made from white sugar and water. He had a drink made from roasted wheat which we called "Bennett Coffee." We had dinner at K——'s, tea, bread, and corn syrup. Relief allow-ances were always so low that food was very scarce at the end of the month, they complained. We went to E—— T——'s for the night. I had known E—— when I taught school at Davidson 15 years before. Dry years drove him north. He had a small 2-roomed log house.

Sunday, March 31

What poverty! Their tea kettle sprung a leak last Fall and the trouble with the relief system, said F——, was that it as-sumed that people never required a new lamp chimney, tea kettle or wash basin. For five years they had been seeing one utensil or implement after another wear out without being able to replace it.

Mr. and Mrs. J—— P—— kept us for the night. J—— home-steaded near Strasburg about 30 years ago. He put up good buildings—later bought another quarter on which he paid $2,000 cash. Finally he lost the half [section—360 acres] be-cause he could not meet his payments. Mrs. P—— in her early fifties is almost blind because she cannot get the necessary medical care for her eyes.[25]

Saskatchewan lost about 155,000 people to other parts of Canada and foreign countries.[26] While the population of Canada increased 1,140,000 from 1931 to 1941, that of Sas-katchewan dropped from 921,785 to 895,992. The remainder of the decline is derived by adding the natural increase of births over deaths for that period. Within one decade, at least one-fifth of the people were forced to leave their homes in order to obtain a livelihood.

The drought cycle ended in Saskatchewan in 1939, coinciding with the end of the world-wide depression and the outbreak of the Second World War. The depression in wheat prices did not, however, end until 1943, as the war cut off some of Canada's export markets. The price of wheat per bushel was 54 cents in 1939, 53 cents in 1940, 53 cents in 1941, and 69 cents in 1942.[27] These were years of revival for the farmers, however, as they could at least eat well and begin to rehabilitate their farms.

The war years after 1942 brought abundant crops and higher prices for farmers. The year in which the CCF took office, 1944, was also the year of the highest farm income in Saskatchewan history; the gross income per farm was $4,516. Much of the increased income of the 'forties has been used to rehabilitate the farms. Estimates of the effects of the depression on farm machinery alone indicate that there will be an annual expenditure of $25,000,000 for many years to replace worn-out machinery.[28] Payment of debts and taxes accumulated during the depression is only now ending.

Saskatchewan is riding the crest of the economic and climatic cycles, but it is still thinking in terms of the 'thirties. As one interviews the residents of rural Saskatchewan today, one cannot help being impressed by their ever-present fear that prosperity will not last, that a new drought or depression will set them back again. At farmers' conventions, at "bull sessions" in the local stores, the discussion always turns to the control of wheat prices, to crop insurance, and to the politicians who are believed to have power to prevent another catastrophe.

NOTES

1. Bank of Canada, *Report of the Financial Position of the Province of Saskatchewan* (Ottawa, 1937), p. 3.

2. *Prairie Population Possibilities—A Study Prepared for the Royal Commission on Dominion-Provincial Relations* (Ottawa, 1939).

3. William Allen, and E. C. Hope, *The Farm Outlook for Saskatchewan* (University of Saskatchewan, 1934), p. 2.

4. *Ibid.*, 1935, p. 2.

5. *Ibid.*, 1936, p. 2.

6. *Ibid.*, 1938, pp. 1–2.

7. *Ibid.*, 1939, p. 1.

8. *Ibid.*, 1940, p. 1. (Italics mine.)

9. University of Saskatchewan, College of Agriculture, "Changes in Farm Income and Indebtedness in Saskatchewan during the Period 1929 to 1940," *Agricultural Extension Bulletin 105* (Saskatoon, 1940), p. 13.

10. Province of Saskatchewan, *A Submission by the Government of Saskatchewan to the Royal Commission for Dominion-Provincial Relations* (Regina, 1937), p. 187; G. E. Britnell, *The Wheat Economy* (University of Toronto Press, 1939), p. 97.

11. *Report of the Royal Commission on Dominion-Provincial Relations: Canada, 1867–1939* (Ottawa, 1940), Book I, p. 164.

12. Britnell, *op. cit.*, p. 170.

13. *Ibid.*, p. 171.

14. D. B. MacRae and R. M. Scott, *In the South Country: A Reprint of a Series of Articles Which Appeared in the Winnipeg Free Press, Regina Leader-Post and Saskatoon Star-Phoenix in September, 1934, as a Result of a Tour of the Drouth-Stricken Districts of Saskatchewan and Manitoba* (Saskatoon *Star-Phoenix*, 1934), pp. 18–20.

15. *Ibid.*, pp. 7–14.

16. Province of Saskatchewan, Department of Telephones, *Annual Report* (Regina), 1930–39.

17. Gertrude S. Telford, "Livingstone: A Social Survey" (unpublished master's thesis, McMaster's University, 1931), p. 34, quoted in Britnell, *The Wheat Economy*, pp. 179–80.

18. Dominion Bureau of Statistics, *The Prairie Provinces in Their Relation to the National Economy of Canada* (Ottawa, 1934), p. 109.

19. *Ibid.*, p. 115.

20. Legislative Assembly of Saskatchewan, *Journals* (Regina, 1937), p. 174.

21. MacRae and Scott, *op. cit.*, p. 18.

22. G. E. Britnell, "Economic Conditions in Rural Saskatchewan," *Canadian Forum*, March, 1934, p. 210.

23. Carolyn Rose, unpublished manuscript in possession of author.

24. Britnell, *The Wheat Economy*, p. 202.

25. Quoted in *ibid.*, p. 212.

26. *Report of the Saskatchewan Reconstruction Council* (Regina, 1944), p. 115.

27. Province of Saskatchewan, Department of Agriculture, *Fortieth Annual Report* (Regina, 1945), p. 167.

28. *Report of the Saskatchewan Reconstruction Council*, p. 80.

6

THE MOVEMENT GROWS TO POWER

THE YEAR 1932 saw the Saskatchewan farmers and the social-ist movement united in a national attempt to establish so-cialism in Canada. Joining with other groups in the rest of Canada did not greatly affect the Saskatchewan movement beyond giving it a base from which to take part in national elections. The Saskatchewan group called itself the Farmer-Labor Group, and did not officially adopt the name Coopera-tive Commonwealth Federation for provincial usage until 1935. The new CCF was to remain essentially a federation of provincial parties, each of which had its own approach to socialism and politics and did not interfere with the activities of other provincial sections.

The creation of a mass socialist party in Saskatchewan was not, therefore, the local extension of a new national move-ment but, rather, an endemic movement having its roots in Saskatchewan. A small group of convinced socialists in key positions in the farmers' movement prompted action in the face of the double catastrophe of depression and drought. These socialists attempted to use this opportune moment to make a drastic change in the thinking and organized actions of farmers and workers. They hoped to build a radical social-ist party that would completely change the social and eco-nomic structure of Canada.

The early radical promotion group, many of whom had socialist ideas as a result of earlier experiences in other social-ist movements or because of intellectual contact with socialist ideas, was only a small segment of the new party. These so-cialists, however, gained an influence that was out of propor-tion to their numerical strength in the new Farmer-Labor Group because of the obvious failure of other attempted solutions to the farmers' economic problems, especially the efforts at economic cooperation and political pressure on old party governments. This suggests that proposals for radical change tend to get a hearing only after the more moderate possibilities have been exhausted. Radical reformers who believe that they can get people "rationally" to reject efforts at moderate and ameliorative reform without trying them succeed only in isolating themselves from any influence in the later development of a movement, as the experience of American socialism well demonstrates. Men like E. A. Partridge, George Williams, and M. J. Coldwell were able to retain their influence with the agrarians because they had participated actively in the earlier nonsocialist efforts, even though they were confident that socialism was the long-term solution to the farmers' problems.

The willingness of agrarian activists in the U.F.C. to place themselves under the command of the socialists, who appeared to have a new and workable answer to their problems, can be seen in the selection, by the joint convention of the U.F.C. and the I.L.P. in 1932, of M. J. Coldwell, the leader of the urban socialists, as the provincial leader of the new Farmer-Labor Group. The socialist leaders of the new party also succeeded in getting the movement to accept their proposals on most questions of policy and ideology. The convention of 1932 instructed the Saskatchewan delegates to the "New Party" national conference in Calgary to vote for "Socialist Party of Canada" as the name of the national party. The predominantly rural delegates voted down all objections to the word "socialist."[1] The position of the socialist leaders was stated by George Williams, the foremost rural socialist in the party. "The history of socialist groups elsewhere showed that, where an effort was made to camouflage under a vote-catching label, disaster followed. The Labor Party [of England] had striven for power and neglected socialist education. They gained power, but when the crisis came, the people in their ignorance elected a Conservative government."[2]

The new party advocated socialization of all private industries in Canada. This applied to land as well, since the U.F.C., under the impact of the depression, advocated a form of land nationalization in which the state would hold title to the land

and the farmers would be given a use-lease title. This appealed to many agrarians as a means of preventing foreclosures by banks and mortgage companies, and it satisfied the socialists' desire for government ownership.

The U.F.C. and the I.L.P., working together as the Farmer-Labor Group, began an intensive campaign to win the next election, which legally had to be called by 1934. The U.F.C. was in charge of the work in rural areas, while the I.L.P. campaigned in the towns and cities. The joint provincial organization was controlled by a board of seven representatives from each organization and seven elected at the annual joint conventions of the two groups. It was difficult to raise money for an active campaign in a province as poverty-stricken as Saskatchewan, but the party depended upon active support from local farm leaders who could campaign during the slack seasons. Speakers and organizers preached the gospel of a new social order. The opposition did not take the new party seriously at first; but as the party succeeded in holding large meetings and constituency nominating conventions, the old parties turned a large part of their fire against the socialists.

The most vulnerable plank in the program of the party was its sponsorship of socialization of land. Both Liberals and Conservatives concentrated on making farmers believe that the new party would take away their land and set up state farms similar to those in the Soviet Union. As a Liberal speaker declared, "The CCF debt policy means surrender of the Torrens title . . . and you are not going to get it back. . . . You will have your land only as long as you are a good socialist. . . . If you do not agree with the state you are in a position where the state will dictate to you. Once in power the CCF will socialize everything and not wait for votes."[3]

The U.F.C. and the I.L.P. were repeatedly attacked as communistic and revolutionary and were forced to dissociate themselves from Russia and the Communists. They bitterly fought this campaign of insinuation. Frank Eliason, the secretary of the U.F.C., wrote to the editor of the Regina *Leader-Post* in September, 1931.

You, sir, either know or you do not know that there is no connection between the Soviet Union and the U.F.C. If you know there is no connection, the paragraph [in a previous issue] is not only a base insinuation, but is a deliberate untruth uttered in an effort to discredit the U.F.C. . . .

So far from the U.F.C. being under the influence of Moscow, as you suggest, prior to the issue of your editorial we had prepared a severe criticism of Communism. . . . The only kind of revolution the U.F.C. stands for is a revolution by constitutional means, viz., the use of the ballot.[4]

The opposition used every available method to defeat the new party. The Regina public school board, controlled by local business and professional men, ordered M. J. Coldwell, who was then a principal of a Regina school, to withdraw from politics or be discharged. This was a serious threat, since Coldwell had an invalid wife. Coldwell refused to give up his political rights as a citizen and was discharged by the board.

The two old parties, all the daily newspapers of the province, and most of the weeklies circulating among farmers made repeated attacks on socialism and the new party. They tried continually to drive a wedge between the farmers' demands for economic changes and their desires to retain control of their farms.[5] The Liberal Party, which was the opposition party provincially and federally, campaigned as a progressive, nonsocialist reform party that would give farmers what they wanted—higher farm prices, increased relief, and protection against foreclosures—without threatening their position as landowners.

The Catholic Church joined in the attack. A letter read in all Catholic pulpits in the province just before the election of 1934 clearly repudiated socialism.

Catholics will be guided by the words of Pius XI, "Whether Socialism be considered a doctrine, or as a historical movement, if it really remains socialism, it can not be brought into harmony with the dogmas of the Catholic Church . . . the reason being that it conceives human society in a way utterly alien to Christian truth . . . the hierarchy of Canada has recently issued a collective warning that Catholics of this country be ever on their guard."[6]

Various Catholic priests throughout the province publicly attacked the CCF both inside and outside their pulpits.[7] Members of the party among students at Notre Dame College at Wilcox, Saskatchewan, were told they must resign either from the school or from the CCF.[8]

Though opposition to the CCF was great, the leaders of the party firmly believed that they would win the election and convert the province to socialism. They were convinced that the desperate economic conditions in the province had destroyed all faith in the old order. On election day, in June, 1934, the CCF received 103,582 votes, almost 25 per cent of the total. The triumphant Liberals obtained 206,191; the Conservatives, who had previously formed the government, fell to 114,973. In spite of finishing third in the popular vote, the CCF became the official opposition in the legislature, because the Tories failed to win a single constituency, whereas the CCF won five.[9]

In rural districts the CCF won almost 30 per cent of the vote, and was a close second to the victorious Liberals.[10] Many predominantly rural constituencies were lost because of the overwhelming vote for the old parties in small towns and villages. The large rural vote polled by a new party advocating socialism and state ownership of land is an indication of the effect of the depression and drought on the farmers of Saskatchewan. This vote was achieved by a party that had little funds, no regular press, no representatives in the legislature, and the opposition of two powerful and experienced party machines, as well as the Catholic Church, all the daily newspapers, and almost the entire urban middle class.

To the CCF leaders, however, both agrarian and socialist alike, the election was a great defeat. They had been sure that they would win and form the first socialist government in Canada. Some of the leaders were so overwhelmed by what they considered a repudiation by the electorate that they seriously thought of abandoning politics. The agrarian leaders in the executive of the U.F.C. began to consider withdrawing from the CCF and resuming their original role of a farmers' pressure group which attempted to influence all parties on the farmers' behalf.

Before the Saskatchewan CCF could assess its position, it was thrown into the federal elections of 1935, the first na-

tional election that it contested. The national party was much
weaker than the Saskatchewan organization. With the exception of British Columbia and Alberta, the new party had little
strength in the rest of Canada. The Trades and Labor Congress (A. F. of L.) opposed it, and it therefore had little
urban support outside the old socialist strongholds of Winnipeg and Vancouver. The party was obviously not a realistic
alternative to the incumbent Conservatives, and faced the traditional danger to third-party movements on this continent—
the fear of would-be supporters of wasting their vote by voting
for a hopeless candidate.

The situation was further complicated on the prairies by the
appearance of the Social Credit Party. The Social Crediters,
under William Aberhart, swept the Alberta provincial elections early in 1935 and then proceeded to organize in other
provinces.[11] They had been able to make more headway than
the CCF because their reform program did not involve socialization. The Social Credit promise of $25 a month to
every person and the abolition of interest on debts appealed
to many impoverished farmers, and the threat of losing their
land was not involved.

In Saskatchewan as well as in Alberta, many CCF agrarian
supporters and some party leaders were attracted to the electorally more successful Social Credit movement. Like the
CCF, the Social Credit Party was opposed to eastern financial
control and favored immediate action to save farms from
foreclosures. Local Social Credit associations were formed
throughout Saskatchewan, and in many areas, especially those
close to Alberta, CCF organizations joined the Social Credit
movement.

A movement developed, both within and without the CCF,
for unity between the two third-party western protest groups.
The nonsocialist agrarian leaders in the CCF, who had accepted the leadership of the socialists in 1931 and 1932, did
not recognize the existence of any important differences between the two movements. They viewed both as fighting the
"interests," as being against the Grain Exchange and other
traditional enemies of the farmers. In two Saskatchewan federal constituency organizations the unity movement resulted

in the nomination of joint candidates by the CCF and Social Credit parties.

A rift developed within the party as the socialists in the CCF bitterly opposed the movement to merge with Social Credit. They believed that Social Credit was a "reformist capitalist" party, and that more far-reaching changes were necessary to create a stable society. Various leaders of the party, such as "Jake" Benson, an agrarian progressive who had never accepted socialism, were expelled for cooperating with the Social Credit Party. The point of view of the socialists is expressed in an extract from a letter by Tom Johnson, a party leader, to the CCF executive.

I am firmly convinced that our future strength depends upon the organization repudiating any candidate that departs from our principles in the hope that by doing so he may get elected at this time. Compromise will mean ultimate defeat. We have told the people that socialism is the only way out. Any departure from that position would brand us as a party that wants to get office and will grasp at any straw.[12]

The 1935 election in Saskatchewan resulted in a greater defeat for the CCF than that of 1934. The party elected only two members of Parliament from the twenty-one seats in the province. One of the victorious CCF candidates had been endorsed also by Social Credit. The total strength of the CCF declined from 25 per cent in the provincial election of 1934 to 19 per cent in 1935. Social Credit took away much of the socialist support in western Saskatchewan, and received a slightly higher provincial vote than the CCF. The total vote of the two third parties was, however, 39 per cent—larger than that of either of the old parties.[13]

Rural Saskatchewan was beginning to make a definite break with the two old parties. In the rural areas close to half of the total vote went to parties favoring economic change beyond the program of the Liberals and the Conservatives. The 1935 vote and the unity movement within the CCF indicate that the protesting farmers had not become socialists. They were ready, however, to support radical economic innovations. Some of them wanted to try the solution of Social

Credit, as they earlier had tried cooperation and the Progressive Party. Here again is evident the characteristic fumbling of the western farmers as they turn to different ways of solving their economic problems.

The defeat of 1935, coming on the heels of that of the year before, had a drastic effect on both agrarian and socialist leaders of the Saskatchewan CCF. True to the traditional reformer's weakness, they had been counting too heavily on the rational persuasiveness of their cause. They believed that socialism was the correct solution to the social and economic problems of the day and that, if it were honestly presented to the people, it would be accepted. Previous Saskatchewan reform movements, such as the Progressive Party and the Wheat Pool, had succeeded in winning majority support in a few years. It galled the CCF leaders that the "opportunistic, reformist" Social Credit Party could so easily upset the young socialist movement. They had been psychologically unprepared for rejection by the people whom they were trying to help.

The party leaders concluded from the setback that they were overvaluing the political realism of the common man. Since the farmers were apparently not yet ready to support a complete socialist program, a definite choice had to be made: Should the CCF continue as an independent socialist party preaching that socialism is the only hope for a decent society, until the pressure of events brought the majority over to them? Or should the party compromise its program by modifying its radicalism in order to win an electoral majority for a program of immediate reforms that would put the party in power?

Faced with these alternatives, even the veteran socialist leaders of the Saskatchewan CCF chose the path of compromise. Accordingly, the 1936 convention adopted a new provincial program that contained no mention of socialism and dropped completely the plank calling for nationalization of land.[14] It also reversed its previous policy on cooperation with other political groups by adopting the following resolution:

Whereas we believe that a victory for democracy and progress can only be won by the cooperation of the various progressive political organizations of Saskatchewan, and

Whereas it is most desirable that the initiative to secure this unity should be taken by the CCF,

Be it resolved that this convention urge upon the Provincial Council the advisability of issuing a call to all progressive organizations, political, cultural and economic to meet in convention to seek to discover common ground upon which we may unite for action and a common goal to which we may unitedly move.[15]

The earlier agrarian emphasis on immediate reforms to alleviate the consequences of the economic constraints on farmers had again won out. George Williams, former U.F.C. president, who had become provincial leader of the party in 1935 after M. J. Coldwell was elected to the federal House of Commons at Ottawa, together with the other agrarian and socialist leaders of the party, drastically changed their policy to one of uniting with Social Credit and "progressive" Conservatives against the incumbent Liberals and "eastern interests," even if it meant dropping socialism temporarily.

M. J. Coldwell was the only prominent Saskatchewan leader who vigorously opposed the swing in policy. He was joined in his opposition by J. S. Woodsworth, the national leader of the CCF, the foremost socialist in Canada. Woodsworth told the Saskatchewan convention in July, 1936, in no uncertain terms, that his socialism and Social Credit did not mix: "Social Credit stands for capitalism. I am a socialist and I'm not going to enter into political alliances with those who uphold capitalism."[16]

It is highly significant, therefore, that the proposal to reverse CCF policy and unite with other "progressive" parties met very little opposition from the convention delegates. Only 8 votes out of a total of 312 were cast against the unity resolution.[17] The agrarian reform tendencies in the Saskatchewan farmers' movement had overwhelmed the original hopes of the small socialist promotion group. The farm leaders wanted immediate economic action and political power, and did not care whether or not the goal was socialism.

The Saskatchewan CCF was the only provincial section of the national party to modify its socialist policies significantly at this time and to favor political alignments with other parties.[18] This was a consequence of two factors. (1) With the exception of the old Marxian British Columbia section, the Saskatchewan party was the only division of the CCF that had hopes of gaining political power within a short period of time. The other sections were small minority parties with little mass support. There was, therefore, very little pressure on these organizations to engage in practical politics. They could afford to be "pure," as they had no vested political position to lose. (2) The Saskatchewan CCF had fewer doctrinaire old socialists in proportion to its total membership than other sections of the party. In every other province the party was led by men who had been in small, isolated socialist parties for years before the CCF was organized and who were, therefore, comparatively unaffected by a new defeat. In fact, for those old socialists, such as Woodsworth, the establishment of a national party, which received 10 per cent of the national vote, was a major socialist victory, not a defeat, and did not necessitate political compromise.

The subsequent national convention of the CCF in 1937 defeated efforts to get the party to form alliances with other groups. Saskatchewan, however, was permitted to continue its independent course of favoring coalitions, because of the CCF principle of provincial autonomy. Between 1936 and 1938 the Saskatchewan CCF entered into repeated negotiations with all the provincial parties opposed to the Liberals, that is, Social Credit, Communist, and Conservative. Repeated efforts were made to secure a real coalition that would sweep the Liberal government out of power and replace it by a "progressive" administration pledged to help the farmers.

In 1937 the CCF provincial executive sent greetings to the Social Credit convention: "Through the medium of this message of greetings, the Saskatchewan CCF desires to extend to your organization an invitation to meet a committee from the Saskatchewan CCF to canvass the possibility of cooperation, in order to prevent the forces of reaction again sweeping Saskatchewan by splitting the reform vote."[19] The Social Credit organization, which was under the influence of Premier William Aberhart of Alberta, refused to consider a coalition because of the bitter attacks on the Alberta government which the Alberta CCF was continually making.

The CCF also attempted to secure an alliance with the provincial Conservative Party, which as an opposition party had adopted a reform program. The *New Era,* the organ of the Saskatchewan CCF, in defending such an alliance even went so far as to comment:

But, says the *Leader-Post* [leading Liberal daily], the mixture is a little strange. What of those Conservatives who denounce the CCF and all its policies!

We might say in reply that there are no such Conservatives. The western Conservatives who are opposed to a farmers' wheat board and a marketing act are very scarce. The Conservatives who oppose electoral reform as embodied in proportional representation and the single transferable ballot are scarcer still. The Conservatives who would sooner see our present reactionary government retain power than the election of one of a more progressive nature are non-existent. . . . Our Liberal Government has become a reactionary Tory organization and most of the Conservatives have gone far to the Left.

. . . It is quite clear that consideration of ways and means to split the progressive vote has occupied the attention of the Liberal Board of Strategy. Perhaps the Weyburn nomination [a joint CCF–Conservative candidate] is an indication of the reply that can be expected to the forces of reaction.[20]

These statements indicate the effect of coalition tactics on a radical party. The participants in any coalition are obliged to defend one another. The Saskatchewan CCF, which was organized under the Conservative government of J. T. M. Anderson, was now forced to say that Anderson and his party, which the CCF had castigated as a business-controlled party, were progressives. The Alberta CCF, which was attacking the Social Credit government in that province as a fraudulent reform administration that did not actually fight big business, found the ground removed from beneath it by the alliances of the Saskatchewan party.[21] The whole purpose and program of the CCF had therefore changed. It could no longer carry on a systematic attack on capitalism and all its institutions. The party had become a farmers' pressure group seeking to win agrarian reforms.

CCF efforts to secure cooperation among the opposition parties floundered in the sea of competitive politics. The local organizations of the opposition parties found it difficult to agree on which party should get the nomination. Actually, no over-all agreement was reached with any other party. However, in a large number of constituencies one or another of the parties made no nomination, but simply supported the group that did. The CCF contested only 30 seats out of the 52 in the province, the Social Crediters ran candidates in 41 constituencies, and the Conservatives nominated 25. In six districts, unity candidates backed by two or more parties ran.

As the CCF moved away from orthodox socialist principles and tactics, it ceased being the butt of vigorous attack from all sides. The opposition forces concentrated their main fire on the Liberal government. The former Conservative Premier of the province, J. T. M. Anderson, in an appeal for CCF support in areas where it was not running its own candidates, went so far in 1938 as to repeat the contention of the CCF *New Era*, that the CCF program and the Tory one were similar. Appealing to the supporters of the CCF, he stated, "Every plank in the CCF platform is ours and there is no reason why the members of the [CCF] party can not conscientiously support us in this effort to rid the province of a discredited administration."[22]

The Liberals, on the other hand, concentrated their fire on the Social Crediters, who had polled the largest vote of the opposition parties in 1935 and were contesting the most seats. Of the Liberal propaganda attacking the other parties in the election of 1938, ten pamphlets were directed against the Social Credit Party, two against the CCF, and none against the Conservatives.[23] The Catholic Church had apparently lost its fear of the consequences of CCF victory, for there is little evidence of continued overt opposition to the CCF from the Saskatchewan hierarchy.[24]

The election results gratified the CCF as much as the earlier ones had depressed it. The party won eleven out of the thirty seats which it contested, and received 11,000 more votes than Social Credit, though it ran in eleven fewer constituencies. In fact, Social Credit succeeded in electing only two candidates, while two unity candidates supported by all three opposition parties were also elected.[25]

Again, the CCF leaders had guessed wrong. They had feared that the Social Crediters, supported by their Alberta party, would become the largest opposition party in the legislature. The Social Crediters apparently lost their appeal to the Saskatchewan agrarians as a result of the failures of the Alberta government to fulfill its original promises of $25 a month and the cancellation of all interest. Social Credit had had three years of power in Alberta and had done little in the way of reform.[26] The continuing depression and drought, the weakness of the Social Credit government, and the fact that the scare propaganda against the CCF disappeared, all enabled the CCF to grow, in spite of the pessimism of its leaders.

The CCF was now the leading opposition party in Saskatchewan. The Conservatives for the second time had failed to elect a single representative and could therefore be ruled out as a major factor in Saskatchewan politics. Social Credit had finished a bad third in the election and its provincial organization soon disintegrated, with many of its supporters going over to the more successful CCF.

The CCF strength in 1938 brought about almost as complete a reversal in policy and tactics as had resulted from CCF weakness in the elections of 1934 and 1935. Many leaders of the party felt that they had made a mistake in compromising with the other opposition parties. Actually, the period before the election, 1937–38, had been the worst years of the 'thirties, as virtually the entire province suffered from drought in 1937. The average crop yield was under three bushels an acre, and two-thirds of the farm population received relief during this period. (See chap. 5, p. 123.) The farmers were restless and bitter over the low relief allotments and, as the 1938 election revealed, actually moved left again. But so preoccupied were the CCF leaders with efforts at unity and removal of the stigma of radicalism that they failed to sense the renewed readiness for a more radical program.

But immediately after the elections of 1938, the party plunged into an organizing drive, looking forward to the 1940 federal elections. They refused all offers of unity with other "progressive" opposition groups. The party leaders had learned their lesson. This time it was to be a CCF government or nothing. The basis for this policy was made clear in a letter of May 29, 1939, from George Williams, the provincial leader, to a member who had urged continuation of the unity program.

. . . a few years ago we had a Saskatchewan Provincial Convention mandate to cooperate with other Progressive groups. We tried that and no one can say that we did not sincerely do our best to make it work. The results were not only disappointing but even possibly disastrous. It being now admitted that had we gone our own way with a full slate, . . . we might now be the government.

The 1939 provincial convention ratified with little opposition the new change in policy, as set forth in the following resolution:

Resolved that this Convention reiterates its faith in the CCF platform, the CCF organization and in the ultimate victory of the CCF, and instructs its officers and members to do everything within their power to ensure that CCF candidates contest every election and by-election in order to elect a CCF government for Saskatchewan and a CCF government for Canada.[27]

This reaffirmation of independent action did not include a revival of the earlier doctrinaire socialism in the CCF platform. Rather, it represented the recognition by its leaders that the party had become the sole voice of agrarian protest in the province and therefore did not have to compromise with other opposition groups. CCF leaders adhered to the views, formed after the election defeats of 1934 and 1935, that emphasis on socialist principles does not win elections. In the sober light of experience it seemed wiser to eliminate issues and symbols likely to antagonize the voters. As George Williams stated this conclusion, "I believe the growing popularity [of the Saskatchewan CCF] . . . is caused by the policy we have adopted. We have purposely and painstakingly avoided theoretical discussion and we have addressed ourselves to the task of offering worthwhile and practical suggestions as to the solution or alleviation of current problems."[28]

Before the Saskatchewan CCF could reorganize to take advantage of its new, powerful position, the outbreak of the Second World War disrupted the unity of the party. Nationally, the CCF had from the beginning favored an antiwar, neutral policy for Canada. The national leader, J. S. Woodsworth, was a convinced pacifist who had vigorously opposed the First World War. Upon the outbreak of war in 1939 the CCF movement split into three groups on the war question: one minority, following Woodsworth, was opposed to Canadian entry into what it considered to be an imperialist war; a second even smaller minority favored all-out support of the war; the majority of the party's national leaders backed the position of M. J. Coldwell in supporting Canada's declaration of war but opposing the sending of troops overseas.[29]

The National Council of the CCF voted in September, 1939, to support Coldwell's position. All the CCF members of the federal House of Commons, except J. S. Woodsworth, voted for war. Woodsworth, though the national leader, received the permission of the party to cast a personal vote against the war.[30]

In Saskatchewan the same three-way split occurred. The majority of the Provincial Council voted in favor of the Coldwell middle-of-the-road position. It adopted a compromise program of immediate domestic demands, which neither supported nor opposed the war. Members of the party were left free to take any position they desired.[31]

A federal election was called early in 1940. The strength of the CCF appeared at a low ebb because of its dissension over the war question. During the campaign, some members of the Saskatchewan CCF ran on an antiwar platform, some on an all-out support of the war, and still others on the party program of economic but not military aid to the Allies.

The election results were surprisingly favorable to the Saskatchewan CCF, for it elected five members of Parliament out of a possible twenty-one members in the province. This represented a gain of three seats from the previous election in 1935. Outside Saskatchewan the CCF succeeded in winning only two constituencies. In the fifteen Saskatchewan seats, which were predominantly rural, the party received 101,450 votes, compared with 104,441 votes for the Liberals.[32] This meant that the CCF was the first party among the agrarians, as the vote included small towns and villages that were overwhelmingly opposed to the CCF.

The CCF was again definitely on the upswing as the party of rural Saskatchewan. Economic conditions in the province were beginning to improve, as the disastrous drought of 1930–39 had ended, but the price of wheat remained very low, being 54 cents a bushel in 1939, and 53 cents in 1940.[33] The CCF was the major Saskatchewan opposition party fighting for higher wheat prices, while the incumbent Liberals were blamed for the continuation of low prices. The farmers were being squeezed by the rising costs of manufactured products. To them, the fact that the CCF was fighting the economic battle of agriculture in Parliament and in the legislature was evidently more important than the party's confusion on the war question.

The years 1940–41 proved to be a turning point in the fortunes of the CCF. Again, the fight for higher wheat prices was responsible. Economic conditions were continuing on a depression level in Saskatchewan, although prosperity was returning to the rest of Canada. The fall of western Europe to the Germans had destroyed the European wheat market and resulted in a continuation of low wheat prices. In response to these conditions, the Wheat Pool committees demanded that a Saskatchewan delegation be sent to Ottawa to seek higher prices; 185,000 signatures and $40,000 were collected to support the delegation. Many farmers who had previously supported the Liberal Party took part in the campaign, including old W. R. Motherwell, the first president of the Saskatchewan Grain Growers' Association and a former Liberal Minister of Agriculture in the national government.[34] The CCF was, however, the only political party to give all-out support to the farmers' demands. As a result of the campaign, the federal Liberal government agreed to raise the price of wheat to 90 cents a bushel—as against $1 a bushel, which was demanded by the Wheat Pool and the CCF.[35] In the course of the struggle the CCF actually doubled its

Agrarian Socialism

membership, although, with no election pending, membership figures could normally be expected to decline.[36]

The year 1941 also witnessed change in the leadership of the provincial party—the third since 1932. Increasing resentment had developed within the party against George Williams, who had led it since 1935. Williams had antagonized many in the party by his attempts to extend his control over all facets of party activity.[37] He had assumed the positions of party legislative leader, president of the provincial organization, director of the party newspaper, and head of the party's organizational and office staff. Many felt that Williams was ambitious for power, and that he had deliberately attempted to eliminate prospective rivals from influence in the party. An attempt was made in 1940 to defeat him as provincial president, but it failed. Shortly thereafter, Williams enlisted in the army. At the 1941 convention, T. C. Douglas, a CCF member of Parliament, was elected provincial president over a candidate endorsed by Williams.

Douglas was a Baptist minister, who had first been elected to Parliament in 1935 from Weyburn. He had been one of the early members of the Saskatchewan I.L.P. He was by far the best and most popular orator in the party. Many of the provincial leaders who sponsored his election believed that Douglas' popularity and oratorical ability could unify the party and give it a leader acceptable to all groups in the province. His skill as a public speaker was no small advantage in an agricultural community where public debate is popular and campaign meetings are well attended.

The CCF was now firmly convinced that it was on the road to power. In 1942 Saskatchewan had the largest wheat crop in history. Prices, though still considered low by the farmers, were higher than in previous years as a result of the Wheat Pool campaign. The farmers strongly resented the provincial and federal Liberal governments, which held down the price of wheat and symbolized the terrible depression years. Money began to pour into the CCF treasury, and the party was able to put paid organizers into almost every constituency in the province and to start a weekly newspaper. The membership grew rapidly. Many prominent individuals in the farm and labor government who had shied away from identification with the CCF when it was a struggling young radical movement now climbed on the band wagon, seeking party nominations. Local politicians, officials of the Teachers' Federation, Wheat Pool employees, and trade-union leaders openly identified themselves with the party; and some became candidates.[38]

Nationally, the CCF had lagged behind its Saskatchewan Section. In the federal election of 1940 it had elected only two members of Parliament outside Saskatchewan and received about 9 per cent of the popular vote. The Canadian Gallup Poll indicated that national party support remained constant for the first three years of the war, until 1942.[39] Outside Saskatchewan, the party had stagnated in terms of popular vote from 1932 to 1942.

Suddenly, in 1942, the CCF began to grow rapidly in all parts of the country. It won a series of federal and provincial by-elections, and in August, 1943, won a major triumph in Ontario, gaining 34 of the 90 seats in the legislature, compared to none in the previous election. The Gallup Poll indicated that CCF support rose from 8 per cent in the beginning of 1942 to 29 per cent in September, 1943.[40] Party membership also increased greatly, from less than 20,000 in 1942 to about 100,000 in 1944.[41]

It is difficult to explain this dramatic rise in the fortunes of the national party. The factors involved relate mainly to the end of the depression and the war. (1) Canadian unions doubled in membership from 1939 to 1943. The Canadian Congress of Labor (C.I.O. in Canada) was founded in 1940, and many of its new unions were led by members of the CCF. The Ontario victory in 1943 was in large degree a result of trade-union leadership. (2) The end of the depression gave many workers and farmers the economic and psychological security to begin to think in long-range terms rather than in immediate, personal ones, and therefore the CCF program of postwar reforms to prevent a new depression could receive support. (3) The rising cost of living and increased taxation created resentment against "war profiteers" and the government, which benefited the CCF since it called for increased controls of profits and prices. (4) Canada had not had any middle way or New Deal reforms during the depression. Because it was dependent on foreign trade, it suffered more from the depression than had countries of greater self-sufficiency. Relief standards were lower than in the United States. The incumbent Liberal government symbolized the deprivations of the 'thirties, and the opposition Tories were a right-wing party. The CCF, as the party of reform, was the logical instrument of the desire of many Canadians to obtain the benefits of social security legislation, economic planning, labor legislation, and guaranteed minimum prices for farm products.

The effect of the absence of a reform administration in Canada during the depression can be seen in the significant differences between the responses of Canadians and Americans to the following Gallup Poll question: "After the war, would you like to see many changes or reforms in Canada (the United States), or would you rather have this country remain pretty much the way it was before the war?" In September, 1943, 71 per cent of the Canadians polled favored changes or reforms. The majority specified better employment and working conditions, social security, and "more even distribution of wealth." In the same month, only 32 per cent of the Americans polled favored postwar reforms, and about half of these suggested a return to the era before the New Deal, with tighter controls over trade-unions, less government bureaucracy, reduced taxes, and a free hand for business enterprise."[42] Apparently, the "go slow and muddle through" policy of Mackenzie King resulted in greater support for far-reaching social reform than did the liberal reform program of Roosevelt, which was bitterly opposed by American businessmen and supported by many American socialists and liberals.

The growth of the CCF nationally strengthened the Saskatchewan movement and gave it greater assurance that it was on the eve of forming a provincial government. This point of view was shared by the incumbent Liberals. Under Saskatchewan law, a provincial government has to call an election at least once every five years. An election was due in 1943. The Liberals, fearing defeat, passed a law extending the life of the legislature to 1944, arguing that the war made it inadvisable to hold an election. This excuse only increased the opposition to the government among many nonpartisan people, and strengthened the morale of the CCF.

The party leaders tried to make the CCF a broadly based farmer-labor opposition to the government. While maintaining CCF independence of other political groups, they welcomed the adherence to the party of many prominent persons who had not previously supported the movement, and even gave some of them nominations. The weakened Conservatives, who nominated in only half the constituencies in the province, were urged to vote CCF to get rid of the Liberal "machine."[43]

The party realized that its program for the elections would probably be a program of a government, not of an opposition, party. They therefore appointed research committees to examine realistically the potentialities of the provincial government. The eventual program was based on the need for extended social security and welfare work, educational facilities, farm security legislation, trade-union rights, and minor experiments in socialization. Though still mentioning the goal of socialism or a cooperative commonwealth, the party campaigned primarily as a social reform movement.

As the 1944 elections drew near, it became increasingly clear that the CCF would win the province. Its meetings were large and enthusiastic. The party membership grew to include one out of every twelve voters in the province.[44] On election day, June 3, 1944, the CCF carried 53 per cent of the voters of Saskatchewan.[45] After thirteen years of organization, the Saskatchewan CCF took power as the first "socialist" government in the United States or Canada.

The development of a mass socialist movement in Saskatchewan seems to follow more or less logically from previous socioeconomic conditions and a history of agrarian protest. The question may be raised, however, why Alberta and North Dakota—Saskatchewan's neighbors, which have a similar history and social and economic structure—did not develop the same response to the severe predicament of the 'thirties. It is necessary to isolate the significant differences among these three wheat areas which resulted in different patterns of behavior. However, in comparing the political scenes in the three areas, one is struck less with the differences than with the similarities. Each of these governmental units elected agrarian radical governments as a result of the depression. Alberta, in 1935, replaced the old United Farmers of Alberta government, which had been in power since 1921 and proved inept at coping with the depression, by the monetary reform government of the Social Credit Party; while North Dakota returned the agrarian, semisocialist Non-Partisan League to power in 1932.

Social Credit, the N.P.L., and the CCF were like responses to very similar conditions. Each movement represented an attack by western farmers on the economic power of eastern big business and sought to preserve their economic and social status by preventing the foreclosures of farm mortgages. The movements offered the farmers a scapegoat, in the form of external economic constraints, on which to blame their difficulties, and at the same time presented a solution that was "logical" in terms of the historical experiences of the organized farmers' movement. Nevertheless, there were important differences among them, differences of ideology, tactics, and objectives, which were largely a result of the variations in the historical backgrounds of the areas, and in the men who commanded community leadership.

In Alberta the political option of forming a class-conscious agrarian party out of organized farmers' movements, as the U.F.C. did in Saskatchewan, was almost impossible, since the Alberta equivalent of the U.F.C., the United Farmers of Alberta (U.F.A.), was in power when the depression began. Though the U.F.A. adopted a socialist program in 1933 and affiliated to the CCF nationally, the option of a U.F.A.-CCF government did not represent a new and radical alternative to the people of Alberta. The radical new choice was presented by William Aberhart, a radio evangelist, who became an advocate of the Social Credit doctrine and succeeded in winning the support of the majority of the rural electorate by a combination of religious fervor and economic radicalism.

In North Dakota the radical Non-Partisan League had been out of power during the middle and late 'twenties. It was, therefore, able to make a political comeback as the expression of the discontent of the 'thirties. A description of the political situation in 1934 indicates the political temper of the state during the depression.

Farmer loyalty to William Langer [N.P.L. Governor] . . . is explained by Langer's proclamation, in April, 1933 of a moratorium on the foreclosures of farm and home mortgages . . . the farmers regard it as a *coup d'etat* against Money. The banks, insurance companies, and all other out-of-state creditors are naturally horrified at North Dakota's official attitude toward sanctity of contract. Everyone—borrowers and lenders alike—accepts moratorium as a breach in the walls of capitalism. And the farmers are not disturbed.

Why should we worry about property rights, the farmers ask when you suggest that they are striking at the fundamental economic structure. . . . When your farm is covered with mortgages, your cattle tied up with a barnyard load, your machinery attached by a chattel mortgage, your previous year's taxes unpaid, and your coming crop covered by a seed lien—and then you get no crop—you fail to see just what it is you may lose with the collapse of capitalism.[46]

The Social Credit Party, while attacking the Grain Exchange and eastern financiers, did not propose a fundamental change in the going capitalist system. It hoped to make capitalism work by nationalizing the banks and pumping new currency into circulation whenever prices fell. The N.P.L. was prepared to socialize much of the industry within North Dakota and to support nationalization of large-scale industry, but its leaders, for electoral reasons, refused to break with the Republican Party. The Saskatchewan CCF, therefore, was the only one of the three movements that sought to make fundamental changes in the political and economic structure of the country.

Many of the farmers, however, did not see vital differences in the program and tactics of these movements. In Saskatchewan, farmers, inside and outside the CCF, sought to force the party to unite with Social Credit, and it actually did so for two years. In the federal elections of 1935, Social Credit received more votes than did the CCF in Saskatchewan, and carried many districts that had voted CCF the year before. The existence of a strong Social Credit movement in Alberta has completely blocked the growth of the CCF in that province. It has still to carry a single rural constituency in Alberta.

In North Dakota the same confusion of agrarian ideology exists. Norman Thomas, running as the Socialist candidate for president in 1932, received an insignificant number of votes, while the then extremely radical N.P.L. was sweeping the state. Though N.P.L. leadership was aggressively socialist in 1932 and 1934, proposing government ownership of many industries within the state, a N.P.L. congressman, William Lemke, won 13 per cent of the state vote as the Union Party's candidate for president in 1936.[47] The Union Party, which was founded by Father Charles Coughlin, was in many ways the American equivalent of Social Credit, and, like it, was antisocialist and opposed to government planning, but was also against the eastern "financial interests."

Each movement—the Social Credit Party, the CCF, the N.P.L., and the Union Party—provided a functional definition of the situation within the cultural framework of the wheat belt. Each interpreted the depression as being caused by eastern "capitalism," "vested interests," or "financiers." Within that framework, however, one could apparently build either a leftist or a rightist ideology. The radicalism and strength of the N.P.L., which remained a faction of the Republican Party, waned after economic prosperity began to return and the farmers received their immediate economic objectives of a guaranteed parity price and crop insurance from the federal government.[48] No real basis for a permanent radical movement was created, since the specific socialistic program of the N.P.L. was never integrated into a philosophy that required a new social order and permanent political action. Social Credit became the conservative and antisocialist party, and large sections of it accepted many of the anti-Semitic and semi-Fascist ideas of Major Douglas, the founder of the international movement.[49] Anti-Semitism—specifically, opposition to Jewish financial interests—could be linked to the opposition of western agrarians to eastern bankers. The myth of the powerful Jewish financiers has also received strong support in North Dakota, where it was propagated by the Coughlinites.[50] In Saskatchewan, however, the fact that socialists obtained control of the agrarian protest and directed it into a new national socialist party gave farmers a different interpretation of the nucleus of external economic power, though essentially it played the same role of providing an external scapegoat for the personal misfortunes of farmers.

The situation of different ideologies playing the same functional role is not peculiar to the western wheat belt. In Latin America, various ideologies—Peronism, Apristaism, socialism, communism, and old-fashioned military nationalism—win support from the miserably exploited peons. Each of these movements has a different economic and social program, but concentrates its propaganda on attacking external imperialist control as the cause of the poverty of South America. Like the western farmers, the lower classes south of the Rio Grande follow different variants of anti-imperialism as a purported solution of their ills.

Economic determinists may still insist that there is some variable peculiar to the economic structure that creates the variations in the ideological superstructure. This is not so in western Canada, unless one includes chance factors such as the tactics pursued by different persons in comparable situations within a deterministic theory. For example, the reason that Alberta elected a farmers' government in 1921, whereas Saskatchewan did not, appears to lie in the fact that the Alberta provincial election of that year was called after the United Farmers of Alberta had decided in favor of independent political action in the province.

In Saskatchewan the incumbent Liberal government realized that a farmers' party could defeat it, and called the provincial election before the Saskatchewan Grain Growers' Association could meet in convention to launch a provincial party. That strength for a farmers' government existed in Saskatchewan as well as in Alberta is indicated by the fact that independent farmers' candidates carried twelve of the thirteen seats for which they ran. This occurred in spite of the fact that each candidate was running independently of any party organization. It seems likely, therefore, that, had the election been held a short time later, Saskatchewan, like Alberta, would have had a farmers' government in the 'twenties. A Saskatchewan farmers' government would have been as helpless before the onslaught of the depression as the Alberta government, and would probably have gone down to a similar disastrous defeat before Social Credit or some comparable new variant of agrarian protest.

NOTES

1. Minutes of the First Convention of Delegates Representing U.F.C. Lodges, Branches of I.L.P., and Provincial Constituency Organizations, 1932, p. 14.

2. Saskatoon *Star-Phoenix,* July 28, 1932, p. 4.

3. Regina *Leader-Post,* June 8, 1934, p. 9.

4. *Ibid.,* September 15, 1931, p. 4.

5. See esp. Regina *Leader-Post,* Regina *Star,* and Saskatoon *Star-Phoenix,* 1931–34.

6. Regina *Leader-Post,* March 3, 1934, p. 2.

7. *Ibid.,* May 13, 1934, p. 8.

8. *Ibid.,* May 17, 1934, p. 3.

9. *Official Election Results,* Secretary of Executive Council, Province of Saskatchewan.

10. *Ibid.*

11. J. A. Irving, "The Evolution of the Social Credit Movement," *Canadian Journal of Economics and Political Science,* August, 1948, pp. 321–41.

12. October 9, 1935.

13. *Canadian Parliamentary Guide, 1937,* pp. 234–357.

14. Minutes of the 1936 CCF Convention, pp. 13–14.

15. *Ibid.,* p. 20.

16. Regina *Leader-Post,* July 17, 1936, pp. 1–2.

17. Minutes of the 1936 CCF Convention.

18. Interviews with CCF leaders.

19. Letter from CCF Provincial Council, October 6, 1937.

20. "A Challenge to Reaction" (editorial), *New Era,* February 16, 1938, p. 2.

21. B. T. Richardson, "CCF in Saskatchewan Would Pull with Social Credit, Not So in Alberta," Regina *Leader-Post,* October 14, 1937, p. 4.

22. Regina *Daily Star,* May 14, 1938, p. 9.

23. See 1938 campaign literature, Liberal Party file, Regina.

24. Interviews with CCF leaders. Unlike the campaign of 1934, in the 1938 campaign there were no newspaper accounts of statements of Catholic leaders opposing the CCF. See Regina *Leader-Post* and Saskatoon *Star-Phoenix,* January–June, 1938.

25. *Canadian Parliamentary Guide, 1939.*

26. Irving, *op. cit.*, p. 333.

27. Minutes of the 1939 CCF Convention (Saskatchewan Section), p. 12.

28. Unpublished address before the CCF National Convention, 1937.

29. Interviews with CCF leaders.

30. Interviews with CCF leaders.

31. Interviews with CCF leaders.

32. *Canadian Parliamentary Guide, 1941.*

33. Data from Secretary of Statistics, Department of Agriculture, Regina.

34. Saskatchewan Cooperative Producers, Ltd., *Submission Made to Prime Minister King and His Cabinet in Support of the Saskatchewan Agricultural Petition Bearing 185,000 Signatures* (Regina, 1942). See also Saskatchewan Cooperative Producers, Ltd., *Eighteenth Annual Report* (Regina, 1942).

35. Saskatchewan Cooperative Producers, Ltd., *The Wheat Pool and Its Accomplishments to 1946* (Regina, 1946).

36. In August, 1941, according to the membership and financial records of the Saskatchewan CCF, there were 4,460 paid members. In July 31, 1942, the paid membership rose to 9,813. The financial report also indicates a growth of the CCF. In 1933 the revenues collected were $2,134; in 1934, $3,053; in 1941, $6,325; in 1942, the year of the March on Ottawa, $13,605.

37. Interviews with CCF leaders.

38. Interviews with CCF leaders.

39. Canadian Institute of Public Opinion, *Report* (Toronto).

40. *Ibid.*, 1943.

41. Records of CCF National Office, Ottawa, 1945.

42. See the Canadian and the American Institute of Public Opinion, *Report*, October, 1943.

43. "A Big Job for the Tories" (editorial), *Saskatchewan Commonwealth*, January 19, 1944, p. 4.

44. According to the records of the Saskatchewan CCF, membership in 1944 was 25,925; it rose to 31,858 in 1945.

45. *Official Election Results,* Secretary of Executive Council, Province of Saskatchewan.

46. Datus C. Smith, Jr., "North Dakota Seeks a Demagogue," *New Republic,* October 3, 1934, p. 205.

47. *World Almanac* (New York *World-Telegram,* 1947), p. 170. Lemke obtained less than 2 per cent of the national vote.

48. John Gunther, *Inside U.S.A.* (New York, Harper and Brothers, 1947), p. 241.

49. Irving, *op. cit.*, pp. 336–41.

50. Gunther, *op. cit.*, p. 244.

7

IDEOLOGY AND PROGRAM

THE IDEAS that guide a new political movement like the CCF are a combination of primitive doctrine, promotional slogans aimed at holding and recruiting members, and the general values of the culture in which it has arisen. These ideas had been accumulated, in part by trial and error, over the thirteen years in which the party emerged into power. The meaning of this CCF socialism can be appraised by studying the changes through which the party ideology passed.

The collectivist reform program of the organized farm movement of Saskatchewan was unified after 1931 under the general heading of "socialism." This did not mean that the agrarian leaders who accepted the term as a description of the kind of economic society for which they were fighting had suddenly adopted a new economic or philosophical doctrine. To many of them the socialist proposals seemed the same as the program that the organized farm movement, especially the U.F.C., had worked out from 1902 to 1930.

In reply to the question "When did you become a socialist?" one old farmer answered:

Why, I've been a socialist all my life, and so were most of the farmers around here. Of course, I didn't know it until after the CCF was started, and the Liberals began telling us that government marketing of wheat and ownership of the banks and railroads was socialism. Don't let anyone tell you that the farmers aren't socialists. They all are, even those who still vote Liberal. The trouble is that all the propaganda around gives them a wrong idea of what socialism is.[1]

The socialists in the farm movement and the urban Independent Labor Party were able to capture the ideological control of the new Farmer-Labor political movement as a result of the catastrophic depression and drought and the obvious inadequacy of the accepted rural institutions to cope with them. Economic conditions in 1931 and 1932 were desperate, and the militant agrarians of the U.F.C. were not in a mood to quibble over a program or a specific statement as being too radical. They were even willing to call the new party the "Socialist Party of Canada." (See chap. 6, p. 135.) The period up to the elections of 1934 and 1935 was distinctly a radical, agitational stage. The old socialists would brook little compromise and secured the acceptance of a program calling for a completely socialized society, including the ownership of land.

When campaigning for the new party in 1933–34, however, the leaders soon found that to many people the word "socialism" had unfortunate connotations of atheism, confiscation of land, and dictatorship. Some of the agrarian CCF candidates realized that greater strength could be achieved for an independent farmers' party that opposed the eastern capitalists than for a socialist party. Even before the first election in 1934, party leaders began to omit all reference to socialism in their propaganda. Some rural leaders tried to discourage urban socialist speakers from mentioning socialism, Russia, and other tabooed topics when they visited rural areas. One very successful CCF candidate admonished such campaigners: "You can say anything you want about capitalism, the banks, and so forth. Be as radical as you want. But you can't speak here if you are going to talk about socialism. The farmers here hate the C.P.R. and the Grain Exchange and will fight like hell for the co-ops. . . . Socialism to them means Russia and antireligion."[2]

Propaganda in a rural constituency in 1934 reveals the conscious attempt to avoid using socialist terms that might lose votes.

Do not be misled by false and malicious propaganda spread at your expense by the Liberal and Conservative parties about the Farmer-Labor (CCF) movement.

There is no difference between the Liberal and Conservative parties. They are nothing but servants of the money lord—bankers and the financial magnates. They want power to carry on the collecting of money for their masters and thereby further impoverish you. They have exploited the people of Canada and its resources. They have forever mortgaged your homes, your farms, and your future to the financiers and the capitalists.

VOTE FOR A NEW DEAL

Canada is on the verge of total collapse. Save Saskatchewan from the curse of either Fascism or Communism.[3]

This was typical of CCF campaign leaflets in many rural districts. The provincial organization of the party, however, which was controlled by convinced socialists, such as M. J. Coldwell and George Williams, continued to emphasize socialism, the overthrowal of the capitalist system, and the socialization of all industry.

The electoral defeats of 1934 and 1935 and the rise of Social Credit as an opposition reform movement destroyed the confidence of many of the socialists in their program. Actually, the theoretical socialists in the top leadership of the provincial party now felt that they were wrong in attempting to force their program and terminology on the farmers. They accepted the arguments of agrarian leaders that converting farmers to complete socialism was a task of many decades and that a successful political movement must concentrate on immediate demands.

How pointedly all reference to socialism was removed from CCF propaganda appears in the following paragraph from a leaflet published in 1936. It is identical with a party pamphlet of 1934, except that the 1936 version substitutes "CCF" for each mention of the word "socialism."

[The opposition claims] That the *CCF* Will Destroy the Home and Substitute Free Love for Marriage.—This is the last argument of a dishonest person. Many honest people do not at first understand *CCF* ideas, but no honest person has ever charged the *CCF* with a desire to abolish marriage and return to a state of barbarism; nowhere in the literature of the *CCF* is such an absurd thing even hinted at. The *CCF* believes that women are not now possessed of all the rights to which they as human beings are entitled. We propose that when it is possible for all men to have employment, as it will be under the *CCF,* that the same opportunity shall be open to women. She will be an equal and a partner.[4]

The campaign literature of the CCF between 1936 and 1938 avoided the word "socialism." The party leaders were trying to popularize the CCF by speaking in the traditional language of agrarian radicalism, as in a radio speech by George Williams, the then provincial leader.

My friends, is it not fairly obvious that the only way to get people into office who will do something for the *west* is to elect men and women of a *western* party, such as the CCF, who are not continually looking for a cabinet position in Ottawa and willing to sell out their *western* principles in order to get it. . . . Elect a truly *western* government that will really fight for Saskatchewan and it will be done.[5]

The implications of the CCF's shift from being a socialist to a social reform party can be seen most directly in the crucial area of nationalization of industry. In Western democratic society, the foremost difference between socialist movements and progressive nonsocialist movements is their attitude toward changing the power structure of society by government ownership of industry. The original objective of the Saskatchewan CCF in the early 'thirties made it clear that the party believed in a completely socialized economy.

Objective:
The social ownership of all resources and the machinery of wealth production to the end that we may establish a Cooperative Commonwealth in which the basic principle regulating production, distribution, and exchange will be the supplying of human needs instead of the making of profits.[6]

In explaining this clause the CCF provincial leadership made it clear that they were not prepared to compromise on the issue.

The wording of the objective is "Social Ownership of all resources and the machinery of wealth production." This, therefore, includes all industries. We recognize the rights of the individual to own personal property which he can use for his comfort and well-being. Personal property is inclusive of home, clothing, furniture, etc.

. . . in compensating industries taken over, we will have due regard to the interests of society as a whole, and at the same time protect the individual in society. We will compensate small bond-holders in full in order to give them a reasonable purchasing power. And in compensating large holders of capital or bonds, our discount will be continuously heavier in order that we will not build up capital in the hands of one to the detriment of the whole.[7]

This forthright objective had been inserted in the program by the more socialist elements in the party; but this extreme statement on complete nationalization and the manner of compensation was not part of the traditional agrarian ideology favoring public ownership of only the more important industries, especially those that affected agriculture. Gradually, under the pressure of opposition criticism and electoral defeat, the socialists dropped the insistence on a totally socialized society. By the election year 1938, the CCF policy emphasized government planning more than ownership. It no longer directly attacked private ownership and profit, as the rewording of the party objective indicates.

The purpose of the CCF is the establishment in Canada of a Cooperative Commonwealth in which the principle regulating production, distribution, and exchange will be the supplying of human needs.

To this end a CCF government in power in Saskatchewan would substitute social planning in the place of the ruthless competition now practiced under capitalism.[8]

Instead of "all industries" under public ownership, the party now proposed a "sane policy of Public Ownership, of governmental assistance to the needy, governmental regulation of Big Business, and governmental assistance in creating publicly owned Cooperative Institutions."[9] A later publication by the leader of the Saskatchewan CCF in 1938 made it clear that the party was interested primarily in regulating industry and in preventing undue exploitation rather than in widespread government ownership.

A CCF government will say to timber operators, "We are not interested in the title to the mills, but we are interested in the price at which you sell your timber, because we want it to be produced for use, and we are interested in the wages you pay, because we want these men to be able to buy goods, and we are interested in the preservation of our Timber Resources; therefore, although we are not taking the title to the mill, we are going to insist that you plant two trees to take the place of every one you cut, and we are going to set your wage scale for your workers in order to prevent exploitation, and we are going to develop some Cooperatives and State Mills in order that, by competition, we may fix prices where they ought to be, by creating some non-profit institutions." . . . In that case *the Government would have brought about Socialism, although they did not touch the title,* because they would have forced these people to sell their products at a reasonable price and pay wages high enough to enable the workers to buy the goods.[10]

The CCF did not return to its advocacy of widespread public ownership after the 1938 elections. The provincial platform of 1944, the one upon which the party won power, urged government ownership only for natural resources and public utilities. In analyzing Saskatchewan CCF propaganda for socialization from 1936 to the present, it is significant to note the nature of the industries concretely marked for socialization, as contained in extracts from various party publications.

Socialization of the banking, credit, and financial system of the country together with the social ownership, development, operation, and control of utilities and natural resources.[11]

. . . the national issue and control of currency and credit.[12]

. . . [public ownership of] coal, clay, mineral, water-power, oil, and timber resources.[13]

Public property will consist of the Natural Resources, the Timber Lands, the Mines, the Oil Fields, Public Utilities such as the banking system, transportation systems, Power Plants, etc.[14]

The Social Ownership of public utilities such as transportation. . . . The Public Ownership and development of certain of our Natural Resources—mines, electric energy, waterways, large-scale lumbering.[15]

We believe, for instance, that the banking system ought to be owned and operated by the people of Canada through their federal government. . . . There are other great monopolies such as our railways, packing plants, milling concerns, the tobacco and farm implement industries, which have become so powerful that they can now set the price for both the producer and consumer and, consequently, exploit both of them. The CCF contends that such monopolies should be owned by the people through the federal government.

In the same manner there are economic activities which ought to be owned by the people through their provincial governments. Already hydro-electric power has been taken over by the government in some provinces—we think that this should be extended. We believe that other forms of power such as natural gas, coal and oil wells should belong to the people of a province rather than to a privileged few.[16]

Proposals to place almost all the foregoing industries under public ownership appeared repeatedly in the program of the Saskatchewan farmers' movement long before the CCF was formed. The Saskatchewan Grain Growers' Association, the Farmers' Union, the United Farmers of Canada (Saskatchewan Section), and the Progressive Party, all urged the nationalization of banking, transportation, and public utilities. (See chap. 3.) Oil wells, mines, timber resources, and packing plants were added to the list of industries to be nationalized. Nonprofit government operation of these industries would reduce production costs for the farmer and make him less subject to external economic control. In continuing to advocate the nationalization of such industries, the CCF was not clashing with any of the private property values of the agrarians, but rather had become the political voice of the traditional agrarian economic protest movement.

While modifying its goal of total socialization, the CCF has continued its emphasis on the extension of the social services rendered by the state, such as social security, health, and education. These services assume major importance in a province like Saskatchewan, where health and educational facilities tend to be poor because of the sparseness of the population. The farm movements of the province have always demanded more government aid for such services. All CCF literature and programs since the start of the party have urged government protection against illness, accident, old age, and unemployment, increased funds for education, and socialized medicine. These social security aspects of the party's program gradually assumed greater importance in its propaganda as the stress on socialism declined, until today it is the most important part of the provincial program.

Both program and propaganda for social services have remained fairly constant. Party policy on education, however, changed drastically with the other shifts designed to accommodate to existing values. Many socialists in the party believed that the educational system was biased in favor of capitalist social and economic values. Under their influence, the party in its 1933–34 program advocated not only increased expenditures for education but also basic changes in curriculum.

Education Program . . .
(*d*) The teaching of the principles of cooperation.
(*e*) The teaching of the origin of money and its function as a medium of exchange.
(*f*) Elimination of all glorification of war, and to substitute calisthenic drill in place of cadet training.[17]

This plank was not a minor part of the early program. The *Handbook for Speakers,* put out by the party in 1933, laid especial emphasis on it.

This is one of the most important planks in this particular program. If we are going to establish a Cooperative Commonwealth, we must have cooperation definitely taught. If a Farmer-Labor Government is returned to power in the Province of Saskatchewan, one of the first things that the Head of the Department of Education would have to do would be to call together the teachers of the various points in the Province, explain cooperation to them, and then tell them to go into the schools and teach cooperation.[18]

M. J. Coldwell, the provincial leader, reiterated this point in a campaign speech: "We propose to stop teaching capitalism in the schools. We will substitute teaching cooperation for competition."[19]

The proposal to change the school curriculum met vigorous criticism from opponents of the CCF, who charged that it meant introducing politics into the classroom. The socialists answered that politics already existed in the classroom in the form of a pro-capitalist history and economics. After the disastrous defeats of 1934 and 1935, the educational proposal was dropped. No mention of curriculum revision was made in the election programs of 1936 to 1938. The 1944 program suggested some general curriculum changes, but did not revert to the original platform.

Curriculum Revision: The CCF proposes to revise the school curriculum so that the material of school studies may prepare students adequately for intelligent participation in the life of their community and not, as now, inadequately for a University to which the majority will never go.[20]

The basic cultural conservatism of the Saskatchewan CCF, the fact that it was an outgrowth of significant permanent forces within western Canada rather than a new radical movement seeking to make far-reaching changes, can best be seen through analysis of the impact of religious beliefs on the party. Socialism has traditionally been identified as basically materialist and antireligious. Marx's classic statement, "Religion is the opiate of the people," has been reiterated by European socialist parties; for the tenser political situation in Europe showed the fundamental opposition of authoritarian religions and socialism more clearly than it has in Canada and the countries of the British Commonwealth. European socialism, accordingly, has been able to win its way in spite of its antireligious stand, because in many of these countries the church was identified in the minds of the lower economic groups with the upper class or with the state. In Germany the Lutheran Church was a state church; in Russia the same was true of the Greek Orthodox Church; in southern Europe the Roman Catholic Church possessed tremendous wealth and political power; in France anticlericalism was a deep and bitter heritage from the French Revolution, which had fought the clergy as a part of the privileged class.

The socialist and working-class movements of the self-governed countries of the British Commonwealth have, on the other hand, been unique in their ability to gain the support, or at least the real neutrality, of the churches toward their political efforts. This happened for three main reasons: (1) the Anglo-Saxon left-wing movements never accepted a Marxist theoretical approach to socialism with its initial antagonism to organized religion; (2) the strong nonconformist churches in the British countries were primarily poor men's churches, whose ministers often took part in the organization of workers' parties; and (3) the Catholic Church has been relatively weak in the British Commonwealth.[21]

The same factors have operated in Canada—outside French Quebec—and in Saskatchewan in particular. The largest Protestant church in western Canada, the United Church of Canada, resulted from an amalgamation of Presbyterians, Methodists, and Congregationalists because of the thinly scattered population of the frontier provinces. Coming out of the nonconformist British tradition, many of the United Church ministers stressed the social gospel rather than a fundamentalist view of salvation, and were sympathetic to the social and economic strivings of their rural members. The ministers lived close to their parishioners and shared their fortunes and misfortunes. In May, 1931, after depression and drought had hit the province, the Saskatchewan conference of the United Church adopted this resolution: "We believe that the competitive system must be transformed into a cooperative system and that production and distribution, together with the whole fiscal system, must be democratically controlled in the interests of human needs, rather than for private profit."[22]

As had been true in nineteenth-century England, many of the leaders of the CCF were former ministers. J. S. Woodsworth, the first national leader of the CCF and the foremost socialist of western Canada, was a Methodist minister who had been engaged in missionary and social welfare work among poor immigrants. His socialism was based on a conviction that there was a contradiction between the ideals of Christianity and the poverty and insecurity in contemporary society. Woodsworth preached the message of an idealistic Christian socialism at hundreds of farmers' meetings and conventions. Both the Farmers' Union and, later, the United Farmers of Canada arranged lecture tours for him in Saskatchewan during the 'twenties.

Two of the five members of Parliament elected by the Saskatchewan CCF in the 1940 elections were ministers. One of them, T. C. Douglas, who was first elected in 1935 and later became the leader of the Saskatchewan party and Premier of the province, expressed a point of view that appealed to many Saskatchewan ministers who became active members of the CCF.

The religion of tomorrow will be less concerned with the dogmas of theology and more concerned with the social welfare of humanity. . . . When one sees the church spending its energies on the assertion of antiquated dogmas . . . but dumb as an oyster to the poverty and misery all around, we cannot help recognize the need for a new interpretation of Christianity. . . .

[We have] come to see that the Kingdom of God is in our midst if we have the vision to build it. The rising generation will tend to build a heaven on earth rather than live in misery in the hope of gaining some uncertain reward in the dim distant future.[23]

It is not surprising, therefore, that, like British socialism, the Saskatchewan CCF, from the time of its formation and right down to the present, has had a moralistic and religious emphasis. The CCF stresses its support of Christianity and the fact that many of its leaders are religious; and it makes political capital of the fact that some churches are anticapitalist. Since the CCF is dominated by those who think that socialism and Christianity are but secular and sacred versions of the same philosophy, the few in the party who hold Marxist materialist views have kept these in the background. The majority of the party agrees on the necessity of winning the religious people, and the British tradition has made it both easy and logical to abolish the antireligious connotation of socialism.

In fact, the Saskatchewan CCF has consciously suppressed any expressions of irreligious attitudes by its members. In January, 1936, the *Research Review,* a magazine published by a group of young CCF members in Regina, published an article, "Socialism and the Church," by George Webster, a Marxist socialist who belonged to the more radical British Columbia party. The article criticized the clergy for having a conservative outlook resulting from their social position, and contended that "they may tend to be too readily satisfied with reformist half-measures." This statement brought prompt, open repudiation in the legislature from George Williams, the leader of the party. The provincial executive of the CCF urged its leading members on the *Review* to resign.

The following extract from a CCF leaflet is typical of the CCF attempt to identify its teachings with those of the Christian churches:

The question is not so much whether the CCF is opposed to Religion as to whether Capitalism is opposed to Christianity. The Anglican, Roman Catholic, and United Churches have declared that the Capitalist system is opposed to Christianity. On one side of the fence—Christianity; on the other—the social system under which we live. . . .
If the Anglican, Roman Catholic, and United Churches are right, then those who are fighting Capitalism's battle are fighting against Religion and Christianity.[24]

Such statements gave support to the CCF contention that it was "the true Christian party," and allayed the apprehensions of many religious people. But although the CCF was successful in identifying itself with the Christian social gospel, it met the active resistance of the Catholic hierarchy. Cardinal Villeneuve of Quebec, the leading Catholic dignitary in Canada, stated in 1934 that a good Catholic could not support the CCF. This was followed up in Saskatchewan by a pastoral letter, issued just before the elections, warning Catholics against socialism, and pressure was placed on Catholics in the CCF to leave the party. The CCF leaders did not react to this opposition by becoming anticlerical, though some of its members did. Rather, they sought to convince both the members of the hierarchy and lay Catholics that the CCF was not the type of socialist party condemned in the papal encyclicals. M. J. Coldwell, as leader of the Saskatchewan party, made this clear in answering Cardinal Villeneuve in 1934.

> The CCF was socialist in the sense that the British Labor and Socialist Party and the New Zealand Labor Party are socialist parties, for we share their philosophy and have a similar program.
> Yet the Prime Minister of New Zealand and four members of his cabinet are devout Roman Catholics, and the late Cardinal Bourne of England stated explicitly that the British Labor Party, though a Socialist Party, did not fall within the category of those movements condemned by the Pope. Why, therefore, should the CCF receive condemnation from Cardinal Villeneuve?[25]

Following the CCF's ideological shift to the right in 1936, the Catholic Church dropped its overt hostility to the party. In private, however, members of the Saskatchewan hierarchy have continued to put pressure on leading Catholics not to support the CCF. A few devout Catholic members of the CCF have made significant gains in campaigning in Catholic districts by completely eliminating the scare word "socialist" in their party propaganda. One such Catholic, Joseph W. Burton, formerly member of Parliament from the predominantly Catholic district of Humboldt, succeeded in winning the constituency by presenting the terms "cooperative order" and "new social order" as objectives of the CCF.

> The founders of the CCF were moved by the thought that there could be an abundant life for all. . . . Fundamental to this is the Christian idea of mankind. Has he not been created by almighty God as His masterpiece, made to His image and likeness? Was he not to be crowned with glory and honor and placed over the works of the Maker's hands? What of the fulfillment of the Divine destiny, what did they find? They

found that for the past hundred years the homes men lived in, the nutrition they had, the clothing they wore, the wages they received, the education and security they enjoyed were far from being commensurate with their dignity and honor. It was such conditions that made men like J. S. Woodsworth think of a new order to supersede the old.

You and I have the responsibility of laying the foundation for the new structure and that foundation must be social justice, because only in social justice can social security be built. That will be the new order.[26]

Besides its socialist and social reform propaganda, the CCF concentrated on demonstrating that it was the only party that fought for the immediate economic interests of the people. To do so, it evolved a program supporting the economic demands of the three class groups to whom it directed its electoral appeal: farmers, urban workers, and small businessmen. The socialists drew up programs designed to convince each of these groups of their place in a completely socialized society. Such proposals were dropped after the election defeats. An analysis of the propaganda addressed to these groups is further confirmation of the thesis that the CCF grew culturally conservative as it moved toward power.

Historically, security of landownership is the farmer's deepest demand. The fact that he puts his own work into improving his land makes the tract on which his life depends more than a job. But single-crop farming makes the dependence of the Saskatchewan farmer on the price of wheat a more prominent factor in his political thinking than are prices in diversified farming areas: the whole life of the community depends perilously and visibly on a single price which the farmer is powerless to influence. This has meant that CCF ideology in Saskatchewan has to be based on two principles: long-run tenacity of landownership and the short-run, perennially fresh fighting issue of the price of "this year's" wheat.

The depression and drought of the 'thirties demonstrated to many farmers the comparative worthlessness of owning land if it would not produce an income. As tens of thousands of farm families were forced to leave the province or to trek to the northern bush frontier to earn a living, fear spread throughout the province. It is impossible to overemphasize the farmer's continuing fear of losing his entire means of livelihood. He was unable to pay the accumulated interest on his debts and taxes. The number of actual foreclosures and tax sales was, however, very small. The economic disaster was so overwhelming and universal that mortgage companies and banks could gain nothing by foreclosing, as a forced sale would bring little in return. The provincial government would have had to stop any mass wave of foreclosures, for no government could have remained in office if it permitted its citizens to lose all they had.

Debt-ridden farmers did not, however, stop to think logically. The threat of foreclosure was very real to each farmer who could not pay his debts. Between 1928 and 1932 the interest owed on debts in rural Saskatchewan rose from one-tenth to nearly three-quarters of the net cash operating income of the farmers. The threat to the farmers' ownership of land seemed to come from the mortgage companies. Many Saskatchewan farmers literally had "little to lose but their mortgages."

The militant agrarians' party, the CCF, concentrated on an effort to convince the farmers that it was the only party that could protect them—provincially, through government action to stop foreclosures, and federally, by government marketing of farm products, a guaranteed minimum price, and crop insurance. The CCF endeavored to identify the old parties with the banks, the Grain Exchange, the railroads, and eastern manufacturing interests. It contended that only a people's party, like the CCF, which was not dependent on campaign contributions from large corporations, could be expected to help the farmers. "He who pays the piper calls the tune" became the favorite propaganda attack on the old parties by the CCF.

It would be impossible without interviewing a large sample of the Saskatchewan farming population to discover what the CCF meant to the people who supported it. The CCF leaders were sure that land security and prices were the two most significant problems, and their propaganda concentrated on these issues. Though there were many changes in program and ideological appeal in the thirteen years between the time the CCF was organized and the time it was elected, there was no slackening of emphasis on these basic farm issues. The CCF was a farmers' party and reflected the primary concerns of its members.

The socialists in the party succeeded, in the early period of the movement, in getting the farmers in the U.F.C. to accept the principle of nationalization of land. This proposal, however, was never suggested as a means of making farmers employees of the state or even members of cooperative farms. The CCF farmers accepted it as a means of guaranteeing permanent land tenure to working farmers. This can be seen clearly in the wording of the plank on use-lease titles in the 1933–34 program.

Security of tenure to be obtained by institution of perpetual "use-hold" on homes and lands instead of patents or Torrens' title. Substitution of perpetual "use-hold" for home and land titles when and if requested by the present registered owner, or dispossessed owner who now occupies under a lease. The prevention of immediate foreclosures, due to arrears of mortgage installments or purchase agreements with mortgage, land and investment companies and private individuals, by an exchange of provincial non-interest-bearing bonds for equity based on actual economic value of the land and homes.[27]

Though CCF leaders presented the program as one designed to protect the agrarian's control of his farm, the sheer suggestion of nationalization of land was the most controversial aspect of the program. The party leaders, therefore, dropped it in 1936, and concentrated on protection of the farmer's equity in his land. The CCF sought to appeal to the farmer in terms of his basic desire to become or to remain a property holder. Socialism for the farmer was henceforth to mean the protection of his property by control of the rest of the economy, and especially big business. This goal was clearly stated in all party literature after 1936. "The CCF believes in the family farm as the basis of rural life. Living standards for farmers must rise with those in the rest of the community."[28]

T. C. Douglas, the provincial leader after 1941, often promised that a CCF government would resign if a single farmer was evicted from his farm. The first and major plank in the party platform in 1944 was security of landownership.

Insecurity for farmers in Saskatchewan may be summed up in two words, *debt* and *eviction*. That this is true, is shown by the fact that in 1940 the Saskatchewan Debt Adjustment Board permitted 1,753 foreclosures; in 1941 it permitted 830 foreclosures; in 1942 it permitted 741. The fact is that the farms of Saskatchewan are passing into the hands of mortgage and loan companies, and farmers are becoming tenants rather than owners. The CCF is determined that this policy of making a farmer a tenant on his own land must cease.

To provide protection and security for farmers on their land, a CCF Government in Saskatchewan will take the following steps:

1. It will stop foreclosures and evictions from the farm home.

One of the first acts of the CCF Government will be to use its legislative power to prevent the eviction of Saskatchewan farmers and thereby give them security on their farms.

2. It will introduce legislation to protect them from seizure of that portion of a farmer's crop that is needed to provide for his family.

A CCF Government will consider it a first duty to pass legislation to provide that the farmer shall have enough of his crop to buy necessities for his family and pay his bills to his local merchant.

3. It will use the power of debt moratorium (that is, of suspension or postponement) to force the loan and mortgage companies to reduce debts and mortgages to a figure at which they can reasonably be paid at prevailing prices for farm products.

The CCF believes that every settlement of farm debt should take into account the years of toil that a farmer has put into his farm, and that this equity should be protected. A CCF Government will call a halt to foreclosures while the settlements are being worked out.

4. It will prevent the accumulation of new debt.

A CCF Government will pass legislation to provide that all existing and new land contracts shall contain a crop failure clause stating that in any year in which the farm income falls below six dollars an acre (*a*) there shall be no interest chargeable; (*b*) there shall be no instalment of interest payable; and (c) the length of the contract shall be extended one year. In this way both debtor and creditor will share the burden of crop failure and loss, and the crushing weight of accumulating interest debt will be lifted from Saskatchewan farm homes.[29]

Sheer ownership of land meant little, however, in a commercially oriented farm economy without decent prices and crop insurance. The farmers' movement had been fighting for three decades to eliminate fluctuations in income, and the CCF as its new political voice took over the battle. CCF members of the federal Parliament from Saskatchewan have consistently fought for higher guaranteed prices to agriculture through government marketing boards.[30] The following statements are typical of provincial programs and literature.

It [a CCF government in Saskatchewan] will press for the closing of the Winnipeg Grain Exchange and the setting of Parity Prices for agricultural products. The CCF believes that there should be no speculation in food, and for that reason it has consistently urged that the Winnipeg Grain Exchange be permanently closed. In its place, the CCF advocates the setting up of appropriate Marketing Boards upon which the producers should have majority representation. Parity Prices will assure that the farmers receive their just share of the national income.[31]

The significance of the fact that the CCF was the only party that uninterruptedly concentrated on increasing farm prices through government action can be seen in the growth of the party in 1941–42. Once the drought and its immediate threat to the farmers' basic livelihood had ended, Saskatchewan farmers became concerned with increasing their income. The CCF was able to double its membership and proceed to power as a result of its cooperation with the Wheat Pool's "March on Ottawa" campaign. (See chap. 6, p. 149.) Here was concrete evidence that the agrarian protest aspect of the CCF program was more significant in the minds of farmers than its general program of total social reform.

The second element to which the CCF has appealed is the urban working class, 20 per cent of the population of the province if one includes all employees. The original (1932) name of the party, Farmer-Labor Group, indicates the basic concept of the unity of the producing classes, farmers and workers, against their common economic enemies. Despite these gestures toward urban workers, however, the party was basically agrarian from the start. Success or failure for the new movement depended mainly on winning a majority in the rural districts. It is characteristic that the only appeal to workers in the first program of the provincial party for the 1934 campaign barely mentions labor in the course of a 1,500-word statement.

Social Legislation to secure to the worker and the farmer:—
(a) An adequate income and leisure, with an effective voice in the management of his industry.
(b) Freedom of speech and the right of assembly.[32]

Specific labor planks such as an eight-hour day or a minimum wage were lacking. The speaker's handbooks and propaganda leaflets rarely mentioned labor, and then only incidentally.

The party was badly beaten in the cities and towns of Saskatchewan in the 1934 and 1935 campaigns; this led it to abandon the urban field in the 1938 election. No CCF candidates ran for the six seats in Regina, Moose Jaw, and Saskatoon. The revised program of 1936 contained only one three-word plank for labor—"Work with Wages." The basically rural orientation of the CCF can be seen from this statement in a pamphlet explaining the party platform. *"Work and wages is generally considered to be an urban problem. Possibly we think of it in that light because the farmer has plenty of work. We suggest, that he should have some wages along with his work. Primarily this plank is a labor plank."*[33]

Obviously, labor was not conceived as basically part of the core of the movement. The attitude toward this outsider whom "we" were trying to convert was characteristically expressed in an interview by a leading agrarian in the CCF.

Do you think that the workers will ever become socialists? It's easy to convince farmers of the value of socialism. They can see that, if the state takes over the monopolies, farm-implement industries, and railroads, and markets wheat without a profit, their income will be much higher. But how can we get the workers to recognize that the CCF will benefit them also? All they care about is higher wages and they think that they can get them through their unions. Personally, I doubt if we'll ever win the government at Ottawa, for the workers just won't vote for us in the big eastern cities.

After its victories in the 1938 elections, the CCF began to gain working-class support. The leaders of the small trade-union movement in the province became interested in a party that professed to be more prolabor than the two old parties and now appeared to be capable of forming the next provincial government. As a result, the enlarged trade-union wing of the party drew up a complete labor program setting forth the traditional demands of organized labor, with the addition of certain social services.

1. The Right to Organize:
The CCF will make it compulsory for employers to enter into collective bargaining with the labor union selected by the majority of their employees.

2. Minimum Wage Act:
The CCF will increase the rates of wages established by the Minimum Wage Board and will take action to enforce their payment and to extend the act to protect the employees in other low-paid industries.

3. Workmen's Compensation Act:
The CCF will eliminate the three-day waiting period before benefits are paid, and will raise the compensation to a higher percentage of regular wage paid.

4. Labor Representation on Boards and Commissions:
The CCF will appoint Labor representatives to all boards, commissions or other bodies dealing with Labor matters, and will consult with the official organizations of the Trade-Union movement before making such appointments.

5. Department of Labor:
The CCF will set up a Department of Labor with a Minister of Labor in charge.

6. Socialized Health Services:
The CCF will provide a complete system of socialized health services so that all will receive adequate medical, surgical, dental, nursing, and hospital care without charge.

7. Old-Age Pension:

The CCF will raise the amount of the Old-Age Pension and will bring pressure to bear on the Federal Government to reduce the age to 65 years.

8. Housing Program:

The CCF will press the Federal Government to institute a National Housing Plan to provide low-cost and low rental homes.

9. Security:

The CCF will provide for the workers security of tenure in their homes, and will bring about adjustment of debts for urban dwellers as well as for the farmers.

10. Unemployment and Postwar Reconstruction:

Mass unemployment in wartime is not tolerated. In peacetime it should be equally intolerable. The CCF demands that our natural resources, now being used to bring about Victory, shall be used in peacetime to bring about security and a higher standard of living. The CCF is determined that we shall not drift back into the chaos of unemployment and depression which preceded the war; and therefore will formulate definite practical plans for postwar reconstruction and adjustment of our social and economic life.[34]

It is significant to note that this is basically a trade-union program, not a socialist one. There is no mention of the advantages to labor under socialized industry, nor of the possibilities of labor representation in the management of industry. Labor leaders, like the farmers, were primarily interested in the party as a means of advancing their own economic objectives.

The cooperation of organized labor and farmers may appear strange in terms of the popular stereotype of rural antagonism to labor. Actually, this stereotype, like many others, includes diverse groups and patterns of behavior. There are numerous farm groups on this continent, each with separate economic interests and social values. In Ontario and in the eastern part of the United States, the economically stable farmers are usually associated with the economic and social middle class of the neighboring towns, and they tend to accept the urban middle-class fear of a powerful labor movement. The economic power of big business is not so apparent to the eastern farmer, and the efforts of unions to secure a larger share of the national income seem a threat to him.

In the western wheat belt, however, farmers have often been involved in economic and political struggles with eastern big business. Organized labor has been a small group, which does not constitute a visible threat to farmers. The railroads, banks, grain exchanges, and manufacturers who increased prices, on the other hand, have been highly visible exploiters of agrarians. Grain growers, therefore, having identified their enemy as "the interests," have tended, when organized in class-struggle groups, to view labor as a potential ally rather than as an opponent. This fact is borne out by the history of the Greenbackers, the Populists, and the Non-Partisans in the United States, and of the Progressives and the CCF in Canada. (See also chap. 1.) The Non-Partisan League, representing the overwhelming majority of North Dakota farmers, actually signed a closed-shop agreement with the revolutionary I.W.W. in 1917, in which the N.P.L. agreed that its supporters would hire only "wobblies" as harvest hands, while the I.W.W. pledged that its members would work only for N.P.L. farmers.[35] In the United States today the Farmers' Union, which is largely a grain-growers' movement, has been continuously prolabor and works with the C.I.O. on political issues.

In Saskatchewan the farmers' movement frequently co-operated with labor before the CCF was organized. The Farmers' Union passed resolutions supporting various strikes, and even contributed to the strike funds of the Nova Scotia coal miners in 1923.[36] During the Wheat Pool campaign, the unions reciprocated by permitting the farmers to use the office facilities and staff of the local Trades and Labor Councils (A. F. of L.).[37] Although sources of friction have existed and still do exist within the Saskatchewan CCF, there has rarely been a significant objection from either group to the demands of the other. The unionists recognize that unless they have the backing of the farmers they cannot receive state help from the province, which controls all labor legislation; while farm leaders know that without trade-union support nationally they cannot hope to gain federal power, which they need to secure higher prices. It has, therefore, been in the interest of the organized groups on both sides to dissuade any latent rank-and-file hostility.

Farmer-labor cooperation is further strengthened by the fact that many of the older rural settlers are former workers with trade-union experience; while many of the younger workers are migrants from farms and have relatives who are still engaged in farming. This has made both groups more receptive toward supporting each other than would be true in older and more industrialized areas.

Though cooperating with urban labor, Saskatchewan farmers have a tradition of antagonism to all middlemen, including small businessmen. The consumers' cooperative movement, which first appeared early in the present century, is designed to eliminate the profits of retailers. In its early radical period the CCF advocated the complete elimination of private business. A pamphlet issued in 1933 made this explicit:

Our cooperative organizations in Canada are far too insufficient to allow us to have much hope of setting up distribution on a cooperative basis with the cooperative system we now have. We might have a State distributing agency, for instance, in which the present storekeeper would become a civil servant and have his salary paid by the State, and the prices governed by the State to give people a decent standard of living.[38]

Propaganda issued before the 1934 elections reemphasized state distribution and the employment of retailers as civil servants:

Business Men

You have always voted Grit and Tory

Because

You thought you were in business for Profits

You Never Made Any

The postmaster is sure of his income

Why not be sure of yours, under a planned economy,

in which you will be guaranteed an income

as a distributor.

Vote CCF[39]

There were few small merchants in the new party, and there was no vocal opposition to the desire to eliminate their businesses. But in the 1934 and 1935 elections, merchants voted overwhelmingly against the CCF. (See chap. 8, pp. 199–200.) Many constituencies were lost to the party because the old-party plurality in the small urban areas outweighed the CCF lead in the country. Moreover, Social Credit was able to secure the support of many businessmen who were attracted to its policy of increasing purchasing power by distributing money.

The Social Credit gains among small merchants and professional men showed that these people could be won away from the old parties. The CCF leaders, seeking votes, decided to attempt to win over small business to their own ranks. This necessarily involved the adoption of a policy designed to protect small business against the monopolies. The economic goal of the CCF, "Production for Use and Not for Profit," was changed by dropping out the last four words. George Williams, the provincial leader, clearly stated the reasons for the change: "The farmer and the small businessman in Saskatchewan have difficulty in understanding the CCF manifesto when they come to the section which sets out that production under socialistic policies can only be carried on when it is 'not for profit.' "[40]

This new appeal of the CCF to small business has never been dropped. The party conceives of the people for whom it speaks as farmers, laborers, and small businessmen. The following are typical of the efforts to attract small business.

The CCF intends to break the power of the Canadian monopolies which are exploiting our people—but has no intention of interfering with the retail merchant in the conduct of his business. The CCF has no desire to curtail the wages he receives as a distributor—but rather—CCF policies will increase his sales. . . .

What does this [the CCF program] do for the retail merchant? It does not interfere with his legitimate income as a merchant, but it does increase his income—for is it not obvious that every government development which pays out wages to workers, every pension paid out of new wealth created increases the amount of business done in our stores, and it does it without resorting to a taxation of Peter to clothe Paul, and without increasing the Public Debt.[41]

Though CCF leaders seek the support of the urban middle classes, the latter make little response. There is an essential conflict between the party's support of the large consumers' cooperative movement and its appeal to small merchants. In Saskatchewan, cooperative stores are as great a menace to private country stores as are chain stores. The overwhelming majority of rural members of the CCF are cooperators; as such, they are not very friendly to businessmen. This cleavage between the two groups is minimized, however, in party ideology. Here, then, is another example of ideological compromise to gain an electoral majority. In practice, most of the agrarian members ignore the party's appeals to small business and remain critical of private enterprise while working to build the cooperatives.

In spite of its programmatic appeals to small business, the CCF, after 1936, laid increasing stress on its identification with the cooperative movement. Organized by people active in the cooperatives, the party was able to capitalize on the previous acceptance by a large proportion of Saskatchewan farmers of non-profit enterprise as superior to private capitalism. The very name of the party, the Cooperative Commonwealth Federation, meant to many that it was the political arm of the cooperatives, an idea which the CCF did not try to dispel. The *Saskatchewan Commonwealth,* the party newspaper, stated this explicitly in 1944.

The growth of the cooperative movement in Saskatchewan during the past few years as shown by articles in this and the last issue of the *Saskatchewan Commonwealth* is a most inspiring picture for those who believe in the necessity for extending the cooperative movement from the political as well as from the economic or commercial angle.

We cannot urge too strongly upon our readers that they should continue to organize what might be called the two great departments of the cooperative movement, and to express the hope that neither department will be neglected, but that the two will go forward hand in hand until the economic security which is possible through the further development of both departments of this great movement is within the reach of all.[42]

Every election program of the CCF and most of the speeches by party leaders stressed this relationship between the CCF and the cooperatives. Anyone listening to CCF speeches or reading CCF literature by 1944 would think that he was asked to vote for the cooperatives' party, as an excerpt from an article in the *Commonwealth* makes clear.

This movement [the CCF], founded by the people, has also grown by leaps and bounds, just as did the original cooperative movement, and it is now being viciously opposed by the same vested interests which oppose cooperation of any sort. The issue is, however, clear cut. The people are being asked to make their choice between cooperation and competition and the majority are choosing the former.

That which is founded on a just principle can not be stifled and so the cooperative movement—commercial and political— marches on.[43]

There can be little doubt that this propaganda has been effective in overcoming the prejudices against the CCF as a socialist party. Some CCF leaders publicly assert that they are cooperators and not socialists. In most places in the province there is a strong interrelationship on the local level between CCF leaders and the cooperatives. The same men often lead both.

Though the CCF leaders tried to eliminate discussions of socialism and to drop ultraradical aspects of their program, the opposition groups would not let them do so. Socialism and the CCF platform before 1936 formed the major core of the Liberals' attack. Reporters on the Regina *Leader-Post*, the leading Liberal daily in the province, were ordered to play up stories in which members of the CCF anywhere in Canada were reported to have talked about socialism or the nationalization of industries.[44] In 1944 the Liberals reprinted the twenty-four-page *Handbook for Speakers* issued by the CCF in 1933; these booklets were distributed in the thousands to remind farmers that the CCF had once stood for total socialization.

It is ironical that one of the major factors in popularizing the concept of socialism in rural Saskatchewan was the attacks made on it by the daily press and the old parties. Liberal propaganda continually attempted to associate the CCF with red radicalism, as in the heading of a party leaflet in the 1944 campaign:

THE CCF PLATFORM
MEANS THE SAME TODAY AS IN 1934
SOCIALISM AND DICTATORSHIP

These attacks were not very successful among the farmers by 1944. The daily papers were distrusted because of their earlier opposition to farmers' movements such as the Progressive Party and the Wheat Pool in the 'twenties. The Regina *Leader-Post* was known in many areas as "the Misleader" from Wheat Pool days. (See chap. 3, p. 85.) Invectives against the CCF, while the party fought in the legislature and the House of Commons for higher prices for wheat, debt reduction, and increased social services, only served to make socialism palatable to the farmers. If socialism meant $1 a bushel wheat as it did in 1941, while Liberalism meant 70 cent wheat, then socialism was not so bad. Many farmers explicitly reported that they began to think of themselves as socialists as a result of the attacks on socialism by groups whom they considered enemies of the farmers.

As the CCF moved toward power in the 1940's, some of its leaders again began to speak of socialism as the ultimate objective of the party. The opposition's attacks on socialism forced the CCF to defend it on the public platform. The increasing strength of the party in spite of the strenuous redbaiting by the Liberals convinced party leaders that socialism was no longer the handicap they had imagined it to be in the 1930's. Party propaganda, however, consisted mainly of a series of specific reforms to which the CCF committed itself when it should become the government of Saskatchewan. The new socialist order, though it was mentioned, remained in the background. The electors were asked to vote for security and reform, not for a socialist society. In 1944 the CCF still found it possible to appeal to the supporters of the Conservative Party as follows: "The problems which face us all, both now and in the postwar period, are too vital and important to become the football of ambitious party leaders. If the Conservatives are desirous of ridding themselves of the yoke of Liberalism, then there is only one sure way of doing it, and that is by supporting the CCF candidate in their riding."[45]

The CCF movement in Saskatchewan won majority power after thirteen years of organization and propaganda. During that period the ideology of the movement was in a state of continuous adjustment. Aspects of the original program that were risking popular support by challenging basic social values were eliminated. In summary, the significant changes in the CCF program and ideology were as follows:

1. The virtual dropping of the explicitly socialist goal and its replacement by phrases such as "a new social order" or the "cooperative commonwealth."

2. The elimination of any suggestion of land nationalization, succeeded by emphasis on protecting the owner's title.

3. The withdrawal of plans to socialize all, or even the majority, of private industry. This was replaced by a stress on state economic planning and the socialization of public utilities and industries directly infringing on the rural economy.

4. An increased emphasis from 1936 through 1944 on social security.

5. The inclusion of small businessmen as a group whose status would be preserved and strengthened under a CCF government.

6. The elimination of plans to change class biases in the educational system.

7. The development in the 1940's of a complete labor and trade-union policy as a consequence of the increase in urban CCF organization.

The formal aims of the party in 1944 were a compromise between the original goals of the small nucleus of socialists in the leadership of the U.F.C. and I.L.P. in 1932, and the basic political, social, and economic values of the farmers. The socialists had attempted to convert the people of the province to the necessity of a fundamental societal change that would affect the entire economic structure of the country. They soon learned, however, that the majority of farmers and many of their original followers were more interested in immediate reforms that would improve their economic position than in a new social order. The strong appeal in the middle 'thirties of the Social Credit and progressive coalition movements was clear evidence that the particular ideology of socialism was not important to farmers. If Social Credit would fight "the interests" and give security to the farmers, they would become Social Crediters like the farmers of Alberta.

When one considers the changes in CCF policy, together with the constant emphasis of the Saskatchewan CCF members of the House of Commons on raising the price of wheat, it becomes clear that the CCF has gradually changed, under external and internal pressure, from an agrarian socialist party to a liberal agrarian protest movement, following in the direct tradition of the Populists, the Non-Partisan League, and the Progressives. No single modification of party policy and emphasis was sufficient to change the character of the movement, but taken together they constitute a qualitative change. The socialists had won power, but the method and conditions under which they succeeded had in large measure adversely affected their socialism.

This process was not confined to the Saskatchewan Section of the CCF, though it initiated some programmatic changes before other sections. This resulted mainly from the fact that the Saskatchewan CCF was closer to power and had a smaller proportion of doctrinaire and intellectual socialists. Actually, many in the CCF outside Saskatchewan reprimanded the provincial party for its "opportunism" during the 1936–39 period. The national CCF and its provincial sections began, however, to change their orientation during the war, when the party gained electoral strength throughout the country.

It is not part of this study to analyze the national party, but its programs and propaganda literature issued from 1933 to 1948 clearly reveal the attempts to win majority power by eliminating aspects of socialist ideology that might antagonize significant sections of the electorate. The turning point in the development of the national party can probably be centered in the withdrawal from politics and subsequent early death of J. S. Woodsworth, the leader of Canadian socialism from 1921 to 1940. Woodsworth, who had spent a large part of his life in political isolation trying to build a socialist party, resisted all efforts to achieve rapid party growth through ideological compromise. The newer and younger socialists who joined a going movement wanted power and proceeded to try to gain it.

Karl Mannheim has pointed out that a new doctrine can succeed only if it is based on attitudes already present in a society.

Only when the utopian conception . . . seizes upon currents already present in society and gives expression to them, when in this form it flows back into the outlook of the whole group, and is translated into action by it, only then can the existing order be challenged by the striving for another order of existence. Indeed, it may be stated further that it is a very essential feature of modern history that in the gradual organization for collective action social classes become effective in translating historical reality only when their aspirations are embodied in utopias appropriate to the changing situation.[46]

The CCF in Saskatchewan is a "class" party in the objective sense, since its program reflects the aspirations of a class created by constraining economic forces. As a result of the depression, it became the political voice of angry, exploited, rural Saskatchewan. Like the Russian Bolsheviks in 1917, the CCF adapted socialism to "currents already present" in agrarian society. This generalization still leaves the problem of deciding how far such present "currents" can be extended. There were plenty of currents in Saskatchewan that a socialist utopia could use—and the Social Credit movement shows how easy it is to hitch different utopias to existing needs. It is one thing, however, to attach the provocative title of "socialism" to a movement, and another to create the ideological structure capable of sustaining far-reaching social changes. It may be said of most political innovators not content with the role of a permanent minority that they err on the side of underplaying the potentialities of "currents already present." The problem of major social and political change balances between what one can surely get as a short-run objective and what one dares hope to gain by boldness. To choose the former, as democratic socialists traditionally have done, may mean to forego the possibilities of realizing the latter.

From the short-range point of view, it was the particular

good fortune of the Saskatchewan CCF that, unlike other socialist parties on this continent, it did not have a powerful core of doctrinaire leaders who forced the movement to adopt an ideology that did not grow out of "currents already present in the society." Most of the earlier socialist parties in Canada and the United States—the Socialist Labor Party, the Socialist Party, and the Communist Party—were movements that sought to transfer to the North American environment the ideology of European socialism.

These movements failed to win significant national support for a variety of reasons that would take another series of studies to elaborate. It is significant, however, that the most successful socialist or semisocialist parties in the United States —the Socialist Party of Oklahoma, the Non-Partisan League, the Farmer-Labor Party of Minnesota—based their attack on the capitalist economic structure, not in terms of a Marxian doctrine of class struggle, but as a continuation of the traditional struggle of farmers and workers, the common people, against "the vested interests" of eastern bankers and Wall Street, the symbol of concentrated wealth. North Americans have shown their willingness to organize against capitalist power in order to protect their opportunities to have a good job or to run their own farm or small business; but propaganda designed to appeal to a permanently exploited proletariat of workers and landless or mortgaged farmers has made little impression.

Myrdal has pointed out the extent to which the values of the American creed of equality, of freedom of opportunity, of democratic classlessness have permeated every aspect of the culture. One would expect, therefore, that a successful socialist movement on this continent must basically be one that does not attempt to destroy the American creed, but presents its program for change in terms of amplifying and extending American values to all parts of society.

In Europe, where social and economic class lines were more firmly drawn as a result of a feudal past, labor and socialist parties basing their doctrines on a fundamental conflict of interests were successful in appealing to the proletariat. In most of the European countries the upper classes never accepted freedom of social mobility as part of their publicly proclaimed values. Class differences were openly recognized by all groups. Socialist and Labor parties were able, therefore, to be radical in both economic and cultural spheres. As class-conscious Marxists they rejected the capitalist or ruling-class culture around them. They built their own culture, with their own flag, songs, plays, and educational program, and rejected the traditional values of religion and patriotism.

While still in the early agitational stage, these movements demanded total revolutionary change. But this stage could last only so long as the movements were illegal or comparatively small radical sects. Once a movement achieves legality and wins broad lower-class support, it finds that an ultrarevolutionary, antisocietal approach tends to repel groups who want a change but are not completely dissatisfied with the *status quo*. At this stage, radical parties must make a choice: either continue to try to win majority support for an all-out radical socialist program, without compromising the original revolutionary doctrine, or seek to win votes for a limited set of objectives by compromising and modifying the parts of the program that challenge the basic values of the more stable groups.

This choice cuts across the traditional division of the socialist movement into revolutionary and democratic socialists. Revolutionaries such as Rosa Luxemburg in Germany and Bela Kun in Hungary would stand for no compromise; Lenin and the Russian Bolsheviks are examples of a revolutionary group that concentrated on power rather than program. Lenin, realizing that the Russian peasants would not support the Marxist program of nationalization of land, changed it to "Land to the Peasants," whereas Luxemburg and Kun continued to advocate the nationalization of land.[47]

On the other hand, the Austrian Social Democrats and the Socialist Party in the United States, though they were democratic socialists in philosophy, adhered in large measure to the uncompromising school of socialism.[48] The American Socialists before the First World War had many leaders who were suspicious of the support which the party received from Midwestern farmers, and these leaders prevented the party from appealing to the farmer on the basis of his interest in keeping his land. The Socialist Party also opposed the First World

War, and this action was contrary to the patriotic principles of many potential supporters.

These two types of radical parties never exist in a pure form, except for a few doctrinaire socialist sects such as the Socialist Labor Party. The distinction between the two is useful, however, in partially explaining the development and the success or failure of left-wing movements. No uncompromising Marxian group has ever won majority power in any country in the world. Every nominally "socialist" governing group —Russia, Britain, China, Yugoslavia, Sweden, New Zealand, Australia, Saskatchewan—immediately before they won power had programs appealing to most sections of the population in terms of the latter's own immediate values. The Communist Party of France, which is the largest electoral Communist Party in a democratic country, dropped many parts of its original internationalist and leftist program during its election campaigns in 1945–47. It appealed to the peasants as the party that desired to protect private landownership, and to the middle class as the party that wanted to protect small business from the trusts.[49]

The history of most leftist parties has been largely an evolution from the class-conscious internationalist Marxist position to an "opportunistic" national appeal in which large segments of the population are wooed with specific planks directed to their own interests. Socialist parties originally envisaged socialism as a society in which there would be some form of social ownership of all industry, business, and land. This concept has gradually been modified until today many socialist movements stand for national economic planning, state ownership of certain large-scale monopolies, private ownership of most of industry and the distribution system, and the maintenance and extension of family-owned farms.[50]

With this change in economic doctrine has come a shift in the cultural and philosophic phases of socialism. Antagonism to religion has died away, and efforts have been made to link socialism and religion. Opposition to patriotism and symbols of nationalism has also disappeared. Antagonism to the monarchy has died among the socialists of the British Commonwealth and Scandinavia and, until they consolidated power, among the Communists of Rumania.

Official contempt for "bourgeois" sex mores and family system vanished long ago among leftist movements. In Italy the Communists opposed the establishment of divorce laws. The press description of the inauguration of a Communist, Klement Gottwald, as "president" of Czechoslovakia, indicates clearly the conscious recognition by the leaders of the Cominform that, while they are in the process of securing power, they must compromise with institutions they oppose.

The new president [Gottwald] swore allegiance to the Peoples' Democracy constitution, . . . crossed back into the courtyard where Catholic Archbishop Josef Beran greeted him and Mrs. Gottwald at the door of St. Vitus cathedral.
The archbishop shook hands heartily with the presidential couple and then escorted them into the church for a Te Deum (thanksgiving) mass. . . .
The government-controlled Catholic People's party commented that the cathedral service "was an extraordinary novelty in the history of presidential elections and the faithful will receive it with great satisfaction."[51]

The social changes introduced by *democratic* radical movements appear to result more from objective pressures in the society for such changes than from a small doctrinaire minority converting the majority of the population. The stronger a radical social movement becomes in a democracy, the less radical it appears in terms of the general cultural values. As it captures society, society captures it. The amount of change that the movement introduces into the culture as a result of assuming power appears relatively slight compared to the original goals.

This may not hold true, however, for totalitarian groups such as the Communists, who set up a dictatorship after taking power. These groups have two programs—one with which to win power and the other to go into effect while in power. In order to win power, the Communists (and the Fascists as well) publicly modify their goals in the direction of culturally approved objectives. Once having gained power and no longer subject to public opinion, they introduce changes which the electorate has never approved. The Russian Bolsheviks, for example, proceeded to nationalize land in 1929, though Stalin stated as late as 1928 that private agriculture would be desirable for at least another fifty years.[52] In order to force changes against the will of large sections of the population, however, the dictatorial "reformers" must use police measures continually against discontented elements. This strengthens the totalitarian nature of the state and destroys the original goal of an ultimate total democracy.

The democratic socialist party bidding for actual power or newly come to power is also placed in a difficult position, which is well illustrated by the British Labor government as this is written (1949). The winning of votes, particularly the decisive marginal votes of the middle class, calls for a policy of ideological opportunism and gradualism. But the pre-election period, which presents the threat of socialism during the continued operation of capitalism, invites loss of confidence by businessmen and, more dangerous, active sabotage of the socialist program. Thus the means employed by democratic radicals to secure power are as likely as are those of dictatorial "reformers" to endanger their original objective.

NOTES

1. Interview with a CCF member.

2. Interview with a CCF leader.

3. CCF campaign leaflet (Regina, 1934).

4. CCF (Saskatchewan Section), *The Cooperative Commonwealth—Conservative and Liberal Objections Answered* (Regina, 1936), p. 2; *The Most Frequent Objections to Socialism Answered* (Regina, 1934).

5. *New Era,* February 3, 1948, p. 2. (Italics mine.)

6. Saskatchewan Farmer-Labor Group (CCF), *Handbook for Speakers* (Regina, 1933), p. 21.

7. *Ibid.,* p. 12.

8. *Handbook to the Saskatchewan CCF Platform and Policy* (Regina, 1938), p. 1.

9. CCF (Saskatchewan Section), *The Growth of the Provincial Platform* (Regina, 1938), p. 2.

10. George Williams, *Social Democracy in Canada* (Regina, 1938), pp. 40–41. (Italics mine.)

11. Federal program adopted by the Saskatchewan Farmer-Labor Group, 1933.

12. *Provincial Platform, 1938.*

13. *Ibid.,* 1944.

14. Williams, *op. cit.,* p. 39.

15. Gertrude S. Telford, *What Happened to David Jones?* CCF (Saskatchewan Section) (Regina, 1939), p. 39.

16. T. C. Douglas, *Towards a United Canada* (Regina, 1944), p. 5.

17. Saskatchewan Farmer-Labor Group (CCF), *Economic Policy* (Regina, 1933), p. 4.

18. *Handbook for Speakers,* p. 14.

19. Regina *Leader-Post,* June 16, 1934, pp. 1–2.

20. *Provincial Platform,* 1944.

21. See Franz Lindner, *Sozialismus und Religion* (Leipzig, Tauchnitz, 1932), for a discussion of the British Labor Party's attitudes on religion.

22. CCF (Saskatchewan Section), *Religion and the CCF* (Regina, n.d.).

23. "Youth and the New Day," *Research Review,* June, 1934, p. 2.

24. *Religion and the CCF,* pp. 1–4.

25. Regina *Leader-Post,* December 3, 1938, p. 1.

26. Excerpt from radio speech, April 20, 1943.

27. *Economic Policy,* p. 4.

28. CCF (Saskatchewan Section), *The Farmer and the CCF* (Regina, n.d.), p. 3.

29. CCF (Saskatchewan Section), *The CCF Program for Saskatchewan* (Regina, 1944), pp. 2, 3.

30. Ottawa, House of Commons Debates: "The Address and Purchasing Power," *Speeches of M. J. Coldwell* (1937), pp. 4–5; M. J. Coldwell and T. C. Douglas, *Saskatchewan Conditions* (1938), pp. 3–4; also, by the same authors, *A Plea for Democratic Government* (1944), pp. 6–7; and CCF Parliamentary Group, *Fighting for Democracy on All Fronts* (1940), pp. 5, 8–10, 26–28.

31. *The CCF Program for Saskatchewan,* p. 3.

32. CCF, *Provincial and Federal Program* (Saskatoon, 1933).

33. *The Growth of the Provincial Platform,* p. 4. (Italics mine.)

34. CCF (Saskatchewan Section), *Labor and Urban Security* (Regina, 1944), pp. 2–4.

35. Andrew A. Bruce, *The Non-Partisan League* (New York, Macmillan Co., 1921), pp. 142–44.

36. Minutes of the 1923 Farmers' Union Convention.

37. Interviews with U.F.C. leaders.

38. *Handbook for Speakers,* p. 13.

39. CCF (Saskatchewan Section), election leaflet (Regina, 1935).

40. Saskatchewan Liberal Party, *The CCF Platform* (Regina, 1938), p. 3.

41. George Williams, *Problems Confronting the Retail Mer-*

chants of Western Canada (Regina, January 4, 1939), pp. 2–3. A published address.

42. "The Cooperatives" (editorial), *Saskatchewan Commonwealth*, February 12, 1944, p. 4.

43. *Ibid.*, January 11, 1944, p. 4.

44. Interviews with members of *Leader-Post* staff.

45. "A Big Job for the Tories" (editorial), *Saskatchewan Commonwealth*, January 19, 1944, p. 4.

46. Karl Mannheim, *Ideology and Utopia* (London, Routledge and Kegan Paul, Ltd., 1936), p. 187.

47. Rosa Luxemburg, *The Russian Revolution* (New York, Workers Age Publishers, 1940), pp. 17–22.

48. Julius Braunthal, *In Search of the Millennium* (London, Victor Gollancz, Ltd., 1945), pp. 267–68.

49. Gelo and Andrea, "French Letter: The November Elections," *Politics*, December, 1946, pp. 378–79.

50. See W. E. Walling, *Socialism As It Is* (New York, Macmillan Co., 1912), for a discussion of ideological shifts of socialist parties before the First World War. See also Franz Borkenau, *Socialism, National or International* (London, G. Routledge and Sons, Ltd., 1942).

51. Toronto *Star*, June 14, 1948, p. 1.

52. Sir John Maynard, *The Russian Peasant and Other Studies* (London, Victor Gollancz, Ltd., 1947), pp. 180–83, 279–88.

8

CCF SUPPORT

THE ANALYSIS and understanding of a social movement necessarily involve a discussion of the support the party receives as well as the nature of the opposition it meets. The CCF is ideologically a farmer and labor party attempting to replace the political and economic hegemony of big business by "the rule of the people." The movement has three important aspects: primarily, it represents the latest historical phase of the almost continuous struggle of western grain farmers with eastern business interests; second, within the Saskatchewan setting the movement is an outgrowth of the conflict between farmers, as consumers and producers, and middlemen who derive profits from them; and lastly, within the larger urban centers, it reflects the hostility between employers and workers.

The class-struggle aspects of the CCF are brought out clearly by the results of the three provincial elections contested by the party before it took office in 1944. The difference between the vote received by political parties in rural areas and that received in the small trading villages and towns reflects the fact that the urban middle class and the farmers divided sharply in their reaction to the CCF.

The majority of the urban middle classes in the trading enclaves in Saskatchewan remained hostile to the CCF in every election, in spite of the fervent overtures of the party leaders. It is significant to note that this cleavage in voting behavior between town and countryside occurred in other agrarian movements, as in the Non-Partisan League.[1]

The urban gains of the CCF in the elections of 1938 and 1944 are in part a result of its changed ideological position. As we have seen, the party in 1938 entered into formal and informal coalition agreements with the Social Crediters and

TABLE 13

PERCENTAGE OF VOTES RECEIVED BY CCF

Elections	Rural areas	Small urban districts*
1934	29.8	12.9
1938	36.3	26.8
1944	58.1	38.8

Raw data in *Official Election Results*, Secretary of Executive Council, Province of Saskatchewan.
* Population less than 1,000.

the Conservatives against the Liberals who were in office. This led many supporters of the other parties to vote CCF in constituencies where their own candidates were not running. As table 14 makes clear, the CCF received a large portion of the Conservative and Social Credit vote.

The urban support of the CCF was still very low where it did not receive the support of members of other opposition parties. In constituencies where all four parties ran, the CCF received 17.5 per cent in small urban centers, as compared to 31.7 per cent in rural areas. The Social Credit Party, which promised to end the depression by issuing monetary dividends to all, became the party of the urban middle-class group that wanted reforms in the economic structure.

By the election year 1944, it was clear to everyone in Saskatchewan that the CCF was the only opposition party that could succeed the Liberals. The Conservatives nominated candidates in only half of the constituencies in the province, while the Social Crediters withdrew from the provincial field. The CCF was able, therefore, to win the votes of many people who wanted to get rid of the incumbent Liberals and could do so only by voting CCF. This accounts in part for the growth of the CCF among middle-class groups.

The gain of the CCF in the small towns probably does not indicate any significant lessening of the cleavage between countryside and trading center. The election statistics for small towns and villages conceal a conflict within the urban areas, for the CCF received a higher vote from small-town workers and farmers than from business and professional people. This is indicated by the electoral data in towns that are large

TABLE 14

PERCENTAGE OF VOTES IN SMALL URBAN DISTRICTS,* 1938

Party	All parties running	Three parties running	Two parties running
CCF	17.5	23.2	43.0
Liberal	45.9	51.7	57.0
Conservative	14.9		
Social Credit	21.7	25.1	

Raw data in *Official Election Results*, Secretary of Executive Council, Province of Saskatchewan.

* Population less than 1,000.

enough to have separate polling centers for different districts. The CCF was appreciably stronger in working-class sections than in districts inhabited by business and professional men.[2] CCF organizers report that their strength in the villages of Saskatchewan comes from workers and farmers who live in the towns.

The same internal class cleavage existed in the larger urban centers. In every city of the province, CCF strength was considerably higher in working-class districts than in middle-class areas. The election results for the city of Regina indicate this clearly.

The attempt of various CCF leaders to unite small businessmen, farmers, and workers in one party was foredoomed to failure, for it ignored the fact that in Saskatchewan small businessmen are the only immediate representatives of the "profit" system and, therefore, are resented by the farmers, who desire to eliminate them rather than to win their support. The cooperative store and the Wheat Pool elevator are the core of emotional loyalty for the CCF farmers. The general store, the bank, and the insurance office are symbols of economic oppression.

Business and professional men, on the other hand, tend to identify themselves with large capital rather than with workers and farmers. Objectively, the urban middle classes may have, in the monopolists, a common enemy with other groups, but, in fact, local merchants, doctors, bank managers, and lawyers regard themselves as superior to both farmers and workers, and aspire to the status of the upper classes in the large cities.

The country grocer or butcher in the small villages of the wheat belt is in the highest social class in his community, even though his economic compeers in the large cities are probably

TABLE 15

PERCENTAGE DISTRIBUTION OF VOTES IN REGINA

Party	Working-class polls*		Middle-class polls*	
	1934	1944	1934	1944
CCF	25.5	61.6	19.4	32.2
Liberal	44.0	29.7	45.5	52.3
Conservative	30.4	8.7	35.1	15.5

Raw data in *Official Election Results,* Secretary of Executive Council, Province of Saskatchewan.

* The difference between the polls was based on information obtained from interviews with officials of the city of Regina and from local politicians and old residents.

in the lower middle class.[3] This tends to give the small-town merchant a greater social stake in preserving the *status quo* than his big-city brother, and it is more difficult to recruit him to a radical social movement. Furthermore, the program of the CCF to take over retail distribution, medicine, banking, and insurance, under cooperative or government ownership, seemed to adversely affect a large group of the small-town middle class. They therefore remained actively hostile to the new party.

Before the CCF was organized, the urban middle classes dominated the political life of the province. They were and still are the leaders of the Liberal and Conservative parties. The political machines of the old parties were centered in the towns and cities, and were operated by lawyers, insurance men, and other members of the middle class. (See chap. 9, p. 236.) The CCF represented a threat to the political control and influence of the urban middle classes, as well as a challenge to their economic interests. The change in the class base of political control in Saskatchewan which the CCF introduced is clearly indicated in table 37 (p. 237).

The election statistics cited tend to confirm the interpretation that the CCF has been primarily a farmer-labor party. In every election that it has contested, the party received more support from these two groups than it did from the urban middle classes. These data, however, reveal little of the dynamics of the growth of the CCF. An analysis of the shifts in electoral behavior within the working class and the farm population is necesary in order to understand the real significance of Saskatchewan radicalism. Fortunately, the Canadian census makes such an analysis possible, as it supplies social and economic data for rural municipalities, which do not include organized urban communities.[4]

CCF rural support doubled between 1934 and 1944. The party received 29 per cent of the farm vote in 1934, and 58 per cent in the election that swept it to power. One possible interpretation is that these gains reflect the changes in the party program between 1934 and 1944, that the party won the support of the extremely poor farmers to whom it addressed its propaganda in the early radical period, and later gained the more substantial middle-class agrarians by modifying its radicalism to win the support of the conservative and well-to-do elements. Many political observers, including some CCF leaders, made this interpretation of CCF growth.

Actually, the exact opposite occurred. CCF supporters in 1934 came from the groups in the rural population which had the highest social and economic status. The party's vote was highest in prosperous farm areas where land-tax assessment was high and tenancy was low. Strong CCF districts were also characterized by being predominantly Anglo-Saxon and Protestant. Though the correlations between the various ecological factors and the CCF votes are not very great, as can be seen from table 16, an analysis of these factors by the Lazarsfeld latent-attribute method reveals that the cluster of factors that make for high status in Saskatchewan was highly interrelated with the CCF vote in 1934.[5]

The differences between the support of the CCF and of the Liberal Party may be explained on the basis of cultural attributes: the Liberals derived more of their support from the poor non-Anglo-Saxon and Roman Catholic elements than did the CCF. The Conservatives, who were traditionally the party of the Anglo-Saxon Protestants, continued to receive most of their backing from that part of the population. The CCF, however, was supported by the well-to-do, Anglo-Saxon Protestant areas, while the Tories were found in the poorer districts.

TABLE 16

CORRELATIONS OF CENSUS DATA FOR RURAL AREAS OF
SASKATCHEWAN WITH POLITICAL PARTY VOTE, 1934

Group	CCF	Conserva-tive	Liberal	Assessment of Land	Tenancy	United Church	Roman Catholic	Anglo-Saxon
CCF	x	−.23	−.65	.25	−.11	.40	−.29	.44
Conservative	−.23	x	—	−.04	.20	.33	−.37	.35
Liberal	−.65	—	x	—	.03	−.43	.25	−.40
Assessment of Land	.25	−.40	−.20	x	.18	.57	−.27	.51
Tenancy	−.11	.20	.03	.18	x	.19	.14	.08
United Church	.40	.33	−.43	.57	.19	x	−.45	.85
Roman Catholic	.29	−.37	.25	−.27	.14	−.45	x	−.50
Anglo-Saxon	.44	.35	−.40	.51	.08	.85	−.50	x

The shifts in the electoral strength of the political parties between the elections of 1934 and 1938 are difficult to analyze because of the multiplicity of parties and the coalitions among them. In some constituencies in 1938, the CCF ran against three other parties—Liberals, Conservatives, and Social Crediters; in others it received the support of Social Crediters or Conservatives against Liberals. The CCF, in turn, did not contest 22 out of the 52 seats in the province and supported, formally or informally, one or the other of the opposition parties. The entry of Social Credit as an alternative protest party greatly complicated the picture, for in areas where the Social Crediters ran against the CCF, the party's vote declined below that received in 1934, while in constituencies where the CCF alone opposed the old parties, its vote went up.

The principal change in CCF support in the 1938 election from that of 1934 was that it tended to receive the support of many poorer Anglo-Saxon Protestants who had previously voted Conservative. This was probably a result of the fact that the Conservative Party did not contest half the seats in the election, and its rural supporters tended to vote CCF where their party did not run. As in 1934, the CCF was opposed by the poorer non-Anglo-Saxon and Catholic areas. Catholic farmers either continued to vote for the Liberal Party or backed the Social Credit movement, which had more appeal to dissatisfied Catholics than did the socialist CCF.

As the depression came to an end, the CCF recruited many more supporters from the socially and economically depressed part of the rural population that had previously supported the old parties. In the election of 1944 the party made most of its electoral gains from the low-status groups, the poorer and non-Anglo-Saxon farmers, as table 17 indicates.

The inconclusive correlations between the CCF vote and the ecological variables resulting from the 1944 election returns are due to the fact that CCF gains canceled out the effect of the original (1934) CCF support. The party made its greatest gains in the areas where it had been weakest in 1934, and the ecological analysis of the 1944 vote does not reveal significant differences between CCF and anti-CCF areas.

The data cited above raise some interesting questions about the nature of radical political activity. It is popularly assumed that radical political action in a crisis is related to poverty and low social status. Marxists have traditionally believed that revolutionary action would be brought about by increasing economic misery. The Saskatchewan situation suggests, however, that within an exploited economic group, such as the prairie wheat farmers, those who possess economic and social status within the class are most resentful of a threat to their security. The poorer, socially outcast groups, when they are seriously affected by economic reverses, are likely to be politically

TABLE 17

CORRELATIONS BETWEEN CCF VOTES IN 1934 AND 1944, AND CCF GAINS

Group	CCF votes		CCF gains between 1934 and 1944
	1934	1944	
Assessment of Land	.25	−.08	−.26
United Church	.40	.10	−.27
Roman Catholic	−.29	−.10	.06
Anglo-Saxon	.44	.04	−.42

apathetic rather than rebellious. In Saskatchewan this group did not organize for remedial action but had to be organized from the outside by leaders of the more prosperous farmers. In 1934, in the depths of the depression, low-status farmers— the poor, non-Anglo-Saxon, and Catholics—tended to remain loyal to the Liberal Party.

There is a second related explanation of the differences in 1934 between supporters of the CCF and of the old party. The CCF was organized mainly by men who had been active in farmers' movements: the Wheat Pool, the Saskatchewan Grain Growers' Association, the Farmers' Union, and the United Farmers of Canada. Studies of rural cooperative and economic class organizations in the United States have indicated that such organizations are composed primarily of well-to-do farmers of Anglo-Saxon or northern European extraction. Poorer agrarians and those belonging to low-status ethnic groups have not generally participated in organized farmers' movements.[6] The battle for higher prices and a better economic return for their labor has been conducted by the farmers who need it least.

This is true of Saskatchewan as well. An unpublished study, the source of which is confidential, has shown that members of the Wheat Pool and consumers' cooperatives in the province are predominantly well-to-do farmers. The ethnic settlements have long been obstacles in the path of the cooperative movement. The comparatively wealthy Anglo-Saxon farmers had learned, before the CCF was organized, to react through class organizations to economic problems. The CCF was founded in 1931 as the newest in the long chain of such protest movements, and as such it received the support of the more economically and politically class-conscious agrarians.

The less prosperous Saskatchewan farmers began to support the CCF only after the depression had ended and economic conditions had improved. The combination of a long economic depression that had deprived them of all material rewards and a subsequent economic boom was necessary before they could turn to political action on their own behalf. These developments challenge the assumption that radicalism necessarily wanes during economic prosperity. Often, as in Saskatchewan, an upswing in the business cycle may prove to be the stimulus that gives the depressed members of society enough personal security to engage in politics.

Farmers in the lower stratum, once aroused, however, seem to become stronger supporters of the radical movement than well-to-do farmers. CCF field organizers confirm from their campaign experiences the indications of the election results. Those interviewed almost invariably reported that it was difficult to organize the poorer farmers during the 'thirties, but that during the war they became stronger supporters of the party than many of the wealthy grain growers.

The implications of these data for theories of radical political behavior are not limited to farmers. A similar pattern exists among urban workers. The data were obtained by dividing the city of Regina, the largest urban area in the province, into three sections: the East End, composed mainly of foreign-born, unskilled workers; the North End, inhabited by better-paid, skilled Anglo-Saxon workers; and the West End, a middle- and upper-class section. The differences in the electoral behavior of the two working-class sections are similar to those found in rural areas.

In 1934 the CCF's greatest support in Regina came from the upper strata of the working class, while the poorer, the unskilled, and the unemployed workers in the East End remained as loyal to the old parties as did the business-class district. It was only when the depression ended that the lower strata turned to the CCF.

Ethnic and religious factors appear to play an important role in distinguishing CCF support and its opposition. It is

TABLE 18

PERCENTAGE DISTRIBUTION OF VOTES IN REGINA

Party	West End* middle class	Per cent gain or loss	N. End* skilled workers	Per cent gain or loss	East End* unskilled workers	Per cent gain or loss
			1934 Election			
CCF	19.4	....	33.2	....	19.5	....
Liberal	45.5	....	32.9	....	52.8	....
Conservative	35.1	....	33.9	....	27.7	....
			1944 Election			
CCF	32.2	64.9	60.8	83.1	62.1	218.5
Liberal	52.3	14.9	26.9	−18.2	31.5	−40.3
Conservative	15.5	−55.8	12.2	−64.0	6.4	−76.9

* Raw data in *Official Election Results,* Secretary of Executive Council, Province of Saskatchewan.

impossible, however, to obtain correlations with which to analyze the effect of these factors because the different cultural groups are concentrated in a few areas. The 58 per cent of the rural population who are non-Anglo-Saxon live in ethnic enclaves, and most census areas (rural municipalities) do not contain more than one or two ethnic groups in significant numbers. It has been necessary, therefore, to examine the municipalities that have a large proportion of cultural subgroups, and compare them with the general population in order to estimate the role played by cultural background in CCF support.

The ecological data indicate that the Anglo-Saxons and the Scandinavians of the province have tended to be members of the CCF. This is probably because supporters of the cooperatives and the farm movement are generally CCF voters. The

TABLE 19

CCF SUPPORT IN RURAL SASKATCHEWAN MUNICIPALITIES WITH HIGH PROPORTION OF SCANDINAVIANS
(Percentages)

| | Scandi-navians* | CCF votes† | | |
		1934	1938	1944
All rural areas in province	10.1	29.6	36.3	58.1
Scandinavian rural municipalities	31.9	40.0	45.0	58.6

* *Farms and Farmers in Canada: Facts from the Census, 1941 and 1931* (1944), p. 10.
† Raw data in *Official Election Results,* Secretary of Executive Council, Province of Saskatchewan.

TABLE 20

CCF SUPPORT IN RURAL SASKATCHEWAN MUNICIPALITIES WITH HIGH PROPORTION OF FRENCH CANADIANS
(Percentages)

| | French Canadians* | CCF votes† | | |
		1934	1938	1944
All rural areas in province	5.0	29.6	36.3	58.1
French-Canadian rural municipalities	29.5	24.2	31.7	49.6

* *Farms and Farmers in Canada: Facts from the Census, 1941 and 1931* (1944), p. 10.
† Raw data in *Official Election Results,* Secretary of Executive Council, Province of Saskatchewan.

Anglo-Saxons tend to be cooperators because of their superior economic position, which enables them to invest in cooperatives. Many of the Scandinavians have had favorable experiences with the cooperative and socialist movements in their home countries and consequently joined these movements in Saskatchewan. CCF organizers report that the Scandinavians were the easiest group to organize into the party.

Other non-Anglo-Saxon ethnic groups have been more difficult to organize. Many have remained loyal to the Liberal Party, the traditional party of the minority ethnic groups in Canada, as contrasted with the Protestant Anglo-Saxon Tories. The French Canadians of the province, who come from traditionally Liberal Quebec and live in French-speaking enclaves, have remained more strongly opposed to the CCF than the rest of the population.

The Mennonites, who comprise 4.6 per cent of Saskatchewan's population, are also strongly opposed to the CCF. Many of them are refugees from the Russian Revolution and identify the CCF with the hated communism of Russia from which they escaped. The largely Mennonite constituency of Rosthern is the strongest anti-CCF seat in the province.

The vote of the Ukrainians is the most difficult to explain. Though the majority are Roman Catholic by birth, they tend to be less influenced by the Church than other Catholic groups. The Ukrainians, in fact, are the only predominantly

TABLE 21

CCF SUPPORT IN RURAL SASKATCHEWAN MUNICIPALITIES
WITH HIGH PROPORTION OF MENNONITES
(Percentages)

	Mennonites*	CCF votes† 1934	1938	1944
All rural areas in province	4.6	29.6	36.3	58.1
Mennonite rural municipalities	46.7	19.4	31.9	45.0

* *Eighth Census of Canada, 1941,* Bulletin A-5, pp. 2–3.
† Raw data in *Official Election Results,* Secretary of Executive Council, Province of Saskatchewan.

Roman Catholic national group whose support of the CCF is commensurate with that of the general population. The strong CCF vote may be an indication of the weakened position of the Catholic Church among the Ukrainians, rather than of Catholic support for the CCF. A large minority of Ukrainians belong to the Greek Orthodox Church and therefore are exposed to different religious pressures. The so-called "Red" Ukrainians, who ideologically support the Soviet Union, are mostly agnostics and atheists.

The Ukrainians live in the poorer northern and central districts, since they were comparatively late settlers. They were not among the early strong supporters of the cooperative and farmers' movements, as can be seen from their voting behavior in 1934. In succeeding elections, however, the CCF was able to make great gains among the poorer Ukrainians after concentrated organizational work in these districts. Today the Ukrainians are among the strongest supporters of the CCF.

Persons of German extraction constitute the largest non-Anglo-Saxon ethnic minority in Saskatchewan. They are divided between the Roman Catholic and the Lutheran churches. It is difficult to ascribe any significance to the voting data for the German areas. Like most of the other ethnic

TABLE 22

CCF SUPPORT IN RURAL SASKATCHEWAN MUNICIPALITIES
WITH HIGH PROPORTION OF UKRAINIANS
(Percentages)

| | | CCF votes† | | |
	Ukrainians*	1934	1938	1944
All rural areas in province	10.3	29.6	36.3	58.1
Ukrainian rural municipalities	59.6	21.1	42.7	59.6

* *Farms and Farmers in Canada: Facts from the Census, 1941 and 1931* (1944), p. 10.
† Raw data in *Official Election Results,* Secretary of Executive Council, Province of Saskatchewan.

TABLE 23

CCF SUPPORT IN RURAL SASKATCHEWAN MUNICIPALITIES
WITH HIGH PROPORTION OF GERMANS
(Percentages)

| | | CCF votes† | | |
	Germans*	1934	1938	1944
All rural areas in province	15.1	29.6	36.3	58.1
German rural municipalities	57.7	24.0	34.5	54.0

* *Farms and Farmers in Canada: Facts from the Census, 1941 and 1931* (1944), p. 10.
† Raw data in *Official Election Results,* Secretary of Executive Council, Province of Saskatchewan.

minorities, the Germans tend to be more opposed to the CCF than those of Anglo-Saxon extraction. German Catholics are reputed to be highly resistant to the party's appeal.

The evidence indicates that Roman Catholic opposition to socialism is the most significant of the ethnic and religious factors involved in the Saskatchewan vote. Catholics have been and remain the backbone of the Liberal Party's support in the province. In every election they give less support to the CCF than do the Protestants. A Saskatchewan Catholic priest who is engaged in a study of the CCF and has studied the attitudes of both lay and clerical Catholics indicates the causes of their hostility to the party.

The mentality of most Catholics I have met across Canada, including the clergy, is infected with a terribly distorted view of the CCF *reality*. The result is that Catholics generally are afflicted with a deep-rooted, though unconscious, prejudice against the CCF. It is virtually identical with the kind of prejudice against Catholics found in the typical Ontario Protestant of twenty years ago. Catholics by and large condemn the CCF for something it is not; they are enslaved by the tyranny of a single word—"socialism." If I may generalize on the fairly large sample I have interviewed across the continent, then the overwhelming majority of Catholics are unconsciously banded together in a compact political unity based on an illusion. (I suspect that this is not true of Nova Scotia, due mainly to the enlightened leadership given the people by the priests of Saint Francis Xavier.) The result is that Catholics tend to fall into a mould of political and economic thought quite out of line with that of the encyclicals. Enslaved mentally by the tyranny of that awful word, they are virtually forced to devour with avidity all the "anti-socialist" propaganda dispensed so generously and freely by the forces of reaction. And we come to the sad and tragic paradox where we find that Canadian Catholics, by and large, have divorced themselves from those constructive and creative forces about which Maritain has written so well, and which are the only hope we have of winning the peace. Outside of Joe Burton of Humboldt, there is not a single Catholic in a place of influence or leadership in the Saskatchewan CCF movement. With rare exceptions the same is true all across Canada. The influence of Catholic leadership, both clerical and lay, and a considerable portion of the Catholic vote is thus spent in prolonging what Maritain has called the agony of the modern world.[7]

The decline in overt clerical hostility to the CCF in recent years has been associated with CCF gains in Catholic areas. It is questionable, however, whether the change in the official attitude of the Church is a cause of the increased Catholic support of the party. The hierarchy in Saskatchewan still believes, as Father Cullinane has indicated, that CCF socialism is evil and represents a threat to the Church.

The increasing support of the CCF, both Catholic and non-Catholic, has led Catholic leaders to recognize that the CCF has become a permanent factor in Saskatchewan and Canadian politics and that the Church cannot afford to antagonize a prospective governmental party. The Church also has been under pressure from lay Catholics, who joined the CCF, to cease her opposition to the party. The decline in the CCF's aggressive radicalism both in Saskatchewan and across Canada has reassured Catholic leaders that the CCF does not necessarily represent a threat to the Church. At present, however, there can be little doubt that members of the Canadian hierarchy prefer a non-CCF government and that this feeling is reflected in Catholic voting.

The influence of the Protestant churches on Saskatchewan political behavior is more difficult to analyze; with the exception of the United Church, no one Protestant sect has a sufficiently large proportion of the population to lend itself to a statistical analysis from census data. Two factors do stand out, however: membership in the United Church tends to be consistently and positively associated with CCF support, and there is some evidence that Anglicans are opposed to the movement.

The United Church of Canada is comparable to the nonconformist workingmen's churches of Great Britain. It has stressed the social-gospel aspect of Christianity. Many of its leaders have been active in secular reform activities.[8] A number of church conferences have officially attacked private capitalism as "un-Christian." Since it has the least fundamentalist and conservative creed, the United Church tends to attract and influence those who believe in a liberal Christianity that is concerned with establishing "the good life" on earth. Many

CCF members of the United Church explicitly state their belief that a good Christian must be a socialist.

The Anglican Church has remained "essentially an English institution, maintaining English traditions and a close relationship with England."[9] It is more of an urban, middle-class church than is the United Church. Its adherents tend to be more conservative and traditionalist than do those of other denominations. They are prone, therefore, to be found in the ranks of the Conservative Party, which is associated in the minds of many people with strong Empire ties. A Gallup Poll sample (see p. 220) indicates that Anglicans constitute the largest group of Tory supporters in the province, and that they are overwhelmingly opposed to the CCF.

Veblen has suggested that the capacity of a society for change "depends in large measure on the degree . . . of exposure of the individual members to the constraining forces of the environment." The process of social transformation will be retarded, however, "if any portion or class of society is sheltered from the environment in any essential respect, [for] that portion of the community or that class will adapt its views and its scheme of life more tardily to the altered general situation."[10]

The western rural community possesses Veblen's prerequisites for social change more than any other group in the United States or Canada. Saskatchewan comes closer to being an economically undifferentiated society than most rural or urban areas, for almost every farmer is dependent on wheat for his basic source of income. When, in the price decline of the early 'thirties, the cost of the production of a bushel of wheat came to exceed its sales value, the deficit of larger and more prosperous farmers was greater than that of small farmers. (See table 8, p. 121.) Some of the wealthiest rural districts in the province were among the worst afflicted by hard times. Nearly every farmer was forced to accept some form of government relief.

This situation meant that the threat to the basic social and economic values of rural Saskatchewan was experienced more or less equally by all sections of the population, for climatic and economic forces played few favorites. A unity of suffering and interest existed despite differences in economic status. As in most wheat areas during crises, there was no "sheltered" group in rural Saskatchewan in the 'thirties. Most of the rural community, therefore, supported the movement for change.

In urban areas, in contrast, the population is unequally affected by economic depression. The upper and middle classes retain their relative social and economic position, though their total income may decline. Sections of the middle class and working class may actually experience an increase in real income as a result of the decline in prices. Only a minority of workers are ever unemployed. Thus a new movement for social change cannot appeal equally to all classes or even to all sections of the working class.[11] The fact that economic crises have given rise to successful agrarian parties more often than to workers' protest parties is partially a result of this difference between the rural and the urban community.

The effect of a depression on the farmer, especially in Saskatchewan, and on the urban worker differs also in another important respect. The relations between the "uncontrollable" external forces and the farmer's plight are more directly visible than they are in an urban economy. The worker who cannot get a job has been taught to blame his own ineptitude for his failure.[12] As a result of economic crisis, many of the unemployed lose confidence in themselves and become apathetic. Farmers, however, are more apt to lose confidence in the traditional values of society under extreme economic conditions. The farmers of Saskatchewan could not be blamed for the economic problems that threatened them. It was not their fault that they could not raise crops because of the drought or the decline in the price of wheat.

Saskatchewan differed also from rural areas where large variations in types of farming exist. Such variations usually create differences in economic and political interests and behavior. Ecological studies of agrarian voting behavior in the United States indicate that the most important factor differentiating rural districts supporting protest movements from those opposing them has been the type of crop: there has often been a significant difference between the vote in wheat areas and in corn or mixed-farming regions.[13] The last large agrarian party in the United States, the Non-Partisan League, was able to win majority support only in North Dakota, a state that is similar to Saskatchewan in having a one-crop wheat economy, and it secured only minority support in states where farming was more diversified. Fluctuations in economic conditions affect different farming regions unequally, and are reflected in the voting and organizational behavior of the population.

The most significant feature of the growth of the CCF has been the apparent contradiction between the pattern of CCF growth and the belief that radical movements are based on the poorest segment of the population and grow best during economic depressions. The earliest support of the party came from the upper layer of farmers' and workers' groups. Among the more depressed strata its greatest growth came in a period of rising prosperity. The phenomenon of intensified radical behavior in a period of prosperity following a depression has been paralleled in other parts of Canada. Nationally, the CCF did not gain much between 1935, the year of the first federal election which it contested, and 1940, when the depression receded. It had about 10 per cent of the vote on both occasions. The party began its rapid national growth in the latter part of 1942. It won a series of by-elections all across Canada and increased its representation in the Ontario legislature from no seats in 1937 to 34 seats in 1943.

Canadian workers and farmers apparently learned the economic lessons of the depression only after the event. During the depression, poverty, insecurity, and unemployment did not stimulate mass upheaval. A research study on the effect of unemployment in Marienthal, Austria, throws some light on this problem. The workers, instead of becoming more radical when the town's leading factory closed, became politically apathetic. They tended to withdraw into the family circle and lose interest in the outside world.

Those who are on the bottom of the economic scale will not revolt if they are pushed down further. A person must have a certain amount of security to fight for a larger share. Those who have nothing to lose but their chains are too closely chained, psychologically, to the desperation of their lot to generalize their predicament, face the consequences of a malcontent position, or otherwise add to their suffering by striving for social change. They are too deeply concerned with the all-absorbing, time-consuming, dismaying problem of getting by on "handouts" to afford the luxury of thought and effort for a distant eventuality, however promising. The authors of the Marienthal study point out that

[unemployment in Marienthal resulted in a] drop from the higher cultural level of political struggle to the more primitive level of mutual individual animosity . . . the few who are politically active, especially among the young people, are still at work. The group of Socialist Working Youth has 37 members; of these only 7 are unemployed. As soon as an official of this group becomes unemployed he gives up all his duties and, tired of politics, withdraws. . . .

It is typical of the whole situation when a leading political functionary of the place reports:

"Previously I used to know the *Arbeiterzeitung* [the Socialist Party newspaper] by heart; now I look at it just a bit and then throw it away, in spite of the fact that I have more time."

As a matter of fact, from 1927 to 1930 the subscriptions to the *Arbeiterzeitung* have dropped about 60 per cent. This is not, as one might suppose, to be interpreted as a mere economical counting of pennies, for the *Arbeiterzeitung* issues an unemployed subscription that costs only four groschen per copy; it is the interest in politics that has lessened. The subscription to the *Kleinen Blatts,* which has the same political direction, only in general is more concerned with entertainment than politics, has declined only by about 27 per cent in spite of its higher price—10 groschen per copy.[14]

It is the people who have something to lose in the form of economic and social status who fight back. Well-to-do farmers and skilled workers will resist economic adversity. They know that loss of farm income or reduced wages are not their fault. They are more likely to join or support a new radical movement than are the poor farmers or unemployed workers.

Emile Durkheim has pointed out that sheer poverty does not lead to lack of adjustment with society.

. . . poverty . . . by its very nature . . . acts as a restraint. Whatever one may do, one's desires are obliged, in some measure, to reckon with the available resources; what one has acts in part as a guide in determining what one would like to have. Consequently, the less one possesses, the less he is inclined to extend endlessly the range of his wants. By subjecting us forcibly to moderation, poverty habituates us to it, and besides, where mediocrity is a general condition, nothing occurs to excite envy. Wealth, on the other hand, by virtue of the power which it confers upon its possessor, creates the illusion that we can rise simply by our own efforts. By reducing the obstacles which are placed in our way, riches lead us to believe that such obstacles can be mastered indefinitely. Now the less a man feels himself restrained, the more intolerable any actual restraint seems to him. It is not without reason, then, that so many religions have glorified the benefits and the moral worth of poverty. Poverty is, indeed, the best school for teaching a man self-restraint.[15]

The return of prosperity removes the main cause of political apathy among the poorer farmers and workers. The radical movement is able to capitalize on the adverse experiences of the poorer classes during the depression. The CCF in Canada was able to convince many workers and farmers that a change in the economic system would prevent a new depression. The resentment of the lower strata of the population over their treatment during the depression was therefore channeled during prosperity.

The effects of the depression on political behavior in other countries would seem to contradict this general theory. Radical parties made headway in many European countries, in New Zealand, and in North Dakota and Minnesota during the 'thirties. It must be remembered, however, that the Labor Party in New Zealand, the Social Democratic Party of Sweden, the Farmer-Labor Party in Minnesota, and the Non-Partisan League in North Dakota, which achieved power in the depression period, were not depression-born movements. Each was the largest opposition group in its country or state before the depression. As the alternative government, it capitalized on the discontent with the government in power. Leftist governments that were in power when the depression started, as in Australia and England, also lost office because the government in power was blamed for troubles that began while it held office.

The development of political class consciousness is similar to the emergence of economic class consciousness, or trade-unionism. The greatest growth of the latter usually occurs during an economic upswing following a depression. A depression weakens working-class morale and makes it almost impossible to recruit workers into unions. The immediate objective of workers becomes simply to have and hold a job. The worker is not open to new ideas, such as those of trade-unionism or a radical political party.[16] Only after the worker's economic position has been fortified by some degree of security is he free to consider ways and means of improving his position or of preventing a recurrence of past evils.

Once the process of radicalization develops—a conscious discontent with one's lot and a conviction that economic and social conditions can be improved through collective class action—the poorer section of the working and farming classes appears to become the firmest base of the class movement. Additional moves in a leftist direction may now come from the more depressed elements. This can be seen in Saskatchewan, where the Labor Progressive Party (Communist) gained what little strength it has in the poor sections on the northern frontier and in the East End in Regina.[17] A farmers' strike in the autumn of 1946 in Saskatchewan and Alberta was, for the most part, a movement of the smaller and poorer farmers who were dissatisfied with the price of wheat and supported strike action to gain immediate economic benefits.[18]

NOTES

1. Stuart A. Rice, *Farmers and Workers in American Politics* (New York, Longmans, Green and Co., 1924), p. 165.

2. The election results of a number of Saskatchewan towns were analyzed with political leaders of these towns. They invariably

indicated that the poorer and working-class areas supported the CCF, whereas the business-class districts backed the old parties.

3. Jean Burnet, unpublished doctoral thesis, University of Chicago, 1948; Jim Giffen, unpublished master's thesis, University of Toronto, 1947.

4. Rural municipalities are about eighteen miles square. The province is divided into more than 300 municipalities of this size. Their population varies from about 800 to 5,000. The municipalities average six election polls each. The election results were calculated for each municipality by adding the results for the polls within municipalities. When a poll overlapped municipal boundaries, each municipality was assigned a proportionate part of the vote.

5. The Lazarsfeld latent attribute is a method of analyzing the relationships among a number of variables. It indicates the presence or absence of a common underlying factor.

6. J. H. Kolb and E. de S. Brunner, *A Study of Rural Society* (New York, Houghton Mifflin Co., 1935), p. 353.

7. Letter of the Rev. Eugene A. Cullinane, C.S.B., Professor of Economics, University of Saskatchewan.

8. England has a similar pattern. The Methodists, who are the largest group in the United Church of Canada, were the backbone of the British labor movement.

". . . it seems to me that it still remains true that, in the silent solid membership of every popular movement in the country, from Trade-Unionism and Cooperation, from Friendly and Temperance Societies, right up to the rapidly growing Labour Party itself—no less than among their active local organizers and leaders—perhaps the largest part is contributed by the various branches of the Methodist community." Sidney Webb, *The Story of the Durham Miners, 1662–1921* (London, Labour Publishing Co., 1921), p. 24.

"The training in self-expression and in the filling of offices and the control of public affairs which these [Methodist] Societies provided for a great host of working men and women was invaluable as a preparation for industrial combination and for the future work of Trade-Unionism. The Dissenting Chapel and the Methodist Society were the pioneer forms of the latter self-governing labour organizations, and they became the nurseries of popular aspirations after place and power in civic and national government." A. D. Belden, *George Whitefield the Awakener* (London, S. Low, Marston and Co., Ltd., 1930), pp. 247 ff.

9. G. E. Britnell, *The Wheat Economy* (University of Toronto Press, 1939), p. 188.

10. Thorstein Veblen, *The Theory of the Leisure Class* (New York, Modern Library, 1934), p. 193.

11. G. D. H. Cole explained the failure of English socialism in the 1930's as a result of the fact that "distress is to a great extent

now localized in the so-called 'special areas,' and affects comparatively little the major portion of the population, or even of the working class. Over most of the South, indeed, the sense of crisis was only acute for a few months at most; and actually a majority of the British people, including nearly all those who have been able to keep in regular work, has enjoyed a higher purchasing power during the depression than ever before . . . so great was the effect of this fall [in the price of foodstuffs] that even the reduced wages paid to the employed workers enabled them to buy more than they could afford when times were better." *Socialism in Evolution* (London, Penguin Books, Ltd., 1938), p. 224.

12. "I assumed the role of one who was out of work and had become a communist because I couldn't get a job. I was told frankly and with great emotion that I could get work if I wanted it, that I was simply lazy and wanted a handout from people who had energy enough and ambition enough to work for a living even though it meant twelve to sixteen hours a day." E. Wight Bakke, *Citizens without Work; A Study of the Effects of Unemployment upon the Workers' Social Relations and Practices* (Yale University Press, 1940), p. 61.

13. C. O. Ruggles, "The Economic Basis of the Greenback Movement in Iowa and Wisconsin," Mississippi Valley Historical Society, *Proceedings,* Vol. 5; Benton H. Wilcox, "An Historical Definition of North-Western Radicalism," *Mississippi Valley Historical Review,* December, 1939; Raymond C. Miller, "The Economic Basis of Populism in Kansas," *ibid.,* Vol. 11 (1925); Rice, *op. cit.;* Jerry Nepresh, *The Brookhart Campaigns in Iowa: 1920–26* (Columbia University Press, 1932).

14. Marie Lazarsfeld-Jahoda (Paul Lazarsfeld), *Die Arbeitslosen von Marienthal* (Leipzig, S. Hitze, 1933), pp. 35–37.

15. Emile Durkheim, *Selected Readings of Anomie* (trans. by W. C. Bradbury, Jr., from *Le Suicide, étude de sociologie*), Part V, reprinted from *University Observer,* Winter, 1947.

16. The greatest gains in the Socialist Party vote in the United States were in 1902, 1904, and 1912—periods of economic expansion. "On the other hand, the panics of 1907 and 1913 did not make it possible for the party to get recruits or money in abundance and to wage as good a campaign as during better times. Workingmen are not militant if they are out of work or threatened with loss of work, unless the condition lasts for a long time. . . . The Socialist Party made no gains in 1908 and lost votes in 1914." Nathan Fine, *Labor and Farmer Parties in the United States* (Rand School of Social Science, New York, 1928), p. 217.

17. A random sample of 549 Saskatchewan farmers made after the federal election of 1945 tends to confirm the interpretation that the poorer farmers are now the farthest to the left.

DIFFERENCES IN SUPPORT RECEIVED BY SASKATCHEWAN
POLITICAL PARTIES IN 1945*
(Percentage)

	CCF	Liberal	Conservative	Others
Socioeconomic status:				
Above average	42.6	31.3	22.7	4.4
Average	45.5	32.3	19.3	3.9
Below average	49.3	27.6	19.2	4.9
Religion:				
Catholic	38.1	48.7	1.9	2.3
United Church	52.0	23.7	24.6	0.7
Anglican	36.4	31.5	28.8	4.3
Ethnic Origin:				
Anglo-Saxon	47.4	37.7	32.2	3.7
Central European and French	45.3	42.9	7.2	5.6

SOURCE: Sample of 549 farmers interviewed.
* Original data in files of Canadian Institute of Public Opinion, Toronto, Ontario.

18. Interviews with leaders of the U.F.C. (Saskatchewan Section).

9

CCF LEADERS

THE ELECTION data presented in chapter 8 contradict theories which assume that radical parties are movements of the "down-and-outers," the bottom level of society. To what extent are similar stereotypes about radical leaders correct? It has been suggested that the nucleus of leadership in a social movement comes from marginal groups, with their concomitant of economic, social, or personal maladjustments.[1] These groups should be most likely to accept a new radical program for social change in a period of social disequilibrium such as depression or drought, while the old community and class leaders attempt to maintain the *status quo*.[2] Actually, however, research data on the nature of leadership in new social movements are scanty and inconclusive.

In Saskatchewan it has been possible to trace the social and economic backgrounds of leaders of an organized protest movement. Information was obtained about the social, economic, and political backgrounds of delegates attending CCF provincial conventions in 1945 and 1946. These delegates, who were elected from forty-five constituency conventions held throughout the province, represented the best large-scale cross section of secondary party leaders. Of the 800 delegates who attended these conventions, 628 filled out questionnaires. Of these, 71.8 per cent were farmers or farmers' wives; 11.0 per cent, workers; 10.5 per cent, business or professional men; 2.7 per cent, teachers; 4.0 per cent, miscellaneous or unknown.

The backgrounds of the 431 rural CCF convention delegates explain in large measure the reasons for the comparatively rapid growth of the CCF in rural Saskatchewan. These active secondary leaders of the party were also the rural community leaders. Three-quarters of them held some position in

TABLE 24

431 Rural Delegates to CCF Convention Holding Posts
in Cooperative Movement, 1946
(Percentages)

Post	All delegates	Delegates over 45 years old	Delegates under 45 years old
Any in a cooperative	73.6	77.9	66.1
Wheat Pool committee	60.4	64.8	54.4
Chairman or secretary, Wheat Pool committee	34.1	39.2	25.0
Wheat Pool delegate	10.4	13.7	3.6
Director consumers' cooperative	39.2	39.2	39.2
Director provincial cooperative	10.0	13.7	3.6
Director Credit Union	5.7	5.9	5.4

a local or provincial cooperative. Official positions in the cooperative movement are a good index of community leadership, as the cooperatives are the major rural organizations in Saskatchewan. At the end of 1944, the year in which the CCF came to power, the cooperatives had 299,686 members. This meant that there were approximately two cooperative members for every farmer in the province.

The interrelations between CCF and cooperative leaders suggest that the cooperative leaders started the CCF or that CCF supporters succeeded in replacing the old cooperative leadership as radicals achieved wider influence in the rural community. From the fact that 58.9 per cent of those CCF delegates more than 45 years of age in 1945 held posts in cooperatives *before* the CCF was organized, it is clear that the CCF did not win control of the cooperative movement from the outside, but rather that the existing cooperative leaders organized the CCF. Further evidence in support of this conclusion can be found in the fact that the average number of years of membership of the older CCF delegates in the Wheat Pool, the largest cooperative in the province, was 20.4 years, and the median period was 21.7 years. The majority of them joined the Pool in 1923 and 1924, when it was first organized and was the major agrarian protest movement.

Another index of the leadership of CCF men in the community is their participation in farmers' educational organizations: the Saskatchewan Grain Growers' Association, the Farmers' Union, and the United Farmers of Canada (Sas-

TABLE 25

FARMERS' EDUCATIONAL ORGANIZATIONS OF 1945 AND 1946
CCF DELEGATES OVER FORTY-FIVE YEARS OLD
(Percentages)

Organization	Members	Officials
Saskatchewan Grain Growers	56.4	19.4
Farmers' Union	33.7	11.8
United Farmers of Canada	78.9	30.5
None	18.8	59.1

katchewan Section). These organizations have been in the forefront of all the struggles of the farmers since 1901. They supported the formation of most of the cooperative ventures and independent political efforts in the province. Since the organization of the CCF, the present farmers' educational organization, the U.F.C., has declined greatly in membership and influence because most of its supporters have become active in the CCF. This transfer of participation from the educational organization to the political party is clearly shown by the organizational backgrounds of the CCF leaders who are old enough to have taken an active part in these educational associations before the organization of the CCF.

CCF leaders were active in farmers' educational organizations before the formation of the CCF. Of the older group of CCF delegates, 70.1 per cent were in one or more of these organizations before 1931, when the CCF was formed in Saskatchewan, and 55.1 per cent of those who belonged to these organizations before the formation of the CCF held official positions in them.

The rural areas of Saskatchewan have their own separate nonpartisan governmental institutions. The CCF delegates, as table 26 indicates, are also leaders in this form of community activity. The overwhelming majority of rural CCF officials are community leaders, but it could not be concluded from this information alone that the CCF rural leaders and the community leaders are the same. It is conceivable that those who are active in all three provincial political parties are community leaders. To examine this possibility, information was gathered about the political backgrounds of officials of the cooperatives. Two sets of data were obtained. From persons

TABLE 26

PUBLIC POSTS HELD BY RURAL DELEGATES TO 1945 AND 1946 CCF CONVENTIONS

Public post	Percentage of all delegates	Percentage of delegates over 45 years old	Percentage of delegates under 45 years old
Reeve (mayor)	10.5	17.8	3.5
Rural municipal councilor	19.5	33.9	5.3
Hospital board	9.5	9.9	7.0
School board	55.8	73.3	35.1
Telephone board	34.2	39.6	17.5
Any public post	67.4	84.2	51.8

active in the cooperative movement of the province, information was obtained about the political affiliations of 113 out of 165 subdirectors or delegates of the Saskatchewan Wheat Pool, the largest and most important cooperative. Moreover, questionnaires similar to those given to the CCF delegates were filled out by 122 delegates to the conventions of two of the more important cooperative organizations. The two sets of data, presented in table 27, are strikingly similar.

Though the cooperative movement is officially neutral in politics, there can be no doubt that its leaders are largely supporters of only one party, the CCF. These cooperative supporters are not recent adherents of the party. Of the 122 delegates who filled out questionnaires and indicated their support of the CCF, 87.8 per cent had backed the movement before 1936, and 64.6 per cent in 1933 or earlier. The close ties between CCF and cooperative leaders are further indicated by the fact that most cooperative leaders have held some post in the CCF party. These CCF cooperative leaders, like the delegates to the CCF convention, were active also in the three farmers' educational organizations; 75.3 per cent of them belonged to, and 52.0 per cent have held official positions in, one or more of these organizations.

TABLE 27

PARTY AFFILIATION OF DELEGATES TO WHEAT
POOL AND TWO OTHER COOPERATIVE
CONVENTIONS, 1946
(Percentages)

Party	Wheat Pool delegates	Cooperative convention delegates
CCF	84.9	82.9
Liberal	10.6	10.6
Conservative	1.8	1.6
Social Credit	1.8	0.8
Labor Progressive	0.9	0.0

TABLE 28

CCF PARTY POSITIONS HELD BY RURAL
DELEGATES TO TWO COOPERATIVE
CONVENTIONS, 1946
(Percentages)

CCF position	Cooperative delegates
Any CCF post	69.1
Poll committee member	56.7
Secretary, poll committee	14.4
Chairman, poll committee	7.2
Zone organizer	14.4
Constituency committee member	38.1
President of constituency	7.2
Provincial Council member	7.2

That the CCF's earliest electoral support came from the more prosperous farmers is clearly reflected in the economic background of the party's local officials.

More than 50 per cent of Saskatchewan farmers are members of minority ethnic groups. Studies of radical movements have indicated that a disproportionate number of leaders come from such groups. In terms of the earlier data concerning the CCF, one would expect to find, however, that CCF rural leaders come from groups that have superior status in the community. This expectation is confirmed by the data in table 30.

TABLE 29

ECONOMIC STATUS OF RURAL DELEGATES TO CCF CONVENTIONS AND TO TWO COOPERATIVE CONVENTIONS

	Total population, Saskatchewan, 1941*	CCF delegates	Cooperative delegates
Size of farm (acres)	433.2	673.7	689.4
Value of farm	$6,435.0	$12,983.4	$14,189.9

* *Farms and Farmers in Canada: Facts from the Census, 1941 and 1931* (1944), pp. 3, 10.

TABLE 30

ETHNIC ORIGIN OF RURAL DELEGATES TO CCF CONVENTIONS AND TO TWO COOPERATIVE CONVENTIONS
(Percentages)

Nationality	Rural population 1941*	CCF DELEGATES			Cooperative delegates
		All	Over 45 years old	Under 45 years old	
Anglo-Saxon	41.9	59.8	63.0	52.8	75.3
German	15.1	10.3	9.6	11.1	5.6
Ukrainian	10.3	2.5	0.9	4.4	0.0
Scandinavian	10.1	16.3	16.4	16.1	11.2
French	5.0	2.0	1.8	2.2	1.1
Dutch	3.8	1.8	2.2	1.1	3.3
Polish	3.2	0.5	0.0	1.1	0.0
Others	10.6	6.8	6.0	8.3	3.5

* *Farms and Farmers in Canada: Facts from the Census, 1941 and 1931* (1944), p. 10.

Scandinavians, who are the social equals of Britishers in the West, and Anglo-Saxons are disproportionately represented in the CCF rural leadership. In a culture dominated by Anglo-Saxons, persons of British descent tend to be chosen for leadership. Prejudice against "foreigners" makes those of other origins shy away from exposing themselves to criticism by becoming leaders. The same trend holds true if country of birth is considered. Although, according to the census of 1941, 36.0 per cent of Saskatchewan farmers of forty years and over were born in non-English-speaking countries, this was true of only 17.8 per cent of the CCF delegates forty-five years of age or over in 1945.

It is interesting to note that ethnic cleavages seem to be disappearing among the younger generation of CCF leaders. There are 10.2 per cent more non-Anglo-Saxons among the group under forty-five years than among those above that age. The younger members of ethnic groups, who were born in Canada and speak English well, are beginning to assume their proportionate place in rural society. The increase in non-

TABLE 31

RELIGIOUS AFFILIATION OF RURAL DELEGATES TO CCF
CONVENTIONS AND TO TWO COOPERATIVE CONVENTIONS
(Percentages)

		CCF DELEGATES			
Religion	*Total rural population, 1941**	*All*	*Over 45 years old*	*Under 45 years old*	*Cooperative delegates*
Protestant	64.2	86.8	90.2	78.9	90.8
Roman Catholic	30.3	11.7	7.9	17.7	9.2
Greek Orthodox	5.0	2.3	1.5	3.4	1.1

* *Eighth Census of Canada, 1941*, Bulletin A-5.

Anglo-Saxons among the younger and more recent CCF leaders may also reflect the increased electoral support for the CCF among minority ethnic groups.

CCF leaders, as a group, differ significantly from the general rural population in religious affiliation. Here again the minority groups are underrepresented. The relative absence of Catholics among CCF leaders is due to a number of factors, some of which were cited earlier. In the early period of the movement the traditional hostility of the Church toward socialism was directed against the CCF in Saskatchewan. This undoubtedly prevented many Catholic supporters from aligning themselves with the party. Another reason is that most of the Saskatchewan Catholics come from minority ethnic groups—Ukrainians, French, Polish—and therefore are likely to be underrepresented in rural leadership. Protestant prejudice against Catholics is another factor in accounting for the lack of Catholic CCF leaders. The CCF as a movement is not anti-Catholic, but anti-Catholicism has deep roots among many Protestants in Saskatchewan. This religious prejudice has served to keep Catholics out of leading positions in many community institutions. But resistance to the participation of Catholics in the CCF and in community institutions may be decreasing. There are more than twice as many Catholics in the group of CCF leaders below forty-five years of age as in the older group.

The influence of religious affiliation on political behavior becomes even clearer if the denominational differences among Protestants in the CCF are examined. The data in table 32

TABLE 32

PROTESTANT DENOMINATIONS OF CCF
RURAL DELEGATES
(Percentages)

Denomination	Protestant rural population*	Protestant CCF delegates
United Church	34.8	54.5
Lutheran	21.8	20.4
Anglican	16.4	11.5
Mennonite	7.3	0.0
Presbyterian	8.1	6.4
Baptist	3.1	3.0
Total Protestants	100.0	100.0

* *Eighth Census of Canada, 1941*, Bulletin A-5.

reinforce the interpretation of the election results, that membership in the United Church is conducive to support of the CCF, while Anglicans tend to be opposed to the party.

It is significant that the social and economic characteristics of cooperative leaders differ from those of the general rural population in the same way as do those of CCF officials. (See tables 29 and 30.) The cooperative officials and the CCF party leaders are predominantly well to do, Anglo-Saxon, and Protestant. Wealth, Anglo-Saxon origin, and Protestantism are the main objective social factors that one would expect to be associated with status in our culture.[3]

The sample of non-CCF cooperative officials was not large enough to justify any conclusions about the backgrounds of farm leaders who do not support the CCF. Only twenty-one, or 17.7 per cent, of the cooperative delegates who filled out questionnaires were not CCF supporters. One difference between them and the backers of the CCF does stand out, however: 38.1 per cent of those who did not support the CCF were Roman Catholics, which suggests anew that the opposition of the Church to socialism has been a major factor in deterring Catholic farmers from backing the CCF.

These facts tend to confirm the earlier interpretation that the CCF is not a radical movement for change within the rural social structure, but the spokesman of the rural com-

TABLE 33

OCCUPATIONAL BACKGROUND OF 230 URBAN CCF LEADERS
(Percentages)

Occupation	Convention delegates	Constituency executives	Provincial Council and constituency presidents	Total (230)
Workers	45.9	63.6	52.2	50.0
Business and professional men	43.4	24.7	38.1	34.3
Teachers	11.2	11.7	9.6	11.3

munity organized on a class basis to preserve itself by changing the larger social order of which it is a part. The CCF movement is a direct continuation of the earlier efforts of the Saskatchewan rural community to create a stabilized rural economy. It is the political voice of the rural community, and is led by the "normal" community leaders.

CCF support in the urban districts of Saskatchewan is largely from the working class. This urban base is reflected in the backgrounds of the party's nonfarmer leaders. Most of the working-class leaders of the CCF are skilled workers:

84.0 per cent of the worker delegates to the 1945 and 1946 conventions were members of skilled trades, as were 89.5 per cent of the working-class members of the constituency executives and the Provincial Council. These leaders of the CCF were among the higher-paid labor groups in the province, earning an average of $2,454 a year in 1945.

Of all the CCF labor leaders about whom there are data, 51.3 per cent were railroad workers. The six CCF labor members of the 1944 legislature were all railroad employees. Skilled railroaders in western Canada have a special status. They are among the highest-paid workers, often earning as much as many small businessmen. Their trade-unions are the oldest and strongest in the nonindustrial, agricultural West. For a long time the westerners' only direct contact with organized labor was through the unions of railroad workers. When the CCF was first organized, the railroaders virtually symbolized "Labor" to the farmers. They were the "Labor men" whom the agrarians in the CCF sought out to form joint Farmer-Labor committees, as the following statements from a CCF leader indicate.

I had an opportunity to confer with one of the leading *Railway* men at Wynyard regarding the political situation and I am told that the matter of political action has been discussed and that almost everyone of the *Railway employees* has stated at one time or another during the past six months that they will never again vote for the two existing political parties.

In my opinion the Wynyard Constituency Committee should appoint a delegation to call upon Mr. Elliott Sherman, who is Mayor of the town of Wynyard, and suggest to him that the *Labor men* be called together for a conference and appoint a representative of *Labor* on your Constituency Committee. I trust that you will take immediate action in this matter because although some of the *Railway men* at Wynyard have been known to be closely allied with the Liberals and Conservatives, it is very apparent to me that they have now changed their mind, and in a political fight every vote counts.

I may say for your information that I have had a number of meetings with *Labor people* here, and we are forming a branch of the Independent Labor Party in Saskatoon. We have been working at night and have drafted a Federal and Provincial Policy. We are meeting again on Friday night to draft a Civic policy. After the Organization Committee have drafted a full program, we will call the members together and complete the organization. I am in hopes that when the party is formed, they will advise the *Labor people* at points such as Wynyard to lend their support to the Farmers' candidate, and we in turn will advise farmers in City Constituencies to join with the *Labor people*.[4]

Many of the railroad workers entered the CCF at a fairly early date as representatives of Labor. The depression had reduced their income greatly, and the new Farmer-Labor Party gave them an opportunity to join the organized agrarians in a political bloc that would give them added strength. The urban areas were, therefore, won to the CCF in the same way as were the rural districts. The upper strata of the working class, the organized skilled workers, joined the movement first and became its leaders. This is confirmed by the organizational affiliations of the group. Of working-class leaders of the CCF, 60 per cent were members of trade-unions, and 40.0 per cent have held official posts in union locals.

CCF working-class leaders are similar to rural leaders in their personal background also. Working-class leaders belong to the culturally dominant group of Anglo-Saxon Protestants. Their religious affiliations indicate the positive relationship between United Church membership and CCF support as well as the negative influence of the Catholic Church on the movement.

TABLE 34

ETHNIC ORIGIN AND RELIGIOUS AFFILIATION OF WORKING-CLASS CCF LEADERS

Ethnic origin	Percentage	Religious affiliation	Percentage
Anglo-Saxon	77.8	United Church	53.8
Scandinavian	11.1	Anglican	15.4
French Canadian	2.2	Lutheran	11.5
German	4.4	Baptist	3.8
Ukrainian	3.3	Presbyterian	3.8
		Roman Catholic	3.8
		Greek Orthodox	7.7

The urban business and professional groups overwhelmingly support the Liberal and Conservative parties, though a growing number of them have been voting CCF in recent years. The contrast in the class electoral support of the three main parties is reflected in the economic backgrounds of their leaders, as indicated in table 37. The majority of leaders of the old parties belong to the urban middle class, while CCF leaders are predominantly farmers, and to a lesser extent workers.

The CCF has made overtures in recent years to small businessmen, urging them to support the new party to protect themselves from the monopolists. This appeal has not been very successful. The rural members of the CCF regard the small merchants as part of the exploitative profit system which they would like to eliminate through cooperatives. The small-town merchant, in turn, looks upon the cooperatives as a major threat to his security, at least as great a threat as chain stores and mail-order houses. This identification of the CCF with the cooperative movement prevents the party from appealing successfully to small businessmen.

The fact remains, however, that a minority of the business and professional groups do actively support the CCF. The data available about the backgrounds of these people are scanty, but they suggest certain interesting hypotheses about the causes of this deviant class behavior. Urban middle-class leaders of the CCF differ significantly from farming and

TABLE 35

ETHNIC ORIGIN OF CCF LEADERS
(Percentages)

Nationality	Farmers	Workers	Business and professional men
Anglo-Saxon	59.8	77.8	36.7
German	10.3	4.4	10.0
Ukrainian	2.5	3.3	20.0
Scandinavian	16.3	11.1	13.3
French	2.0	2.2	3.3
Dutch	1.8	....	6.7
Polish	0.5	....	3.3
Others	6.8	....	6.7

working-class leaders in one essential respect—ethnic origins.

The data are suggestive of the relationship between a marginal social position and radical political behavior in members of an upper economic class. The CCF in Saskatchewan is the party of workers and farmers. Economic constraints on these two groups led them to accept the need for widespread social reform designed to better their economic condition. They were led into the new social movement by men of their own class who had both status and organizational experience.

The business and professional groups, on the contrary, decisively rejected the new party, which was directed against them as the local representatives of the capitalist system. To support the CCF, therefore, would be abnormal class behavior for a member of the urban middle class. The few who did so were regarded as "crackpots" by other businessmen. Most of the social and economic coercions on middle-class individuals tended to keep them supporting the old parties, which were controlled by men having the same class background.

The middle-class people who joined the CCF were, however, precisely those who were not accepted socially in the urban business community. They belonged, predominantly, to minority ethnic groups; these groups were not part of the urban "upper class," which in Saskatchewan is largely Anglo-Saxon. This is true even in areas where the population of the surrounding countryside is composed overwhelmingly of members of minority ethnic groups.[5] The non-Anglo-Saxon businessmen are often newcomers to the business life of the towns, being former farmers or children of farmers. They tend to retain their ties with the minority ethnic group of the surrounding countryside, and remain socially marginal to the business community. This was clearly brought out in a study of a small, predominantly Anglo-Saxon town in a Ukrainian farming district. According to one young Ukrainian merchant, "The Anglo-Saxons made it plain that they were better than the Ukrainians and didn't want us, so the Ukrainians said, 'To hell with you, we can get along by ourselves.' "[6] The two CCF Ukrainian members of the Saskatchewan legislature in 1944 were small-town merchants who came from farm families. Both reported close ties with the Ukrainian rural community.

The data suggest that "deviant" class political behavior can be explained partially by other "deviant" sociological characteristics. Socially, the businessmen of the ethnic minority are part of the lower-class group of the Saskatchewan population. They are not exploited economically, but they are deprived socially of many of the privileges that usually go with business status. The cleavage between them and the Anglo-Saxon "upper class" is often as great as the split between the farmers and the business community. Subject to the cross pressures of contradictory statuses, many members of the minority groups have seen fit to identify themselves with the political party which is opposed by the "upper class" and which promises to strike at the community power of these dominant groups.

The acceptance by some CCF agrarians of the minority ethnic members of the business community as party leaders is probably related to the fact that in Saskatchewan ethnic ties within groups which are rejected by the majority of the community outweigh economic class cleavages. The CCF Ukrainian farmer will accept the guidance of a Ukrainian merchant, whereas the Anglo-Saxon farmer will not follow a businessman from his own national group.

Members of a dominant economic class who belong to a minority cultural group and are not socially accepted by the rest of their class tend to participate disproportionately in political movements whose programs appear to be inconsistent with upper-class economic interests, but which give minority-group members of the upper class the possibility of assuming higher social status, or of striking at those who deny them the status that should be a concomitant of their economic position. The contrast between the ethnic backgrounds of CCF and old-party urban middle-class leaders leaves little room for doubt that this is true in the province of Saskatchewan.

The Saskatchewan CCF data on the backgrounds of "upper-class" radical leaders are similar to those found in European socialist movements. Robert Michels, the foremost analyst of Social Democracy before the First World War, re-

TABLE 36

ETHNIC AFFILIATION OF BUSINESS AND PROFESSIONAL MEN WHO
ARE LEADERS OF SASKATCHEWAN POLITICAL PARTIES
(Percentages)

Nationality	CCF leaders*	Liberal leaders†	Conservative leaders‡
Anglo-Saxon	36.7	84.7	96.4
Ukrainian	20.0	1.7	0.0
French Canadian	3.3	10.2	0.0
Scandinavian	13.3	1.7	1.2
German	10.0	0.0	2.4
Mennonite	6.7	1.7	0.0
Polish	3.3	0.0	0.0
Others	6.7	0.0	0.0

SOURCE: *Canadian Parliamentary Guide*, 1935, 1939, 1945; and interviews with leaders of the three political parties.

* 68 convention delegates, 1945 and 1946; constituency officials, 1946.

† 83 members of the legislature and candidates in 1938 and 1944, and 1946 constituency officials.

‡ 59 members of the legislature in 1934, candidates in 1944, and constituency officials in 1946.

ported that the Jews, who constituted the principal minority group in the ethnically more homogeneous European countries, played a disproportionate role in the socialist movement. Middle-class and upper-class Jews, who had an inferior social status, were attracted to a movement that promised to eliminate the causes of Jewish inferior status. Michels' explanation of the position of the Jew in the socialist movement also suggests that deviant economic class behavior is related to marginal social status.

The origin of this predominant position [of the Jews in the European socialist movement] is to be found, as far at least as concerns Germany and the countries of Eastern Europe, in the peculiar position which the Jews have occupied and in many respects still occupy. The legal emancipation of the Jews has not been followed by their social and moral emancipation. In large sections of the German people a hatred of the Jews and the spirit of the Jew-baiter still prevail, and contempt for the Jew is a permanent feeling. The Jew's chances in public life are adversely affected; he is practically excluded from the judicial profession, from a military career, and from official employment. . . .

Even when they are rich, the Jews constitute, at least in eastern Europe, a category of persons who are excluded from the social advantages which the prevailing political, economic, and intellectual system ensures for the corresponding portion of the Gentile population: Society in the narrower sense of the term is distrustful of them, and public opinion is unfavorable to them.[7]

The question will naturally be raised, If the CCF is the party of the leaders of the Saskatchewan rural community, where do the two old parties get their leaders? Unfortunately, no data comparable to the material on the CCF could be obtained, as neither of the old parties held a convention during the course of the field work. A statistical breakdown of biographical material in the *Canadian Parliamentary Guide* and of data obtained in interviews with Liberal and Conservative leaders suggests that in the older parties the leaders come from the business and professional groups, even though Saskatchewan is preponderantly a rural area. The data in table 37 help confirm the interpretation that the political cleavages in Saskatchewan life are closely related to economic class cleavages.

There are, however, large numbers of Saskatchewan farmers who did not support the CCF in 1944. Obviously, this large anti-CCF rural minority must have a leadership structure. One can, however, do little more than suggest tentative hypotheses as to its nature. Many of the non-CCF rural leaders may be comparable to the CCF urban middle-class leaders; that is, they are not so well integrated in the rural community as their CCF neighbors and are therefore exposed to a larger number of noneconomic cross pressures. Since the old parties are predominantly urban middle-class organizations, the farmers who are active in those parties may have stronger social or economic ties with urban life than do the members of the CCF. This may come about through active membership in a church such as the Anglican or Catholic churches, where religious ties outweigh class cleavages, or through membership in lodges and fraternal orders such as the Orange Order.

Second, there are a large number of cultural subgroups within the Saskatchewan rural community that are not sup-

TABLE 37

DISTRIBUTION OF OCCUPATIONS OF LEADERS OF
SASKATCHEWAN POLITICAL PARTIES
(Percentages)

Party	Business and professional men	Farmers	Workers	Teachers
Liberal:				
Executive, 1946	65.0	20.0	5.0	0.0
Constituency presidents, 1946	41.0	41.0	6.0	2.4
Members of legislature, 1934	46.5	46.5	2.3	2.3
Members of legislature, 1938	56.2	34.4	3.1	3.1
Conservative:				
Provincial Council, 1946	63.9	26.7	5.3	2.7
Members of legislature, 1929	58.4	20.8	4.2	4.2
Candidates, 1938	54.2	20.8	4.2	16.7
Candidates, 1944	30.0	45.0	5.0	7.5
Social Credit:				
Candidates, 1938	45.0	20.0	10.0	10.0
CCF				
Constituency Executive, 1946	5.1	75.1	13.1	2.4
Provincial Council and constituency presidents, 1946	13.1	65.6	17.9	3.3
Members of legislature, 1944	6.4	59.6	12.8	14.9

SOURCE: *Canadian Parliamentary Guide*, 1930, 1935, 1939, 1945; and interviews with leaders of the Liberal, Conservative, and CCF parties.

porters of the CCF. The Mennonites, the French Canadians, the Catholic population as a whole, and other minority groups have never been completely integrated into the general rural community. They therefore have an independent leadership structure, which differs from the dominant cultural group in its reactions to external social and economic pressures.

A third possible source of anti-CCF rural leadership may come from the large group of farmers who have had personal ties with, or received favors from, the Liberal Party, which dominated the political life of the province and of the nation during most of the twentieth century. The well-organized provincial Liberal machine placed many farmers under personal obligation as a result of its effective distribution of patronage and Tammany Hall type of service.[8] Until the CCF came on the scene in the 'thirties, most of the officials of the rural municipalities were connected with the Liberal Party, and many of them probably remained loyal to the Party. These personal relations with the Liberals undoubtedly constituted one of the effective cross pressures working against the CCF in the rural community.

The suggestions about the sources of Liberal leadership, however, must remain in the category of unproved hypotheses until further research is done on the Saskatchewan political scene in particular and on the effect of cross pressures on political behavior generally. We know that group affiliations determine the social behavior of individuals, but we know little about the strength of group affiliations, especially those related to class actions in cross-pressure situations. Marxists assume that class position always takes priority. This may be true in terms of long-run historical analysis, but we have no systematic information on what happens in concrete situations in different societies.

The growth of the CCF was a result of a drastic shift in the political loyalties and attitudes of two economic classes, farmers and workers. This change may be related to the economic constraints on these classes.

Anyone who is required to change his habits of life and his habitual relations to his fellow-men will feel the discrepancy between the method of life required of him by the newly arisen exigencies and the traditional scheme of life to which he is accustomed. It is the individuals placed in this position who have the liveliest incentive to reconstruct the received scheme of life and are most readily persuaded to accept new standards; and it is through the need of the means of livelihood that men are placed in such a position. The pressure exerted by the environment upon the group, and making for a readjustment of the group's scheme of life, impinges upon the members of the group in the form of pecuniary exigencies; and it is owing to this fact—that external forces are in great part translated into the form of pecuniary or economic exigencies— . . . that we can say that the forces which count toward a readjustment of institutions in any modern industrial community are chiefly economic forces; or more specifically, these forces take the form of pecuniary pressure.[9]

It is obvious that social change is not a simple reflex action. Economic pressures, like all other social forces, operate through individuals. The degree to which an individual or group is affected by such pressures varies according to position in the social structure. The question of who is most affected by changing social pressures, who leads the members of a group or class to accept a change, has never been answered satisfactorily. Various theorists have suggested that receptivity to new ideas is related to marginal social status. Such an acute observer as Karl Mannheim has stated that psychopathological types are the innovators, the leaders of change.

There can be little doubt that maladjusted persons are prone to accept the need for change before the rest of society. It is highly dubious, however, whether they are actually the informal molders of new opinions at the "grass-roots" level. The statistical data on the backgrounds of CCF leaders demonstrate that in Saskatchewan a radical movement for economic reform was led at the grass-roots level by those possessing status within the farming and working classes. The local leaders of the party were not the marginal or deviant members of the society, but rather the old class leaders. This process was very apparent in the rural communities of Saskatchewan, since class and community leaders were largely the same people. A class or a community will not usually accept the leadership of its deviant members. The CCF was able to grow rapidly in Saskatchewan because the "normal" class leaders were the first to become members of the party.

Recent sociological researches have cast some light on the social forces that determine public opinion. Studies of voting behavior indicate that group membership is the foremost factor in affecting vote decision; that is, persons in the same religious group or social class tend to vote similarly. Paul Lazarsfeld suggests that individuals who belong to formal organizations composed of persons with the same social and economic background as themselves are more likely to vote with the majority of their socioeconomic group than are individuals who are not integrated into their class through formal organizational affiliations.[10]

Concretely, this meant, in the United States, that the proportion of Republicans was larger among those with high socioeconomic status, who belonged to various high-status organizations, than it was among those with the same class background who were not members of such associations. Among the working class, those who belonged to trade unions were more likely to be Democrats than were the nonjoiners. These facts are explained by Lazarsfeld as follows:

. . . people who live together under similar external conditions are likely to develop similar needs and interests. They tend to see the world through the same colored glasses; they tend to apply to common experiences common interpretations. They will approve of a political candidate who has achieved success in their own walk of life; they will approve of programs which are couched in terms taken from their own occupations and adapted to the moral standards of the groups in which they have a common "belonging."[11]

The research findings on the effect of group structure in reinforcing the political attitudes of members are based on analyses of comparatively static electoral situations in the United States. The basic core of Democratic and Republican strength has not changed since it has been under the observation of social scientists. In Saskatchewan, however, where fundamental shifts have taken place within a comparatively brief period, the data on CCF electoral support and leaders would appear to contradict the findings reported in *The People's Choice*. In 1934, in Saskatchewan, the CCF was a minority party among all social classes. On the basis of Lazarsfeld's analysis of a comparatively static situation, those who belonged to class organizations, such as cooperatives and trade-unions, should have voted for the old parties, as did the majority of the class. In fact, however, the members of class organizations were the leaders and first supporters of the CCF.

The data indicate that when the attitudes of a class are in flux, because of changing social and economic pressures, those who are most thoroughly integrated in the class through formal organizations are the first to change. In Saskatchewan it was the local leaders of the Wheat Pool, of the trade-unions, who were the first to join the CCF, the first to become cognizant of the need for change. Their position made it incumbent on them to make decisions and set new patterns of behavior when traditional methods were no longer adequate. These leaders were in the best position to realize the long-range implications for people in their economic position. The unorganized mass became CCF supporters only gradually, following the organizationally active members of their class.

A study of Saskatchewan voting behavior today would, however, probably result in findings similar to those obtained by Lazarsfeld from the 1940 elections in the United States. The political situation in Saskatchewan is now relatively static. The "normal" class behavior for workers and farmers is to vote CCF. An unpublished study of cooperative members in Saskatchewan indicates that about 75 per cent of the members of the Wheat Pool and other cooperatives voted CCF in 1944, though only about 58 per cent of the total farming population did so.[12] Those who now belong to formal organizations among the farmers are more prone to vote with the majority of the class than are those who are isolated. Among urban middle-class groups, however, isolated individuals are more likely to be members of the CCF than those who are integrated in organized group activity.

It is necessary, therefore, to modify the assumptions about the marginality of leaders of new social movements. When a large social class or group is changing its attitudes, the normal integrated leaders of the class are the first to change. They are more exposed to the social pressures on the class than are marginal, deviant, or apathetic members. The relationship between marginal social position and radical political behavior holds true only for radicals who come from the upper classes.

In small, isolated political parties such as the Communist parties of the United States and Canada and the Socialist Party in the United States, one would probably find, as Harold Lasswell did in his study of the Communist Party of Chicago, that the members and the leaders of these groups are disproportionately maladjusted socially. This is true, however, only of small parties, which are not genuine expressions of large-scale social pressures. These small parties are themselves marginal to the total society. If a small radical party succeeds in becoming the political voice of a large group, it will necessarily attract the normal, integrated members of the class. The CCF, starting as a large movement, was therefore led from the beginning by the normal class leaders.

NOTES

1. "By the very nature of their role reform leaders tended to be people devoid of 'respectable' attributes. . . . The influences which prompted people to break from established institutions and to take up the case of reform often increased opposition against them. Desire to escape from the boredom of routine tasks, inability to secure a living or recognition in any other way, love of power which was experienced in swaying large audiences or large reading publics, and personal 'grudges' against persons in authority, may have mingled, along with other motives, with the sincere conviction of doing good." S. D. Clark, *The Social Development of Canada* (University of Toronto Press, 1942), pp. 14–15.

2. A study of members and leaders of Communist organizations suggested that they come from marginal groups, i.e., they tend to be members of minority, foreign-born, or ethnic groups, or people who are personally insecure. Harold Lasswell and Dorothy Blumenstock, *World Revolutionary Propaganda* (New York, Alfred A. Knopf, 1939), pp. 277–300.

3. The findings in this study of rural cooperative and CCF leadership in Saskatchewan are similar to those of other sociological studies of rural leadership. In the United States, higher economic status and farm ownership are correlated with active participation and leadership in farmers' organizations. Dwight Sanderson, *Rural Sociology and Social Organization* (New York, John Wiley and Sons, 1942), pp. 598–600. "Cooperatives are more successful in enlisting the better educated, the more experienced, wealthier farmers than the others, and farm owners will join more readily than tenants. . . . In the main, cooperators belong to more organizations like churches, farm bureaus, lodges, and have a higher standard of living, more conveniences and more equipment than noncooperators." J. H. Kolb and E. de S. Brunner, *A Study of Rural Society* (New York, Houghton Mifflin Co., 1935), p. 353.

Ethnic influences in the United States are similar to those in Saskatchewan. Segregated ethnic colonies participate much less in organizations such as the Farm Bureau and cooperatives than do the Anglo-Saxons. Farmers of Scandinavian and Teutonic origin participate more than those coming from Slavic or Latin countries. E. de S. Brunner, *Immigrant Farmers and Their Children* (New York, Doubleday, Doran and Co., 1929), chap. v.

4. Letter from Frank Eliason to William Thomson, president, Wynyard Local Council, U.F.C., August 6, 1931, p. 2.

5. Jim Giffen, unpublished master's thesis, University of Toronto, 1947.

6. *Ibid.*

7. Robert Michels, *Political Parties* (New York, Hearst's International Library Co., 1915), pp. 260–61.

8. Escott Reid, "The Saskatchewan Liberal Machine before 1929," *Canadian Journal of Economics and Political Science,* February, 1936, pp. 27–40.

9. Thorstein Veblen, *The Theory of the Leisure Class* (New York, Modern Library, 1934), pp. 195–96.

10. Paul Lazarsfeld, Bernard Berelson, and Hazel Gaudet, *The People's Choice* (2d ed.; Columbia University Press, 1948), pp. 145–47.

11. *Ibid.*, pp. 148–49.

12. The sources of this study, based on a random sample of the Saskatchewan population, are confidential.

10

SOCIAL STRUCTURE
AND POLITICAL ACTIVITY

VARIOUS OBSERVERS of the North American scene have called attention to the problem of mass passivity and political apathy in our culture. Myrdal has pointed out that the masses in America "are accustomed to being static and receptive. They are not daring, but long for security. They do not know how to cooperate and how to pool risks and sacrifices for a common goal. They do not meet much. They do not organize. They do not speak for themselves: they are the listeners in America. They seldom elect representatives from their own midst to Congress, to state legislatures or to city councils. They rather support friendly leaders from the upper strata, particularly lawyers."[1]

Myrdal's description is accurate for most parts of the United States and Canada. It does not, however, give a picture of Saskatchewan political activity. The Saskatchewan CCF has succeeded in involving more people in direct political activity than any other party in American or Canadian history, with the possible exception of certain similar farmers' parties.[2] In 1945 the party had a dues-paying membership of 31,858, or approximately 4 per cent of the total population and 8 per cent of the 1944 electorate. CCF membership in the province has reached the equivalent of a national dues-paying membership of about 500,000 in Canada and 6,000,000 in the United States. One can hardly speak here of mass passivity. An examination of the factors related to the attainment of so large a membership should throw light on some of the reasons for political apathy in other areas of the continent.

The most important single factor differentiating the Saskatchewan social scene from other regions is the high degree

TABLE 38

ELECTIVE POSITIONS, RURAL SASKATCHEWAN

Position	No. of local groups	No. of officials in each	Total
Municipal council	304	7	2,128
School-board member	5,184	3	15,552
Hospital-board official	79	6	474
Telephone-board director	1,127	5	5,635
Wheat Pool and other marketing cooperatives	1,257	10	12,570
Cooperative store	519	8	4,152
Community hall	203	5	1,015
Miscellaneous cooperatives	48	5	240
United Farmers, etc.*	....	..	......
Lodge*	....	..	......
Church group*	....	..	......
Political party*	....	..	......
Minimum total			41,766

* Figures not available.

of individual participation in community organizations in rural districts. There are from 40,000 to 60,000 different elective rural posts that must be filled by the 125,000 farmers. There is, then, approximately one position available for every two or three farmers. Table 38 indicates the nature of these posts.

The large number of positions in rural Saskatchewan does not mean that one out of every two or three farmers is a community official, for many rural leaders are active in a number of organizations. In most communities the same people are on the rural municipal councils, the boards of directors of local cooperative stores, and the executive of the United Farmers of Canada (Saskatchewan Section). A rough estimate, drawn from many interviews and more than 800 questionnaires filled out by Saskatchewan rural leaders, indicates, however, that at least 15 per cent of the farmers hold community posts to which they have been elected by their neighbors. This proportion of formal community leaders to total population is much larger than has been attained in any urban area. It is probably also greater than that found in other rural areas, for Saskatchewan has the largest cooperative movement on the continent and more local governmental units than any other American rural state.[3]

This situation is a result of an almost unique combination of factors that have created the formal structural conditions for widespread individual participation in community affairs. The farmers have been faced, in the forty years since the province was created, with a series of major social and economic challenges requiring the establishment of a large number of community institutions to meet them. Pioneering on the unsettled prairie in the two decades before the First World War, farmers had to establish local rural governments, hospitals, schools, and a telephone system. They were faced with the hazards of a one-crop wheat economy that was subject to extreme fluctuations in income because of variability in grain prices and climatic conditions. Their position as isolated individual producers and consumers at the end of the distribution system left them exposed to monopolistic exploitation by the railroads, the grain companies, and the retailers. Through the formation of cooperatives and political pressure groups, Saskatchewan farmers sought to improve their competitive position in the fluctuating price economy and to reduce the cost of the articles they bought. All these community and economic associations had to be organized by a handful of people.

The area of effective community action in the wheat economy of Saskatchewan is necessarily limited by distance. Wheat farms are large, and wheat regions are consequently sparsely settled. The rural municipalities, the local governmental units, contain less than 400 families, and each municipality (about eighteen square miles in area) contains a number of distinct communities. There are about 1,500 railroad stops, over 1,100 rural telephone companies, and more than 5,000 local school districts in Saskatchewan.[4]

The sheer need for extensive community organization would not necessarily result in widespread participation in community affairs by farmers. In many rural areas on this continent, the community institutions serving farmers are controlled by members of urban business and professional groups of the neighboring towns. County government positions and consolidated school-district posts are open to non-farmers in many agricultural districts. Within the rural areas of the Southern States or in parts of California, where significant social and economic cleavage exists within the rural community, the wealthier and upper-class farmers are the formal community leaders, and the bulk of the poorer farmers are politically apathetic.

Rural Saskatchewan, however, is socially a "one-class" community. Differences in income and status do exist within individual rural communities, but they are not large enough to bring about the emergence of distinct social classes. The wheat farmers have more in common with each other economically and socially than with any other group. The organized community life of the agrarian population is conducted independently of the activities of neighboring towns and cities. Very little intermingling takes place between the cliques of the town and those of the countryside.[5] Almost all the formal community positions must be held by farmers. Neither the rural municipal councils nor the rural school boards are legally open to town lawyers or other members of the urban middle class. The cooperatives are almost completely rural organizations.

Under these conditions, any farmer who has executive ability is forced to accept community responsibility. A large portion of the population has become accustomed to playing an active role in different organizations. Rural leaders must conduct meetings, write reports, make speeches, and recruit members. One informant described the effect on his father of being in a leading position:

My father was elected vice-president of the S.G.G.A. local early in the 'twenties. He hadn't wanted the job, but he was a leading farmer in the district and had been a member for a long time, so some of the other officials prevailed on him to take the post.

Shortly after he was elected, the local sponsored a meeting by a Progressive M.P. The chairman of the lodge took sick and my father was told that he would have to preside over the meeting. He tried to get out of it, for he had never made a speech in his life. He couldn't, however, and had to preside. For days before the meeting he stopped all work and went around the house reciting a five-minute speech which he had memorized. The family almost went crazy listening to it.

On the day of the meeting, he delivered the speech and

afterward was complimented on his ability by the M.P. After that he lost his fear. He would chair meetings and gradually began to make speeches for the organization. By the time the CCF was organized he had no fear in facing a meeting of hundreds and speaking for hours. Before he died he must have delivered hundreds of speeches at CCF meetings, co-operative meetings, and other farmers' gatherings.

As officials in cooperative and governmental units, local farm leaders study and make decisions on the policies of larger organizations and governments. The members of school boards, hospital boards, and rural municipal councils become acquainted with the problems of taxation and administration, and with the policies of provincial and federal governments. The leaders in farmers' cooperatives and educational organizations must act on the policies of governments that affect them. The 11,000 or more Wheat Pool committeemen are kept up to date by the Pool's educational department on all national and international aspects of the wheat problem. They learn at once of government decisions that may affect their economic position. The Pool has sixteen field men who visit the committees periodically to keep them informed of problems of the cooperative movement.[6]

This structure of grass-roots participation provides direct channels of communication between the mass of farmers and their leaders. The Saskatchewan rural community is highly receptive to outside pressures and can be quickly mobilized by its leaders. A striking example of this mobilization took place in 1941–42. Wheat prices were fixed by the Canadian federal government at 70 cents a bushel in 1941. The Wheat Pool had demanded a higher price, but the government refused because the Nazi conquest of Europe had closed many Canadian markets. Crop conditions were bad and the farmers who had anticipated a period of war prosperity began to fear that 1941 would be another depression year for them, though the prices of goods they bought were rising. Wheat Pool committees passed resolutions demanding that the provincial organization take action to gain a higher price and crop insurance. The Pool leaders organized meetings throughout the province to discuss the problem. "Farmers by the thousands flocked to these meetings, leaving their threshing machine standing idle in many instances, in order to raise their voices in the interests of a better deal in agriculture."[7]

The Wheat Pool officials, who are relatively conservative, desired to limit the farmers' protest to resolutions and to personal pressure on members of Parliament. This, however, did not satisfy the farmers of Saskatchewan. A grass-roots demand for action swept the province. One militant old farmer described what happened at one Pool meeting.

When in 1941 things got intolerable and we resorted to mass meetings I was at the one in Swift Current. I was never at a meeting where the audience was so hostile to the platform. You could feel it like a chill through the church and there were noted men on it too.

A little old fellow got up and moved that we send two men from each sub-district to Ottawa and demand dollar wheat. There was a loud guffaw, but he soon got a seconder and it carried unanimously. The point I want to make is this: it was right from the grass roots, there were no paid officials on this, though there was one on the platform. The idea went through the Province like a prairie fire. Forty thousand dollars were collected in spite of the determined opposition of the Liberal machine. Four hundred men were sent to Ottawa; preachers, sinners, and lawyers. Twenty cents more per bushel was eventually secured.[8]

The "March on Ottawa" is but one of a number of movements which the dirt farmers began and carried through against the opposition of the bureaucracy of farmers' organizations and of the government.[9] Though the forces making for bureaucratic control of the farmers' movement exist in Saskatchewan as they do elsewhere, the structural conditions for rank-and-file participation and for resistance to such control are stronger there than in most other areas. There are comparatively few paid positions in the farmers' cooperative and educational movements. The secondary leaders of all the farm groups are working farmers who are just as much affected by economic pressures and general currents of opinion as are the rank and file. Unless these leaders express the feelings of their neighbors, who have chosen them, they will be replaced by others who do. The extent of direct participation means that the farmers' movement must always be receptive to the needs of the members. Further, it results in heightened awareness by the farmers of large-scale political and economic events.

This widespread activity makes for rapid political changes. Its effects can be seen in the influence of the "March on Ottawa" movement on the growth of the CCF. In 1941 the CCF was the only party to support fully the demands of the organized farmers. The federal Liberal government refused to meet some of them. This fact was known to the rural leaders and, through them, the knowledge spread to most of the farmers of the province. Between August 31, 1941, and July 31, 1942, the period of the agitation resulting in the "March on Ottawa," CCF membership rose from 4,460 to 9,813.[10] This increase is highly significant, for it occurred between elections at a time when there was no prospect of another election and party membership normally could be expected to decline.

In the past the social organization of the economy—the fact that almost all the farmers were wheat farmers and therefore had common interests and problems—meant that "solutions" to problems in one area were rapidly accepted in others. Each rural community in Saskatchewan is a replica of every other. An example of rural flexibility in adopting a common solution to a community problem can be seen in the rapid spread of the municipal doctor scheme, which began in the early 'twenties. Saskatchewan farmers have always found it difficult to secure adequate medical care at a reasonable cost. There was often a rapid turnover in physicians and it was difficult to get good ones. In 1921 the rural municipality of Sarnia decided to hire a doctor on salary, so that farmers could be assured of medical services and the physician would be guaranteed his salary.[11] This plan proved successful, and gradually spread until, by 1944, in spite of opposition from the organized medical profession, one-third of the rural municipalities of Saskatchewan had doctors on salary. Once it had proved itself in a few areas, the system was accepted and advertised throughout the province by the organized farmers' movement. The United Farmers of Canada (Saskatchewan Section) spread circulars and other propaganda materials, such as the following:

At present we are committed to pooling our wheat and other farm products. The municipal doctor scheme is in reality a pooling of our doctor bills. Or we might look on it as an insurance against unduly high doctor bills in any one year—an equalization scheme. . . .

In no case where the municipal doctor scheme has been tried has there been any complaint from either ratepayers or doctors. In —— Municipality during eight years under this scheme their death rate is much below the average for the province and they have had no maternal deaths during this time. . . .

For additional information before voting on this important question, attend a meeting to be held in the Orange Hall on Friday, December 7, at 3 P.M. sharp. The meeting will be addressed by Mr. —— of the Research Department of the United Farmers of Canada. Mr. —— and Mr. ——, Secretary-Treasurer and Reeve, respectively, of the Municipality.[12]

The rapid acceptance of new ideas and movements in Saskatchewan can be attributed mainly to the high degree of organization. The small rural communities are forced to adjust to changing economic and social situations. Interest in political and economic matters is continually being stimulated. Farmers derive most of their ideas and knowledge of larger problems and policies from well-informed neighbors who hold community posts.

The Wheat Pool, the cooperatives, the agrarian Progressive Party of the 1920's, and the CCF were all built rapidly through this structure of organized farmer opinion. The role of the social structure of the western wheat belt in facilitating the rise of new movements has never been sufficiently appreciated by historians and sociologists. To the economic and cultural factors usually associated with the development of these movements should be added the variable of social structure. Repeated challenges and crises forced the western farmers to create many more community institutions (especially cooperatives and economic pressure groups) than are necessary in a more stable area. These groups in turn provided a structural basis for immediate action in critical situations.

Though it was a new radical party, the CCF did not have to build up an organization from scratch. It was organized from the start by the local "class" and community leaders of rural Saskatchewan. The fact that the province was so well organized on an occupational basis enabled the new party to obtain the support of the politically conscious community leaders. By the early 1940's, CCF committees, composed in the main of the same people who were the officials of the other rural organizations, were operating in almost every district in the province. It was this "machine" that brought the CCF to power.

Today the CCF has become the political voice of the organized agrarian community. The organized farmers are brought into direct contact with "their" government by active participation in a class political party that controls the state.

The basic unit of political organization in rural Saskatchewan is the poll, the smallest voting district. Each provincial constituency is divided into from one hundred to two hundred polls. The CCF has attempted to build up in each district a working committee of two or three people who will take charge of CCF educational work among the one hundred to two hundred voters in the poll. Above the local organizations is the constituency. A CCF constituency has a committee of twelve to twenty-five members and an executive committee of seven to twelve members. The committees are elected at annual conventions, which are attended by three delegates from each poll. The leading body of the entire party is the Provincial Council, which has representatives from each constituency and meets several times a year. The provincial party organization supervises the work of each constituency body. Between Council meetings, the party is governed by an executive body of nine. This provincial organization is controlled by the annual provincial convention. Each constituency convention elects ten delegates to the provincial convention. The convention elects top party officers and determines policy.[13]

If the formal pattern of the CCF party organization were actually followed, about 24,000 people would be active party members, either as members of poll committees or as delegates to the party conventions and committees. Actually, this optimum figure is never reached, for many districts have no active poll committees. In recent years the average attendance at the fifty annual CCF constituency conventions has been about 100 delegates, 5,000 people in all. Many more electors, however, are active in the local organizations than attend as convention delegates. One could safely estimate that between 10,000 and 15,000 people take part in the actual operation of the party.

Between elections, this activity does not include much formal party work. Poll committees usually meet once or twice a year to discuss the work of the local and larger party bodies. They arrange public meetings for party leaders and enroll new members. In some areas, committees meet regularly to discuss party policy and to analyze books and outlines suggested by the provincial office. The constituency committees, which have about 1,000 members, have much greater responsibilities and consequently meet from six to twelve times a year. These committees are the grass-roots bodies which influence the work of the CCF members of the legislature and the provincial party.

The fact that the majority of CCF members and officials are not continuously active in party work does not mean that they are not acting politically in other community roles. Most of the active CCF members have administrative tasks in rural organizations. They are members of local cooperative store boards, Wheat Pool committees, and U.F.C. executive bodies, and do not differentiate between their activities in these organizations and in the CCF. One informant expressed this feeling clearly.

It's really all one movement that we have here. We are building socialism through the Wheat Pool, through our co-op store, through our U.F.C. local, as well as through the CCF. They are all part of one movement, the "people's movement." Sometimes one organization or fight is more important than the other, but we need them all. The fact that our poll committee doesn't meet except before conventions doesn't mean the CCF'ers here don't care about the party. We feel that we are building the CCF when we build our co-op store, and we are building cooperation and destroying the profit system when we build the CCF.

At first glance the relationship between the CCF and other rural community organizations appears similar to the pattern of party-society relations advocated by the Communist Party. Communists want to be the vanguard of the working class, the class leaders. To accomplish this, they attempt to permeate working-class organizations and become their officials. In the Soviet Union, Communists are placed in key positions in trade-unions, cooperatives, and local governments. In democratic countries they use the tactics of "boring from within" to achieve positions of leadership.[14]

In Saskatchewan, however, the "vanguard," the leaders of the farming community, started the CCF. As a result, CCF activity and community activity are closely interrelated. This situation is not a result of any planned action, but is, rather, a consequence of the tight organization of the farming community on an occupational basis. The CCF is the class party, the farmers' party, and thus controls the farmers' organizations. Many leaders of the CCF and of rural organizations are not aware of this close interrelationship. The party makes no direct efforts to influence other institutions and has no explicit policy for its members to follow in them. There are no CCF caucuses in the cooperatives or other rural groups. In practice, however, most of the secondary leaders are CCF members and therefore support the policy of the party and the CCF government. The leaders are, in fact, continually engaged in political activity.

The relationship between the CCF and rural community organizations is a two-way affair. CCF leaders in their capacity as local government officials and cooperative leaders know the needs of the community and the effect of government policies on the rural community. They use the party organization as a direct channel of communication to the legislature and the cabinet. A stream of resolutions moves constantly from local and constituency committees to the Provincial Council and the government.

Since the election of 1944, interest in CCF conventions and governing committees has grown greatly. Through participation in this organization at least 10,000 people are led to feel that they are taking a direct part in the establishment of government policy. The vitality of grass-roots participation in rural Saskatchewan leads to vigorous criticism of the activities of the government and the party. The active members in the CCF are mainly experienced local leaders, who represent the grass-roots, not the summits, of the rural community. The CCF differs from many European socialist parties and the nonsocialist parties in the United States and Canada in that its secondary leaders are unpaid and receive little additional status from their party position. The party officials had status in the community before they became CCF leaders, and therefore are relatively independent of top control. This pattern of grass-roots democracy runs through all the farmers' movements in Saskatchewan, and the CCF is only continuing it. In order to perpetuate interest and loyalty to the party, CCF leaders are almost forced to encourage criticism and suggestions from the rank and file. Many CCF leaders, from Premier Douglas down, reiterate that they are only the servants of the majority of the party. Theoretically, the party leadership and the government must accept any policy adopted by the provincial convention.

Many members of the CCF now conceive of government as a tool to be manipulated by the people. They come to constituency conventions fully prepared to let the government know their opinions. The resolutions adopted at conventions reveal the operation of this conception of direct democracy:

That the Government investigate and pass legislation which will stop completely the overloading and crowding of live stock in stock cars, trucks or any other vehicle.

That a stop be made to the shipping of live stock unfit for human consumption to packing houses or stock yards. The only exception being stock clearly designated for purposes other than human consumption.[15]

Whereas the Department of Health is prepared to go to considerable work and expense to have all citizens tested for T.B. to have the disease controlled and

Whereas after the test has been taken and even if your family shows no signs of the disease they may go home and drink milk from a diseased cow

Therefore be it resolved that the Government make an extensive test of all cattle as soon as possible regardless of whether the present veterinary profession have time to do it all or not.[16]

That we the delegates of Saltcoats Convention, especially the women members, desire the Government to investigate the possibility of the Woolen Mill handling woven materials, as blankets from this class of goods fulfill many useful purposes on the farm.[17]

The lack of inhibitions in criticizing government policy can be seen in a number of resolutions.

Be it resolved that we consider the five CCF Cabinet Ministers who talked and voted against the resolution to exempt single men up to $1,200 and married men up to $2,500 on the Federal Income Tax, were badly out of line, . . . especially Mr. Fines, who actually implied that he would tax the lower paid classes exactly as the Capitalist King Government is doing.[18]

Whereas the existence of natural gas and oil in commercial quantities in the Province of Saskatchewan has been proven conclusively;

And whereas the CCF as a Socialist Party believes in and advocates the public ownership of the natural resources of this Province for the benefit of the people of Saskatchewan;

And whereas a resolution was passed at the 1945 Provincial Convention urging the Government of Saskatchewan to undertake the development and distribution of natural gas and oil in this Province;

And whereas natural gas and oil in the Province of Saskatchewan continues to be extensively exploited by private persons and concerns;

Therefore be it resolved that the Government of Saskatchewan be called upon to show cause why the exploitation of these resources has been allowed to fall into private hands.

And be it further resolved that the Government of Saskatchewan be immediately called upon to place these resources under social ownership, control and operation for the immense benefit of the people of Saskatchewan.[19]

Free forums, such as the constituency conventions provide, strengthen the CCF in innumerable ways. The top leaders can never depart far from the thinking of the rank and file without being made aware of it. The conventions serve, also, to preserve the vitality and support of the party. In interviews many CCF members stressed this existence of direct democracy through the party.

Well, what did you think of that speech? I really made B. [a Cabinet minister] squirm. Don't misunderstand it though. I think B. is doing a good job, but like all men, he makes mistakes and he has to be told about them. That's the wonderful thing about this party. The members really run it. No one in this room would have the least hesitation about telling anyone from Coldwell or Douglas down that he is wrong if he thinks so. Can you see any Liberal supporter doing that to old Gardiner? Why, did you know the Liberals haven't had a convention since 1933?[20]

To what degree can the formal structure and appearance of grass-roots democracy in the CCF be said to be real? Do the people really govern? One cabinet minister, in discussing the role of conventions, said:

They are today the most important part of the CCF organization. I think we are doing good work and that the majority of the people approve our policies. However this will not keep us in power. A lot of good governments have been defeated and lost power. Our people will not actively support and work for the CCF once their feeling of "Get the Rascals out" is over. . . .

The one thing that maintains our active support is the feeling that the people run the government, that we are only their servants. The conventions reinforce that feeling every year. It is therefore important that we never refuse to carry out anything demanded at the Provincial Convention unless we have a darn good explanation. Our supporters will put up with mistakes or with inefficiency, but they won't stand for dictation. The one thing that can kill the CCF is the idea that we are another party like the Liberals and Conservatives, that the government is composed of another group of politicians and "heelers" who come around every four years for votes.

Cabinet ministers and party leaders appear to act on these

principles. *This does not mean that they do not make policy.* In fact, almost all important provincial policies are set by the cabinet and the members of the legislature. At provincial conventions the final form of resolutions, suggesting changes in policy, is usually determined by top leaders. This control, however, is exercised by men who combine superior oratorical ability, status, and information. When the leaders oppose a resolution they are able to control the overwhelming majority of delegates.

In the 1946 convention a resolution proposing government ownership of gas and oil appeared to be favored by the majority of the delegates, for it had been a traditional demand of the farmers' movement and of the CCF. Two cabinet ministers armed with statistical data were able to convince the convention that the oil and gas fields were not yet proved commercial fields and that the cost of developing them as a risk investment was beyond the financial ability of the province.

On certain issues, however, government and party leaders have been voted down and accepted their defeat. The 1946 provincial convention adopted two resolutions recommending changes in government policy that had previously been rejected by the cabinet and the CCF legislative caucus: one supported the right of married women to work for the government, and the other urged the forty-four-hour week for labor with no reduction in pay. At the following session of the legislature both proposals of the convention were adopted.

There has been, however, one major issue in which the government has not completely followed convention instructions. The 1945 and 1946 conventions urged the government to fill all policy-making positions in the civil service with persons who support CCF ideals. The cabinet at first refused, but gradually has been making concessions to the pressure from the conventions.

Direct democracy in the CCF and other Saskatchewan farm organizations is limited by the extent of the knowledge, experience, and interests of the secondary leaders. CCF conventions fail to pass resolutions on a multitude of important problems because the delegates lack opinions about, or knowledge of, these problems. The conventions rarely bother with the details of a government health scheme, the methods of operation of government industry, the problems of debt refunding or repayment, priorities in economic planning, or provincial proposals to Dominion-provincial conferences, though these administrative details may be more important than the broad over-all policies with which the resolutions deal. Other important issues neglected by the conventions are foreign policy and other aspects of national affairs that do not affect agriculture. The overwhelming majority of resolutions reflect the day-to-day economic and social concerns of farmers and workers: farm regulations, provincial tax legislation, roads, liquor laws, and social services.[21]

The extensive grass-roots discussion of governmental problems is not new in the history of the province. Long before the CCF was formed, the Saskatchewan Grain Growers' Association met in annual district and provincial conventions to adopt policies to be urged on governments. The annual meeting of the S.G.G.A. was known as the "Farmers' Parliament" and was well attended. The Liberal Party, which then controlled the province, paid close attention to the actions of these conventions and wherever possible implemented the recommendations of the S.G.G.A. In order to maintain the support of the organized farmers, it offered cabinet posts to Grain Growers' officials.[22] The provincial Liberals lost their hold on the farmers' movement when the Progressives were formed in 1920, because the federal Liberal Party would not meet many of the agrarian demands.

The fact that extensive participation in the Saskatchewan CCF is not a result of the growth of a new political movement or of some characteristic inherent in the CCF becomes clear if the organization is compared with the party elsewhere in Canada where it has been successful. Of those voting for the CCF in Saskatchewan, 15 per cent were party members. The British Columbia CCF, which is largely an urban working-class movement, won 39 per cent of the total vote in the 1946 provincial election, but less than 5 per cent of its supporters are members of the party. In one Vancouver constituency that has elected socialist or CCF candidates since 1930, party leaders do not know who their supporters are, and only a handful of them are in the party.[23] In Toronto the CCF received 133,443 votes in 1945, but has never enlisted more than 3.8 per cent of this figure in the movement. Actually, the Toronto CCF has considerably less than 1,000 active members. The growth of the CCF movement in Toronto and Vancouver has not been the result of, nor has it resulted in, an increase in direct political participation by the masses. The party in these cities resembles the traditional North American parties, with little direct contact between the organization and the major part of the electorate.

If one notes the differences between the community structure of Saskatchewan and that of cities such as Toronto and Vancouver, the relationship between structure and the extent of political activity becomes clear. The 600,000 rural residents of Saskatchewan elect 2,100 members of municipal councils and 15,000 members of school boards. Large cities, however, have an insignificant number of community positions compared to their total population. The 800,000 citizens of Toronto elect only 24 members of a council and 18 members of the school board.

In most North American cities the majority of political and community posts are held by members of the middle and upper classes.[24] The city councils are filled with lawyers and other business or professional people. Many community organizations such as hospital boards, Y.M.C.A. boards, and community chests are dominated by members of the upper classes. This again is in striking contrast to rural Saskatchewan, where farmers must fill these posts themselves.

Trade-unionism is the major institutional exception in urban life in which workers are given an opportunity to hold office and take responsibility. The ratio of officials to total union membership, however, is often very low. There are many union locals with thousands of members and two to twenty officials. In Saskatchewan the ratio of members to officials in the cooperatives and educational organizations ranges from five to one to twenty to one. The Saskatchewan Wheat Pool, the largest farm organization, has a total membership of 60,000 to 70,000. About 11,000 farmers are elected members of Wheat Pool committees in their localities. One out of every six members of this organization, which most closely approximates a trade-union in rural Saskatchewan, is a local official who meets regularly with others from six to twelve times a year to discuss and act on local, provincial, and national matters. Local members usually attend meetings twice a year. The average local Pool organization has about sixty members.

The cooperative movement is extremely weak in the urban areas of Canada and the United States. In contrast with Europe, cooperatives in America have not succeeded in interesting many workers. The cooperatives, therefore, do not serve as a basis for training leaders and creating channels of communication between workers and larger institutions. The few urban cooperatives that do exist tend to be led by members of the middle class. The breakdown or absence of real neighborhoods in urban centers has also served to prevent the formation of a local corps of leaders. The political machine has provided the only effective urban leadership group, and it could hardly be expected to be a vehicle for new ideas and for social change. Outside the factory, the urban working class is dispersed. There are few channels for genuine intraclass communication.

The building of a new mass political organization is, therefore, much more difficult in a city than in a rural community or small town. It is almost impossible to locate the informal leaders of the lower classes. The people are not accustomed to making political decisions. In the anonymity of city living, organized person-to-person political contact is difficult.

If it is true that popular interest and participation in political activity are facilitated by the wheat economy of Saskatchewan, one should expect similar patterns of behavior in comparable areas. Saskatchewan's neighbors permit such comparisons. The state of North Dakota, economically and geographically, is almost a replica of Saskatchewan. It is sparsely settled, has a one-crop wheat economy, and is rural for the most part. The environmental and economic challenges which forced the farmers of Saskatchewan to establish many different organizational structures were similar in North Dakota. This state should therefore be expected to have a high degree of political activity.

The historical facts tend to confirm this expectation. In that state the Non-Partisan League secured its greatest strength and membership. At its height, in 1920, it had 50,000 members, which was 7.7 per cent of the total population. The League won more than 1,000,000 votes in various states and had 300,000 members, but in no other state was the ratio of its membership to population or to its electoral support so high as in North Dakota.[25] Today the Farmers' Union, which is politically the most active of the major farmers' organizations, is strongest in North Dakota.

The Farmers' Union is by far the biggest single force in the state, and its North Dakota unit is probably the strongest farmers' organization in the whole country on a state level. . . . Of the 57,000 farmers in North Dakota, more than 30,-000 are members, which must be something of a record for saturation in any movement.[26]

Fifteen hundred local groups of the National Farmers' Union [of North Dakota] meet with staff organizers once or twice a month for discussions on local, national and world problems. . . . Each year with wives and children over sixteen voting in addition to the farmers themselves, the locals elect their officers and their delegates to the state convention where the next year's program is planned.[27]

In Canada, Saskatchewan's neighbor on the west, Alberta, is somewhat similar in economic and social structure. It too has widespread community participation through local governments and cooperatives. Politically, also, Alberta tends to resemble Saskatchewan. The last thirty years have seen the growth of three large social movements: the Progressives and the United Farmers of Alberta in the 'twenties, the Social Credit Party in the last decade, and a growing CCF movement today. Alberta farmers, like those of Saskatchewan and North Dakota, are quick to react politically when a threat to their society or economy arises.

Manitoba, Saskatchewan's eastern neighbor, however, has had much less community and political activity. Its cooperative movement is considerably weaker than those of the other provinces. There has not been a significant farmers' political movement in Manitoba since the early 'twenties. It is the only one of the three Prairie Provinces that does not have a farmers' educational and political pressure organization such as the U.F.C. (Saskatchewan Section) or the United Farmers of Alberta. The differences between Manitoba and the rest of the Prairie Provinces help to confirm our hypothesis as to the causes of political apathy.

Manitoba has been less exposed to the vagaries of weather and price fluctuations than the rest of the northern prairie region. Only a small part of Manitoba is in the drought belt. The province is no longer a one-crop wheat region. Many of its rural residents practice mixed farming and have a large immediate market in Winnipeg. This tends to reduce economic hazards. The economic need for a large cooperative movement is not so great.

A second reason for the smaller degree of political participation is the strength of urban influence in rural Manitoba. The inhabited portion of Manitoba is a much smaller area than that of either Alberta or Saskatchewan. Much of the rural part of the province is close to the large city of Winnipeg. The important community and provincial institutions are concentrated in the one city that is accessible to most farmers. The need for duplicating the community services that exist in urban areas is not so great in rural Manitoba as it is in Saskatchewan and, consequently, local activity is weak. The Manitoba Wheat Pool has only two districts as compared with Saskatchewan's sixteen.

Manitoba is the oldest of the Prairie Provinces. Its pioneer days are almost a generation behind those of Saskatchewan. The striving to create and maintain basic community institutions ended long ago. Other things being equal, older organizations tend to enlist less participation and interest than new ones. It is significant that during the period between the 1890's and the early twentieth century, when economic and ecological conditions in Manitoba approximated those of Saskatchewan and Alberta today, the Manitoba agrarian political movement was strong. In the 'nineties the wheat farmers organized a strong third party. The Manitoba Grain Growers' Association and later the United Farmers of Manitoba were large and powerful pressure groups which made and unmade governments and built the first large cooperative movement in western Canada.

A Saskatchewan informant who took part in a recent CCF

election campaign in Manitoba indicated clearly the effect on political life of the lack of community participation.

I was in Manitoba at the last Federal election in Russell, the home of Hon. J. A. Glen, and was able to see the CCF in operation. Many of the conditions were akin to Saskatchewan, but the ground work was missing. No trained speakers were at hand. Many were poorly equipped to conduct a meeting. No experience had been gained like Saskatchewan's Wheat Pool Delegates and field men had gained in meeting the exacting demands of the farmers under contract to the Pool. If Glen had been running in a Saskatchewan riding he wouldn't have lasted as long as a snowball in hell.

They have no system of carrying on cooperative education in Manitoba like in Saskatchewan. The farmers just aren't used to attending meetings and discussing their problems.

Myrdal has described the relationship between political apathy and the lack of community organization in America.

In local politics, America has, on the whole, not spread political responsibility upon countless citizens' boards, as have, for example, the Northern European countries (including England), thereby widening political participation and making politics more anonymous and less dependent on outstanding leadership. Much more, not only of broad policy making, but also of detailed decisions are, in America, centralized in the offices of salaried functionaries. *Political participation of the ordinary citizen in America is pretty much restricted to the intermittently recurring elections. Politics is not organized to be a daily concern and responsibility of the common citizen.* The relative paucity of trade unions, cooperatives, and other civic interest organizations tends to accentuate this abstention on the part of the common citizens from sharing in the government of their communities as a normal routine of life. In this essential sense American politics is centralized.[28]

A description of the Saskatchewan scene is the inverse of Myrdal's description of the American scene. The tendency in local politics has been to spread political responsibility among countless citizens' boards; this has brought about wider political participation and has made politics more anonymous and less dependent on outstanding leadership. *Political participation of the ordinary citizen in Saskatchewan is not restricted to the intermittently recurring elections. Politics is organized to be a daily concern and responsibility of the common citizen.* The relatively large number of farmers' organizations, cooperatives, and other civic-interest organizations encourages common citizens to share in the government of their communities as a normal routine of life. In this essential sense, Saskatchewan politics is decentralized.

Widespread community participation and political interest have developed in Saskatchewan in response to the environmental and economic problems involved in creating a stable community. No one factor—the small units of government, the vulnerable one-crop economy, the "one-class" society, the sparse settlement of the area, the continual economic and climatic hazards—developed because of an interest in maintaining an active grass-roots democracy or a concern for politics. The combination of all these factors, however, has made for a healthy and active democracy. Unplanned structural conditions have facilitated rapid popular response to economic and social challenges and the acceptance of new methods and ideas.[29]

The Saskatchewan pattern, while offering confirmation of the "small democracy" theories, provides no panacea for those who would plan society so as to create the basis for popular community activity. Early in the nineteenth century Thomas Jefferson advocated "general political organization on the basis of small units, small enough so that all its members could have direct communication with one another and take care of all community affairs."[30] This and similar proposals have been ignored, for small communities were not functional in the development of a great industrial nation. In the nineteenth century, anyone who objected to the growth of large cities was called a "reactionary" or a "utopian" trying to block the march of civilization.

The small agrarian community in Saskatchewan has been preserved only because this pattern was functional in the wheat economy. The grain companies, the cooperatives, the political parties, and the farmers, all would have preferred larger communities and more centralization. They would laugh at the rational democrat's argument for their type of living and their type of economy. To the people of the West, decentralization has meant poor community services and little access to many material and cultural values. They welcomed the automobile and better roads, which are resulting in the breakdown of the smaller communities and the growth of large towns and cities. It remains true, however, that the smaller the community and organizational unit, and the less economically and socially stratified the society, the better are the possibilities for grass-roots political activity. Saskatchewan demonstrates that widespread and continuous political interest is not incompatible with efficient, large-scale organization.

NOTES

1. Gunnar Myrdal, *An American Dilemma* (New York, Harper and Brothers, 1944), p. 714.

2. Nathan Fine, *Labor and Farmer Parties in the United States* (Rand School of Social Science, New York, 1928); John D. Hicks, *The Populist Revolt* (University of Minnesota Press, 1931), p. 80; Paul Fossum, *The Agrarian Movement in North Dakota* (Baltimore, Johns Hopkins Press, 1925), pp. 85–86.

3. The cooperative organizations of the province have 477,000 members, though there are only 125,000 farmers. See Saskatchewan *News*, March 22, 1948, p. 3; also Department of Municipal Affairs, *Report* (Regina, 1948).

4. G. E. Britnell, *The Wheat Economy* (University of Toronto Press, 1939), p. 188.

5. Jean Burnet, "Town-Country Relations and the Problem of Rural Leadership," *Canadian Journal of Economics and Political Science,* August, 1947, pp. 395–419.

6. Hugh Boyd, *New Breaking* (Toronto, J. M. Dent and Sons, Ltd., 1938); Saskatchewan Cooperative Producers, Ltd., *Annual Report* (Regina), 1924–47.

7. Saskatchewan Cooperative Producers, Ltd., *The Wheat Pool and Its Accomplishments to 1946* (Regina, 1946), p. 12.

8. George Robson, "Letter to Editor," *Western Producer,* January 30, 1943, p. 2.

9. In the past, many agrarian protest movements succeeded despite the initial opposition of the top officials of the organized farmers. The Grain Growers' Grain Company was organized in spite of the fact that the heads of the Saskatchewan Grain Growers' Association opposed it. After the First World War, independ-

ent political action was forced on the leaders of the S.G.G.A. The Wheat Pool succeeded despite the early reluctance of the officials of the S.G.G.A. and the Saskatchewan Cooperative Elevator Company. The 100 per cent pool plan was adopted in 1929 and 1930, though the leaders of the U.F.C. and the Wheat Pool were opposed to it. See chaps. 3 and 4.

10. Records of Saskatchewan CCF.

11. C. Rufus Rorem, *The Municipal Doctor Scheme in Rural Saskatchewan* (University of Chicago Press, 1931).

12. *Ibid.,* pp. 83–84.

13. CCF (Saskatchewan Section), *Handbook* (Regina, 1946).

14. Commission of the Central Committee of the Communist Party of the Soviet Union, *History of the Communist Party of the Soviet Union* (New York, International Publishers, 1939), pp. 46–49.

15. CCF (Saskatchewan Section), *Provincial Convention Delegates' Handbook* (Regina, 1945), p. 33.

16. *Ibid.*

17. *Ibid.,* 1946, p. 51.

18. *Ibid.,* p. 45.

19. *Ibid.,* p. 51. It should be noted that the last two resolutions were passed at constituency conventions at which cabinet ministers were present.

20. The Saskatchewan Liberal Party held a convention in 1947.

21. CCF Convention, *Handbook,* 1945, 1946, 1947.

22. Hopkins Moorhouse, *Deep Furrows* (Toronto, George J. McLeod, Ltd., 1918), pp. 230–33, 265.

23. From interviews with CCF leaders.

24. Myrdal, *op. cit.,* p. 714.

25. S. Roy Weaver, *The Non-Partisan League in North Dakota* (Canadian Reconstruction Association, Toronto, 1921), p. 13.

26. John Gunther, *Inside U.S.A.* (New York, Harper and Brothers, 1947), p. 242.

27. Henry Wallace, "Report on the Farmers," *New Republic,* June 30, 1947, p. 12.

28. Myrdal, *op. cit.,* p. 717. (Italics in original.)

29. Similar results were found in an unpublished study of a small, self-contained housing community in an industrial area. Craftown, a community of 2,500, was found to be much more active politically than neighboring urban areas. The community, like rural Saskatchewan, was a small, relatively homogeneous town, with four-fifths of its population industrial workers. Similarly, it faced a series of problems that demanded organized action. Because of the lack of public services, the working-class citizenry had to start volunteer police and fire departments and a cooperative store. These associations provided opportunities for learning collaborative techniques and leadership skills which were also put to use in political action.

"Joined in an interlocking complex, these factors of the manageable size of the local community, a new and flexible social structure, a continuing flow of problems visibly common to the group and a nucleus of men and women equipped through experience with skills of collaboration all contributed to the building of an actively participating citizenry." Robert K. Merton and Patricia Salter, *An Interim Report: The Lavenburg-Columbia Research on Human Relations in the Planned Community. The First Year's Work—1945–1946* (New York, 1946). Mimeographed.

30. John Dewey, *Freedom and Culture* (New York, G. P. Putnam's Sons, 1939), p. 159.

I I

POLITICS AND SOCIAL CHANGE

THE CCF has held office in Saskatchewan for six years, from 1944 to 1950. It has had the opportunity of demonstrating to the people of the province as well as to the rest of Canada how successful a new party based on the support of the farmers and workers can be in carrying out its goals of a more democratic society. Its overwhelming parliamentary majority has meant that there were few formal restraints in the path of enacting and administering its program.

It is obvious that democratic reform governments are more a result than a cause of social change. As a result of breakdowns in the integration of existing value structures, community mores gradually change. The need for explicit formal institutional changes gradually becomes recognized by different strata of the population who are adversely affected by the breakdown in the old community integration. The organizations or persons who propose reforms that appear to fill the needs of maladjusted groups win influence and, if the crisis is widespread, power. In a stable democracy, however, the reformer will gain power usually after all elements, even the more conservative ones, recognize the need for change.

Many societies, of course, become so unstable in their structure that agreement on widespread reforms is impossible. This is especially true when the socially defined "needs" of one class necessitate the elimination of the power, wealth, and influence of another class. This was true in China and much of eastern Europe during the past thirty years, and in pre-Hitler Germany. In more stable societies, however, where no class has to make far-reaching changes in the position of another group to accomplish its aims, compromise on objectives is usually reached. The situation that leads workers or farmers to demand new forms of economic security also changes the values of the dominant groups. This shift in the publicly proclaimed values of the upper strata is made grudgingly in order to maintain power and influence, as in Great Britain today. This fact, however, does not change the significance of the basic agreement on objectives by rival democratic political movements.

The radical party in a stable society, therefore, is not on the left side of a fundamental cleavage, but is on a point in a continuum. Where real cleavage as to aims occurs, the revolutionary situation makes the continuance of democracy difficult. The actions of most electorally successful radical parties have, therefore, not differed greatly from the policies that were acceptable to their conservative oppositions. History has shown that socialists come to power democratically only when their opposition is almost "socialist." Conservative parties in Norway, Sweden, England, New Zealand, and France, in the years after the Second World War, accepted the nationalization of various major industries and the extension of social welfare. The attitude of English Conservatives to the policies of the Labor government is a good example.

In Britain's hour of need for leadership, the loyal Opposition does not want to take power. . . . the Tory futility is rooted in something far more significant for Britain's future than the political manoeuvres of the moment. The hard truth is that Big-C Conservatives have lost their faith in small-c conservatism. They are now economic and political agnostics, with no new belief to replace their lost faith in free enterprise.

British Tories agree almost unanimously on the necessity of thorough public controls. They quarrel mostly with the degree and not the principle of public ownership. They believe that free enterprise has gone out of their lives; and a sizeable minority believes that it is a good thing. . . .

The Conservative Party may continue for a while to be an alternative to a Labor Party. But it is now clear that it will be conservative in name only. Said one grim Tory M.P. last week: "When we get back into power, we'll show them how to run Socialism properly."[1]

Henry Wallace, who is considered to be on the left side of

the American political spectrum, found himself on the right in many European countries when discussing economic policies. In England he described himself as a "Progressive Conservative," and in Norway he spoke at a meeting "whose chairman explained that he was a Conservative. . . . But labels mean little; in many ways, the student [chairman] was politically to the Left of myself [Wallace]."[2]

Many European governments that do not have a "socialist" majority have nationalized part of their economy. The breakdown of the European economy and the loss of overseas investments have apparently caused many groups in countries like England and France to recognize the need for state planning and government ownership. "Socialist planning" has been instituted only when all parts of the community accept it. This is not to imply that there are no serious political and class cleavages in European countries. The conservatives and the old ruling classes are struggling, often successfully, to maintain much of their old power and privileges in the new planning state by retaining control of important positions in the new government industries and power structure.

The general climate of opinion determines what is radical or conservative at a given time and place. The introduction of major changes in the economy may not necessarily be radical for one community, though similar reforms would outrage the sentiments of other regions. With few exceptions, democratic leftist parties have implemented only those aspects of their program which met little popular resistance. The radical party, however, does a more thoroughgoing job of introducing change than would its conservative opposition, because the radicals believe in the changes.

In Saskatchewan and other Prairie Provinces, political climates of opinion have usually been to the left of the rest of the country. Before the First World War, the old party governments of the Prairie Provinces engaged in experiments in government ownership and supported the growing co-operative movement. In Saskatchewan, following the Progressive upswing after the First World War, the Liberals and the Conservatives attempted to regain their influence with the farmers by becoming markedly more radical than their fellow party members in eastern Canada.[3]

Saskatchewan representatives of both old parties supported, at least verbally, government-guaranteed higher farm prices (parity), government crop insurance, debt reduction and moratoriums on farm debts during crises, lower tariffs, government loan agencies, public ownership of power and other public utilities, state or socialized medicine, increased social welfare and pension benefits, and the expansion of the co-operative movement.

The only parts of the CCF program that were not duplicated in old-party platforms were the proposals for government ownership. This difference is not so great as it appears, however, for many old-party Saskatchewan leaders supported government ownership of organizations that affected farmers, such as banking, transportation, and marketing. During the depression the former Conservative Premier of Saskatchewan, Dr. J. T. M. Anderson, put forth the following program for his party in order to win left-wing support:

1. Work and wages. . . . If industry will not absorb them [the unemployed] the Government must in a definite way do so, even if it means the *Government itself establishing new industries.* . . .
3. Drastic reduction in urban as well as rural indebtedness.
4. State medicine made available to all.
5. Equal educational opportunities. . . .
6. Increased social services. . . .
7. Support of cooperative marketing. . . .
12. Development of our natural resources in the interests of the province rather than in the interests of a few favored individuals.[4]

We believe in the policy of public ownership as shown in the matter of the power commission. Over 11,000 were built during the first year of [the Anderson Conservative] government and more would have been done had not some of the present private companies got so deep-rooted before we took office.

Nothing would please us more than for the government to be able to put $10,000,000 in the hands of the power commission.[5]

The linkage between the Saskatchewan Liberal and Conservative parties and their more conservative national organizations tended to discredit their efforts in the province. There is no doubt, however, that the provincial old parties are to the left within their national parties. Reforms that are still "radical" in Ontario or Quebec are well established on the prairies.[6]

The social and economic conditions of the wheat-growing areas of the Great Plains of North America have produced a self-interest economic radicalism that has resulted in different types of semisocialist experimentation by such movements as the Non-Partisan League, the Farmer-Labor Party, the United Farmers, Social Credit, the CCF, certain old party governments, and the great cooperative movement.[7] How radical has the work of the CCF government in Saskatchewan been? The question must be raised in the context of the society within which it developed. What were the social and economic options for the CCF? Has the government attempted to use social reforms to create the basis for a new socialist society with a new value orientation, or is it simply innovating in areas where there is specific public demand for change? For the purposes of this discussion, the ideal socialist society is defined as an economically equal one, with socially cooperative instead of competitive values. It is not maintained that such a society is necessarily possible or that the CCF has the power to create it, but rather that a socialist movement can and should be evaluated on the degree to which its reforms lead to such a society.

Agriculture is by far the most important element in Saskatchewan society. Growing out of the farmers' movement, the CCF has attempted to carry out in legislation and administration those aspects of the program of the farmers' organization that lay within provincial power. Immediately upon taking office, therefore, the CCF legislature enacted farm security legislation providing that no farmer could lose the basic 160 acres on which he lived because of nonpayment of debt. It also stated that in any year in which the total income of a farmer's land fell below $6 an acre, he should not have to pay the interest owing on any mortgage for that year.[8] The purpose of this legislation was to make the mortgage company share the economic and climatic risks of farmers. The Provincial Debt Mediation Board, by using its power to recommend debt moratoriums, forced many mortgage holders to reduce debts, which had mounted during the depression.[9] The entire force of the government was put behind the pledge of Premier Douglas that "no farmer shall be evicted from his farm under a CCF government."[10]

The government is further aiding the security of farmers by establishing seed and fodder banks in which supplies can be stored from good crop years, so that drought will not ravage the province. It has greatly raised appropriations for scientific farming and has increased the number of agricultural field representatives.[11] The provincial government and the CCF members of the federal Parliament have continually put pressure on the federal government to retain government marketing of wheat, which was established during the war.

Two aspects of the Saskatchewan CCF policy—security of tenure and stability of farm income—have been part of the western agrarian program for decades. In themselves they are not radical, except as they involve decreasing the income of other hitherto more powerful groups for the benefit of farmers. All farmers' governments in the grain belt have attempted to effect similar policies. It should be noted, therefore, that the program of the Saskatchewan CCF is designed to maintain the social and economic structure of the rural area, not to change it. In fact, the CCF program is *conservative* within the rural economy. The party has done nothing to change the comparative position of tenant farmers or to equalize the economic status of the poorer and smaller farmers. Indirectly, farm security legislation makes it more difficult for the poor farmer to buy new land than for the well-to-do farmer, since the latter has more cash to pay for new land. An owner of farm land, to defend his own interests, will prefer to sell to those with greater assets, since the government is protecting farmers who cannot pay their mortgage debts.

Second, the CCF policy of a guaranteed profitable price benefits the large farmer more than the small one, as the former's production costs per bushel of wheat are lower and his profit therefore greater. This enables the wealthy farmer to increase the size of his holdings and the amount of his equipment. These policies of the CCF may, therefore, eventually lead to the creation of a class of large wealthy farmers and the elimination of the small farmer.

No one who knows the Saskatchewan farmer could realistically suggest the socialization of land as an alternative to CCF agricultural policy. The Communist dictatorships of eastern Europe could enforce land nationalization only because they could ignore the sentiments of their disenfranchised electorate. A democratic socialist government must accept the desire of farmers to retain title in their farms. There are, however, two ways by which a radical government can prevent increased rural stratification: restriction of the size of farms, and experiments in voluntary cooperative farms.

Some of the more radical CCF leaders have suggested legislation restricting the size of individually owned farms and placing discriminatory taxes on absentee-owned farms.[12] The government and the majority of the legislative caucus have voted down such equalitarian proposals for two reasons: first, the party leaders fear that any proposals that affect land tenures will be regarded by many farmers as steps leading to nationalization of land; and second, most of the CCF rural leaders belong to the more prosperous group who own large farms. They are as much concerned with mortgages, interest rates, reducing the cost of manufactured goods, and raising wheat prices as are the poorer farmers. The wealthy farmers, however, do not desire to equalize the position of all farmers at their own expense. The party, therefore, is under no pressure from its active members to become an equalitarian agricultural party.[13]

The same internal antiequalitarian bias of the Saskatchewan farmers' movement and the CCF can be seen in the operation of the cooperative movement, which the government supports. The Saskatchewan government has given enthusiastic support to the growth of the large cooperative movement of the province.

Since the party took office, cooperative organization has increased greatly.[14] The major reason is the general prosperity of the rural areas, which enabled farmers to raise share capital for initial investments. There can be little doubt, however, that the CCF government of Saskatchewan, by its enthusiastic support of cooperatives, has played an important part in the growth of the movement. It established a separate Department of Cooperatives with its own cabinet minister. Almost every new cooperative that I visited during my stay in Saskatchewan had been organized by members or supporters of the CCF. There are now about 500,000 members of cooperatives, an average of four memberships per farmer.

The growth of cooperatives creates the same dilemma for the development of rural society as do the CCF agricultural policies. Cooperatives have been organized mainly by the upper strata of the farming population.[15] The poorer farmers either do not have the necessary share capital to start their own cooperatives or do not have the cash reserves to use them. They patronize the private companies, which give higher immediate benefits, rather than wait for an annual patronage refund. This has meant, in practice, that the larger farmers receive a higher price for their wheat and pay less for the goods they buy. Like the farm security legislation, the cooperatives aid the farming community against outside exploiters, but *within* the rural community they help well-to-do farmers more than poorer ones.

Recognition of the fact that cooperatives unduly aid one section of the rural community has led some in the CCF to advocate that the government take over certain functions of cooperatives. They argue that the CCF position that cooperatives and government developments are both forms of "nonprofit" ownership is not true, for the question remains unanswered: Who is to obtain the profit from the "nonprofit" organizations? These radical members of the CCF suggest that profits from socially owned institutions should go to the government and be used for increased social services to benefit the neediest elements of the population. Ardent cooperators in and out of the CCF, however, state that those who produce the wealth deserve the benefits, and therefore the profit should be returned in the form of patronage dividends. This problem has never been formally resolved by the CCF, but in practice the party is committed to giving cooperative principles a free hand in marketing and distribution, and in whatever other fields cooperatives had preempted before the CCF was elected.

The CCF government has advanced only one agricultural

equalitarian proposal—voluntary cooperative farming. A small minority in the party have suggested that the cooperative farm is the real form of socialism in agriculture, since it lessens the individualistic work of the farmer and necessitates a more cooperative value system. The government, through the Department of Cooperatives, has given financial and research assistance to a few experimental farms. Neither the party nor the government nor the cooperatives, however, are engaged in any widespread program to educate farmers on the advantages of cooperative living on the sparsely settled prairies. Several cabinet ministers believe that cooperative farms are not feasible in the provinces. One of them stated in an interview: "Our farmers are too individualistic. They couldn't work together on a farm under a manager. There is no sense in antagonizing them by trying to get them into it."

The members of the Economic Planning Board of the government are also opposed to cooperative farms, because they cannot see how such farms could create more goods. They feel that government funds should be used in measures to increase economic security, as in irrigation and in seed and fodder banks.[16]

Most CCF leaders assume that if farmers are given economic security and increased social services they will continue to support the movement in its efforts to socialize the rest of the economy. Experiences in other countries do not lend weight to this assumption. In fact, the contrary seems to be true—farmers tend to become conservative when they achieve their economic goals. The farmer is radical vis-à-vis the larger society when his economic security and land tenure are threatened. He may join other exploited groups, such as the workers, to win his own economic demands. However, once the farmer achieves these immediate goals and becomes a member of the secure property holders of society, he resents government controls and labor or tax legislation that interfere with the expansion of his business.

New Zealand farmers supported the guaranteed price policy of the Labor Party in the depths of the depression in 1935, when low prices threatened their security. When the depression ended, however, the rural districts turned against Labor's planning program, which called for maximum farm prices as well as minimum ones, and increased incomes of the poorer groups.[17] In the United States, President Roosevelt established the guaranteed parity prices and crop insurance demanded by organized farmers. In so doing, however, he lost the support of the rural areas, including the once-radical wheat belt.[18] In Russia the Bolsheviks lost the support of the peasants after they gave them title to the land. The well-to-do peasants (*kulaks*) sought to increase the size of their holdings and to restore capitalist labor relations; they objected to controlled prices.[19]

In Saskatchewan a rift of interests may be developing between small and large farmers. The large farmers, who have highly mechanized and economically efficient farms, can operate with a profit at a lower wheat price than the small farmers. The well-to-do farmers, therefore, can afford to buy more and more land, aided by the provincial government's farm security legislation. This is creating a potentially serious cleavage between big farmers and small and tenant farmers. At present the United Farmers of Canada (Saskatchewan Section) is reviving as an organization representing small farmers. The U.F.C. sponsored a farm strike for higher prices in 1947. This farm strike was opposed in the wealthier farm areas and supported in the poorer ones.[20] The organization differs from the CCF in its belief in rural strikes.

This growing cleavage can result in one of two possibilities: the CCF, under pressure from the small farmers, will turn to the left; or the party will continue to aid the farming community vis-à-vis the larger society, but thereby strengthening the middle and wealthy section of the rural population. Another serious depression or drought, however, would probably re-create the unity of action of the Saskatchewan grain growers. The possibility still remains, nevertheless, that, like the Russian Bolsheviks during the N.E.P., the New Zealand Laborites, and the Roosevelt New Deal, the Saskatchewan CCF is sowing the seeds of opposition to socialist change.[21]

Though labor's electoral power in Saskatchewan is comparatively slight, the CCF's hope of gaining national power rests on the support of the labor movement outside the province. Organized labor, therefore, has had an appreciable influence in determining government policy. At the first session of the legislature after the electoral victory in 1944, the government enacted a Trade Union Act, which was drawn up by the unions and is probably the most pro-union legislation in the democratic capitalist world. The whole trend of government labor action is biased in the direction of supporting trade-union organization and demands.

The Trade Union Act makes collective bargaining mandatory on the part of the employer. It gives maintenance of membership and the compulsory check-off to any union which is the bargaining agent of the majority of the workers voting in a Labor Relations Board election. It outlaws various anti-labor practices by employers, and requires them to prove that they did not discharge an employee for union activity, thus placing the burden of proof on the employer rather than on the union.[22] An employer who consistently violates the orders of the Saskatchewan Labor Relations Board may have his plant expropriated by the government. This actually occurred in 1946, when the government took over the Prince Albert Box Factory after the owner had persistently refused to abide by the decisions of the Labor Board and had discharged his entire force in order to by-pass the Board's decision.[23]

The effect of Saskatchewan's labor legislation on trade-union organization is strikingly demonstrated in table 39. In the four years of CCF government, trade-union membership increased by 118.5 per cent. In the same period the unions of the entire country increased their membership by only 25 per cent.

Besides aiding trade-union organization, the CCF government has passed laws to strengthen the economic position of workers. The minimum weekly wage was raised to $18.50, one of the highest in Canada. Workmen's compensation payments were increased to 75 per cent of the worker's salary, given without a waiting period. This is the highest compensation rate on the continent. Two weeks' vacation with pay is now required by law, as well as a forty-four-hour week with no reduction in weekly pay.[24]

Most of the legislation benefiting workers was passed during the first year of the government, in the "honeymoon" period following the CCF's tremendous election victory. Since then, however, party support of labor's demands has been

TABLE 39

DISTRIBUTION OF TRADE-UNION MEMBERSHIP DECEMBER 31, 1943–47

Province	1943	1944	1945	1946	1947	Per cent gain 1943–47
Nova Scotia	41,982	35,095	31,982	33,233	36,575	−12.9
New Brunswick	18,232	17,980	18,238	18,659	22,295	22.3
Prince Edward Island	383	925	721	823	714	86.4
Quebec	188,714	175,993	171,203	208,546	210,260	11.4
Ontario	211,970	210,952	204,399	236,729	286,981	35.4
Manitoba	29,664	33,100	34,106	38,681	40,327	35.9
Saskatchewan	11,124	16,557	19,290	21,756	24,306	118.5
Alberta	28,975	28,504	28,578	33,662	38,202	31.8
British Columbia	87,485	90,702	83,823	99,466	115,230	31.7
Yukon	116	295	157	249	200	72.4
Unspecified	10,019	9,510	10,092	9,401	10,479	4.6
Totals	628,664	619,613	602,589	701,570	785,569	25.0

SOURCE: Department of Labour, *Annual Report on Labour Organization in Canada*, 1945–49.

waning. Many of the rural leaders of the government feel that they have done more than enough for labor. Electorally, they feel that the legislation has injured the party with small businessmen and many of the farmers. The rural leaders argue that a provincial government has little or no power to increase the income of farmers, since that is a federal matter, and therefore it is unfair to farmers to continually better the economic position of urban labor. They suggest also that Saskatchewan, as a province surrounded by governments with "bad" labor practices, will not be able to maintain industries that must compete with the rest of the country. The CCF legislative caucus in 1946 refused the request of the unions for a forty-hour week, and enacted a forty-four-hour week only after the trade-union delegates to the CCF provincial convention of that year insisted on the compromise.[25] Under pressure from businessmen and members of the legislative caucus, enforcement of labor legislation has somewhat weakened, the longer the government remains in office.[26] The trade-union members of the provincial party have been fighting this trend away from support of labor, but it is very doubtful whether the Saskatchewan CCF, as a farmer's government, is free to enact further legislation helping labor.

The one area in labor relations in which the government is comparatively free from public opinion is in its internal administrative policy in the civil service and the government-owned Crown corporations. The policy of the government is to be a model employer, encouraging workers to join unions and giving the unions a closed shop and higher wages. In spite of this policy there have been a number of labor disputes in the Crown companies. Two groups of workers, those at the Prince Albert Box Factory and at the Government Insurance Office, actually went on strike against the government, and employees of other Crown corporations have threatened to do the same in the past four years.

A basic conflict exists in the interpretation of the essential purposes of socialized industry from the managerial and employee standpoints. The government and its managerial personnel are primarily concerned with the financial success of their industries and thereby hope to demonstrate to the rural electorate that government-owned industries can operate as

efficiently as private enterprise. As a result, government officials fear to inaugurate any experiments in labor relations that
might injure the financial success of the Crown companies.
They do not want to yield any aspect of control into the hands
of potentially "irresponsible" workers' representatives. The
government, believing that nationalization is benefiting the
workers economically, expects them to work hard and cooperate with management.

The workers, however, have different criteria of success
for socialized industry. Many of them, especially those who
were socialists before the CCF victory, expected a change in
their status as workers, in their interpersonal relations with
their superiors. They felt that social ownership implied that
workers would be consulted on industrial policies. As one
worker in a Crown corporation expressed it,

We have been working here for a long time. Why ——
knows more about the operation of this plant than anyone in
the office. Before the government took over no one cared
whether the plant was operating efficiently or not. Afterwards
we thought a labor-management committee would be set up.
No one, however, asked us our opinion about anything. . . .

As far as the people in the office are concerned, we are
just so many machines who must produce. ——, the Minister,
came down once and gave us a pep talk on the necessity to
prove social ownership can work. That's just a lot of talk so
far as we are concerned. Why should we kill ourselves so ——
[the manager] can get all the credit.

J., an official in the same Crown corporation, expressed his
view on the effect of government ownership on labor.

The men have become impossible since the government
took over the plant. The union is always demanding higher
wages, shorter hours, rest periods, and extra overtime. Their
demands are ridiculous.

There is sure to be a clash between the union's desires and
the government's demands that we show a profit. The government must show a profit to satisfy the voters. Unless we crack
down on the union now, the government is going to be in
trouble later on.

If Saskatchewan gets another drought or the wheat market

drops, we will have a hard job making revenues meet expenditures. The workers don't realize this. They think because revenues are high now we can give them anything.

This executive was unaware of any desire on the part of his workers for participation in management. It is interesting to note that the employees in this plant complained that the management did not consider their feelings, but interpreted their grievances purely on an economic, dollars-and-cents level. The same pattern recurred in other government factories.

Virtually all the managerial personnel in Saskatchewan Crown corporations had previously been employed in private enterprise. Though most of them think of themselves as being friendly to labor, they cannot conceive of sharing authority with the worker. The worker is someone to be helped rather than consulted. Experience with trade-unions has tended only to make government managers fearful of yielding authority. Relations between unions and management have been concerned primarily with wages, hours, and working conditions, and the unions have necessarily taken a "hard-boiled" bargaining position in such negotiations. The managers, in turn, are convinced that the unions are not interested in the success of social ownership, for they appear willing to endanger it by insisting on uneconomic wages.

This situation has created a conflict in the minds of many government workers who belong to the CCF. Socialism to them meant a change in the status of labor in the factory. Since this has not happened, they either had to change their conception of socialism or refuse to accept their particular experience as an example of socialism in practice. A small proportion of the workers in the Crown companies have begun to believe the Communist arguments that the CCF is not a truly socialist party. The majority of vocal, active unionists felt certain, however, that the managers were "reactionaries" who were sabotaging the CCF government and should be removed from their jobs. In at least two government-owned plants, a committee of workers attempted to convince the cabinet minister in charge of their industry that the manager was a saboteur. When a minister supported the manager, many workers argued that the minister was not a "real socialist." Others believed that he was surrounded with reactionary advisers who were giving him false information. During my stay in Saskatchewan almost every manager, regardless of political affiliation, was charged by the workers in his plant with being "reactionary and antisocialist." Managers who had been active socialists for years before they were employed by the Saskatchewan government were criticized just as vigorously as nonsocialist managers, indicating that the cleavage between workers in the Crown corporations and the managerial staff was a result of structural rather than ideological differences.

Both top management and the workers' representatives have stated their belief in a new pattern of social ownership that will benefit both workers and the community. In practice, the managers, who remained under government ownership at the top of the industrial structure, define their day-to-day goals as making a profit, demonstrating to their immediate political supervisor that they are doing a good managerial job, and, if they are socialists, convincing the public that social ownership helps everyone. The workers, viewing "socialism" or government ownership from the bottom of the industrial structure, define their goals in terms of "personal dignity," "equality," "not being shoved around," and "the right to make suggestions," as well as higher income.

Conflicts in the attitudes of workers and management in government industry have not been peculiar to Saskatchewan. In England there is increasing recognition of this problem as one of the most crucial which the Labor government faces. The *Economist* pointed out this difficulty in discussing a coal miners' strike.

The real issues which are being fought out at Grimthorpe, where the miners have now been on strike for more than three weeks, can be summed up as a struggle between rationalization and syndicalism. The argument over the extra working at the coal face appears to be merely the pretext for a showdown on whether control is to be exercised by an all-powerful Board, or whether the workers are to be given a measure of influence in the management of their own pits. Many miners expected nationalization to result in workers' control;

instead it has resulted in a large bureaucratic machine leaving the individual miner face to face with the same managers with whom he has been wrangling over the past twenty years.[27]

Many workers in Saskatchewan government industries had never been part of the organized labor movement before the CCF was elected, and had little conception of the procedures for labor-management cooperation. Even the comparatively few workers who were old socialists had no definite idea of what they meant by "workers' control of industry." Both groups, however, did expect a greater sense of personal significance in the industrial structure under a socialist government. Some developed grievances against the CCF management of their plant, which they probably would never have voiced against private owners.

Workers felt that arbitrary management decisions on overtime work versus Saturday work, sick leave, and similar problems contravened the fundamental principles of the government. The first major strike in government industry occurred primarily because, in the words of some of the workers, the manager was "shoving his weight around too much." Attempts by workers in one factory to abolish various practices of restricting output, after the CCF government bought the plant, broke down completely because the active CCF members in the factory were not able to discuss changes in work procedure with the management.

The failure of the CCF to make innovations in the social structure of the factory has caused resentment. A change in the formal ownership of industry does not end the basic social frustration of the industrial worker if he feels he is merely a puppet in a dictatorially controlled industry. Unless socialist governments adopt methods that give workers a sense of democratic participation in the life of the factory, they may find, as the British and Saskatchewan governments have, that they will be faced with as much "sabotage" and "restriction of output" in socially owned industry as in private, capitalist enterprise. In fact, the sense of grievance of the worker in a plant owned by a socialist government may be greater than his grievance against management in a capitalist concern, since the worker's expectations are higher where "my government" owns the factory. Such working-class grievances may be of greater danger to the professed goals of a socialist government than the disturbances that result from changing managerial functions and status.

The basis of the educational program of the CCF government is similar to that of its labor and farm policies. The government is, in effect, carrying out the policies advocated by the *organized* teachers of the province, just as it has enacted the programs of the *organized* farmers and workers. The Minister of Education was president of the Saskatchewan Teachers' Federation for the three years immediately preceding his appointment. The policies and some of the personnel of the Federation were transferred to the Department of Education.

The new minister introduced changes in technical administration and in the curriculum. The first included raising the minimum salary of teachers from $700 to $1,200, providing free textbooks for students, setting up large school districts so that the cost of education should be more evenly spread between wealthy and poorer districts, establishing vocational high schools, and increasing scholarship funds for the provincial university. Most of these reforms were part of the program of the organized teachers and were advocated by farmers' groups as well. They were introduced soon after the CCF took office, and were pressed with vigor, so that today the educational facilities in Saskatchewan compare favorably with those in any rural area on the continent.[28]

The second aspect of the education program goes beyond the reforms demanded by clients of the department, and involves the ideology of the CCF movement. Many in the CCF believe that the present educational system is geared to uphold the existing social order, and that the social sciences, especially, are biased in favor of the capitalist system. They argue that the "real causes of wars" are not taught in the schools, that students do not learn of the power position of monopoly capital in an erstwhile democracy, and that the achievements of the cooperative movement and of socialist governments in other countries are played down in the textbooks. The party and the government, however, have long tended to avoid anything that might be construed as bringing politics into the school. Here again, fear of antagonizing sections of the electorate has limited the actions of the government.

The Minister of Education, Woodrow Lloyd, has shown, however, that such sentiments are not completely dead in the CCF.

I suggest that in the past, education has been neutral. . . . On the great issues facing the people, peace, prosperity, social justice, education cannot be neutral. Surely history has illustrated the fallaciousness of neutrality. Generally speaking, public opinion was neutral as it watched the degradation of China, Ethiopia, and Spain. While it is not suggested that education should accept all the responsibility for this neutrality of feeling, it must be admitted that neutrality could not have existed had education been more inclusive, more adequate, vital, and vigorous in outlook.[29]

The Department of Education has been acting to a limited extent on the principles laid down by the Minister. The high-school curriculum has been revised to include a positive orientation toward international cooperation, national planning, and the cooperative movement. The Department has organized an Adult Education Division "to help clarify the thinking of citizens on the fundamental issues confronting modern society." This division has sponsored conferences on cooperative farming, government health plans, and farmer-labor institutes designed to bring urban workers and farmers together.

The most important single social reform of the government is socialized medicine. The CCF has been committed to state medicine since its origin. Immediately after taking office, the government proceeded to initiate a state medical plan, which was later to become a most completely socialized system. All pensioners—the aged, the blind, and those receiving mothers' allowances—are now entitled to receive free medical, hospital, and dental services. Certain diseases, either costly to treat or a community danger, are treated free. These include cancer, tuberculosis, mental illness, and venereal disease. On January 1, 1947, a free hospitalization plan was inaugurated through which all residents of the province receive hospital services in return for the payment of a per capita tax of $10.

The CCF's long-term health policies are the only ones that involve a direct clash with powerful "vested interests." The party leaders originally envisaged a medical system in which all doctors would work on a salaried basis, and in which the emphasis would be changed from curative to preventive measures. Under such a system, many physicians, besides suffering a loss of income, would be forced to readjust their methods completely. They would be paid to keep people well rather than to treat their ailments. The members of the medical profession who treasure their incomes, traditions of practice, and personal independence have uncompromisingly opposed the implementation of any government scheme that would fundamentally alter their status.

In most parts of North America the organized medical profession has resisted any form of state medicine. In Saskatchewan, however, doctors have been forced to accept the basic premise of the need for state provision of medical care, since almost every section of public opinion favored it. The lack of decent health facilities in the sparsely settled rural regions made farmers acutely conscious of the need for government provision of such services, and the conventions of farmers' organizations since the First World War have requested state medicine. The Liberal and Conservative parties of the province also have repeatedly gone on record as favoring the change.[30]

The extent to which the public has accepted the necessity for socialized medicine is best illustrated by the municipal-doctor scheme, which began in 1921. By 1944, in 101 out of 303 rural municipalities, as well as 60 villages and 11 towns, having a total population of 200,000, doctors were working on a salary basis, treating all residents free of charge.[31] In effect, then, one-third of the rural municipal governments in Saskatchewan had a local version of socialized medicine. Research studies revealed that morbidity rates in municipal-doctor areas were lower than in comparable private-practice districts.

In view of the public support of state medicine, the Saskatchewan College of Physicians and Surgeons, the local medical body, has given support to the principle of government payment for medical care. The major conflict in Saskatchewan when the CCF took office was not, therefore, whether there should be state medicine or private medicine, but what kind of state medicine there should be. The physicians favored health insurance under which they would continue to practice exactly as they did under private medicine, except that they would send their bills to the state instead of to the patients.[32] The CCF, however, has long maintained that health insurance was no solution to the problem of adequate medical care. A pamphlet issued by the party in 1937 makes this position clear.

The matter of payment or non-payment for medical services is probably not the most pernicious evil. With all the advances of medical services we cannot make them available to a very large number. In our present system of practice, preventive medicine is largely neglected because the members of the [medical] profession are almost wholly engaged in the curative end of practice, so that preventable deaths are not being prevented and correctable conditions are not being corrected. . . .

If we are to have an all-inclusive system the state must necessarily assume control. In this Province much has been done. The direct control by the state of Tuberculosis has resulted in such advance in the treatment and prevention of Tuberculosis that it is amazing. . . . In the municipal doctor scheme much good has resulted, but there is no coordination in the scope of the work or the salary paid the doctor or in many other features. . . . The fact that the Governments of this Province have felt it necessary to undertake such schemes now mentioned, and many others to which reference might be made, indicates the great need of state or socialized medicine to provide for all the individuals in the state, an all-inclusive, coordinated, well functioning system of medical services.

The objective of a State Medical system should be to prevent disease and promote physical and mental health, and thus increase human efficiency, effectiveness and happiness. Prevention should be the foremost endeavor of any system because by it there will ultimately be a limitation of disease and its severity. . . . Disease or proneness to disease could be discovered at its source and measures undertaken before any advancement of ill-health began. . . . The doctor could then do the work for which he is best suited and especially trained and then he could devote his energies not to the competition of securing a living, but to the striving after better results in his work. The nurse could also be employed, when the necessity of the patient requiring special attention is the reason for her employment and not the financial position of the patient, irrespective of need.[33]

Soon after the CCF took office in 1944, the conflict between the government and the medical profession began to take shape. The government appointed a Health Services Planning Commission to draw up a detailed program of socialized medicine. The Commission, composed mainly of CCF experts, made two basic recommendations, which it considered essential to the success of the project, but which were in fundamental conflict with the policies of the organized medical profession. These were, first, that the program should be under the direct control of the government, and second, that the physicians should be paid by salary. The Commission explained its recommendations as follows:

The formulation of any policy that might be termed *"state medicine"* must be the duty of the Department of Public Health. Of all agencies interested in matters pertaining to the health and the medical care of the people of the province, it alone is responsible to the people, and it alone has the sanction of the law to make its policies effective.

Much has been said about the desirability of creating an independent non-government body to develop a province-wide health scheme. While such an organization has proven satisfactory in the case of the Anti-Tuberculosis League, there are certain features of it that make the extension to include all health services inadvisable:

(*a*) The powers of policy making with regard to matters pertaining to the health of the people of the province are delegated by the constitution to the Provincial Government. It is true that these powers may be delegated to other agencies, but it would seem to be a most doubtful practice to delegate a matter of such importance to any group other than the elected representatives or those immediately responsible to them;

(*b*) In so far as such an agency served any administrative function, it would be empowered to dispose . . . public funds. Again, it is doubtful if it is the best practice of representative government to permit any agency not directly responsible to the people or their representatives to control the spending of public revenues.[34]

One of the essential reasons for the Commission's insistence on direct provincial control of the scheme was omitted from the report for political reasons. The organized medical profession insisted that any state medical scheme should be controlled by an independent nonpolitical commission staffed largely by the profession. The Planning Commission, however, feared that such an "independent" body would be dominated by physicians who were hostile to the objectives of the plan and would therefore oppose measures that might jeopardize their own interests.

The second major recommendation that was opposed by the organized medical profession concerned the basis of remuneration.

The general practitioner service should be a salaried service. The municipal doctor system now in operation, despite its shortcomings has proven to be, on the whole, satisfactory. In support of a salaried service we may mention:

1. It has proven itself in Saskatchewan as a satisfactory method of providing medical care in small urban centers and rural areas.

2. It is an incentive to the physician to do preventive work, since he gains from health, rather than from illness. Surveys have shown that municipal doctors do relatively more preventive work than other rural physicians.

3. It removes the possible temptation for the physician to do unnecessary work, or work for which he is not well qualified.

4. It does not necessitate the constant supervision and redtape which would be necessary under a fee-for-service payment. . . .

9. When graded salaries are possible, the incentive to do good work will be furnished not only by pride in good results but by the increased salaries which may be earned on the

completion of a post-graduate course, the obtaining of a more responsible position, or a specialist's qualifications.[35]

After the publication of the report of the Health Services Planning Commission, the Minister of Health was under continual pressure from the organized medical profession to modify the plan. The Saskatchewan College of Physicians and Surgeons objected to these two recommendations. They insisted that a state medical scheme could operate successfully only if doctors who understood the problems of medical care controlled the scheme, and argued further that a state-controlled system would fail because of political interference. The physicians also insisted that remuneration be on the basis of a fee for service rather than a salary.

What incentives are there under a salaried scheme? It is only human nature not to do as well if one is not paid for it. An adequate financial reward for doctors is necessary if good medical services are to be provided. Competition between doctors is healthy.[36]

. . . the College of Physicians and Surgeons have made a very intensive study of the problem of socialized medicine and have for some time advocated a form of state aided health insurance, administered by a politically independent commission with representation on it from the public, the government, and those providing the service.

The College has opposed any system of state medicine whereby the doctors all become servants of the government on a salary. They have constantly advocated that the patient should have the privilege of choosing his own doctor.[37]

The spokesmen for the medical profession warned the government that the plan would fail unless it were modified. Some doctors even threatened that they would not cooperate or would leave the province to practice elsewhere.[38]

The impetus for implementing the scheme, as originally drawn up, came from within the government itself, from the small group connected with the Health Services Planning Commission. These medical experts, who were newly appointed by the CCF government, and who were thoroughly in favor of a socialized medical system, warned the Minister of Health that health insurance requiring a fee for service would continue the worst features of private medical practice, with its emphasis on curative rather than preventive medicine; and that doctors might overcharge the government through unnecessary surgical operations. They pointed to the failure of the fee-for-service plan in New Zealand, where "numerous abuses [exist], including 'over-consultation,' the speedy examination of patients, some at rates of twelve patients an hour, payment of $6,000 a year for one afternoon's work [during the week], and the charging of a fee for each patient seen on visits to institutions for the aged and invalid."[39]

These cross pressures on the government resulted in a modification of the original proposals of the Health Services Planning Commission. The Minister of Health proposed, instead of the original plan of direct government control, "to have a representative administrative body of all classes of the people . . . set up as a governing body with a small executive body on which the medical profession would be well represented."[40]

The medical profession regarded this concession as a major victory. One doctor suggested that the new plan meant that the government now stood for "health insurance rather than state medicine," and that discussions with the Minister reflected this shift in the government's opinion.[41] The doctors felt that, as experts on a commission meeting with laymen, they would have veto power and could forestall undesirable actions.

The second major compromise from the original proposals of the Planning Commission lay in the crucial area of payment to the doctors. In 1946 an experimental health region was set up in southwestern Saskatchewan, in the Swift Current district, to give complete medical and hospital care. The government agreed to pay the physicians on a fee-for-service basis, paying them 75 per cent of the existing standard rates. The local doctors and the College of Physicians and Surgeons accepted this proposal, which, in effect, gave them most of what they had originally asked for.

A third major government compromise lay in the policy of recruitment and licensing of physicians from outside the province and the country. Saskatchewan has the lowest ratio of doctors to population of any province in Canada except New Brunswick, and one-third of the physicians in the province were more than sixty years old at the end of the war. This fact naturally strengthened the position of the organized doctors. The Planning Commission felt that an organized campaign of recruiting doctors to the province was necessary if any state medical scheme were to succeed. Some government officials suggested that the College of Physicians and Surgeons was discouraging doctors from coming to Saskatchewan by warning them that the future of medicine was dark in the province. Moreover, government medical experts felt that the College was deliberately excluding refugee European physicians by imposing unduly difficult requirements.

A subcommittee of the provincial legislature was appointed to investigate the licensing power of professional groups such as the College of Physicians and Surgeons. Supporters of state and cooperative medicine testified that the College had used its power and influence to prevent doctors from cooperating with state and cooperative medical plans, as well as to keep doctors out of the province.

The legislative committee, which was controlled by a large CCF majority, favored legislation that would take the licensing power away from professional groups and give it to a government board. This suggestion was greeted with widespread protests by various professional groups. Some of the medical leaders again raised the threat of leaving the province. The government, once more, agreed to a compromise that left the professional associations in control of licensing, but required that the profession inform the government of the reason for failing to grant a license.

The medical profession, therefore, still retains most of the legal base of its power to discipline dissident members and its influence over recruitment of physicians. There is little formal evidence that it is abusing that power, but obviously it is not doing its utmost to cooperate with the government in the vital campaign to secure new doctors. Efforts to reduce the shortage of physicians can be effected in four ways: by making conditions of practice attractive to young physicians, by encouraging doctors who believe in socialized medicine to come to Saskatchewan, by admitting refugee physicians, and by stepping up medical training at the University of Saskatchewan.

Instead of encouraging young doctors, such statements as the following are made by reputable physicians: "Saskatchewan's flair for political experimentation leaves the prospective doctor uncertain as to the security of his medical future in this province."[42] Enthusiastic believers in socialized medicine who have expressed their willingness to come to the province have received cold, formal replies from the College, which have discouraged some of them. The leaders of the organized medical profession are still hostile to the idea of bringing in refugee physicians, and require that they undergo prolonged additional training before they are permitted to practice. All these actions must be viewed in the light of the fact that there are not enough doctors in rural areas.

The conflict between the Saskatchewan government and the organized medical profession is the only major clash between the government and a powerfully entrenched and socially necessary "vested interest" group. There are no major industries in the province, and the government, therefore, is not faced with the internal opposition of powerful industrial and financial interests. In embryonic form, however, the struggle with the medical profession is comparable to the problems faced by other socialist governments. The socialization of the medical profession in Saskatchewan is a small-scale equivalent of the problem of the socialization of a key sector of an economy which a controlling group is determined not to yield.

Like all other governments, one of the prime goals of a radical reform government in a political democracy is to be reelected. Any plan of the government will come to naught if it is defeated after one term in office. The elected reformer must, therefore, hold two considerations in mind if he is to achieve the social reforms which his party proposes: first, he must make the changes that are necessary to secure the reforms; and second, he must not antagonize the majority of the electorate. To threaten the power, privileges, or beliefs of any socially necessary key group may lead that group to refuse to continue its work efficiently. Such "sabotage" could temporarily deprive the general public of the services it had previously received.

The Saskatchewan government was faced with the possibility that the socialization of medicine would cause a large number of doctors to leave the province. Members of the government feared that they would then be blamed for the consequent decline in medical standards and services. Similarly, if the British government were to socialize an industry in which the managers were strongly opposed to the plans of the government, the resultant decline in productivity could bring down the government at the next election.

This dilemma has been faced repeatedly by democratic reform governments. The Labor and Social Democratic governments of Sweden, Norway, New Zealand, and Australia have held political power for long periods without making significant inroads on "vested" property and managerial interests. Few industries have been nationalized by these governments, though they all profess socialist objectives. Each of these governments has increased its social services, as Saskatchewan has. Increased social services are an easy solution to the dilemma of the democratic socialist in office, for they improve living standards but do not upset the *status quo* and are not violently opposed by the people with economic power or skill. Thus the medical profession had no serious objection to the establishment of free hospitalization in the province in 1947, for this measure satisfied the popular desire for increased state provision of medical care, but did not affect the position of the physicians.

The problem suggested is a major one in any attempt to secure important social change through democratic channels. Can the state make significant inroads on the power of entrenched groups which are economically or socially necessary without, in the process, giving up democracy? The degree to which a democratically elected government can successfully install far-reaching changes in the face of powerful opposition would seem to depend on the organized popular demand for its program. The British Labor government could not have refused to nationalize the coal mines without suffering a loss of many of its supporters. In Australia the recently defeated Labor government embarked on a campaign to socialize all banks, after being criticized by many of its more left-wing supporters.

The Saskatchewan government, however, is not backed by an electorate that understands or demands qualitative changes in medical care. The people wanted greater and cheaper quantities of the kind of service they already had. The farmers supported "state" medicine, but to them the term meant state payment for medical care, free medicines, free hospitalization, prepayment of medical costs, and medical care of pensioners and indigents. The public, including most of the members and leaders of the CCF, are not and were not aware of the dangerous implications of the professional control of licensing or of the fee-for-service plan for the program of the CCF.

There has been little criticism from members of the CCF of the government's compromises with the medical profession. Party members and supporters enthusiastically approve every step toward the goal of a complete plan of medical coverage. Thus, government officials are faced on one hand with the popular demand for any kind of state medicine, and, on the other, with the threat of sabotage by physicians unless the plan of their organized profession is put into practice. The compromise of the basic goals of reform of medical practice naturally followed.

The dilemma of the reform politician can be lessened only if he wins an enlightened electorate before he assumes office. The pressures of groups opposing social change must be counterbalanced by other powerful groups. The lack of major groups in Saskatchewan opposing the well-organized medical profession has been a large factor in the success of that group. The experiences of the Saskatchewan government indicate that a socialist party may win power by playing down the radical elements of its own program. Many sincere reformers have done this with the intention of educating the electorate and carrying out radical reforms after they took office. Once in office, however, the party learns that it is too late for education, that it must back down before hostile power groups. It then becomes politically necessary to educate the public about the advantages of the compromise, not of further reform.

Like other socialist governments, the Saskatchewan CCF

has extended its social welfare work greatly. There has been little or no opposition to such efforts. The government set up a separate Department of Social Welfare for the first time in the history of the province, and has increased the amount of money spent for this purpose to the highest proportion of the total budget of any province in Canada.

The Department increased old-age pensions $5 a month above those paid by the federal government and granted free medical care to all recipients of government pensions. Mothers' allowances were greatly increased, and the province took over direct responsibility for all unplaced orphan children. A rehabilitation program has been started for the métis (half-breeds), and they are being trained for useful occupations. Old-age homes and the penal system are being modernized. For the first time, trained workers have been hired to staff the Department of Social Welfare.[43]

The only limitation placed on the social welfare work of the government has been financial. The government is afraid to increase taxes sharply for the benefit of social services, since the tax-conscious farmers would resent new direct taxes on land. So far as financial resources permit, however, the humanitarian goals of the CCF movement have been carried out, and have resulted in one of the best social service programs in Canada. These developments confirm the pattern, suggested earlier, of reformers moving farthest in areas of least social resistance.

In explaining the significant difference between the reforms of the CCF and those of various "progressive" nonsocialist governments, CCF leaders point to the socialization of industry. Today the Saskatchewan government owns and operates a large number of enterprises, including electric power, telephones, bus lines, insurance, a printing company, a woolen mill, a fur-marketing service, a shoe factory, a tannery, a sodium sulphate plant, a seed-cleaning plant, liquor stores, two fish-filleting plants, a fish-marketing board, a lumber-marketing board, a box factory, and a brickyard. All except the telephones, liquor stores, and part of the electric power system were acquired since the CCF took office.

The reasons given for government ownership of the different industries vary. The overriding consideration on a provincial level is the desire to obtain funds for extra social services. The CCF looks upon government businesses as one of the best means of increasing the general revenues of the government without raising taxes. Second, the farmers' movement and the CCF have long argued that natural resources and public utilities should belong to the people. The extension of government electric power lies in this category. A third motive given for government ownership has been the desire to keep money inside the province. The establishment of the Government Insurance Office and the replacement of the Greyhound Bus Lines by a Government Bus Company has been defended on the ground that Saskatchewan is keeping its money at home. The government has pointed out that residents of Saskatchewan paid over $50,000,000 in insurance premiums during the depression to non-Saskatchewan insurance firms and received only $19,000,000 in return for losses.[44] A fourth group of industries to be owned by the government are the small-scale enterprises that process Saskatchewan resources: the woolen mill, the shoe factory, and the brickyard.

The government has also set up a number of corporations that could best be described as service companies. These companies were organized to render a nonprofit service to groups that could not obtain the service elsewhere or that were, in the opinion of the government, being exploited by private interests. The fish-filleting plants, the fish-marketing board, the lumber board, the seed-cleaning plant, and the fur-marketing service fall in this category. There is also the Prince Albert Box Factory, which was expropriated as a result of a labor dispute.

There can be little doubt that the government's socialization program does establish a qualitative difference between the CCF and other agrarian reform parties. The socialist ideology and beliefs of the CCF have played a major role in the extent and vigor of the program. After the 1944 victory, party and government leaders indicated a real desire to socialize industry, in spite of the fact that this was played down in the election campaign.

Saskatchewan, however, has no large-scale industry. It has less than 2 per cent of the total industrial production of Canada.[45] Outside of public utilities, therefore, the only areas for potential government investment are businesses that would be considered small in the country as a whole. The Saskatchewan CCF was therefore faced with the choice of leaving the nationalization aspects of the party to a future federal CCF government, which could socialize big business in harmony with the party platform, or of sidestepping that platform and establishing state-owned small businesses. The government chose the latter course, because large sections of the party and its leadership were eager to demonstrate the value of government ownership.

In explaining the program to the people, however, the CCF leaders have defended their activities more in terms of provincial sectionalism, that is, resistance to the industrially dominant East, than in socialist terms of eventual replacement of private ownership by social ownership. It is interesting to note that the Non-Partisan League in North Dakota also embarked on a program of state-owned industry that was defended in similar nonsocialist terms. Many western farmers have considered the lack of industry in the wheat-growing areas of the United States and Canada to be part of the exploitation of the West practiced by "eastern interests."

At the same time that the Saskatchewan government was starting on a program of government industry, it had to continue to support private industry, as the overwhelming majority of industry and future investment would necessarily remain in private hands for many years, and the party desired to win the support of small business. Cabinet members attempted to resolve the apparent contradiction between their promises and their actions by saying that the government would enter only the industrial fields that private enterprise refused to develop, and that where private business would develop an industry, the government would help them to do so.[46] The government set up a fund from which private investors could borrow to start new industries.

This policy of government ownership of small industry was economically dangerous for the government. A number of the small industries that it started, especially shoes and woolen goods, were risky ventures in which private businessmen were afraid to invest. The government has been taking the risks of the marginal producer and has encountered difficulties in competing profitably with older private companies in other parts of Canada, where labor standards are lower than those set by the CCF. Some of these industries have either lost money or are making only a small profit, which will probably disappear with the end of a seller's market.[47]

Faced by these coercions of the market economy, which many of the CCF leaders did not envisage in their early socialist enthusiasm, a number of the government officials have become wary about engaging in further public enterprise. They fear that government industry operating at a loss will lead to a serious decrease in rural support. The government has therefore modified its original intention of socializing the oil fields, for they are still in the category of a risk investment, and private companies are being encouraged to come into the province on long-term leases.

These experiences point up the dangers facing socialist governments that do not have or do not take complete control over the economy. Government enterprise operating in a capitalist market is naturally subject to the same external constraints as private enterprise and reacts in the same way. The attempt to jump into this uncontrolled situation has made many CCF'ers much more conservative in their attitude toward socialization of industry, and may seriously affect the party's action in the federal field. Industrial experience in the province of Saskatchewan seems to confirm the warnings of socialist economists who challenge the possibility of socialists successfully maintaining a mixed economy.[48] It is significant to note that the governments of various Australian states had similar experiences in the 1920's when they established state-owned small industries.[49] Many of these industries had to be sold in the 'thirties because they were losing money.

The experiences of the CCF in power yield significant insights into the processes of social change in a democracy. The types of reform introduced by a political party include three main factors: the ideology of the movement, the power of the forces that benefit from change, and the strength of the opposition. The extent of change in any area under Saskatchewan government control depends primarily on the degree of organized support for reform in comparison with the economic, political, or technical strength of the opposition. The socialist and progressive ideology of the CCF has strengthened the left-wing forces, but it has not changed the usual role of pressure groups in a democratic society.

CCF reforms in education, soon after the government was elected, reflected the strength and pressure of the organized teaching profession. The teachers and the farmers' organizations favored basic quantitative reforms in the educational system. These reforms were brought in quickly and vigorously because there was no organized opposition. Curricular changes did meet opposition and hence such changes have been comparatively minor. The powerful cooperative movement received a government Department of Cooperatives. The organized farmers' movement secured government protection for landownership and support in gaining higher prices. The trade-unions were given what they consider to be "the best labor legislation on the North American continent." The rural demand for state medicine is being fulfilled in a way that meets with the approval of the medical profession.

Earlier in this chapter, the question of the freedom of a radical government in a democracy to innovate beyond the popularly demanded reforms was raised. The experience of Saskatchewan would seem to repeat the pattern followed by other democratic socialist governments. The need of a democratic government to retain the support of a majority of the electorate is a powerful weapon in the hands of groups that wish to prevent social change. Any drastic change in basic institutions may endanger the popular support of the government. Socialist governments, therefore, have followed the path of least resistance, instituting reforms that meet the least opposition from entrenched interests.

Basic institutions are modified only when they have broken down completely. The extensive socialization of industry in Spain in 1936 took place only after the owners of the factories fled Loyalist Spain.[50] The government, however, later returned many of the confiscated industries in order to retain the support of the middle classes. The past or present majority socialist governments of Sweden, Norway, New Zealand, and Australia have not socialized many industries, though they have held power for long periods of time.[51] Socialization has often taken place in these countries as a result of a loss of support to more radical parties demanding the changes. Only those parties that placed the achievement of their "reform" objectives above the maintenance of democracy, such as Communist Russia and Nazi Germany, have succeeded in fundamentally changing the social and economic structure.

A reformer who desires to make drastic innovations must be prepared to face resistance and sabotage from the groups whose power, status, privileges, or traditions he threatens. The democratic radical in opposition will suggest many reforms that appear logical and necessary to him. Once in office he finds that his goal must shift from reform to the maintenance of the equilibrium of the institutional order, unless he is prepared to place the success of his original goals over the possibility of losing power. To explain his refusal to carry out his program on the ground that it is opposed by various groups that make its success impossible is to admit that the proposed reform is utopian, that it never could have been carried out. Few politicians in office will face up to this problem. The result is that their over-all reform program often falls by the wayside.

It is not suggested that the reforms of the CCF in Saskatchewan are not important. The sincere reformist beliefs of CCF leaders have resulted in many actions that would not have been established by the old parties, whose loyalties are to the existing order. No one can challenge the fact that the CCF has made trade-union organization easier, that it is protecting farmers against foreclosure and debt, that it has improved the lot of indigents in Saskatchewan, that it has reduced some of the serious financial burdens that result from illness, automobile accidents, or injuries at work. Actually, the Saskatchewan government has probably done as much to reduce economic hazards as a provincial government with limited powers can do.

The fact remains, however, that with few exceptions the CCF, like many other reform governments, has not innovated where the consequences would endanger its electoral support, because the transition period between the old reform and the smooth operation of a new pattern is, in a democracy, also an electoral period. Left-wing critics of the government, both within and outside the CCF, suggest that the government has been too conservative and cautious in its policies, that it has been afraid to take risks or that it sees risks where none are present. However, even if the government had been more venturesome, the broad, over-all problem would still exist— the problem of maintaining sufficient equilibrium between elections to retain office. The question of how to reconcile the need for change and still keep a basically democratic structure seems to be one of the most crucial issues of our age.

NOTES

1. "Britain, Decay of the Conservatives," *Time,* April 21, 1947, p. 3. See Marquis W. Childs, *Sweden: The Middle Way* (New York, Penguin Books, Ltd., 1948), pp. 142–47, for a description of compromise attitudes of Swedish parties.

2. "Scandinavia—Between Two Worlds," *New Republic,* May 5, 1947, p. 14.

3. See provincial platforms of Saskatchewan Liberal and Conservative parties, 1929.

4. "And the People Are Watching," Regina *Daily-Star,* March 15, 1937, p. 4.

5. Quoted in Regina *Leader-Post,* August 7, 1931, p. 12.

6. The prairies have provincially owned telephone systems, widespread cooperatives, and local rural systems of socialized medicine.

7. Stuart A. Rice suggested the "existence of a radical culture area in northwestern North Dakota, with lines of diffusion extending eastward and southward and again bending westward." See his *Farmers and Workers in American Politics* (New York, Longmans, Green and Co., 1924), p. 181. If we extend Rice's "radical culture area" directly northward, we enter Saskatchewan.

8. *Statutes of Saskatchewan, Second Session, 1944* (Regina, 1945).

9. Interviews with H. K. Warren, chairman of Provincial Mediation Board.

10. Unpublished address by Premier Douglas.

11. Province of Saskatchewan, Department of Agriculture, *Annual Report* (Regina), 1944–48.

12. Interviews with CCF leaders.

13. The proposal to limit the size of farm holdings has never come before a CCF provincial convention.

14. Province of Saskatchewan, Department of Cooperation and Cooperative Development, *Annual Report* (Regina), 1946–48.

15. An unpublished study by a private research organization in 1947 indicates clearly that the members of Saskatchewan cooperatives are upper-income farmers.

16. Interviews with members of the Economic Planning Board.

17. The shift in one decade in rural opinion in New Zealand has been significant.

RURAL ELECTIONS

	1935	1938	1943	1946
Labor	20	15	10	4
Opposition	17	22	27	27

SOURCE: "New Zealand, the General Election," *Round Table*, No. 146 (March, 1947), p, 202.

18. David T. Bazelon, "The Faith of Henry Wallace," *Commentary*, April, 1947, p. 314.

19. Maurice Dobb, *Russian Economic Development since the Revolution* (London, G. Routledge and Sons, Ltd., 1928).

20. *Western Producer*, August 19, 1946, p. 1; and interviews with leaders of the U.F.C. (Saskatchewan Section).

21. This was written before the 1949 elections, which saw the CCF lose support in the rural areas of the province.

22. *Statutes of Saskatchewan*, 1945, 1948.

23. Regina *Leader-Post*, November 2, 1945, p. 1.

24. *Statutes of Saskatchewan*, 1947.

25. Interviews and attendance at the 1946 CCF Convention.

26. Interviews with labor leaders and members of the Department of Labor.

27. "The Issue at Grimthorpe" (editorial), London *Economist*, September 6, 1947, p. 393.

28. Province of Saskatchewan, Department of Education, *Annual Report* (Regina), 1945–49.

29. Unpublished address, p. 3.

30. See provincial platforms of Liberal and Conservative parties, 1938, 1944.

31. Dr. Hugh McLean, *An Address on Medical Health Services* (Regina, 1944), p. 2.

32. Testimony of representatives of Saskatchewan College of Physicians and Surgeons before special subcommittee of Saskatchewan legislature, 1946.

33. *Handbook to the Saskatchewan CCF Platform and Policy* (Regina, 1937), pp. 34–35. (Italics mine.)

34. Health Services Planning Commission, *Report on Regional Health Services: A Proposed Plan* (Regina, 1945), Part II, p. 2.

35. *Ibid.*, Part III, p. 7.

36. Dr. Lloyd Brown, president of Regina Medical Services, unpublished address on Saskatchewan Health Plan, April 26, 1946.

37. Dr. J. G. K. Lindsay, registrar of Saskatchewan College of Physicians and Surgeons, quoted in Regina *Leader-Post*, March 16, 1946, p. 1.

38. Interviews with members of the Department of Health and Saskatchewan physicians.

39. "Medical Rackets Grip New Zealand," New York *Times*, October 7, 1945; "Medical Care Criticized by New Zealand Hospital Head," *Christian Science Monitor* (Boston), September 29, 1945.

40. "Saskatchewan Executive Meets Government," *Trades and Labor Congress Journal*, February, 1946, p. 12.

41. See note 36.

42. Dr. C. J. Houston, president of the Council of the Saskatchewan College of Physicians and Surgeons, quoted in Regina *Leader-Post*, August 7, 1947, p. 13.

43. Province of Saskatchewan, Department of Social Welfare, *Social Welfare in Saskatchewan* (Regina, 1948).

44. O. W. Valleau, *Saskatchewan Government Insurance* (Regina, 1945), p. 1. Mimeographed radio speech.

45. *Report of the Saskatchewan Reconstruction Council* (Regina, 1944), p. 113.

46. C. M. Fines, Provincial Treasurer, *Budget Speech* (Regina, 1948), pp. 12–13.

47. The shoe factory and the tannery were forced to shut down in December, 1948.

48. Oskar Lange and Fred M. Taylor, *On the Economic Theory of Socialism* (University of Minnesota Press, 1938).

49. H. V. Evatt, *Australian Labour Leader* (Sydney, Angus and Robertson, Ltd., 1945), pp. 306, 395, 431, 496–97, 501–11.

50. Felix Morrow, *Revolution and Counter-Revolution in Spain* (New York, Pioneer Publishers, 1933).

51. "No labor leader would repudiate the socialist objective; but none could honestly argue that in practice his socialism had gone beyond a tendency toward using governmental controls as a method of dealing with immediate problems; and toward expanding social services for the mass of the Australian people. We have accepted socialism as a goal, but we have seldom planned a legislative program of rapid and widespread steps toward socialism." Lloyd Ross, *Labor in Australia* (American Council, Institute of Pacific Relations, New York, 1943), p. 17. See also Childs, *op. cit.,* p. 147; Harry W. Laidler, *Social-Economic Movements* (New York, Thomas Y. Crowell Co., 1944), pp. 563–70.

12

BUREAUCRACY AND SOCIAL CHANGE

At almost every CCF provincial convention and Council meeting, the problem of the relationship between the government and the civil service has been raised by party members.[1] Many in the CCF believe that the retention in office of key civil servants appointed by Liberal governments is hampering the work of the government. This conviction is evident in the resolutions they have submitted to various constituencies between 1945 and 1947.

Whereas most of the Civil Service have been supporters of old line parties and most still remain sympathizers of said parties, and

Whereas in the last year under CCF Government, new appointments or promotions to higher positions have been made mostly from supporters of the old line parties because recommendations on a possible new appointment or promotion are being requested from senior officers of said Departments who again are old line party supporters and only naturally recommend their own kind.

Therefore be it resolved that members of the Government in engaging Civil Servants, make appointments, wherever possible, from CCF supporters to at least even up an equal proportion of Civil Servants as between the old line parties and CCF supporters.[2]

Whereas it is quite obvious that certain partisan Liberal employees in the Civil Service are using their inside position to belittle, entangle and obstruct the good work of our CCF Government and

Whereas this can bring about lack of confidence in and place at a great disadvantage our CCF party at the next Provincial election.

Therefore be it resolved that this CCF Convention of the Qu'Appelle-Wolseley constituency do request our Government to be consistently on the lookout for these partisan Civil Servants and have them removed from positions of trust.[3]

Whereas certain recent appointments made by the Provincial Government have brought considerable criticism from the membership, and whereas personnel selected for certain vital positions have not in the past upheld the philosophy of the CCF and are considered doubtful of doing so in the future, and whereas this type of appointment may develop serious opposition in the near future,

Therefore be it resolved that we request the Saskatchewan CCF Provincial Government to be very careful in its appointments in the future, and suggest that socialist minded persons be appointed wherever possible.[4]

Be it resolved that the Government exercise extreme caution in the selection of members to various boards and other appointees holding responsible positions to forestall any sabotage, whether premeditated or because the proposed appointee lacks sufficient grounding in the fundamentals and principles of the Government.[5]

Resolved that the Convention go on record to ask the provincial Government to fill the key positions in the Civil Service with younger people, who are sincere and honest for the cause and principles of the Movement as laid down by our CCF Party Convention.[6]

Whereas our original program for the CCF stated that when elected to power persons holding key positions should be sympathetic to the CCF cause;

And whereas two Provincial Conventions have passed resolutions asking that this be done;

Therefore be it resolved that the Government remove reactionary departmental heads and put in their places persons who are sympathetic to the CCF.[7]

That there should be special attention taken in respect to our public services, which we feel quite sure are being sabotaged in a good many ways by some of the personnel in the different services, which are undermining the interest of the public in a very serious manner;

Therefore we recommend that special investigations be made in these different departments, with special authority to deal with these matters and then clear up.[8]

Whereas the Provincial Government has given all its civil servants, regardless of political affiliations, every consideration, and has taken on new personnel without consideration of their political affiliations, which confirms the original CCF policy;

And whereas it has been found that several of these appointees have been sabotaging the CCF Government in an underhand manner, by giving out incorrect information, which has a mischievous effect in the country, which must be counteracted by local people, and the executive;

Be it resolved that the Government discharge all such officials coming under this class and replace them with loyal cooperators and efficient personnel.[9]

The discussion of the role of the civil servant raises again, this time on the level of the problem of government bureaucracy, the question of how free reform governments are to innovate. Writers and social scientists have long called attention to the fact that in the state and other large social organizations, administrative functions cannot be separated from policy-making power.[10] It is impossible to understand the operation of a government simply by analyzing the goals of the politicians in power and the nongovernmental pressures on them. The members of the civil service constitute one of the major houses of government, with the power to initiate, amend, and veto actions proposed by other branches. The goals and values of the civil service are often as important a part of the total complex of forces responsible for state policy as those of the ruling political party.

The political problem of the power and influence of a permanent civil service with its own goals and traditions was not important so long as the social and economic values of the bureaucracy and the governing politicians did not seriously conflict. The problem becomes crucial, however, when a new political movement takes office and proposes to enact reforms that go beyond the traditional frame of reference of previous governmental activity or which upset the existing set of relations within the bureaucracy. It is especially important today, when the explicit formal goals of many democratic states are changing from the laissez-faire police regulation of society to those of a social-welfare planning state.[11]

The tradition and concept of a merit nonpatronage civil service was related in many countries to the needs of the dominant business groups, who demanded cheap and efficient service from the state. J. Donald Kingsley has shown how in England the policy of a merit civil service grew with the increase in political power of the business class.[12] The business groups desired an efficient state that would facilitate and protect the development of commerce. Permanent, nonpolitical officials insured continuity of government regulations and practices, and made for stable relations with the state, regardless of shifts in party fortunes. This idea of a merit civil service was not challenged as long as party politics remained contests between groups who accepted the basic orientation and activities of the state and the society. The establishment of reform and socialist governments, which propose radical changes in the functions of the state, raises the problem of whether such reforms can be successfully initiated and administered by a bureaucratic structure that is organized to regulate different norms, and whose members possess values that do not correspond with those of the "radical" politicians.

Since the days of Karl Marx, some socialists have maintained that a successful socialist state must destroy the old state apparatus and erect a new administrative organization.[13] In recent times, persons who have served in, or studied, socialist governments have suggested that one crucial reason for their failure to proceed more vigorously toward the attainment of their goals has been the "bureaucratic conservatism" of old civil servants.

In Weimar, Germany, the Social Democratic Party, which held majority power from 1918 to 1920, was not able to make fundamental changes in the power and economic structures. Participants in that government report that the bureaucracy played a major role in obstructing changes, as the following statement by Arnold Brecht, a former important Social Democratic government official, suggests:

One of the finest Labor Ministers in post-war Germany, a great authority in law philosophy, liked to mock himself in relating how the scientific atmosphere of the Ministry of Justice lulled his activity. There were the most admirable experts, modest and seriously prepared to submit to any better argument, intent upon justice and truth, upon science and social achievements, ready to do what they were ordered to do when the arguing stopped. . . . While the political heads changed frequently, the officials as a whole stayed, willing to do anything they were ordered to do. . . . Why not hear them. . . . They would not just say no to new proposals. . . . But they would adjust the political plans to expediency, and would take the fundamentals of the radical proposals and reduce them to cautious experiments in various directions, preserving a conservative trend.[14]

George Lansbury, who was a member of the second Labor government in Great Britain, and subsequently became leader of the Party, unequivocally declared, "All through the life of the late [1929–31 Labor] Government, Treasury officials obstructed and hindered the Ministers in their work. No one can deny this."[15] A study by a political scientist of the work of this government bears Lansbury out.

Philip Snowden's sympathies were with the socialists when he headed the Treasury in a Labor Cabinet, but his budgets might well have been drawn up by Conservatives. . . . the influence of his permanent officials, and of outstanding persons of the City, outweighed that of his cabinet colleagues; and before many months of service, the radical became proud of his conservatism.

George Lansbury, First Commissioner of Works in the second Labor Government, strove for many reforms, particularly in the fields of unemployment, old age pensions, and education. As one of a group of officials called upon to solve these problems, he found the road to reform blocked at every turn by the civil servants. These officials, he said, acted quite constitutionally, refusing to comment on policy, only questioning whether or not a proposed policy would work. But Treasury representatives always found reasons why ministerial proposals could not be carried out. Lansbury soon came to feel the futility of his position and concluded that if a Socialist Government was to succeed, dependence could not be placed on civil servants who were not Socialist.[16]

An Australian participant in a Labor government, V. G. Childe, former secretary to the Premier of New South Wales, pointed to the role of "outwardly obsequious civil servants" in helping to transform the attitudes of Labor ministers.[17] "In

France, too, reactionary officials successfully sabotaged the efforts of the Blum government in finance and foreign affairs."[18]

Saskatchewan is the latest in the series of examples of radical governments attempting to make drastic changes in the direction and functions of government while retaining permanent civil servants in key administrative policy-making posts. There are, however, major differences between Saskatchewan and most other countries in which radical parties have come to power. Civil-service traditions are very different from those prevailing in England and other British Commonwealth countries; they are, in fact, more similar to those of nineteenth-century United States than to those of England. Party loyalty and obligations determine the choice of civil servants, as the following report makes clear.

It is possible to find four main corrupt features in the Saskatchewan Liberal organization, features which are common to most party organizations in Canada, whether Liberal or Conservative: the use of the civil servants as party workers; the patronage system by which party supporters were appointed to the civil service; the use of public works appropriations, particularly the road money, for pork barrel purposes; and the granting of contracts, especially in public works and printing, in return for financial or press support. . . .

The patronage system gave the party the votes of practically all the provincial civil service. Whenever the votes of the civil service can be separated, they appear to have voted en bloc for the Liberals, even in federal elections. For example, one provincial institution, the Weyburn Mental Hospital, cast in the federal general election of 1925, 135 votes for the Liberal candidate, 5 for the Conservative, and 1 for the Progressive. In the rest of the constituency the Liberals received about 4,800 votes, and the other two candidates about 2,000 each. In the federal election of 1921, the Provincial Hospital at North Battleford cast 141 votes for the Liberal, 5 for the Conservative, and 16 for the Progressive. The vote . . . in the rest of the constituency was: Liberal, 4,500; Conservative, 700; Progressive, 8,800.[19]

During the 1930's, administration of relief and awarding of government jobs were more directly partisan than ever before.

Many CCF supporters assert that they were warned by relief inspectors to cease working for the CCF. As a result, the attitude of the CCF toward the civil service differed from that of many European socialist parties. The dislike of the blatant excesses of patronage government led the party, while in opposition, to oppose partisan appointments; but the recognition that the civil service was honeycombed with Liberal politicians made CCF leaders specifically exempt deputy ministers and other major policy posts from civil-service protection. Unlike socialist parties in Europe and Great Britain, which were prevented from advocating changes in the civil service because of the popular acceptance of a politically neutral bureaucracy, the CCF was free, in terms of the political values of Saskatchewan, to advocate the replacement of top-ranking conservative civil servants by CCF experts, and did so in its 1944 program.

The CCF pledges itself to remove party patronage from the public services of Canada. While recognizing that heads of commissions, Deputy-Ministers, etc., *must be in agreement with the policy of the government and should therefore be government appointments,* all other Civil Service appointments should be, and under a CCF government, will be, placed under the control of a nonpolitical commission.[20]

The leader of the party, and later the Premier, T. C. Douglas, in a preelection speech made clear his insistence on having sympathetic experts. "It is most necessary for any government that those in charge of various departments shall be competent and capable of absorbing new ideas and techniques. No matter how good legislation is, if those in charge of administering it are unsympathetic or incapable of a new approach, little good will come of it."[21] Judging by the preelection attitudes of CCF leaders, Saskatchewan should have been a good example of an attempt to institute reforms with a new administrative apparatus. After the election in 1944, both opponents and supporters of the party expected that key posts in the civil service would be filled from the ranks of experts sympathetic to socialist objectives.[22] Some of the new cabinet ministers told party intimates, before the election, that the incumbent deputy ministers were "reactionaries" who could never be expected to carry out CCF policies.

Once in office, however, the new CCF cabinet ministers changed their views. Instead of the expected housecleaning, most of the key civil servants were retained. Few changes in the top administration were made during the first two years of the CCF government. Men who had served under the Liberals were promoted to fill vacancies in the upper levels of the civil service.

Every group of responsible CCF leaders except the cabinet ministers, however, continued to believe that extensive changes in the top-level personnel of the government were necessary if the movement was to carry out its objectives of social reform. This attitude was expressed by members of the Provincial Council, CCF members of the legislature, Saskatchewan members of the federal House of Commons, and every provincial convention since the party took office.[23] The party leaders who formed the government were no less committed to the goals and program of the party. The changes in the objectives of CCF cabinet ministers must, therefore, be dealt with on the structural, rather than the ideological or personal, level.

The difference between the cabinet and the rest of the party hierarchy lay in the fact that the new ministers were exposed to unanticipated pressures. They were faced with the immediate problem of assuming responsibility for departments that had to deal with a multitude of day-to-day problems. No department could stop operating until the new administration rebuilt its working apparatus. The new ministers, like most politicians, were amateurs in their respective departments. None of them had ever had administrative experience in a large organization.

The members of the cabinet were under pressure to implement the legislative and administrative reforms promised by the party platform. This platform, like that of most political parties, was necessarily general, lacking concrete steps to be taken after election. Besides drawing up new legislation, changing administrative regulations of their departments, and taking part in cabinet meetings, the ministers had to continue being active politicians, making speeches and caring for the needs of their constituents.

In any government, such pressures force the cabinet ministers to lean heavily on their civil service.[24] In Saskatchewan, however, many of the cabinet ministers had anticipated deliberate "sabotage" or resistance to their plans by the Liberal civil service. They entered office ready to remove the deputy ministers as soon as they showed signs of opposition to government plans. The key civil servants, on the other hand, expected to be discharged soon after the CCF took office.[25] They knew that the CCF was aware of the partisan nature of their appointments. Some of them had begun to look for other jobs, or planned to retire. The majority, however, in the hope of maintaining their positions, tried to ingratiate themselves with their ministers.

A——, a deputy minister, went to his Minister shortly after the election, and told him that he had been a member of the British Labor Party, thirty years ago, and that he was pleased at the opportunity of working for a socialist government.

B——, who had been an active Liberal, and had been engaged in relief work in the 'thirties, told his minister that he had been unhappy in his job under the old government, because all members of the department had been forced to engage in partisan work. Now that the CCF was in office, he hoped to be really free to do his work. He told the minister stories of the inefficiency of certain parts of the department.

The wives of two deputy ministers began a campaign of wooing the wives of their respective ministers, who were new to Regina. They entertained them and introduced them to various people in the city. The deputies, themselves, offered to assist their ministers in various reforms.

C——, another deputy, came to his minister and offered to draw up the working plans of a major CCF reform.[26]

The leading civil servants did their utmost to convince the cabinet that they were cooperative. In many departments, during the early period of the CCF government, the best "socialists" in Saskatchewan were in the top ranks of the governmental bureaucracy. The administratively insecure cabinet ministers were overjoyed at the friendly response they obtained from the civil servants. To avoid making administrative blunders that would injure them in the eyes of the public and the party, the ministers began to depend on the civil servants. As one cabinet minister stated in an interview, "I would have been lost if not for the old members of my staff. I'm only a beginner in this work. B—— has been at it for twenty years. If I couldn't go to him for advice, I couldn't have done a thing. Why, now [after two years in office] I am only beginning to find my legs and make my own decisions. . . . I have not done a thing for two years without advice."

The failure to change key members of the civil service had important consequences for the future work of the government. Some of the civil servants interpreted it as revealing personal weakness on the part of their ministers and political weakness on the part of the CCF. The deputy ministers, realizing that there was no danger of being discharged, fell back into the traditional bureaucratic pattern. A number of civil servants were able to convince their ministers that certain changes were not administratively feasible or that they would incur too much opposition. Some deputy ministers exchanged information with other deputies on their technique of controlling their ministers. It is difficult to demonstrate concretely —without certain breaches of confidence—which policies were drastically affected by civil-service action, but it is a fact that some key officials boasted of "running my department completely," and of "stopping harebrained radical schemes."

The resistance of top-line civil servants to CCF measures was not necessarily a result of conscious opposition to the party. The most important bureaucratic conservative influence on the government does not seem to be a result of attempts to injure the government in the eyes of the electorate. Many top-ranking civil servants, even though appointed as political partisans, appeared to be honestly concerned with doing their jobs. Their objections to CCF proposals were based on a desire to maintain the stability of their departments and their own positions. These civil servants would probably have attempted to modify Liberal or Conservative schemes which they considered to be unworkable. The bureaucracy, however, had become institutionalized under old party governments. It had a set pattern of reacting to problems. New methods of administration were often designated "difficult" or "impossible" because they had never been tried before or would require revamping the work of a department. In opposing such changes, the civil servant was only taking the easy way out of preserving the *status quo* of his own area of working and living. Harold Laski has pointed this out as a characteristic of bureaucracy in general.

In all large-scale enterprises men who are desirous of avoiding great responsibility (and the majority of men is so desirous) are necessarily tempted to avoid great experiments. In a political democracy this obviously becomes an official habit where there is a . . . bureaucratic system. . . .

The tendency accordingly has been a certain suspicion of experimentalism, a benevolence toward the "safe" man. . . . Administrative codes . . . are applied simply from the conservatism of habit.[27]

Civil-service modification of CCF goals took three major forms: (1) the continuation of traditional and, from the CCF point of view, reactionary procedure in government departments; (2) changes in the intent of new laws and regulations through administrative practices; (3) influence on cabinet ministers to adopt policies advocated by top-level civil servants. Information on the role of the civil service in modifying government activities was difficult to obtain, but, in discussing the work of the government, CCF leaders, cabinet ministers, and civil servants provided significant glimpses into the operation of government policy.

Many local CCF leaders expressed public resentment against the continuation of undesirable practices by local representatives of the government. Informants reported that before the CCF was elected it was common practice in two departments to discriminate against non-Anglo-Saxon groups. These practices continued after the CCF took office, for no one gave explicit orders to the contrary. The ministers were not aware of the fact that discrimination was the informal policy of the department. One cabinet minister changed the procedures in his department when he learned about these practices from local CCF leaders, who had received complaints from people who had been discriminated against. The discrimination practiced by the second department was known only to persons within the department; as no public complaint was ever made, no changes occurred.

Similar charges about the continuation of "reactionary" practices were reported about the work of local field men in government departments. These men had built up a local network of informants over a period of years. Many of the informants were active Liberals or local businessmen. The civil servants continued to rely on them for information after the CCF took office. This sometimes resulted in government actions favoring the preservation of the partisan *status quo* in local administration. One cabinet minister, who has since discharged a large part of his field staff, found as a result of complaints from local members of the CCF that members of his staff continued to grant leases and farming privileges to well-to-do persons who had secured them under previous governments, though it was now government policy to give them to poorer farmers and landless veterans.

The Deputy Minister of Labor was demoted in 1946, after repeated complaints from trade-union and CCF labor leaders, who felt that the Deputy did not understand trade-union objectives, and was hostile to many of them. These labor leaders maintained that the Deputy insisted on carrying out the letter of all regulations, even when the resultant action was contrary to the over-all policy of the government. The unionists, who had expected and had been promised sympathetic and immediate action on their behalf, found themselves frustrated by the slowness of civil-service procedure, and were forced repeatedly to appeal to the Minister and the Premier.

An investigation by the Premier's office in 1946 revealed that patients in government mental hospitals were being neglected by attendants. Facilities that had been erected for patients were forbidden to them and were used by the staff. These practices continued for two years after the CCF took office. The administrators of the mental hospitals, who were responsible for staff appointments, could not be expected to report the need for drastic changes. The defects were remedied only after complaints from CCF supporters who lived near the hospital.

Some time after the government took office, a cabinet minister discovered, during a visit to one of the provincial institutions, that inmates were being fitted with eyeglasses chosen from a large collection gathered from dead inmates. No one had thought it necessary to bring to his attention the fact that money was being saved by depriving people of optometrical services.

Civil-service activities that ran counter to over-all government policy could be checked only when the portion of the public served by the departments could observe what was being done. The permanent civil servant at the top of the administrative hierarchy was too deeply involved in the structure of mutual informal obligations and personal relations that exist in any long-established institution to call to his minister's attention practices that were contrary to CCF objectives. The older civil servants did not realize that many of the practices of previous governments were repugnant to people who believed in the social reform philosophy of the CCF movement, and thus were often not aware of any conflict between practices and objectives.

Cabinet ministers can hope to control the activities of their bureaucracy through reports from clients of government departments or sympathetic party followers. The minister, however, is at the mercy of his subordinates in situations in which the public at large is not aware of government activity. In such situations, civil servants who do not agree with, or do not understand the purposes of, the government are able to modify policy without much fear of detection. Max Weber has pointed out that the absolute dictator is often completely in the power of his bureaucracy, since, unlike the democratic ruler, he has no means of discovering whether his policies are being enforced.[28] Weber suggested that the bureaucracy is less powerful in a democracy, for the governing politicians will be kept informed by the public. This suggestion is only a half-truth, however, for the public can be aware of only a part of the government's activities. The areas of government work that are hidden from the eyes of the public are often closed to the cabinet minister as well. When the clients and the civil servants of a government department both disagree with the minister's policies, there is a great possibility that government policies will not be enforced. Both the clients and the bureaucracy will attempt to convince the minister that his policy is wrong, or they may simply ignore it.

One cabinet minister decided that certain government work that had previously been contracted out to private concerns should be done by government employees whenever possible. His deputy minister, however, continued sending the work out to private concerns. This deputy told confidants that he considered government employees less competent than employees of private firms. Jobs were sometimes done twice, first by civil servants and later by private firms.

It is much more difficult to gather evidence about practices that take place behind closed doors. Members of the civil service have reported numerous examples of the modification of policies by civil servants—in confidence, however, which indicates that those coming to public or ministerial attention are only a small part of the actual efforts to change government policy at the administrative or enforcement level.

The modification of goals through administrative decisions represents only one aspect of the power of the civil service "House" to influence policy. Direct influence over the making of final policy, however, constitutes an aspect of the power of the permanent civil service which is as important as its ability to modify accepted policy through administrative procedure. An outsider cannot scientifically analyze the component elements entering into the decisions of a government department. Both permanent civil servants and new appointees of the CCF report, however, that a number of top-ranking civil servants were able to convince cabinet members that some aspects of the CCF program were impractical to administer. It is impossible to demonstrate that these civil servants were objectively wrong or insincere in opposing specific changes. Their objections to CCF policy were usually based on the honest belief that the changes would not work.[29]

Civil servants, of course, do not operate in a social vacuum. Their opinions about relative "right" and "wrong" are determined, like those of all persons, by pressures existing in their social milieu. A department official is interested not only in whether a minister's proposals can be put into practice, but with the effect of such policies on the traditional practices of the department and on its long-term relations with other groups. A reform which may be socially desirable, but which disrupts the continuity of practices and interpersonal relations within the department, will often be resisted by a top-ranking civil servant. He is obligated to protect those beneath him in the administrative hierarchy from the consequences of a change in policy.

Second, and equally important, the opinion of government officials on the feasibility of any proposal is necessarily colored by their political outlook and by the climate of opinion in their social group. Many top-ranking civil servants in Saskatchewan are members of the upper social class of Regina. Most of their social contacts are with people who believe that they will be adversely affected by many CCF policies. Government officials who belong to professional or economic groups whose position or privileges are threatened by government policies tend to accept the opinion of their own group that reforms which adversely affect the group are wrong and will not work. Cabinet ministers who desire to make social reforms may therefore be dependent for advice on permanent civil servants who, in part, are members of the special-interest group which the ministers oppose. In Saskatchewan, as in other places, civil servants have been known to reduce the significance of reforms directed against their own group. They could hardly have been expected to draw up effective safeguards against "evils" the very existence of which they denied.

The long-term effects of retaining a permanent civil service, when a government attempts to enact a fundamental change in policy, vary. In Saskatchewan, because of the partisan nature of earlier civil-service recruitment, far more of conscious political obstructionism has probably occurred than in a non-partisan merit civil service such as that of Great Britain. On the other hand, the small size of the bureaucracy in Saskatchewan makes it difficult for civil servants to conceal their obstructionist activities. CCF party leaders and members of the legislature have been able to uncover numerous examples of bureaucratic resistance to government policy that would probably have gone unnoticed in a larger structure.

The failure of the government to discharge old top-level civil servants has precipitated a major conflict within the CCF movement between the cabinet ministers and many of the party leaders who do not hold office. The majority of the CCF members of the legislature, of the party Provincial Council, and of delegates to provincial conventions have repeatedly demanded that the government "carry out CCF policy" by replacing old administrators with more sympathetic personnel. The members of these groups cite many examples of actions that they consider to be administrative sabotage on a local or provincial level.

For a long while after taking office, most CCF cabinet ministers refused to admit that they were unduly dependent on the civil service or that they were being deflected from carrying out party policy. They defended the retention of old civil servants on a number of grounds:

1. "It is easier to teach an engineer to be a socialist than a socialist to be an engineer."

2. The CCF stands for a nonpartisan civil service, and to discharge or demote civil servants for their opinions would continue the worst evils of patronage politics.

3. Civil servants only carry out policy, they do not set it. The background of the government official does not matter, therefore, so long as he carries out government policy.

The attacks on the cabinet by the rest of the party and the passing of resolutions demanding action by every provincial convention since 1945 have gradually forced the cabinet to modify its public position and to accept the principle of a partially politicized bureaucracy. Premier T. C. Douglas stated, at the 1946 convention, "We know that people can't carry out a socialist program unless they believe in socialism. We want more socialists in the government service, but they must be trained and efficient. Until we have enough socialists trained for expert jobs, we must use our discretion in using civil servants who are not socialists but who are competent and are only trying to do a job."[30]

The cross pressures of the needs for administrative stability and for party harmony have resulted in a number of concessions to the demand for changes in top-level personnel, while retaining most of the old key officials. At least two deputy ministers and a number of division heads have been removed or demoted because party members disapprove of their activities. Certain of the new agencies created by the CCF government—the Economic Planning Board, the Health Services Planning Commission, and the Division of Adult Education—have been staffed mainly by persons selected because of their sympathies with the objectives of the CCF as well as their technical abilities. As vacancies appear in major posts, the tendency to appoint members of the CCF has increased. These appointments cannot be regarded as the return of patronage politics, since many of the new appointees had not been active in the Saskatchewan party. The head of the Economic Planning Board is an Englishman who belonged to the British Labor Party; two major appointments in public health went to Americans who were supporters of socialized medicine. Many other government appointees are members of the CCF from other provinces.

An unplanned consequence of the struggle in the CCF over civil-service reform has been an experimental test of the theories of those who urge that a radical reform government must have a sympathetic bureaucracy to carry out its program successfully. The Saskatchewan civil service today is a compromise between two approaches to the problem of bureaucracy; the larger part of it is a carry-over from previous governments, but a large minority of top-level positions are held by socialist experts. Many of the older civil servants had resisted changes which the CCF ministers wanted. Some refused to serve on top-level committees where they would be personally responsible for government policies.

Many of the new CCF civil servants, on the other hand, have suggested new policies that would probably never have been proposed if policy formation had been left to the cabinet and the permanent civil service. The ministers did not have the technical knowledge to suggest needed changes, and the old civil servants were not imbued with the CCF values of finding means to reduce the wealth and power of private-interest groups and of using every agency of government to raise living standards. In at least two departments, the differences in orientation of the new and the old civil service resulted in a covert struggle to determine department policy. The permanent civil servants in two departments repeatedly brought their ministers in contact with representatives of the more conservative groups, while the CCF civil servants encouraged supporters of reform to visit the ministers and impress them with the widespread public support for changes.

To specify the innovations initiated as a result of the activities of party experts would compromise the position of informants now working for the government. It is apparent, however, that there is a direct relation between the extent and vigor of reform and the degree to which key administrative positions are staffed by persons who believe in the formal goals of the CCF. If the government had followed its original intention of completely separating the civil service from politics, many of the changes that have been accomplished, both on the administrative and the legislative level, would not, in all probability, have taken place.

In recent years many have become concerned with the problem of bureaucracy in a large-scale society. The sheer size and complexity of social organizations, whether private or public, have created the need for a new "class" of administrators or bureaucrats to operate them efficiently. This new administrative group, necessarily, has been given a large amount of discretionary power. Once entrenched in corporations, trade-unions, political parties, and governments, the administrators develop "vested interests" of their own which may conflict with the interests of those who placed them in office. It seems to be universally true in social organization that men in power seek to maintain and extend their power, status, and privileges. Modern democratic society, therefore, faces the dilemma of making extensive grants of power without at the same time abdicating the right of the democratic constituency to change the policies and the personnel of the bureaucracy.

The justified concern with the dangers of oligarchic or bureaucratic domination has, however, led many persons to ignore the fact that it does make a difference to society which set of bureaucrats controls its destiny. There are bureaucracies and bureaucracies. To suggest, as many social scientists have done, that trade-unions, cooperatives, corporations, political parties, and states must develop a bureaucratic social structure in order to operate efficiently still leaves a large area of indeterminate social action for a bureaucratically organized society. Bureaucrats are human beings, not automatons. The desire to maintain a given bureaucratic organization is only one of the complex series of factors determining their actions. In a given situation, each group acts somewhat differently, according to its background. The reactions of the Russian "socialist" bureaucrats to problems of power were very different from those of the English socialist bureaucrats. A deterministic theory of bureaucratic behavior, such as that advanced by Robert Michels or James Burnham, neglects the implications of an alternative pattern of bureaucratic response.[31]

The focus on a single theory of bureaucracy has been encouraged by the lack of a sociological approach among political scientists. For the most part they have not raised questions about the social origins and values of government administrators and the relationship of such factors to government policy.[32] It is possible that the political scientists' blindness to the sources of civil-service "biases" may be related to their own identification with the government administrator, and their disinclination to accept the fact that the behavior of their own group is determined by personal "prejudice-creating" factors. Political scientists accepted the value of an unbiased civil servant who makes his decisions after analyzing the facts, presents the data to his minister, carries out the policy of the government in power, and then reverses his policy when a new government comes into office. Political history has been analyzed mainly in terms of struggles among interest groups and political parties. The civil service, like the political scientists, was simply a passive, neutral factor.

In recent years, however, political scientists have become aware of the fact that the government bureaucracy does play a significant role in determining policy. They still, however, leave the bureaucrat in a social vacuum. They now recognize that he plays an active role, but the determinants of that role are analyzed purely on the bureaucratic level. The bureaucrat's actions are analyzed on the basis of the goals of the civil service—self-preservation and efficiency. These interests may be defined in terms of prestige and privilege, preservation of patterns of organization or relationships within a department, or maintenance of department traditions and policies. There is little recognition that the behavior of government bureaucrats varies with the nongovernmental social background and interests of those controlling the bureaucratic structure. Members of a civil service are also members of other nongovernmental social groups and classes. Social pressures from many different group affiliations and loyalties determine individual behavior in most situations. The behavior of an individual or group in a given situation cannot be considered as if the individual or group members had no other life outside the given situation one is analyzing.

The direct relationship between class affiliations of members of a bureaucracy and the policies of the government has been demonstrated in the English civil service. J. Donald Kingsley has shown that as England changed from an aristocratically controlled nation to a capitalist state its civil service changed correspondingly.[33] The aristocrats who once dominated the British civil service gradually gave way to members of the middle class.

The experiences in Saskatchewan also indicate the relationship between the background and the actions of the civil service. Trained in the traditions of a laissez-faire government and belonging to conservative social groups, the civil service contributes significantly to the social inertia which blunts the changes a new radical government can make. Delay in initiating reforms means that the new government becomes absorbed in the process of operating the old institutions. The longer a new government delays in making changes, the more responsible it becomes for the old practices and the harder it is to make the changes it originally desired to institute. The problem has not been crucial in Saskatchewan because of the small size of the government and its fairly limited powers. On a larger scale, however, as in Great Britain today, dependence on a conservative bureaucracy may prove to be significant in the success or failure of the Labor Government.

The suggestion that shake-ups in the civil service on the expert policy-making level may be necessary at times for the adequate functioning of democratic government has rarely been considered by North American political scientists. On this continent, the problem of the civil service has traditionally been that of patronage appointment with its resultant inefficiency and malpractice. European social theorists, on the contrary, have been concerned with the implications for social change of a permanent governmental bureaucracy with its own vested interests and social values.

The necessity to face up to the problem of bureaucratic resistance to change becomes urgent only when a "radical" party comes to office. The theory of civil-service neutrality breaks down when the total goals of the state change. A change from the Liberal to the Conservative Party or from the Democratic to the Republican Party does not usually require a civil servant to make any major adjustments.[34] The functions of the department and of the government as a whole remain fairly constant.

The socialist state, however, which has as its goal a reintegration of societal values, giving priority of government services to groups that had been neglected and securing a large measure of government control, may fail in its objectives if it leaves administrative power in the hands of men whose social background and previous training prevent a sympathetic appreciation of the objectives of the new government. "The planning state . . . will require men wholly committed to the purpose the State is undertaking to serve . . . men of 'push and go,' energetic innovators and hard-driving managers."[35]

In American history, the two most significant departures from a merit civil service came during administrations which proposed shifts from the values and purposes of the previous government. Andrew Jackson felt it necessary, as the spokesman of the eastern workers and the western farmers, to break up the old permanent staff of the government in order to effect his program. His actions were based in part on a reasoned criticism of the actions of the civil service of his day, expressed in his Message to Congress in December, 1829.

There are, perhaps, few men who can for any great length of time enjoy office and power without being more or less under the influence of feelings unfavorable to the faithful discharge of their public duties. Their integrity may be proof against improper considerations immediately addressed to themselves, but they are apt to acquire a habit of looking with indifference upon the public interests and of tolerating conduct from which an unpracticed man would revolt.[36]

During the period of the American New Deal in the 1930's, "leaders of the Roosevelt administration privately complained of the difficulty of deflecting the bureaucracy from its ancient ways. The public service machine tended to continue in a straight line in disregard of the deviating influences of different public policy."[37] According to James A. Farley, "Some of the greatest troubles the President had were caused by subordinate officials who were in sharp disagreement with his policies and, rightly or wrongly, were sabotaging the job he was trying to accomplish."[38]

"The Roosevelt Administration was forced to assemble almost a whole new set of officials to carry out the New Deal reforms."[39] Roosevelt felt that these reforms would fail if they were left in the hands of the traditional departments. In 1933, 80 per cent of federal employees were under merit civil service, but by July 1, 1937, the proportion of merit positions had fallen to 63 per cent because of the establishment of over 200,000 new positions in New Deal agencies, many of which were exempt from the rule of merit.[40]

When the Tennessee Valley Authority was set up, its chief exponent, Senator Norris, urged that it be free from civil-service control. He argued that only people who believed in the purposes of the new agency could make it a success. The oath which a T.V.A. employee must take on entering office pledges him to uphold not only the Constitution of the United States but also the ideals of the T.V.A.

There is no simple solution to the dilemma of keeping government administration efficient as well as responsive to the will of the electorate. The increase in the power, functions, and sheer size of modern government necessitates the search for some means of controlling the bureaucracy. It is utopian to think that the electorate's dismissal of the inexpert politician, who formally heads the bureaucracy, will by itself change the course of bureaucratic activities. As Max Weber stated: "The question is always who controls the existing bureaucratic machinery. And such control is possible only in a very limited degree to persons who are not technical specialists. Generally speaking, the trained permanent official is more likely to get his way in the long run than his nominal supervisor, the Cabinet Minister, who is not a specialist."[41]

Government today is a large-scale administrative job requiring experts to operate it. Unless the electorate is given the opportunity to change the key experts as well as the politicians, elections will lose much of their significance. This problem will become more and more significant as efforts are made to increase the economic and social welfare role of the state.

NOTES

1. Interview data.

2. "Resolution Submitted by Canora Constituency," CCF Convention, *Handbook*, 1945, p. 63.

3. "Resolution Submitted by Qu'Appelle-Wolseley Constituency," *ibid.*, pp. 67–69.

4. "Resolution Submitted by Saskatoon Constituency," *ibid.*, p. 70.

5. "Resolution Submitted by Redberry Constituency," *ibid.*, p. 67.

6. "Resolution Submitted by Regina Constituency," *ibid.*, 1946, p. 79.

7. "Resolution Submitted by Regina Constituency," *ibid.*, 1947, p. 71.

8. "Resolution Submitted by Notukeu-Willowbunch Constituency," *ibid.*

9. "Resolution Submitted by Maple Creek Constituency," *ibid.*

10. Harold Laski, *Democracy in Crisis* (London, Allen and Unwin, 1933), pp. 99–104; Max Weber, *Essays in Sociology* (New York, Oxford University Press, 1946), pp. 232–35; Herman Finer, *The Future of Government* (London, Methuen and Co., 1946), pp. 12–13.

11. J. Donald Kingsley, *Representative Bureaucracy* (Yellow Springs, Ohio, Antioch Press, 1944), pp. 287–305.

12. *Ibid.*, pp. 42–77.

13. Marx characteristically expressed this idea in a letter to Kugelmann: "If you look at the last chapter of my *Eighteenth Brumaire* you will find that I say that the next attempt of the French Revolution will be no longer, as before, to transfer the bureaucratic-military machine from one hand to another, but to smash it." Karl Marx and Friedrich Engels, *Correspondence, 1846–1895* (New York, International Publishers, 1936), p. 309. See also Marx, "The Civil War in France," *Selected Works* (Moscow, Publishing Society of Foreign Workers in the U.S.S.R., 1936), Vol. 2, pp. 498–505.

"To destroy officialism immediately, everywhere, completely—of this there can be no question. That is a utopia. But to *break* up at once the old bureaucratic machine and to start immediately the construction of a new one . . . this is not a utopia, . . . it is the direct and necessary task of the revolutionary proletariat." V. I. Lenin, *The State and Revolution* (New York, Vanguard Press, 1926), p. 155.

14. "Bureaucratic Sabotage," American Academy of Political and Social Science, *Annals*, January, 1937, p. 5.

15. London *Daily Herald,* October 23, 1933; quoted in Edgar Lansbury, *George Lansbury, My Father* (London, S. Low, Marston and Co., Ltd., n.d.), p. 197.

16. Charles Aikin, "The British Bureaucracy and the Origin of Parliamentary Policy," *American Political Science Review,* February, 1939, pp. 40–41.

17. V. G. Childe, *How Labour Governs* (London, Labour Publishing Co., Ltd., 1923), p. 16.

18. Kingsley, *op. cit.,* p. 274. Leon Blum himself suggested that the conservative attitudes of the civil service were an obstacle to reform. Blum, *For All Mankind* (London, Victor Gollancz, Ltd., 1946), p. 59.

19. Escott Reid, "The Saskatchewan Liberal Machine before 1929," *Canadian Journal of Economics and Political Science,* February, 1936.

20. *CCF Election Manifesto, 1944,* p. 1. (Italics mine.)

21. "The CCF and the Civil Service," *Saskatchewan Commonwealth,* December 1, 1943, p. 8. Radio address.

22. Interviews with leaders of the CCF and of the Liberal Party, and members of the civil service.

23. Interviews; Minutes of the CCF Provincial Convention, 1945–48.

24. "Consider the tasks which fall upon an important minister in the modern state. He has his own departmental business to get through. He has to make himself acquainted with at least the outlines of the bigger issues before the cabinet. He has to pay all necessary attention to the legislative assembly. . . . He must make party speeches, realizing that from the position he occupies every word he says will be narrowly scrutinized. Ceremonial functions, also, will take up hours of precious time." Laski, *op. cit.,* p. 63.

25. Interviews with civil servants.

26. Information based on interviews with civil servants. These reports are composite pictures of actual cases.

27. "Bureaucracy," *Encyclopaedia of the Social Sciences* (ed. by Edwin R. A. Seligman; New York, Macmillan Co., 1935), Vol. 3, p. 72.

28. Weber, *op. cit.,* p. 234.

29. ". . . [Socialist] ministers are likely to arrive in office, not with a complete body of specific plans, but with some general principles which the departments will be asked to test against the

facts before they are given the share of a concrete measure. The inevitable tendency of the departments will be for the minister's own sake, to minimize the break with tradition. . . . They will be passionately and laudably anxious to save him from failure. Unless they share his own outlook—and this is unlikely enough—they will want time where he demands speed, the attack on the narrow front, where his instruction is for comprehensiveness.

". . . this attitude in the civil service is wholly compatible with its tradition of neutrality. . . . My point is the quite different one that . . . the whole ethos of the service becomes one of criticism which looks towards delay instead of encouragement which looks toward action." Laski, *Democracy in Crisis,* pp. 103–4.

30. Speech before panel on civil service at CCF Provincial Convention.

31. Michels, *op. cit.;* James Burnham, *The Managerial Revolution* (New York, John Day Co., Inc., 1941).

32. Bendix's study of the origins of American federal administrators is the first such study in the United States. He reports that only one similar study was made in Europe. Reinhard Bendix, *Higher Civil Servants in American Society* (University of Colorado Press, 1949). See also Philip Selznick, *T.V.A. and the Grass Roots* (University of California Press, 1949).

33. Kingsley, *op. cit.,* pp. 42–77.

34. In defending a merit civil service, Leonard D. White and T. V. Smith suggest that it is possible to have a neutral bureaucracy in the United States because "the battles between Democrats and Republicans are fought on a narrow stage, with far greater areas of agreement between them than of disagreement." White and Smith, *Politics and Public Service* (New York, Harper and Brothers, 1939), pp. 132–33.

35. Kingsley, *op. cit.,* pp. 304–5.

36. Quoted in White and Smith, *op. cit.,* p. 44.

37. *Ibid.,* p. 57.

38. *Ibid.,* p. 92.

39. Kingsley, *op. cit.,* p. 274.

40. White and Smith, *op. cit.,* p. 53.

41. Max Weber, *The Theory of Social and Economic Organization* (trans. by Talcott Parsons and A. K. Henderson; New York, Oxford University Press, 1947), p. 128.

13

EPILOGUE

THE CCF today represents the culmination of a half-century of political and economic efforts by western grain growers to establish a stable economy. It is the apex of a movement that started with the Territorial Grain Growers' Association in 1902, and continued with the Grain Growers' Grain Company, the Saskatchewan Cooperative Elevator Company, the Progressive Party, the Farmers' Union, the Wheat Pool, and the United Farmers of Canada (Saskatchewan Section). After almost fifty years of organization, the Saskatchewan farmers today have the largest cooperative movement on the continent and the only independent agrarian government. They have probably gone as far as a sectional agrarian group can go within geographic, economic, and constitutional limits to establish direct producers' control over their economy.

No complex society, however, has yet discovered the secret of harmony or equilibrium. Social movements are faced with the dilemma of maintaining their stability and social gains, and at the same time sustaining the base for a continued effort to reach their long-term objectives. The history of the Saskatchewan farmers' movement indicates anew the inherent difficulty involved when a reform organization attempts both to maintain organizational stability and to change the larger society. Each successful social organization creates a new "vested-interest" group, and consequently a new opponent of further change. The leaders of the Saskatchewan Grain Growers' Association feared that the organization of a farmers' marketing company would endanger the survival of their own group. The Cooperative Elevator Company objected to a merger with the Wheat Pool. The S.G.G.A., in turn, feared to launch a new political movement after the First World

War, and the leaders of the U.F.C. (Saskatchewan Section) had to be changed in an internal struggle before that organization would support the compulsory Wheat Pool and independent political action in the 'thirties. (See chaps. 3 and 4.)

The combination of an extremely unstable economic structure and the widespread distribution of secondary local leadership prevented the Saskatchewan rural community from establishing a stable traditional order. The bureaucratic conservatism of the leading agrarian officials rarely succeeded in preventing the farmers of the province from creating new institutional means to attain their economic ends.

The agrarian community now stands in a position similar to its situation in the late 1920's. It is experiencing a period of high prices and good crops. In June, 1948, it gave the CCF a new vote of confidence by reelecting it with a secure parliamentary majority of 31 out of 52 legislative seats. (The drop in CCF support from 1944 was primarily a result of a coalition between the Liberals and the Conservatives and the reappearance of the Social Credit Party as an alternative "reform" movement.)

Ostensibly, therefore, Saskatchewan seems to have remained near the radical peak that it reached in 1944. The government remains socialist. The cooperative movement is larger and stronger than at any time in the history of the province.[1] The actions of the agrarians in continued support of economic and political reform would seem to challenge the generalizations made earlier in this study that farmers (and other groups as well) become conservative after they achieve their immediate economic reforms, as in New Zealand, Russia, and the United States. (See chap. 11, p. 277–78.)

A shift in the direction of conservatism and traditionalism may, however, take two forms. Politically, it may be reflected in a change of support from a radical to a conservative party, as in New Zealand, where the farmers who supported the Labor Party in 1935 were voting for the Conservatives in 1948. (See note 17, p. 305.) More frequently, however, conservatism may increase through the institutionalization of a once-radical organization. The new political movement, as it becomes organizationally stable and achieves some of the goals of its followers, may become a normal integrated part of society. This process has often occurred, as in the shift from sect to church in religious movements and in institutionalization and "bureaucratic conservatism" in organizations like cooperatives, trade-unions, and political parties.

The Social Credit movement in Alberta is probably the most recent example of such a change. It started out only seventeen years ago as the foremost opponent of the "eastern banks" and "vested interests"; today it is commonly recognized as one of the conservative parties of Canada, receiving the open support of the conservative business groups that once opposed it.[2]

The metamorphosis of the Social Credit movement in Alberta from a radical to a conservative movement raises the question of the possibility of the same phenomenon in Saskatchewan. A comparison of the two movements is difficult: the Social Credit Party has been in power for sixteen years, whereas the CCF has held office for only six years. Recent events suggest, however, that conservative forces are gradually changing the character of the Saskatchewan CCF. This generalization can be supported in the areas of social welfare and health, labor, and government ownership.

The government attempted early in 1948 to reduce its contributions to old-age pensioners by $5 a month after the federal government had raised its contribution by a similar amount. This action was reversed just before the election in June, 1948, because of the protest of the politically powerful Old-Age Pensioners' Association. Since the election, the government, instead of giving pensioners free drugs, requires them to pay 20 per cent of the cost. Work on a university hospital in Saskatoon, which would have been the base of a provincial medical school, was stopped in 1948 in order to save funds. No major steps have been taken for two years to implement the original plan of socialized medicine. The government has refused to expand any social services that would require increased taxes.

The CCF government has gradually ended its liberal wage policy in negotiating with unions in government-owned industries. A three-week strike occurred in the Government Insurance Office in November, 1948, when the government refused to increase wages. According to the union, the government would not even negotiate the union's demands until the strike took place. The Insurance Office is one of the best profit makers of the government. Union leaders have stated that resistance to union demands is present in other Crown companies and in the civil service.

The extent to which leaders of the CCF have modified their earlier prolabor attitude can be seen in a press report of the 1948 convention:

Resources Minister J. L. Phelps told the provincial CCF convention Friday, "We appreciate support we received from labor but we must impress upon labor that there are two sides to every question.

"We have sought to drive employers and employees apart. It should be our effort to bring labor and management close together."

Mr. Phelps made his observations when a resolution dealing with labor matters was before the convention.

It called upon the labor department to investigate further ways and means whereby its field staff and inspectors "convey the true intent and meaning of laws and regulations under its jurisdiction to employees in Saskatchewan."

At Mr. Phelps' suggestion, the convention approved the addition of the words "and employers."

The Minister said the CCF on too many occasions had taken the stand labor was always right.

"Perhaps it is not always right," he said.

It was his opinion the CCF should encourage labor to take upon itself more responsibility, because nowadays the employer was not always "the big bad wolf" he was in the past.

Mr. Phelps suggested the reason the CCF may have lost support in rural areas was that the party had moved too fast in its labor legislation to the detriment of those living there.

As long as people lived under a capitalist system, there would continue to be a degree of exploitation by employers, but not all of them were offending, he said.[3]

The government has proposed no new provincially owned industries for its second term in office. Actually, it closed down one of the old ones, the tannery and shoe factory. Since the election in June, 1948, Premier Douglas has made trips to England, eastern Canada, and New York, "to talk to industrialists and heads of mining companies who might be interested in investing some capital in Saskatchewan's development. . . . On his return from Britain, Mr. Douglas announced that British and Swedish capital might be invested in the province and that representatives of these two countries may come to Saskatchewan to investigate the possibilities. On his return from New York he said financial discussions were of an exploratory nature."[4]

The farmers' movements and the CCF once stood for the socialization of oil, but the Saskatchewan government is now encouraging private oil companies to prospect in the province, guaranteeing them long-term leases. The shift in the thinking of CCF leaders is, however, most evident in the fight that Premier Douglas made at the 1948 national convention against the proposal to nationalize the banks.

He [Douglas] believed in ultimate socialization of banks . . . , but he believed the amendment [to obtain control over rather than nationalize the banks] should go through and a CCF government should first try to control the policy of the banks.

Socialization was not an end in itself, according to the Premier, and sometimes the desired results could be obtained without the government taking over a business.

For example, the Premier revealed when the CCF came to power in Saskatchewan, it gave serious consideration to socializing breweries in the province. But they found that as they had the power to set beer prices, license brewers, and otherwise control them, socialization of the industry was unnecessary. He felt the same principle might well work in the case of the banks.[5]

Douglas found, however, that he was in a minority in the national convention. The proposal that a federal CCF government should nationalize the banks passed by 94 votes to 56. If the attitude toward nationalization of banks is to be used as an index of radicalism, the leader of Saskatchewan socialism now stands to the right of the majority of his national party, and opposes a demand made by Saskatchewan farmers' organizations years before the CCF was organized. (See chap. 4, p. 101.)

These changes in the policies of leaders of the CCF in the last few years suggest anew that any evaluation of the present "radicalism" of Saskatchewan must consider not only election results but the changing content of party actions. The socialism of the 1949 Saskatchewan CCF is a far cry from the first years of the movement when the party proposed the complete elimination of private enterprise as its goal.

It is again a question of how much reform can be expected from a "radical" politician in a democracy. (See chap. 11.) The social reforms to which he is committed before taking office often become apparent hindrances in maintaining power. Innovations usually turn out to be more difficult in operation than they seemed in the planning or propaganda stage. In a stable prosperous situation, such as Saskatchewan is now experiencing, stability may seem preferable to innovation. The continued prosperity of the farmers has sharply reduced the popular demand for reform, and adherence to ideological principles may not appear to be worth the danger of losing support if the reform fails. The CCF, which in opposition ridiculed the Liberals' question about the source of the money to pay for increased social services, is now itself engaged in curtailing social services rather than risk the wrath of tax-conscious farmers.

The CCF leaders also face the problems inherent in operating what Premier Douglas once called "a beachhead of socialism on a continent of capitalism." Like the earlier North Dakota Non-Partisan League, it has attempted to try certain socialist experiments with little or no control over the economic structure. A provincial or economically weak national socialist government remains subject to many of the coercions of the old economic system, in much the same manner as a private businessman. Its industries must compete on the free market with other private concerns. It must sell its bonds through regular banking channels. As a thinly populated province, Saskatchewan does not have enough government capital to develop its own resources, such as oil. Such weaknesses force the government to adhere to the regulations of the larger economy.

As politicians, however, CCF leaders cannot afford to admit that they are making "nonsocialist" concessions and that they are not able to carry out their original program. They are, therefore, forced to defend compromises and capitulations as positive goods. They must praise certain segments of private industry, and thereby weaken the force of their long-term socialist arguments. It is difficult for CCF leaders to invite private industry into the province—even subsidize it—and, at the same time, to denounce as exploiters the industrialists or bankers whose money they need.

Dealing with economic problems within the framework of capitalism, the CCF administrator must view many of them as a private businessman does. He, too, must show a profit to his stockholders (the tax-conscious farmers), avoid wage increases if possible, and raise prices. As a result, he sees the businessman's point of view in a new light. J. L. Phelps, who was quoted above as a critic of labor, entered the government as its most radical member. After being placed in charge of most of the new government industries, he gradually became more and more critical of trade-unions. Another high CCF official, who has had many dealings with bankers, stated in an interview that the CCF attitude toward bankers was unrealistic, as they were "only honest men doing a job and did not care what kind of government held power."

These changes in policy do not mean that the party and the government have ceased responding to the needs and demands of its farmer and labor supporters. Compared to the other three provincial political parties, it is still the most "radical" party. The CCF retains a large part of its agrarian and socialist ideology of opposition to big business, and supports organized agriculture and labor in their efforts to secure a higher standard of living in conflicts with private business groups. There can be little doubt, however, that its years in office have tempered the party's radicalism.

The fact that social reform movements rarely succeed in reaching the goals they were ostensibly organized to achieve has long concerned persons interested in the problems of social change. Conservatives have used such facts to demonstrate that radical social movements are utopian, and therefore are not worth the trouble they cause. This thesis has been argued in relation to the French Revolution, the American Civil War, and the Russian Revolution. Radical social thinkers, on the other hand, have cited the negative results of other social movements as evidence for the fact that the leaders of all other movements but their own made serious blunders in strategy. Socialist literature, especially, includes innumerable books and articles explaining the failure of various socialist parties.[6]

The decision on whether a given social movement was worth while is largely a value judgment which no one has the right to make under the guise of scientific or historical objectivity. It is my own belief that, in general, the democratic movements of the left since the American Revolution were and are historically justifiable and necessary to attain the values of an economic and political and social democracy. In spite of their many and obvious failings in terms of democratic values, the alternative to them was a more rigidly stratified and sometimes a dictatorial society.

It is impossible to agree with the efforts of those who would attempt to deal rationally with the problem of the "bureaucratic conservatism" or "institutionalization" of social movements by proposing "logical" solutions to make these movements more democratic or more militant. Socialists, though materialists in their philosophy, become idealists as political citizens, arguing that the movement should do this or that, or avoid doing something else. These solutions are similar to attempts to cure the ills of the present economic system by calling upon all capitalists to be responsible economic statesmen, to collaborate with unions, to pay high wages, and not to discharge employees. Most socialists recognize that the private businessman must act within the coercions of the economic structure. He must make a profit, and therefore treats his employees as impersonal economic commodities. He must buy as cheaply as he can, and sell as dearly as he is able.

The radical politician is in a position similar to that of the private businessman. He cannot change the institutional forces within a few months or even years. Large portions of the provincial, national, and international power structure are retained by nonsocialist or antisocialist groups. The socialist in office is not free, is not all-powerful. Once he accepts the rules of the society, even as a temporary compromise (until the millennial day when he will be free to act), he is caught in a vicious cycle. To stay in power, he must make repeated compromises. Each compromise is in itself unimportant, but eventually he departs so far from his original aims that they cease to be real ends and become only rituals to be observed during election campaigns. The ideals of democracy and a classless society would appear to have become such rituals in the Soviet Union, while the goal of a socialist society in which capitalism is eliminated has now only ritual significance for most of the socialist parties of Europe and the British Commonwealth.

Leon Blum, the former Socialist Premier of France, pointed to the problem of carrying through a program of far-reaching social change in evaluating the work of his Popular Front government:

The Socialist Party was called upon to take its share of the task of government, but it knew perfectly well that it could exercise power only within the framework of bourgeois society. It was, indeed, for this reason that it had avoided power as long as circumstances made this possible. Even when the elected Chamber seemed to be held by a working-class majority, the bourgeoisie kept in its hands methods of resistance which yielded only temporarily to fear, and became effective again as soon as the fears were stilled. It kept its grip on the local Councils, *the Civil Service, the Press, finance, big business.*[7]

The same problem in a German setting was summed up by Fritz Tarnow, a German labor leader, at the German Social Democratic Party congress in 1931:

Are we sitting at the sickbed of capitalism, not only as doctors who want to cure the patient, but as prospective heirs who cannot wait for the end and would like to hasten it by administering poison? We are condemned, I think, to be doctors who seriously wish to cure, and yet we have to maintain the feeling that we are heirs who wish to receive the entire legacy of the capitalist system today rather than tomorrow. This double role, doctor and heir, is a damned difficult task.[8]

The "damned difficult task" is made even more difficult by the fact that the leaders of any organized reform movement have a stake in the existing situation. The organization itself, rather than its formal goal, becomes the ends of men involved in a bureaucratic apparatus. The leaders of the international socialist movement have shown time and time again that, when faced with a choice between fundamental principles or organizational survival, they choose the path that appears to lead to immediate preservation of the strength of the organization. The reversal of the Socialist antiwar attitude immediately upon the declaration of war in 1914 is well known. The policy of Social Democratic trade-union leaders in attempting to come to terms with the Fascists and Nazis in Italy and Germany is an even more convincing and clear-cut demonstration of the way in which the goal of organizational survival can lead men step by step into supporting everything they personally oppose.[9]

These examples of Social Democratic and trade-union "betrayal" of principles are not cited to suggest that there is some special weakness in these movements. Similar examples can be found in the records of the anarchist and Communist movements, as well as in Liberal and Conservative groups. The history of most of the religious sects of the world also bears witness to the power of organization over ideology or theology.

Organizations are always started as means of attaining certain value ends. However, organizations become ends in themselves, which often are obstacles in the achievement of the original goals. This does not mean that organized social effort does not secure many of the value ends that it was set up to achieve. The farm organizations of Saskatchewan have helped to better the economic lot of the agrarians of the province. The trade-unions have increased the living standards of their members. Gradually, however, every large-scale social organization falls victim to the virus of bureaucratic conservatism, and to the fear that a further challenge to the *status quo* will injure its power and status; or the organization may become, as the German labor leaders suggested when proposing collaboration with the Nazis in 1933, "an indispensable part of the very social order . . . increasingly integrated into the state [society],"[10] and as such will be one of the forces resisting further change.

In a world in which the rate of growth of social and economic problems is apparently faster than the increase in our ability to cope with them, conclusions such as these may seem like a counsel of despair. They are not meant to be. An answer to stagnation lies in the bold actions of such men as the "agitators" of Saskatchewan, who are not satisfied with anything but utopia. These men are often destined, as Vanzetti once said, to "live out their lives speaking on street corners to scornful men." They may, on the other hand, like E. A. Partridge, be destined to help form mighty social movements to advance human welfare. As long as there are social organizations that produce men who do not accept the *status quo*, who see "the inhumanity of man to man" as a crime, there will be hope in the human race.

NOTES

1. Province of Saskatchewan, Department of Cooperation and Cooperative Development, *Annual Report* (Regina, 1949).

2. J. A. Irving, "The Evolution of the Social Credit Movement," *Canadian Journal of Economics and Political Science*, August, 1948, pp. 321–41.

3. Regina *Leader-Post*, July 24, 1948, p. 1.

4. *Ibid.*, November 22, 1948, p. 11.

5. *Ibid.*, August 20, 1948, p. 10.

6. Harold Laski, *Democracy in Crisis* (London, Allen and Unwin, 1933); Leon Trotsky, *Stalin* (New York, Harper and Brothers, 1941); Adolf Sturmthal, *The Tragedy of European Labor* (London, Victor Gollancz, Ltd., 1944).

7. Leon Blum, *For All Mankind* (London, Victor Gollancz, Ltd., 1946), p. 59.

8. Quoted in Sturmthal, *op. cit.*, p. 71.

9. Daniel Guérin's description of these events bears quoting here:

". . . immediately after the March on Rome he [Mussolini] invited the general secretary of the Federation [of Labor], D'Aragona to enter his government. D'Aragona accepted. If Mussolini finally had to give up this plan, it was only because his intimates objected. But the union leaders continued to offer themselves. The organ of the railway workers, the *Tribuna del Ferrovieri*, published under the title, 'Without Reservations,' an editorial offering the fascist government the 'collaboration' of the railway unions. For a few months direct negotiations were carried on between the union leaders and Mussolini. In August, 1923, D'Aragona explained to the national committee of the Federation of Labor that the 'collaboration' would not be in any case *political*, but only *technical*. The Federation of Labor would participate in the advisory bodies of the state and in all bodies where problems of labor and production were to be discussed. 'The Federation's policy cannot follow preconceived ideas. . . .' In the meantime, it broke with the Socialist Party.

". . . At the end of 1926, it had to dissolve. Then its leaders substituted for it a Center for cultural association—intended to 'assist by its advice and criticism the social action of the government.' They published a manifesto in which they declared: *'The fascist regime is a reality, and any reality must be taken into consideration.'* The union movement in the past, they explained, could not decide itself either in favor of, or against, the state. However, it was necessary to choose and either wage a struggle for the destruction of the state or collaborate with, and integrate itself within it. They had decided on the second alternative—an alternative that 'implies naturally the abandonment of the principle of the class struggle.' . . .

"When Hitler took power, the Federation's [of Labor] executive committee declared that it 'will await the government's actions.' First of all the Federation broke with the Socialist party, and on March 20th it published a manifesto: 'The union organizations are the expression of an indisputable social necessity, an indispensable part of the very social order. . . . As a result of the natural order of things, they are increasingly integrated into the state. The social task of the unions must be carried out, *whatever the nature of the state regime.* . . . Union organizations make no claim to influence state power directly. *Their task here can be merely to put at the disposal of the government and parliament knowledge and experience acquired in this field.* . . .'

"On April 7, Leipart raised his bid and declared that the unions *'are pursuing the same end as the government, namely to found freedom of the nation at home and abroad on the productive forces of the whole people.'* On April 20, the national committee of the Federation invited unionists to take part in the May 1st celebration as a symbol of the incorporation of the working class into the National Socialist state." Daniel Guérin, *Fascism and Big Business* (New York, Pioneer Publishers, 1939), pp. 126–28. (Italics in original.)

10. *Ibid.,* p. 14.

Part II

TWENTY YEARS LATER

I

AGRARIAN PRAGMATISM AND
RADICAL POLITICS

JOHN W. BENNETT AND CYNTHIA KRUEGER
Washington University and
Brooklyn College
of
The City University of New York

THE Cooperative Commonwealth Federation (CCF) of Saskatchewan, famed as the first major socialist government on the North American continent, won its initial provincial victory in 1944. After enjoying twenty years of provincial power, it relinquished the government to the Liberals in 1964. The total vote for the CCF was not significantly smaller than in the previous election, but it had been declining, and slight shifts in certain districts gave a small majority of seats to the Liberals. Thus Saskatchewan politics came full circle; after twenty years, the party discredited and defeated by the CCF was back in control. The Liberal government, however, has made relatively few changes in CCF-instituted policies and programs. There is no sign of drastic legislative reaction. Apparently, CCF innovations, on the whole, were accepted by the Saskatchewan constituency as needed and desirable, and this political reality has been understood by the Liberals.

It is somewhat early for a definitive assessment of CCF accomplishments, particularly since there is a possibility that the party will regain the government in an early election. Although interim assessments of CCF plans and programs have been made by others,[1] the writers are not, in any case, concerned with the success or failure of the CCF program for Saskatchewan. We are, rather, interested in the ideological significance of the movement, and the nature of its grass roots appeal and strength. Lipset's study of the CCF, *Agrarian Socialism*, sets the stage for this discussion, and while our interpretation of the CCF differs from his, the thoroughness of his research is indicated by the fact that we are primarily dependent on the data presented in his book. We address ourselves to the central assumption of the book, which is to the effect that the CCF was a left-wing or socialist political movement and that this leftward orientation was shared by the majority of Saskatchewan voters.

This procedure requires us to be extremely careful in the use of the term "socialistic" as a description of various institutions and policies.[2] It is our position that the particular ideological flag a political party adopts does not necessarily reveal either the sources of that party's support or its specific programs. Second, we maintain that the term (particularly in the contemporary international situation) carries implications of specific ideological allegiances, and that it should not be used unless these designations are meant. Simple evidence of collective action is not to be equated with socialism: socialism for the Saskatchewan farmer-voter may indeed mean something quite apart from the formal ideology associated with it.

It is our position that regardless of the ideology formulated by the party leaders, the grass roots supporters of the CCF were concerned primarily with specific grievances and the particular reforms sought as remedies. It is a matter of historical record that the CCF, as it approached its first electoral victory in 1944, became increasingly less socialistic in inspiration and doctrine. The paradox in the situation was that this change was particularly true for all policies affecting the interests of its principal supporters, the farmers. While our major evidence for this change will be taken from the history of the cooperative movement in Saskatchewan, an examination of certain events in the history of the party before its election to office also demonstrates this change. For example, the farmers' early attempts to establish pooled marketing and government price controls invited various liberal and agrarian radical movements to focus on the grievances of the farming population. Equally important, however, is the fact that the farmers found it convenient to accept many of these people as spokesmen and organizers. Lipset, in his Chapter 4 ("The Farmers' Movement Goes Socialist") shows how in the 1920's, "the left-wingers, consciously thinking of themselves as such, attempted to involve the organized farmers' movement in new struggles." There ensued a long fight between the right and left wings of the United Farmers of Canada, Saskatchewan Section, which would, according to Lipset, have ended in a victory for the right wing if the depression had not driven down the price of wheat and virtually bankrupted the provincial wheat pools. By 1930, E. A. Partridge, then the honorary president of the UFC, and one of the early prairie socialists, stated that "true cooperation has its final goal in socialism, which is the continual observance of the Golden Rule" (a neat synthesis of the cooperative, radical, and moral influences embodied in the agrarian movement). The left wing advocated a radical platform at the 1930 convention, but this was eventually compromised, under right-wing dissent, to focus on the promotion of cooperatives, the 100 per cent membership Pool, abolition of military training, state medical care, free trade with Britain, and nationalization of public utilities. All these doctrines except the free trade and military training items, which were obviously out of control of provincial governments, later became the program of the provincial CCF. In other words, the victory of the left-wingers was a qualified victory, and one that appears to have gone down the standard Populist line.

However, after this accomplishment, the left wing continued to advocate a more radical doctrine. A left-wing splinter of the UFC, the Farmers' Political Association, advocated solidarity of the farmers and workers and production for use instead of profit. Also, by 1931 the UFC board of directors was supporting a political program that contained more familiar items, such as moratoriums on evictions, the objective of production for use, due to the "inherent unsoundness" of the capitalist system. This item of the program was accepted by the convention—a fact we would interpret as proof of the willingness of some of the farmers to go along with radical sentiment in an economic crisis, but not necessarily support for this item on ideological grounds. In any event, no mention was made of a socialist reform in agrarian entrepreneurship. The final step in the apparent leftward movement of the farmers was signaled when in 1929 M. J. Coldwell, an English Fabian, formed the Independent Labour Party with the miniscule industrial labor force of Regina as its major membership. This organization began to work together with the UFC to create a farmer-labor party. The episode led straight to the famous Regina convention of 1933, when these groups and many others met to form the CCF. The Regina Manifesto was, according to Lipset, "a compromise between the Marxian socialists and the much more conservative farmers' representatives from eastern Canada." The "production for use" slogan was omitted, and each province was left free to interpret the program as it wished.

Lipset interpreted these events as a leftward swing of the agrarian movement. While socialists were in leadership positions, and succeeded, after considerable compromise and persuasion, in obtaining some concessions from the right wing, there is no evidence that the mass of the farmers had been converted to a full-scale socialist program. In these early days, as well as later, there was no departure from sound cooperative principles, no serious advocacy of the collectivization of land, no mention of nationalization of agricultural industries and businesses. In short, the farmers had little to lose by subscribing to the political views of the CCF. At the same time, the CCF, by its attempt to secure the farmers' support, was to increasingly accommodate itself to the interests—some conservative and some "radical," but always pragmatic—of the farmers.[3]

To demonstrate the essentially pragmatic orientation of the Saskatchewan farmer, we may also consider the history and development of the basic form of collective action in Saskatchewan socioeconomic development: the cooperative movement. Since the CCF was required to obtain the support of this movement, and to defend and encourage it after assuming a governmental role, the cooperatives should be seen as central to the increasingly pragmatic political adjustment between the CCF and the farmers.

Cooperation in Saskatchewan is particularly strong; it has been said that "Saskatchewan is simply one big co-op," and this is not far from the truth. No other political entity in North America has so completely accepted the principle and organizational forms of cooperation as a way of adjusting to economic difficulty. Various writers, including, we believe, Lipset, have assumed that the prevalence of cooperation in Saskatchewan is evidence of the left-wing or radical temper of its population; the fact that CCF government helped strengthen and promote cooperatives has been taken as evidence of the socialist identity of the CCF by some commentators. Dean McHenry is typical of a number of writers.[4] He defines socialism as any program with some aspect of public ownership or voluntary collective combination in the economic sphere, regardless of ideological rationale. Only with this purely phenotypic definition would the cooperative movement of Saskatchewan be considered a part of a socialist emphasis in provincial political action.

Such an identification is misleading, in our judgment. While granting that cooperation shares some collectivist elements in common with socialism, it still differs profoundly. First, the cooperative movement does not advocate a basic change in capitalistic institutional structure. It accepts profits and private entrepreneurship; indeed, it seeks to extend the benefits of these institutions to a larger number. Cooperatives are simply described as the joint entrepreneurship of individuals. In Saskatchewan, they have formed a direct practical solution to certain key economic difficulties, principally lack of individual purchasing power (hence the consumer co-ops) and lack of ability to control the price of agricultural products (hence the marketing co-ops). As we shall note in more detail later, the Saskatchewan cooperative movement has been successful only in these two areas. Efforts to establish cooperative farms have failed to impress western farmers, who are predominantly individualistic in their values.

The factors underlying the growth of cooperatives in Saskatchewan indicate that it is a special case. Their formation was immeasurably aided by the presence of many British immigrants who had been members of such organizations in England, but they also had roots in an earlier form of pragmatic mutual aid, a spontaneous neighborliness born from the experience of pioneering in a climate so harsh and so variable as to give one man a crop and his neighbor a failure. These difficulties were compounded in Saskatchewan, because the province was opened up for settlement at a time when the economy of the rest of North America was in an advanced stage. The "last, best West" had to move from frontier poverty to economic establishment in a short period of time, during an era of rapidly increasing costs and an already commercialized agricultural industry. These special hardships bred customs of sharing equipment, exchanging labor, spreading risks, and generally helping out. These customs were more entrenched than in other parts of North America, which were more fortunate in terms of weather or had been settled in earlier times when economic hardships associated with pioneering were not accentuated by modern market and production conditions.

Saskatchewan should not be thought of as qualitatively different from other North American rural cultures in its beliefs and values. These hold that while a man should help himself, some people have bad luck and it is one's duty as a neighbor to give them a hand. These values uphold a free association of equals and oppose governmental, or any other form, of organized compulsion; they are anti-bureaucratic and retain aspects of the frontier tradition of individualism. Such values are widespread in the Saskatchewan population, including the older pioneer generation that established the first cooperative organizations.

The essential point is that the economically homogeneous Saskatchewan farm population responded to critical economic difficulties by cooperative measures of self-help. They looked for solutions to hardship; neither the institutional form nor the ideological rationale was as important as the need for relief. The farmers turned eventually to direct political action, because cooperatives proved to be inadequate to deal with fluctuating world market conditions. Sharp declines in wheat prices taught them the value of political power, power that spoke loud enough to be heard in the councils of the federal government. In the 1930's the CCF became the expression of agrarian self-interest.

Moreover, as the CCF moved toward electoral success, both its leadership and its program changed; it substituted for its original, ideologically pure socialist program the vigorous support of existing farmers' movements and institutions. The CCF knew that it had to get the support of the co-ops, just as the Liberals had found this necessary during the entire history of Saskatchewan as a province (from 1905). Early CCF propaganda emphasized the close relationship between the party ideology and the cooperatives. A CCF pamphlet on "Socialism and Cooperatives," published about 1937, and republished once or twice up to 1944 and then dropped, stated that: "The chief economic object of socialism is to put more money into everybody's pocket so that everybody may own more of the good things of life; the chief economic object of a cooperative is likewise to increase the purchasing power of its members."

The final paragraph of this pamphlet read as follows:

The CCF and Cooperatives

That promise for the future is grounded on the performance of the past and present. Today all over the province CCF people are working and leading in the job of advancing cooperative enterprises; CCF M.P.'s, MLA's, and other leaders have given of their best in support of the Wheat Pool agricultural program; and in the legislature CCF members have asked—alas, in vain—that the Government shall buy all the supplies it can from cooperative organizations. This attitude is significant of the encouragement and support that a CCF government will give to the co-operative movement. The co-operative movement needs socialism; socialism needs co-operatives. Together they bring us nearer to the society of which a great poet has said: "I dreamed I saw a city invincible to the attacks of the whole rest of the earth—I dreamed that was the new city of Friends."

In other publications, particularly the *Commonwealth*, the CCF weekly newspaper, similar arguments were advanced. As it came close to provincial power, the party organ placed great emphasis on its support of the cooperatives; thus, in 1943, we find the following statement: "A reader has written to ask what is the difference between socialism and the cooperative movement. The shortest answer is to say there isn't any difference, but that the first includes the second." Public ownership was only for urban industries and public utilities. Those industries which produced items for agriculture such as farm implements were to be cooperatives. Farmers were told: "They can each own a farm, but they can't each own a packing plant."

After taking office, the CCF party and government continued to promote and foster cooperatives. A list attached as an appendix to this chapter gives the major varieties of cooperative agricultural enterprises and the dates of their establishment; it can be seen that most of the major steps were taken under earlier Liberal governments of the province. CCF contributions to this vast movement consisted of (1) strengthening provincial legislation concerning cooperatives; (2) the establishment of a few cooperative farms; (3) the establishment of fisheries and lumber and fur industries in the north (originally CCF government corporations, which failed and were then reorganized as co-ops). Perhaps most important, the CCF facilitated centralized planning and governmental encouragement of cooperatives by giving definitive power to an existing entity, the Department of Cooperatives and Cooperative Development. This institution continues under the new Liberal government of the province.

The CCF did make an initial bid for the collective ownership of agricultural resources, advocating public ownership of all land. These slogans were dropped as the party neared electoral victory in the early 1940's.[5] Soon after the party assumed office, legislation was passed to facilitate the formation of cooperative farms. The first such farm, the veterans' co-op of Matador, was organized in 1945 in the southwestern part of the province. It has been the subject of studies by social scientists interested in cooperative experiments. Cooperstock's report to the CCF government, later published as a paper in 1961, is a definitive assessment of the difficulties experienced by this farm—troubles which were repeated in most of the other co-op farms established in the 1950's.

The source of the friction was the disagreement over farm management problems and sales policies among farmers who found it difficult to accept shared property ownership as a principle. Dissent about agricultural practices such as field crop production and soil management led to partisan divisions among the members of the farm, and other troubles arose over the withdrawal of equity upon retirement or termination of membership.

It is useful to compare Cooperstock's analysis[6] with Infield's monograph on the same farm.[7] Infield was optimistic and believed it to be a prototype of the future adjustment of farmers to the modern world. The harmony that existed at Matador at the time he studied it was a result of the dedicated, enthusiastic leadership of the farm—which infected the members —in the first year or two after it had been established. Several years later, Wright[8] took a middle position on the question of the future of cooperative farming in Saskatchewan; he acknowledged the troubles but expressed optimism. In the conclusion to his report, Cooperstock wrote that without a deeply rooted ideology, such as that held by communal Hutterian Brethren, the degree of voluntary participation demanded to operate collective or cooperative farms is difficult to achieve.[9]

Under the enabling legislation of 1945, according to data furnished by the Saskatchewan Department of Cooperatives, twenty-nine cooperative farms were organized. Thirteen of them had been dissolved by 1964, and the land sold, either to their own members or to outsiders. Among those still functioning, seven had a history of dissension over issues connected with ownership and decision sharing. Ten of the remaining farms were large family farms made up of nuclear family units. One of them in the north consisted of an entire village of Métis (French Indians), most of whom were related to one another. Among these family farms, three of the cases represented a change from the original group, and the reports note that the related members drove out the non-relatives after disagreement arose. The great majority of the surviving co-op farms are cases in which the enabling laws—which include a number of financial benefits and free services—have been used to establish a family enterprise. Except for one or two of the earliest farms, there is no indication of any important ideological motivation for their organization.

The Saskatchewan Department of Cooperatives attributes the breakup and organizational change of farms to "lack of finances," but also states that "the main objective of most members was to secure through their cooperative farm individual leases on their land," and that "private ownership attitudes were stronger than cooperative ownership attitudes."[10] Thus, the most intense form of production cooperatives did not flourish as a mode of adjustment, and the CCF government did not continue to encourage their establishment.

The Nineteenth Annual Report (1963) of the Department of Cooperatives and Cooperative Development provides statistics that give a concise, overall picture of the contemporary organization of the Saskatchewan cooperatives. In 1963, grain marketing accounted for 39 per cent of the total value of cooperative exchanges. The credit unions were next, and accounted for 18.7 per cent of the total. Cooperative retail sales accounted for 10.1 per cent of all Saskatchewan retail sales. Production cooperatives of all kinds accounted for only .003 per cent of dollar value of services rendered by all cooperative enterprises in Saskatchewan for the year 1962–63. It is clear from this report that agricultural cooperation has flourished only in marketing and consumer organization.

Our second thesis then, is that after it came to power, the CCF government clearly accepted the agrarian cooperatives as pragmatic solutions to the economic problems of the farmer, and at no time during their twenty years in office made any significant attempt to change this orientation. Except for a brief experiment in cooperative farming, their farm policies were those the farmers would accept—security of individual land tenure, stability of individual enterprise and income, and in general, the support of private property.

Set against a farm policy that accepted a status quo position were a number of CCF-sponsored innovations and programs created in the urban and provincial spheres of the Saskatchewan economy. For instance, the CCF invaded the preserve of private capital and production with its enterprises in the fields of insurance, transportation, woolens, bricks, boxes, paint, shoes, house construction, and some minerals. They established government-owned bus transportation, a government insurance office, and various raw materials processing and manufacturing corporations. They passed labor legislation of an extremely liberal, pro-labor type.

In addition to these economic innovations in the areas of public ownership and support for urban labor, the CCF government pressed forward an extensive social welfare program. The majority of the specific measures were comparable to programs offered to people in the United States by the various Democratic administrations, but one, medicare, went further, and eventually led to the doctors' strike in the summer of 1962. Although this plan has been described as socialized medicine and hence as a product of socialist doctrine, the consistent argument of the government on its behalf was rational self-interest. Medicare was presented as financially advantageous to the average Saskatchewan citizen, as productive of better care than private medicine. A full-page newspaper advertisement, for example, begins: YOU CAN RECEIVE FULL QUALIFIED MEDICAL CARE UNDER THE GOVERNMENT PLAN! NO EXTRA CHARGES! NO ADDITIONAL DOCTORS' BILLS! In no sense could this campaign be viewed as a significant deviation from standard trends in liberal state ideology in Canada or the United States. The medicare bill was presented as a progressive piece of legislation, comparable to that favored by the Democrats in the U.S., that would further Saskatchewan's reputation as a North American leader in health programs.

Whether it will be able to formulate a new set of reformist objectives, or will simply become the "left" alternative government to the "conservative" Liberals in a version of the two-party system remains to be seen. The success of the Saskatchewan CCF's pragmatic approach to politics, and its effect on the historical development of the party, led the party away from its allegiance to socialism. In the process of "interplay between current contingencies and historical legacies,"[11] the original socialist ideology was dropped, to be replaced by liberal democratic politics linked to practical expediencies.

This view of Saskatchewan politics rejects the notion that the farmers of the province had reached a pitch of distress and radical fervor, and accordingly voted in a strongly socialist party, but then with prosperity slid down a long slope of increasing conservatism. We have maintained that it is a distorted and oversimplified version of the political process in Saskatchewan. On the contrary, the record shows that the farmers were never really radical socialists. The CCF began compromising its radical doctrine the day after the Regina Manifesto was issued in 1933.

These events in the agrarian political sphere serve to underline the varying functions of political ideology in North America, and perhaps generally. A formal ideology may principally stimulate and determine the course of action to be taken on a given issue; or it may serve as an additional loyalty-producing rationale for actions which are both elicited and accepted on quite different grounds; or it may simply serve to identify the previous role of the sponsors of a particular action. The same ideology may function differently either for the same group at different times, or for different persons or groups simultaneously.

In retrospect, it appears that the early CCF movement suffered from the ideological cosmopolitanism of its leaders,[12] a concern with formulating programs derived from knowledge of the ideology of the national and international socialist movement. Political survival, however, was commensurate with renunciation of these cosmopolitan policies and the adoption of strongly sectional approaches which ultimately led the CCF toward the status of a true provincial political instrument. This could not fail; the deepest grievance of the Saskatchewan farmer concerned what he viewed as the callous indifference and rank ignorance displayed by urban interests with respect to agrarian problems. The Saskatchewan CCF thus became a local party—not a branch of the international and cosmopolitan socialist movement—but a political expression of the local farmers and their needs.

The agrarian movements of the Great Plains taken as a whole can be considered as an expression of native North American rural Populism, insofar as this term is used to describe the three central characteristics of the ideology: anti-monopoly, pro-private agricultural enterprise, and pro-collective action. This Populist spirit assimilated from time to time elements of a Marxist approach, but these were adventitious and did not play an important role in molding the specific action programs. The points of resemblance between Populism and socialist doctrine made it possible for socialists to join forces with the Populist movement, and at times this combination has given the impression that the agrarian movement was in fact radical.

For the majority of CCF supporters, however, the party

was never radical. Rather, it represented economic relief programs for farmers. "A better break for the farmer," "a way to get back something of what we had coming to us," "making it possible for us to compete with the city people."[13] Pre-1964 interviews with supporters of the CCF almost always drifted into discussions of the effects of the depression and the feeling that the CCF was responsible for the present "good times."

In addition, it must be recognized that if ruralities identified the CCF with solutions to their agrarian problems, they to an increasing extent did likewise with regard to the Conservative Federal government's relief measures. Lipset appears to have missed the importance of Prairie Farm Rehabilitation Administration measures and other relief programs introduced by the Federal government in the late 1930's; or, perhaps, favorable sentiment for these innovations was not markedly articulate in the middle 1940's. In the 1960's, and despite some variation, the prevailing pattern of Saskatchewan voting can be summarized by the remark: "They vote CCF in provincial elections, and Conservative in Federal. It makes sense only if you live here." The sense in this situation is clear enough; the farmers voted for those parties that furnished or were associated with solutions to their problems, regardless of ideological doctrine.

In our interviews, the sentiments expressed in favor of CCF policies resembled those voiced in support of the Wheat Pool and co-ops in general. "Like the Pool, the CCF is something we farmers got up." As if to confirm this, conservative opponents invariably said something like this: "That damn CCF government is nothing but a bunch of farmers who took over the province. They don't think of anything but themselves."

Consequently, the socialist label in Saskatchewan political and economic life does not function as a doctrine that incorporates or justifies particular government policies—very few things were done under the CCF government because they were correct socialism. Socialism functioned as an identity tag for the CCF party, helping to distinguish it from the Liberals and the Conservatives. The ideological label facilitated the development of a third political party of enormous vitality, but the CCF government in power represented principally a continuation of accepted policies of public ownership of utilities, and of grass roots cooperation in marketing of agricultural products and the sale of consumer goods, policies pursued by farmer-based parties and movements in other prairie political units, both north and south of the border.

APPENDIX

Résumé of Legislation and Other Developments in the History of the Saskatchewan Cooperative Movement

1890's: Dairy cooperative associations formed with government sponsorship.

1901: Organization of Northwest Territorial Grain Growers' Association, one of the ancestors of the Wheat Pool. Won lawsuit against railroads and forced reforms in grain shipping methods.

1906: Establishment of Saskatchewan as a province. Grain Growers' Association, another Pool ancestor, established by special enabling Act of legislature.

1910: First consumer cooperative organized.

1911: Saskatchewan Cooperative Elevator Company organized on basis of Provincial Act. This was first special Act passed by legislature *in re* cooperatives. Resulted from recommendations of 1910 Royal Commission to investigate handling of grain by railroads and elevators.

1912: Saskatchewan Hail Insurance Act (co-op company).

1913: Saskatchewan Cooperative Associations Act. Basic legislation for all subsequent co-op organizational activities. Amended and supplemented many times since.

1914: Act establishing a Cooperative Organization Branch in Department of Agriculture: ancestor of later Department of Cooperatives and Cooperative Development, a major government agency.

1914: Amendments to Grain Growers' Association Act to permit it to function as marketing and purchasing agent for all associations incorporated under Co-op Associations Act. Beginning of multifarious activities of large marketing co-ops.

1917: Cooperative Creameries Act. Strengthened organizations established in 1890's.

1918: Woolgrowers cooperative founded by sheep ranchers.

1919: Cooperative Stock Yards Acts: established first co-op marketing facilities for livestock.

1921: First cooperative plan for public health: municipal doctor and staff hired by town of Sarnia.

1924: Wheat Pool established by special Act.

1925: Cooperative Marketing Associations Act: strengthened marketing principle.

1925–27: Saskatchewan egg, dairy, poultry, and livestock Pools established by special Acts.

1928: Saskatchewan Cooperative Wholesalers established by special Act.

1931: Milk Pool established by special Act.

1934: Cooperative Oil Refinery built on basis of special Act.

1935: Dominion Wheat Board established; not permanent until 1940's.

1935: Forage crop seed and marketing co-ops established by Act.

1937: Credit Union Act passed by federal legislature. Started development of credit unions in western Canada. Saskatchewan passed own Act in 1941.

1939: New legislation establishing cooperative creameries under producer, not government control.

1940: Canadian Cooperative Farm Implements Company established on basis of federal legislation. New legislation in 1948.

1941: Cooperative Credit Security Act linked credit unions and cooperatives in Saskatchewan into one financial entity.

1944: CCF Government passed Act to establish Department of Cooperatives and Cooperative Development in present form.

1944: Organization of Federated Cooperatives, combining wholesale and production facilities.

1947: Cooperative Guarantee Act: guarantees loans made by credit unions by further linking finances of co-op organizations.

1952: Act setting up Cooperative Trust Company: permitted use of co-op funds for long-term loan business.

1955: Linkage of Federated Cooperatives in Saskatchewan and Manitoba.

1959: Northern Cooperative Trading Services Act. Transfer of CCF-established crown corporations (socialized production) set up in north to co-op management and local ownership.

NOTES

1. Some available studies: Dean E. McHenry, *The Third Force in Canada: The CCF 1932–1948* (Berkeley: University of California Press, 1950); Jim Wright, *Prairie Progress: Consumer Coopera-*

tion in Saskatchewan (Saskatoon: Modern Press, 1956); W. R. Clarke, "Experiments with Socialism," *Canadian Business* (Sept. 1949); Robert Tyre, *Douglas in Saskatchewan: The Story of a Socialist Experiment* (Vancouver: Mitchell Press, 1962).

2. Dean E. McHenry uses the term "socialist party" but means little more than general policy. "A new progressive party, democratic in organization and aspiration, socialist in policy, and pragmatic in politics." We shall hold that save for certain urban innovations, by the time the CCF became a government, most of its socialist policies were changed. McHenry, *op. cit.,* p. 324.

3. Lipset notes at one point that "agrarian radicalism . . . rarely is explicitly socialist, has directed its attack against big-business domination," and also states that "the large measure of 'socialism without doctrine' that can be found in the programs of agrarian political and economic organizations is in many respects more socialistic than the nationalization policies of some explicitly socialist parties." This second statement appears to be his dominant orientation in the book. From our point of view, this conception of the relationship between agrarian reform proposals and socialism is misleading. It masks rather than reveals the character of the farmers' grievances and the nature of the rural values and interests embedded in agrarian reforms. Furthermore, it invites one to explain the farmers' actions as the consequence of formal, socialistic, ideological commitments, which we maintain is either wrong or an exaggeration.

4. McHenry, *op. cit.*

5. Although preparations for a cooperative farming program were under way as early as 1939, there were no important or official public announcements until after the 1944 election. Previous to that time, the CCF newspaper, the *Commonwealth*, repeatedly denied the "rumors" that it was for collectivization of all land and agrarian business, or that "farms would be socialized" (these rumors being based on earlier pronouncements by more radical leaders). In an early issue following the election (9 August 1944), the paper featured a major article on cooperative farming, announcing a research study on the topic and proposed co-op farms for returned war veterans. It should also be noted that the agrarian-based CCF could not obtain much in the way of inspiration from Marxist socialist doctrine, since that doctrine has been ambiguous with respect to agrarian policy. "Peasants" were often interchanged with "workers," in an assumption of their identity of interest, but just as frequently, agrarian people were believed to be too conservative and too capitalistic to be susceptible to socialist ideals (Mitrany 1950; Kautsky 1903). Clearly, the CCF was required to develop a program which had the general objective of economic improvement and prosperity; and do it on the basis of native institutions and existing trends in that direction.

6. Henry Cooperstock, "Cooperative Farming as a Variant Social Pattern," *Canadian Society,* ed. Bernard Blishen, Frank

Jones, Kasper D. Naegele and John Porter (Glencoe, Ill.: The Free Press, 1961), pp. 256–74.

7. Henrik Infield, "Sociometric Structure of a Veterans' Co-operative Land Settlement," *Sociometry*, 10 (1947), pp. 50–70.

8. Jim Wright, *op. cit.*

9. Cooperstock, *op. cit.*

10. A 1959 research conference report, unpublished.

11. Reinhard Bendix, "Industrialization, Ideologies, and Social Structure," *American Sociological Review*, 24 (1959), p. 619.

12. A. W. Gouldner, "Cosmopolitans and Locals: Toward an Analysis of Latent Social Roles—1," *Administrative Science Quarterly*, 2 (1957), pp. 281–306.

13. All are quotations from interviews with Saskatchewan farmers taken by the authors. The senior author has concluded a four-year study of economic and social development of a seven-thousand-square-mile region in southwestern Saskatchewan from an ecological viewpoint. Krueger has done field research on the medicare program and the doctors' strike of 1962.

2

THE DECLINE AND FALL OF
AGRARIAN SOCIALISM

BY

JOHN RICHARDS
Washington University, St. Louis

THE DECLINE of the CCF[1] has often been attributed to the shifts in the social structure of the province, which reduced its potential base of support, and a reduction in the efficacy of the party organization brought about by its inevitable bureaucratization after twenty years of power. This paper purports that at a phenomenological level the above reasons are correct, but that they obfuscate the real problems behind the CCF decline.

There is the irony that the CCF, as an efficient administration, hastened the social changes that deprived it of its rural base, and also that the CCF, as a collection of politically conscious individuals, saw their impending defeat, but could not integrate their analyses and solutions so that it could be avoided. Some attempted to preserve the CCF as a class-oriented socialist party; others tried to revive the flagging youth movement, to inspire the local party organizations, to get more members, to restore the importance of the convention, to reform the *Commonwealth,* to prevent the cabinet from internalizing too many civil-service norms. The importance of the CCF to political sociology is not, therefore, as another case study in the effects of a changing social environment and of bureaucratization, but that the CCF might have created an ongoing political democracy; not that what happened did happen, but that what happened might not have happened.

ENVIRONMENTAL CHANGE

1. "Industrialization"

The relative decline of agriculture in Saskatchewan's domestic product is the most manifest social statistic to explain social change. During the twenty-year CCF reign the ratio of agricultural–non-agricultural value of output fell from over five–one to less than one–one. But because of the negligible importance of manufacturing activities in this development, it is difficult to speak of *industrialization;* I italicize it as a caveat. The economic changes have consisted of new primary industries plus the mushrooming of the tertiary sector, the secondary (manufacturing) being stagnant.

There arose the glamorous new primaries—oil, gas, uranium, potash—and others less so, such as coal and sodium sulfate. They provided non-agricultural employment, and secondary if not primary multiplier effects on income—i.e., their initial capital expenditure usually was for goods produced outside the province, with only their wage and tax payments creating secondary income effects inside Saskatchewan.

More important in terms of political implications was the growth of tertiary industries providing what is needed to live the mass-consumption life, e.g., retailing, distribution, service industries. Typically these industries displayed "economies of scale," i.e., average costs fall with larger units. For example, average retail costs, per dollar of goods sold, fall with the size of the outlet. Therefore urban rather than rural dwellers presumably get the same goods cheaper or better goods for the same price, because the large outlet is impossible without the large market implied by a city. Further, there exist "indivisibilities," i.e., certain consumer goods cannot be provided by small units. They need a minimum market to make operations profitable. An example of this is television, for which the cost is hopelessly high (in terms of cost per viewer reached) without an urban market; the cost falls as urbanization proceeds in the transmission area. When people buy television sets they also need television repairmen, which is a simple example of "complementarity of demand" between the latter and former. Continuing with this example, we can recognize the importance of "transportation costs" (of television repairmen), which limit their travel to the short distances implied by an urban community. An economist would elaborate this genre of argument to show the economic advantages of large units for welfare services (e.g., hospitals), educational institutions (e.g., regrouped school units, central universities), administrative facilities, warehousing, etc.

Large units imply fewness of them, and unless conscious efforts are made to spread them geographically, such industries and urbanization have a positive feedback on each other. They draw labor to the urban communities, forcing the development of an urban community capable of supporting a large, compact population. The development of urban amenities in turn attracts further labor, and assures that new businesses will choose the urban location because of minimal labor and resource supply problems. Since radical political awareness is difficult to arouse in an urban middle class, part of the reason for Saskatchewan's return to the North American political norm may ironically be a consequence of the new urban-based tertiary growth, over which the CCF administered so well.

In the agricultural sector, technological change increased the optimum farm size, although because of its labor-saving character, the family farm has remained a potentially efficient unit, i.e., a family provides sufficient labor to take advantage of new techniques. The better roads and farmers with money to travel on them have, however, destroyed the retailing function of small villages. A town of less than, say, two thousand in 1950 had to fight to keep its population from falling. A town above that threshold could provide sufficient retail outlets and consumer services to "take off" as a regional commercial center. The natural increase, the surplus farm population as the number of farms slowly dropped with increasing size, the youth and the retired from the small towns, all provided potential urban dwellers for Saskatchewan cities—and those of other provinces. Ironically the critical problems surrounding rural society occurred simultaneously, at least toward the end of the CCF reign, with record-high farm incomes.

2. Urbanization

Again, we are presented with one outstanding statistic: Saskatoon and Regina, during the census period 1951–61, were respectively Canada's third and fourth fastest-growing cities, in a province whose population growth was the second lowest in Canada.[2]

Although the economic inducements to urbanization involved in changing farm technology and the phenomenal growth of tertiary economic activity explain much of the urbanization, there are also more strictly sociological reasons. A detailed analysis would seek to subsume these under as few variables as possible, but from a less rigorous standpoint several processes may be mentioned. During the CCF regime there occurred an inversion in the status ranking of urban versus rural occupations—at the expense of the latter. A three-year period in Saskatoon or Regina at the provincial university served effectively for most rural students as a socialization course in urban living.[3] Thirdly, the knowledge of, and the demand for, an urban, mass-consumption life-style grew with the spread of the mass media—from department store catalogues to national magazines and television—and the dramatic rise in incomes during and after World War II. The positive value attached to a mass-consumption life-style was reflected in government programs to minimize the gap between urban and rural living standards, e.g., rural electrification, farm sewage programs, municipal road paving. Such programs represented government attempts to preserve rural communities and stem urbanization, yet both the government and the rural beneficiaries agreed that this could only be done by bringing a mass-consumption life-style to the farm and village, i.e., by making rural life as much like modern urban life as possible. The net effect on urbanization of such programs depended on whether they succeeded in satisfying long-standing rural desires for certain urban conveniences, or whether they increased relative deprivation by instilling materialistic values and raising expectations above what could be achieved in a rural environment.

3. Saskatchewan Class Structure

There had always existed the duality of upper or middle, and lower class, the professional occupations being transitional positions. With continuing urbanization and economic development, any frontier homogeneity in the urban areas vanished. The class structure of the growing cities became more complex and rigid. Immigration has been an important source of the urban lower class, but few upper-class people voluntarily came to Saskatchewan—except persecuted American social scientists. Accordingly, the upper class retained a greater degree of homogeneity than any other class during the changes of the CCF reign. Their noblesse oblige prompted them to continue governing where they could, and to analyze critically the socialists—more comprehensively than they ever had themselves[4]—where they could not.[5]

The lower class grew under the CCF with the increase in manual jobs in the economy. But it failed to gain the sense of class consciousness that the farmers were losing, and that the upper class had. If, as Lipset suggests, occupational homogeneity is essential for class consciousness in rural Saskatchewan, its absence in urban areas may be explained by emphasizing the heterogeneity in work conditions of manual workers. With little industry in the province, many manual jobs originate in the tertiary sector, characterized by relatively small firms, i.e., low employee-employer ratios, facilitating paternalistic work relationships and making unionization difficult. What industrial firms exist are usually small. Thus the working class is divided among many fairly small companies, performing diverse tasks that encourage little solidarity beyond the immediate work group. Those of traditional working-class family background, (e.g., railwaymen) are only a small proportion of the total. The many recent immigrants and people off farms are less likely to become class conscious.

The considerable residential segregation of classes within each city may, however, stimulate class solidarity. Perhaps the highest level of urban class consciousness occurs in inter-school athletics at the high school level. Students at urban high schools are drawn from the environs of the school, and accordingly the schools have the class orientation of their section of the city. In Saskatoon, for example, a Bedford versus Bowman football game is working versus middle class; the latter school is naturally new, the former old.

The rise of the CCF in the 1930's and 1940's implied a new status system, different—almost antithetical—from one correlated with economic class position. Whereas doctors, lawyers, and businessmen are highly respected in the ordinary North American status structure, the agrarian radicals sought an inversion by emphasizing respect for Protestant preachers, teachers, their own politicians (usually), and laborers and farmers (i.e., themselves). Then, in the 1950's, the rapid growth of the urban middle class, resulting from new economic and social conditions, defeated the CCF effort and strengthened a status system positively correlated with class ranking. The growth of the middle class is clearly not an independent reason for the defeat of the CCF—both phenomena should be explained with respect to other variables. Yet North American middle-class occupations, in affording sufficient income to live out a mass-consumption life-style, do offer work conditions orienting people away from the political and social values associated with manual labor.

This emphasis on the urban middle class in analyzing the defeat of the CCF seems initially bizarre, given the pattern of voting which developed in 1964.

TABLE 1

1964 ELECTION RESULTS

	CCF	Liberal	Progressive-Conservative	Totals
Urban[6]	14	6	0	20
Rural	12	26	1	39
Totals	26	32	1	59

The results indicate that the CCF did better in the urban seats, and imply that with continuing urbanization the CCF might again return to power, this time as an urban party. That such optimism is not justified can easily be shown by disaggregating the urban vote into its class components.

The urban upper class, numerically unimportant, has reasserted its political status position—over the middle class completely, and over the working class partially. Accordingly, any political radicalism, inasmuch as it implies an inverted status system, should now decline among the middle class—dying as its older minority of CCF supporters do.[7] There will be little intergenerational continuity, now that the CCF is out of office. Many middle-class parents experienced the ill effects of the depression, and the emergence of reformist pro-CCF agencies, the party itself, the Wheat Pool, consumer cooperatives, trade unions, etc., in a highly politicized atmosphere. But their children attend schools where discussion of politics is avoided by status-conscious teachers, read conservative newspapers, and watch their parents strive, usually successfully, in the booming capitalist economy of modern Saskatchewan.

Among the working class, continuity of CCF support is more likely. The unions continue as socializing agents for the CCF, although other, initially anti-capitalist organizations (e.g., the co-ops) avoid political controversy, which means they accept the reintegrated economic and social stratification of the society.[8] The urban working class is constantly augmented by rural people and foreign immigrants. The former are the poor farmers,[9] more likely to retain their radicalism; the latter are Europeans, often the beneficiaries of stronger radical traditions. At the other end, the working class in an advanced, prosperous, urban economy is always losing members to the middle class, inter- if not intragenerationally.

The continued CCF success in the cities depends on a declining proportion of the urban population, the working class. Among the middle class, as has been discussed, its support will literally die off; among the upper class it was always weak. But because the CCF maintained a plurality in the aggregate, and with one exception never divided the large towns into multiple constituencies,[10] which would have allowed the geographic separation of the classes to become effective in electing candidates of different parties in one city, the party appears to dominate the urban vote. As urbanization proceeded during their administration, the CCF added seats to the multi-seat urban constituencies of Saskatoon and Regina, thereby effecting a minor reapportionment favorable to themselves. Upon returning to power in 1964, the Liberals immediately divided the multi-seat urban areas into single-seat constituencies, on the basis of poll results in the last election.[11]

The prospective decline in urban support of the agrarian protest party may be more easily explained than why rural Saskatchewan has been abandoning the CCF (although perhaps it is doubtful as to who abandoned whom). On a social-psychological level it may be argued that increased rural wealth somehow alienated farmers from politics, and consequently the hard-sell election propaganda of the Liberals could change votes—votes that might otherwise have remained CCF out of habit. Against this hypothesis, however, is the fact that Lipset explained the rise of the CCF before 1944 in terms of increased wealth. He showed that the party began to make real headway after the depression, and that its rural leaders and members were not the poor, but rather the prosperous farmers. Silverstein's analysis of election results from 1952 to 1964 conclusively indicates that rural income or wealth has not been significantly associated with the CCF vote.[12] The first significant disintegration of rural CCF support occurred in the 1958 federal election when the Conservatives under Diefenbaker (himself a Saskatchewan native) reduced the number of Saskatchewan CCF M.P.'s from ten to one[13] at a time when farmers were not particularly prosperous. Perhaps Diefenbaker's image as a western radical broke the rural conviction that the old parties were automatically enemies of farmers.

More important perhaps as a source of CCF decline is the fact that the major, once pro-CCF, non-capitalist economic institutions (Wheat Pool, consumer co-ops, etc.) followed the conservative path that Lipset suggests is common for all purely economic reform organizations during good times. They made peace with the rest of the capitalist Saskatchewan economy, and sought to secure their position in a society returning to the North American political norm. The depoliticalization of cooperative Saskatchewan may have sharply weakened the CCF organizationally, since this process implies a decline in the overlap of leadership between the party and other organizations described in *Agrarian Socialism.*

The corollary of these arguments is the ineffectiveness of the CCF at the constituency level. But I want to suggest that the CCF was not merely a victim of forces larger than itself, but that it failed to exploit all *its* resources in its effort to maintain Saskatchewan socialism; i.e., I do not want to give an entirely exogenous analysis of the decline of the CCF in terms of economic changes, urbanization, etc. Therefore, it is necessary to consider what happened to the internal democracy and the unique institutions the party evolved to handle politics.

SASKATCHEWAN'S POLITICAL INSTITUTIONS

1. Constituency and Below

By 1964 very little CCF organization existed at the subconstituency level, although apart from the ubiquitous women's organization it is difficult to assess how important such organization was in the past. Formal poll committees were extant only in a few constituencies consciously concerned with their political heritage. Nevertheless CCF'ers talk with tragic nostalgia of the party organization as it "used to be"; each constituency had many poll committees, handled membership sales and subscriptions to the *Commonwealth,* and discussed and submitted resolutions to the constituency organization.

At the constituency level formal organization had by 1964 become too much in evidence. Many political activities formerly involving no "bad faith" degenerated to a ritual or a purely executive responsibility. Where the choice of candidate had been competitive, the CCF MLA or candidate often established sufficient charisma so that his renomination was a ritual. Where the formulation of resolutions to go to the provincial convention once involved considerable constituency debate, the responsibility of preparing them now often falls to a committee of the constituency executive, and debate is much reduced. This does not mean that the CCF has become ossified relative to the norm of North American politics, merely that its activities have fallen below the extraordinary level of involvement generated in the 1940's.

Given the importance the party attached to memberships as a symbol of commitment, the membership total in a constituency is a good index of the number of people involved with the party, and the enthusiasm of one constituency relative to another. As a guide to the order of magnitudes involved, consider the 1964 figures. CCF membership was thirty-seven thousand, or an average of over six hundred per constituency,[14] 4 per cent of the total population, nearly 7 per cent of the voting population, and 15 per cent of the CCF vote. Allowing 5 per cent of the voting population for membership in opposition parties, and using this very generous criterion of membership to indicate the proportion involved in provincial politics, there is the depressing statistic that seven out of eight voters were not even paper members of a political party in what had been the most politically conscious province in Canada.[15] These orders of magnitude are worth remembering as the analysis proceeds.

Within the active CCF minority defined by mere membership, a continuum may be defined from the passive, dues-paying, *Commonwealth*-receiving majority, to the active, *Commonwealth*-writing minority. From this minority of activists within a minority, a group that was quite stable over the years, came the constituency executive members and candidates. In the rural constituencies, the party leaders consisted largely of farmers—they had the time, and originally the party had been conceived of as a farmer's movement—but in the cities they were not only union leaders—the natural leaders of a working-class political movement—but with equal frequency, politically deviant middle-class individuals. Political activity under the CCF was sufficiently extensive that the active minority of the party could maintain their inverted, politically defined status system in the face of its general subordination to the class-correlated one. A middle-class professional with a socialist orientation could to a considerable extent opt out of normal society and use the party as his reference group and source of friends. It is difficult to know whether the middle-class activists were socially deviant before they joined the CCF, or whether having become active in it meant that they were no longer socially acceptable to the more conservative members of their class. Trade-union leaders had high political status within the CCF, but could not gain middle-class status even when their income levels qualified them to it. Because of the extensive nature of CCF political activity, they did not bother to try, if closely involved with the party.

The constituency executive was responsible for a vast array of political details, from organizing meetings to nominating candidates, running bake sales and bazaars, formulating telegrams of protest to Ottawa, sending delegates and resolutions to the provincial convention and Council, and establishing liaison between the MLA (if a CCF seat) and the constituency. Despite the power of the central party institutions, great constituency autonomy existed even in 1964: the Kelvington constituency felt free not to renominate their sitting CCF MLA; another rejected the provincial secretary as a candidate (and he accepted their decision with good grace). Constituency representatives at the Council meeting in January 1964 refrained from an open break with the cabinet over government announcement of support to religious secondary schools only because of the impending election, which frightened everyone into a unified silence.

The last example, however, could be interpreted to demonstrate the opposite—constituency subservience—and indeed many constituency activities had become routinely bureaucratic or ritual. When constituencies spent their meetings berating Canada's foreign policy, to the exclusion of formulating solutions to local problems, they were guilty of ritual radicalism that was a denial of their responsibility to attempt to influence the path of their own government in Regina. Apart from this ritualized radicalism, constituency activities became increasingly limited to those immediately functional to election campaigning—the campaign itself, selling memberships, fund-raising activities—to the exclusion of involvement in municipal politics, in discussions of government policies, and in

ν programs to deal with the malaise of a
society.

course, much that was good in constituency
example, the annual membership drive. Although
be argued that membership levels had become goals in
emselves, and that the party had forgotten that membership
was supposed to be a minor formality in the important goal
of involving people in politics, a better analysis would not do
so. In a continent where public commitment to political
deviance is anathema, surely the threshold of political involvement crossed by buying a membership in a third party is not
negligible. Virtually all of the memberships sold in Saskatchewan are individually negotiated every year (union-affiliated
memberships are negligible). They involve the payment of
$2.50 and the signing of a declaration of support. If the
prospective member was personally canvassed, then he would
probably find himself "coerced" into giving an additional do-
nation and subscribing to the *Commonwealth*. Throughout the
year he would receive constituency party propaganda, invita-
tions to attend meetings, to sign petitions, to canvass others,
to bake cakes, etc. The reinforcement of solidarity among the
active members by canvassing is an important additional function. The interaction of canvasser and potential member is a
genuine political act, involving them both in often lengthy
political discussions. Active members, from cabinet ministers
and provincial presidents down, have spent long hours trudg-
ing from house to house in the cold autumn evenings, hopefully searching out new members and bringing old members
back into the fold, engaging in half-hour discussions about
medicare, or cooperative farms, or the box factory.[16] CCF
organizers, responsible for completing a canvass, have be-
rated their canvassers in an attempt to curtail such conversations, but usually in vain. One of the ironies of the CCF defeat
in 1964 is that the membership figure for that year, thirty-
seven thousand, surpassed the former record set in 1945. By
this index, the CCF was never stronger than when it lost
power.

CCF Party Organizations and Interactions, 1964

CCF ADMINISTRATION

PROVINCIAL EXECUTIVE (~ 15 members)

PROVINCIAL COUNCIL (~ 80 members)

CONVENTION (~ 800 delegates)

ORDER-IN-COUNCIL INSTITUTIONS (Budget Bureau Planning)

CIVIL SERVICE

(formal government institutions)

PARTY LEADER

CABINET

GOVERNMENT MLA'S AND CANDIDATES

(parliament)

CONSTITUENCY (52 constituencies)

YOUTH SECTION

POLL COMMITTEES

WOMEN'S SECTION

The preceding diagram is a simplified representation of the institutional interactions specified by the CCF constitution[18] (1–18), and of the expected relationship between parliament and the civil service (19). Although one to eighteen have the concreteness of being written in the party constitution, all are manifestations of party ideology. That performance did not always obey these ideological prescriptions is to be expected; that it did to a considerable extent, is part of the significance of the CCF.

LEGEND

Heavy arrow indicates election of some or all members of "B" by members of "A." Light arrow indicates some other influence of "A" on "B" intended by the party constitution or ideology: e.g., some or all members of "A" automatically being members of "B," "A" having advisory power over actions of "B."

Dotted lines indicate designated institutions and interactions not ubiquitous.

```
┌─────────────────────┐
│    CONSTITUENCY     │
└─────────────────────┘
```

(1) Youth groups send delegates to the provincial convention. (8,3,h)[18]

(2) The constituency organizations directly elect 80 per cent of the delegates to the provincial convention. (8,3,e)

(3) The constituency organizations elect 75 per cent of the provincial Council members. (11,2,b)

(4) The constituency organizations independently elect the constituency candidate for MLA. (10,1,b)

```
┌─────────────────────┐
│     CONVENTION      │
└─────────────────────┘
```

(5) The convention is the supreme source of authority within the party. (8,2)

(6) The convention elects the party leader annually. (8,6,c)

(7) The convention elects ten Council members annually. (8,6,f)

(8) The convention elects the party president and three vice-presidents annually. (8,6,d)

```
┌─────────────────────┐
│     PROVINCIAL      │
│     EXECUTIVE       │
└─────────────────────┘
```

(9) All executive members are delegates to the convention.

(10) The members of the executive (specified by 8) are also automatically Council members. (11,2,a)

(11) The executive controls the party administration. (12,1,4)

```
┌─────────────────────┐
│     PROVINCIAL      │
│      COUNCIL        │
└─────────────────────┘
```

(12) Council members are delegates to the convention. (8,3,a)

(13) The Council has some controls over the cabinet and executive: e.g., the cabinet must allow the Council to review its activities, and the Council must be consulted by the premier before he appoints a new cabinet minister. (12,2,1), (13,1), (13,2)

(14) The Council elects five of its members to the executive. (11,4,b)

PARLIAMENT

(15) All MLA's and candidates are delegates to the convention. (8,3,c), (8,3,d)

(16) The party leader is a member of the executive. (11,1), (11,4,a)

(17) The party leader is a member of the Council. (11,2,a)

(18) The MLA's elect two Council members. (11,2,g)

(19) The government should bring sympathetic administrators into the civil service by direct order-in-Council appointments, and should closely control the rest of the civil service to keep it in hand.

2. Constituency and Above

A description of the elaborate ramification of organizations meeting in Regina best illustrates CCF determination to maintain member control of the party and party control of their politicians (at least on a formal level).

The complicated interactions and limitations of roles one individual could play implied a lack of faith in the extent to which the parliamentary system, left to itself, could provide democratic politics.[17] A party member with a non-government role in one of these organizations might have limited power to force the government to initiate legislation; he clearly had a far more effective regulatory role than, say, many opposition MLA's. Consensus for major policies had to be won not only in the cabinet and among the government

MLA's, but in the various party organizations, the latter consensus often being more difficult to achieve than the former.

The convention is according to the party constitution and ideology, the source of all authority within the party. The potential disruption of the parliamentary system by a political party that takes seriously its formal internal political structure has existed at least since the Marxist theory of the class party. In Saskatchewan, conservative elements occasionally warned the CCF government that it was responsible to the people and not to the members of its political party, but no one ever pushed this theme too much, perhaps for fear of making it too manifest that the democracy Saskatchewan enjoyed existed largely within the processes of CCF institutions. The level of legislative debate was abysmally low, although the opposition leader's fervent anti-socialism[19] usually kept the elder members awake. Other potential sources of democracy were equally discouraging: the Liberal Party, always prone to oligarchic rule, became under Thatcher entirely devoid of any internal democracy; the Progressive-Conservatives were split into upper-class members who secretly admired Thatcher, and lower-class members who secretly admired the CCF; the large urban newspapers belonged to the Sifton family and had been consistently unsympathetic to any of Saskatchewan's unique solutions to political problems for as long as anyone could remember.

As Lipset pointed out, the phenomenon that prevented the authority of parliament or party from ever causing protracted conflict was the charisma of the party leaders, and more particularly, their oratorical skills. It is by no means an unusual situation that potential value conflicts between institutions are contained by the charisma of individuals playing roles in both; what was unusual was the seriousness with which the party considered policy questions and the regulation of the government, and conversely, the concern of the government to convince the convention that it was doing right. Many constitutions of political parties throughout the world contain articles to the effect that a plenary meeting of the membership is the source of all authority within the party, but there is an implicit understanding among all concerned that such ideals are "unrealistic," i.e., cynicism acts to prevent conflict.

Toward the end of the CCF reign, the cabinet became increasingly enmeshed with the professionals of the civil service and took a paternalistic view of convention activities. The party began to hold its conventions in the smart hotels in town, which better fitted the idea of convention week as a chance for rural people to get to town and renew friendships.[20]

Yet occasionally, even in the sixties, the convention debates produced encouraging scenes of cabinet ministers, MLA's, and lesser delegates queuing up for their turn at the microphones placed around the convention floor, and the convention was never an institution to be played with by the party leaders.[21] Its failings, therefore, cannot be blamed uniquely on any group. The influence of the convention waned because nobody in the CCF, from top to bottom, knew what to do with a rich Saskatchewan, or how to make explicit what was valuable in their party processes, so that it could be defended from apathy and professionalism.

> The Executive shall conduct the affairs of the Association in accordance with the policies of the Convention and of the Provincial Council.[22]

According to ideology and practice, the provincial executive was an administrative body; it did not make policy decisions.

> The Provincial Council shall meet at least twice-yearly to review the activities of the Executive and to give direction to the Executive in accordance with the policies and programs of the Association as adopted by the Convention.[23]

> An Advisory Committee composed of three members appointed by and from the Provincial Council, shall from time to time advise the members of the Legislature concerning the implementation of the program of the Association.[24]

> Whenever appointments to a Cabinet are being made, the Political Leader shall submit the names of his proposed Cabinet Ministers to this Committee, which shall act in an ad-

visory capacity, realizing that final responsibility for Ministerial appointments must rest with the Premier.[25]

These quotations are the only written description of the functioning of the Council, perhaps the most interesting CCF institution designed to facilitate membership control of the government. It never met more often than quarterly, but the discussion among the approximately eighty Council members— 75 per cent of them in no way professional politicians—was infinitely superior to legislature debates. Ministers (and federal M.P.'s present) reported, defending their departments and outlining departmental policy in some detail. The provincial treasurer revealed the broad outline of his budget two months before it was presented to the legislature.[26] Each speaker, including the premier, found himself intelligently questioned and sometimes harassed.

The CCF at all levels respected the Council and *wanted* to make it effective. CCF'ers intuitively understood institutionalization as well as a professional sociologist. They also had great fear of co-optation, in the cabinet, the party administration, and especially in the civil service (see note 21). Simple party members, i.e., those without other political roles, were aware of the danger that their leaders would internalize the norms of the professional civil service after years spent in the latter's company. Ministers frequently became aggressive at Council meetings if harassed, feeling that the Council was not sufficiently appreciative of the difficulty of their conflict of loyalties, but if the party had not harassed the government for twenty years, the CCF would have become a typical institutionalized reform movement with democratic ideology and elite control coexisting and all but the "true believers" disillusioned. The Council had the good sense to recognize that the same vigilance had to be extended to the party organization.

Again, charisma was important in reconciling potential conflict about primacy between the Council and the cabinet. The respect accorded to the role of premier-cum-party-leader was enormous; Woodrow Lloyd enjoyed it to as great a degree as T. C. Douglas had. After the 1964 election defeat, there was little specific criticism of Lloyd's leadership, whereas in 1961 he was widely criticized as being Douglas' choice forced on the party. Twenty per cent of the convention delegates voted for another candidate as leader. However, despite charisma and the Official Secrets Act,[27] the Council was perhaps the one body of elected representatives where political issues were argued with a minimum of "bad faith," i.e., there was no implicit understanding by those involved that decisions were to be made elsewhere. At the very end, in 1964, the Council bitterly criticized the cabinet for announcing government support to religious secondary schools without having consulted the party, and effectively ostracized the Minister of Education, who lost a safe seat three months later partially because of Council and membership bitterness at his betrayal of responsibility to the party. Perhaps the support-to-religious-schools issue manifested the extent to which the government had forgotten the importance of its internal party processes[28] and succumbed to an ideology of consensus politics[29] (the Catholics had long campaigned for this measure) and professionalism (the civil servants in the Department of Education were concerned about the lower standard of education among students of religious schools).

With respect to one theme, the fate of the CCF government was analogous to that of the parliamentary system in general. Many political scientists analyze policy initiation as having passed from the legislature to the cabinet to the civil service. With the CCF, it was a question of transfer from party institutions to cabinet to the civil service. The transfer was not simple, and the interaction of three political institutions (party, legislature and cabinet, and civil service) produced results in Saskatchewan dissimilar to those in any other Canadian province.

After 1944 Saskatchewan became a model administration, inspiring left-wing intellectuals from all parts of the Western world to active participation.[30] The reforms attracted professionally trained men, and slowly the "animal spirits"[31] shifted from the party to the new professionals in the civil service. These men had come into government because they found the CCF espousing their ideals, and they worked loyally to translate the ideals into practice. The CCF desperately needed sympathetic administrators, but such men were not aware of the significance of the fact that their ideals were shared not only by a group of politicians but also by the large mass of CCF members, i.e., were not just the ideals of a benevolent elite. The new administrators continued to produce reformist ideas and helped to maintain Saskatchewan's pre-eminence as a model administration, but they ignored—as do all civil servants—the less formal aspects of politics embodied in political parties. The cabinet, with a few notable exceptions, internalized too many of the professionals' ideas about politics. The number of cabinet ministers and senior civil servants was small enough to allow numerous particularistic relationships, which added to cabinet members' role conflict as party member versus department head.

The legislature has been almost completely ignored in this analysis. There are obvious reasons for its insignificance. The CCF has always been highly concerned about presenting a united front to the non-CCF world—conducting its arguments within party institutions and not in the legislature. Little is known publicly about the internal doings of the CCF party caucus in the legislature. The Liberals, for their part, have never considered parliamentary debating overly important. The restrictiveness of parliamentary procedure seems mildly absurd when it requires radical farmers to address each other as the "honorable member for [say] Bengough." It is only when lawyers predominate in an assembly that parliamentary procedure can seem civilized and not cumbersome, and the CCF never suffered from an excess of lawyers. For all these reasons, the level of legislative debate was abysmal.

However, the futility of the role of simple MLA augmented the problem of finding a second generation of CCF leaders. There are few careers with as much insecurity as that of a radical politician in North America, and few young CCF'ers were sufficiently enthusiastic politicians to fight at the constituency level to win the nomination from an entrenched candidate, or, if that fracas were concluded successfully and the election won, to spend dreary years as a backbencher before having a chance to get into the cabinet. If we consider the CCF in this way, the path of a potential professional CCF'er is alien to the idea of the CCF as a spontaneous political movement; but in an organized society, political organization is essential, and presumably it must be partially bureaucratic, with some people playing the bureaucratic roles. Certainly, radicals have had a distrust of professional politicians ever since Robert Michels' *Political Parties* became required reading among educated socialists. But if, as the CCF believed, it is the party that shelters and nurtures democracy, somebody must shelter and nurture the party, and attempt to translate party ideas to professional civil servants. The frustrations faced by professional politicians in democratic politics and amateurs sincere in their political involvement assume neurotic dimensions unless the whole process of bureaucratic organization is made manifest and the potential role conflicts examined so that compromises can be made explicitly, not implicitly.

The problem of preserving the CCF as an ongoing institution was perceived differently by varying groups. Those in the central offices worried about constituency organization, memberships, and electoral support; those in the cabinet worried about electoral support and the continuity of the administration; the activists among the membership worried about institutionalization. Only a very few CCF'ers appreciated the problem of producing a second generation of CCF professionals. Those who did usually manifested it in concern for the faltering young CCF movement.[32] In the 1960's it had a membership ranging from two hundred to three hundred, and was producing neither young CCF members nor professional politicians. After the election defeat, the youth movement naturally knew no better than its elders what was to be done, but ironically that year's convention was very enthusiastic. Membership has trebled since then, now that it no longer has the burden of supporting the government in power.

A unit of organization not previously discussed is the CCF administration. In the 1950's the CCF constructed an impressive headquarters, the Coldwell Building, to house the printing plant of the *Commonwealth* and its central offices. The staff efficiently collected large sums of donations, processed many membership applications, sent out mail, and prepared convention kits. Reputedly, the CCF organization was very efficient (and perhaps was, relative to other parties, before Thatcher organized the Liberals), but its role was too objectified, and the administration staff stopped examining how functional its activities were to maintaining a democratic political party in Saskatchewan. For example, in the medicare crisis, it could not efficiently use its resources to fight the (admittedly much better financed) anti-medicare campaign. At all levels the CCF failed to mobilize efficiently and show solidarity for medicare. In a crisis, the administration could only send out literature to the already committed members. The spontaneous degree of solidarity the convention displayed that year in bolstering the cabinet to fight for medicare was encouraging (see note 21).[33]

The cabinet in early 1964 must have surveyed the political scene, and presumably hoped that all the dysfunctional trends (growth of the middle class, disaffection of the party activists, and more immediately the elaborate advertising campaign of the Liberals) would not have gone far enough to defeat the government if the election were advanced by two months from its usual early June date to April 22. They were wrong.

THEORETICAL CONCLUSIONS

I hesitate to make theoretical statements at the end of a very subjective piece of writing, but at a phenomenological level perhaps the analytical continuum I would like to offer helps to describe the change in psychological orientation toward, and the objective nature of, political action by Saskatchewan citizens. One pole, which may be labeled "functional alienation," is an orientation toward politics where the non-professional in no way involves himself, but accepts (with little conscious questioning) the political environment extant and (via a vote) chooses what appears to be most functional to his apolitical life-style. The professional recognizes (intuitively if not consciously) that the majority of the electorate is alienated from politics, is consciously concerned with it only via very specific acts (e.g., voting, taxpaying), does not conceptualize its political needs or the political aspect of society, except to demand of the politician certain institutionalized public services (e.g., highways for its automobiles) at a minimum personal inconvenience (i.e., lowest possible tax level). Realizing the nature of this functional alienation, the professional exploits it to maintain or advance himself in the political establishment, and has an interest in keeping political consciousness at the simplistic level of his public addresses. If political participation by ordinary people is meaningless, he blesses it paternally; if it is not, he fights it viciously.

The other pole, labeled "politics for itself,"[34] is an orientation that considers one's political role as vital to the well-being of the political system. It implies a pursuance of political action ultimately for the sake of pursuing political action, and not because of a pressing external constraint.

It is difficult to disguise the value judgment in the above continuum, but that criticism need not be fatal. The statements: "Politicians are all crooked"; "Choose the lesser of two evils"; "Time to give the other bunch a chance"; "The Liberals look like they'll lower taxes"; "So long as they leave me alone, I don't care what they do" clearly imply functional alienation. The statement quoted by Bennett from a conservative Saskatchewan rancher: "That damn CCF government is nothing but a bunch of farmers who took over the province"[35] implies that CCF'ers were at the other pole. It is rare that a productive class involves itself in politics to the extent of forming its own party and taking over a government. When that class outnumbered the rest, what could be better?

The tragedy is that the farmers' government presided over the transformation of Saskatchewan into a typical functionally alienated North American region. The medicare crisis in 1962 was the CCF's last great battle against "them." They won, but it was a Pyrrhic victory, and after 1964, no matter how much poetry Douglas quotes ("I'll lay me down and bleed awhile, /And then I'll rise and fight again."), nobody knows whom to fight now; so why not settle back and watch television like everybody else?

NOTES

1. In the 1960's the CCF (Cooperative Commonwealth Federation) became paranoid about its name. In 1961 the reborn federal CCF became the New Democratic Party (NDP), but the Saskatchewan CCF had strong sentimental attractions to the old name, and were familiar with all the uncomplimentary expressions that the letters CCF could be said to stand for—such could not be said for the letters *NDP*. The convention forbade the *Commonwealth* from referring to the federal party as NDP, and adopted for itself the most cumbersome of titles: Cooperative Commonwealth Federation, Saskatchewan Section of the New Democratic Party. This paper will (incorrectly) use the old name, CCF, throughout.

2. Population stagnation has been a prime political issue in the 1960's. Did it constitute a "flight from socialism," as the opposition charged, or is the drawing power of urban centers directly proportional to their size (and accordingly, larger cities outside Saskatchewan could outdraw Regina and Saskatoon), or is it merely a testament to Saskatchewan winters?

3. This latent function, therefore, made it politically dysfunctional for the agrarian-based CCF to have been the most generous of Canadian provincial governments in subsidizing higher education.

4. Escott Reid, "The Saskatchewan Liberal Machine Before 1929," *Canadian Journal of Economics and Political Science,* 2 (1936), pp. 27–40.

5. The pervasiveness of CCF incompetence as an issue, while among civil servants from all Canadian governments the reputation of Saskatchewan's administration was continuously rising, can now be understood. To the upper-class leaders of the opposition parties, it was axiomatic that a bunch of farmers could not govern efficiently, and admittedly, former protest governments in North America have displayed administrative weakness. The tragedy of this antithesis of attitudes affected the CCF, and after the Liberal victory in 1964, poisoned government-civil service relations. Naturally only the incompetence argument had any access to public opinion (see the box factory note 16), and the CCF government, already in an obvious conflict situation between duty to party and civil service, developed obsessions with efficiency and propriety. This social situation is partially the explanation for the government's substitution of professional values for their former concern about party participation in decision making. With respect to the post-1964 civil service, it began immediately to disintegrate, and

the Liberals hastened the decay by harassment of specific individuals. Dozens of dedicated senior civil servants resigned, being snapped up immediately by other governments: e.g., the deputy treasurer became Assistant Deputy Minister of Finance at Ottawa; the chairman of the Medical Care Insurance Commission became deputy treasurer of New Brunswick; the Saskatchewan Power Corporation, renowned throughout North America for its rapid rate of growth and low rates, was chastened by its minister for low profits until its manager resigned.

[6] URBAN SEATS (in order of decreasing size)	CCF	LIBERAL
Regina	5	1
Saskatoon	4	1
Moose Jaw	2	0
Prince Albert	0	1
North Battleford	1	0
Swift Current	1	0
Weyburn	1	0
Yorkton	0	1
Estevan	0	1
Melville	0	1
TOTALS	14	6

7. In my section of Saskatoon, which is predominantly middle class, organizing CCF members to work at the polls was a depressing task. By 1964 there were too many retired couples, not sure if they had the energy, physical or mental, to perform the minor roles of poll clerk and scrutineer.

8. See Lipset's discussion of the evolution toward conservatism of radical organizations: e.g., the SGGA, the Wheat Pool. As a footnote to a footnote, the editor of the Wheat Pool's weekly paper, the *Western Producer,* was by the 1960's an outright conservative.

9. The rich retire into the middle class in British Columbia as frequently as in Saskatchewan.

10. Regina, for the 1964 election, was an exception, since after 1960 the CCF had divided it into Regina North, one seat, heavily working class; Regina West, two seats, working and lower middle class; Regina East, two seats, largely middle class; Regina South, one seat, middle and upper class. Classifying by the 1964 results, Regina North was safely CCF; Regina West was safe, but less so; Regina East, a very marginal CCF seat, involved a recount before the second CCF'er was declared elected; Regina South was the only seat in the entire province where the CCF lost their deposit, i.e., received less than half the votes of the winning candidate.

Regina South also contains a large number of white-collar civil servants, which gives another enigma to explain.

11. After the new boundaries were drawn, a CCF MLA from Regina complained (vainly) that by driving down one street he could go in and out of his constituency four times. Admittedly, the CCF had been guilty of gerrymandering in their differential treatment of Saskatoon and Regina in 1964, but Saskatchewan Liberals have always had a flair for tragicomic corruption in election practices.

As a more detailed example, consider the story of the CCF MLA for Hanley, Robert Walker, ex-attorney general, versus his Liberal opponent, Herb Pinder, briefly MLA and a senior Liberal minister. On election night, April 1964, Walker lost by six votes, but the declared ballots were still to be counted. The summer was spent in acrimonious court proceedings, as the Liberals charged irregularities in these ballots to prevent their being counted. Due partially to Conservative judges, appointed under Diefenbaker, who hated Liberals more than CCF'ers, the Liberals failed, the ballots were counted, and Walker won by two votes. Accordingly, the Liberals now began proceedings to declare the election null and void, at which point Walker offered to resign if a by-election were held at once.

In addition to the Liberal machinations, Hanley illustrated how Saskatchewan politics is "different": in terms of the urbanization, the ideologies of the two candidates, the passions aroused. The constituency was formerly completely rural, but by 1964 counted half its voters in strongly pro-Liberal, middle-class suburban developments of Saskatoon. Walker, as a left-winger of the cabinet, valued the CCF as a class-oriented political movement, and fought against its transformation into a paternalistic, urban-oriented, liberal reform party. Pinder was a dynamic, conservative businessman, who had started and built up a chain of drugstores, and had a passionate desire to save Saskatchewan from socialism. Incidentally, Walker won the December 1964 by-election, and resumed his seat in the legislature.

12. See Sanford Silverstein's essay on the elections.

13. The one remaining, Hazen Argue, defected to the Liberals before the next election.

14. Strictly speaking, there were only fifty-two constituencies, which would give a constituency average of over seven hundred, but dividing by fifty-nine, the number of legislature seats, gives a discount for multi-seat urban constituencies.

15. This is a crude estimate based on none too reliable Liberal membership statistics for 1964.

16. The box factory has been a significant political issue for over fifteen years. It was one of the nationalized industries introduced by the CCF prior to 1948 that failed. For the opposition it has been proof of socialist incompetence; for the CCF, it has been

not only a fardel, but because of the opposition's refusal to let it die, a proof of dirty opposition tactics.

17. After George Williams' dominance, the party constitution stipulated that no elected representative (MLA or M.P.) of the party could simultaneously belong to the executive or Council (except by 16–18 in diagram). (11, 13)

18. All bracketed symbols refer to article, section, and subsection respectively of the 1961 CCF constitution, as amended in 1962.

19. Thatcher, the opposition leader from 1960–64, and Liberal premier from 1964, defected from the CCF in 1955 while serving as a CCF M.P. He has the fervor of all repentant sinners.

20. The 1964 convention was held in Regina at the Hotel Saskatchewan (owned by the CPR) in July, i.e., after the election defeat. The secretary-treasurer reported that the party had come out of the last election "in the black"; the president of the ladies' section reported that the calendar commemorating twenty years of CCF rule had sold well. The shareholders in this prosperous company passed out into the lobby, wall-to-wall crimson carpets to cushion their steps. Nobody knew whom to blame, or what to do; so they argued about foreign affairs and whether the Council should meet three or four times a year.

21. The convention, if incapable of forcing the government to initiate legislation, was to the end capable of passing inflammatory resolutions designed to alienate all but the faithful, and embarrass the leadership. For example, in 1963, the convention passed a resolution calling on the cabinet to fill important civil service posts with socialists, because non-socialist administrators would never work wholeheartedly for socialist programs. That the CCF convention was in session during the negotiations between government and doctors in July 1962 was important in bolstering the government to concede as little as possible to a very well-organized lobby.

22. CCF Constitution of 1961, as amended in 1962; Article 12, Section 1, (4).

23. *Ibid.;* Article 12, Section 2, (1).

24. *Ibid.;* Article 13, Section 1.

25. *Ibid.;* Article 13, Section 2.

26. The significance of this fact can only be appreciated if one knows the sacredness in British parliaments of Budget Day, and that nothing should be revealed beforehand.

27. Ministers could always use this act as a rationale for being professional and withholding information from the Council.

28. Woodrow Lloyd implicitly admitted this in the summer of 1964 by saying that in opposition the CCF had a chance to attend to its internal "plumbing," a task which had been neglected because of the pressures of governing.

29. There is always the possibility that the CCF will return to power as a consensus party of paternalistic liberal reform.

30. The CCF established the Economic Advisory and Planning Board as a home for sympathetic economists, where they could evaluate and suggest policies, and provide the government with detailed social accounts for the province. The Budget Bureau was created with the functions of coordinating budget preparation and acting as an organizational management team within the government, but independent of any particular department. Such innovations were immensely exciting in the 1940's, although admittedly the CCF perpetrated such idiocies as the Labor Department Film Censor. Every year in the budget estimates, after "Gas Inspection and Lighting," and before "Apprenticeship and Tradesmen's Qualifications," appeared "Fire Prevention and Film Censor."

31. An appropriate expression from economics jargon, meaning the initial source of motivation.

32. It would be ungrateful not to introduce a "particularistic" note here, and mention my appreciation of Sandy Nicholson's (the ex-Minister of Social Welfare) concern for and help of the Saskatoon young CCF group to which I belonged.

33. I remember the two boxes of M. J. Coldwell's *Left Turn, Canada* inefficiently buried and forgotten at the Coldwell Building, and the large sums we raised by selling them at one dollar each on the University campus. There was a very personable air about party headquarters. Ruthless efficiency is not everything.

34. The reader must excuse the existentialist terminology, but I want to emphasize that there is no a priori reason to value a society highly involved politically over against one functionally alienated.

35. See John W. Bennett and Cynthia Krueger, "Agrarian Pragmatism and Radical Politics," in this book.

3

THE DOCTORS' STRIKE: CHANGE AND RESISTANCE TO CHANGE IN SASKATCHEWAN

BY

JANET WALKER GOULDNER
Washington University, St. Louis

IN NATURAL ENVIRONMENT, agricultural economy, and in the way the people live, Saskatchewan is similar to the rural Midwest of the United States. But in one important aspect these two cultures differ greatly—in their relations with business and professional groups of urban areas. In Saskatchewan, during the harsh years of the 1920's and 1930's, a great deal of class consciousness and class conflict emerged. The farmers' self-consciousness as a group and the differences they see between their rural interests and those of urban groups continues today and is of the greatest importance in understanding the medicare dispute. Rather than share the respectable, conservative outlook of the business and professional men of the towns, rural Saskatchewan has tended strongly to oppose such values, at least as far as political ideology is concerned, and has fashioned instead a pragmatic variety of agrarian socialism with an emphasis not so much on economic changes as on social reforms.

Urban business and professional organizations have been vociferously opposed to the CCF. Their opposition reflects not only ideological differences, but also resentment over the lack of industrial expansion in the province—a condition businessmen deplore and attribute to the CCF's agrarian socialist policies. Many of Saskatchewan's professional people did not live in the province before the war and have no personal memories of the "dirty thirties." Many doctors of the province are immigrants from Britain; in many cases a dislike of the British national health plan impelled them to leave England, and they are naturally hostile toward similar proposals in their adopted home.

The farmers always had trouble getting and keeping good doctors at a price they could afford to pay. Their medical services have been spread over a thinly populated area, large parts of which become inaccessible during fierce winters. Since most of the province consists of vast rural stretches, it is possible to say that it has been difficult to secure adequate medical service for most of Saskatchewan.

The mayor of a tiny hamlet called Limerick has described a typical rural experience in trying to get medical care:

"We'd get the drifters, d'you see. There was this Irish doctor. The ladies filled his 'fridge with home baking, see. Well, he come here, ate his way through the 'fridge, and went back to Dublin. Then there was the Englishman. Never sober from the day he come to the day he left. We had a Jamaican for a time. Nice young feller but couldn't git along with the old uns. Finally he had a bust-up with Old George, who can't hear too well on account of wax in the ears . . . and off he goes too."[1]

The early community and government programs of the 1930's, designed to help rural communities support a general practitioner, were limited to what a country doctor, working alone, could provide. Other medical service innovations followed, facilitated by provincial legislation, various federal and provincial parties, or community action itself. Health-insurance plans sponsored by doctors were introduced in Saskatchewan in the late 1940's and grew rapidly, but they remained beyond the means of many and were not extensive enough for others. Finally, in December 1959, Premier Douglas announced his government's intention to establish a comprehensive medical care program, in accord with five basic principles: prepayment, universal coverage, high quality of service, administration by a public body responsible to the legislature, and acceptability to doctors and public alike.

There was nothing new or unexpected about the opposition

of Saskatchewan doctors to such a plan. They had been registering their total opposition to what they regarded as "state medicine" in publications of the local medical body, the Saskatchewan College of Physicians and Surgeons, as far back as the early 1930's. In those days, the doctors were a solid part of the hegemonic group of Saskatchewan; that is to say, they were part of the urban elite, whose values dominated the life of the rural province. The farmers, on the other hand, were a marginal group at that time. Their needs and preferences, often at variance with those of the elite group, did not constitute a serious consideration in provincial politics, and they did not have the power to enforce them.

Doctors coming into the province from eastern Canada or England brought with them expectations of the social status and economic rewards that their colleagues got at home. These expectations were fulfilled, even in this predominantly agricultural society, by the high social standing and income of doctors as compared to farmers. The doctors were representatives of an older, urban elite in a frontier world.

Such hegemonic groups typically resist social change; they are committed to preserving the status quo. These groups take for granted the existing social structure, which seems to express the natural order of things. If a crisis occurs they attribute it to some force outside the existing social structure. They feel sure that the disturbance will be removed eventually and life will resume its normal course.

It is the groups that are marginal to a society, groups that do not have a stake in the status quo, that seek radical solutions in a time of crisis. Thus in the 1930's the farmers of Saskatchewan sought radical changes in the existing social structure; the established groups simply tried to hold on until the crisis was resolved.

By the 1940's the doctors and the farmers in Saskatchewan had traded positions. The farmers had become the dominant group. Their ideology had been established in the ruling CCF government. The doctors, although their income and social positions remained high, lost ground politically. The free-competition economic ideology of the doctors, which was once the dominant ideology in the province, was displaced by the prevailing cooperative ideology of the farmers and the workers. The doctors and their allies in the middle class had been displaced from their old positions high up on the power pyramid. Doctors thus became what economist Everett E. Hagen has called a "displaced elite," ripe for radical solutions in time of crisis.[2]

A content analysis of articles and other public pronouncements and proceedings appearing in the *Saskatchewan Medical Quarterly,* the publication of the local College of Physicians and Surgeons, during the 1950's and the 1960's, reveals that, as the CCF came to power and then began to consolidate its power in subsequent elections after 1944, two points of view began to emerge in the medical profession's discussion of health-insurance plans. The first implied the College's recognition of the power of an opposing value system, represented by the CCF government. The assumption now was that health insurance was just "around the corner." The concern of the College was focused, not on whether to have health insurance, but on what type to have and on who should administer it. Labels such as "state medicine," formerly appearing each time the government's part in an insurance scheme was mentioned, disappeared in the *Quarterly*. Where it had formerly insisted that the government should have no authority in the planning and administering of an insurance program, the College now concentrated more on insisting that it be well represented in any committees that the government set up to study and ultimately to organize and administer such a program.

The second point, stimulated by the first, was the College's increasing fear and distrust of the government and its ability to usurp the doctors' base of public support. In response to this, there were more and more references to the need for solidarity within the medical profession and to the importance of good public relations. The doctors were reminded, for example, that they must keep their reputations above reproach.

In April 1960, a few months after Premier Douglas' first announcement, the government declared its intention to set up the Thompson Committee. This committee was instructed to conduct hearings on a plan for prepaid medical services, to study proposals, and to report a plan that could be enacted into legislation. The Committee was made up of twelve people, to represent the public, the government, the medical faculty of the University of Saskatchewan, the Chamber of Commerce, the Federation of Labor, and the College of Physicians and Surgeons. Because of its opposition to the Committee, the College initially did not name men to represent it.

The 1960 provincial election took place less than two months after the Thompson Committee was created. The doctors attempted to mobilize public opposition to the whole orientation of the CCF, not just to medicare. The CCF won the election, but although it retained two thirds of the seats in the legislature, it secured less than 50 per cent of the popular vote. The CCF interpreted the vote as a clear mandate for medicare, while the opposition argued the people's choice was still questionable, since the majority had voted for other parties.

During this time, that is, as the Committee was being created and appointed and the issue was being put to the people during the election, the College was trying to decide whether or not to boycott the Committee. In the doctors' eyes, "the appointment of this Committee seemed another political move on the part of the government, which could have only limited value and objectivity, as the Premier has already announced the basic components of his medical care plan, both in the late fall of 1959 and during the election campaign. The government has obviously already made up its mind about the method of providing medical services to the people, before giving the [Thompson] Advisory Planning Committee its terms of reference."[3] They eventually decided to go along, and named the three men to represent the College, who were then finally officially appointed.

As soon as the election was over the Thompson Committee proceeded with its hearings. As Badgley reports, "of the 43 briefs submitted by organizations to the Committee, groups such as Councils of Commerce, whose membership included merchants, manufacturers, insurance agents, farmers, financial interests and members of various professions were against the medical care legislation proposed by the government. Sharply opposed to this position were organizations representing labor, farmers and the party in power."[4]

The Committee met over the next years and submitted an interim report in September 1961. A majority recommended that a medical-care insurance program be established that would provide for universal and comprehensive coverage, to be financed through taxes, paying the doctors on a fee-for-service basis, and that the plan should be administered by a public commission that was responsible to the Department of Public Health.[5] The medical, professional, and business representatives submitted a minority report, which recommended only that the various voluntary insurance schemes already in existence continue, and that "coverage of persons unable to meet the premiums and all persons over age 65 would be subsidized out of public funds."[6]

Six weeks after the Committee's interim report had been filed, a special session of the legislature was called. On November 17, 1961, the Saskatchewan Medical Care Insurance Act was enacted to go into effect six months later. This meant that the Act would go into effect two years after the Thompson Committee had been established.

As soon as the Act was passed, events began building swiftly to a crisis. The College of Physicians and Surgeons immediately protested the Act, stating that it gave doctors "no rights or privileges," while granting the government "wide powers of control over medical practice." The doctors also protested that Premier Douglas had broken his promise that the plan would be acceptable to those receiving and those rendering the medical services. They announced they would not cooperate with the Act and would, instead, continue to deal directly with their patients. Doctors and their partisans began to form protest groups, and business and professional people from the towns and cities flocked to organizations such as the Keep Our Doctors Committee. Like the doctors, these once-powerful business and professional people felt the squeeze of social change in Saskatchewan. The existence of these protest groups made it possible for doctors to feel doubly justified; they were defending not only their right to private fees, but the whole free-enterprise way of life.

During the following winter and spring months, a few attempts at a reconciliation were made, but both parties clung adamantly to their differences and no compromise was reached. Partly as a result of this impasse, Premier Woodrow Lloyd (who had succeeded Douglas) announced a delay in the implementing of the plan, from April 1 to July 1, 1962. At the same time the government signified its seriousness in going ahead with the plan by announcing, in the middle of April, an amendment to the Act, which designated the Medical Care Insurance Commission as the agent of all beneficiaries in the province and the organization responsible for the remuneration of the doctors' services. This brought more protest from the doctors, who maintained they would disregard the Act and the Commission.

At a meeting of the College in May, the physicians set up their plan to withdraw all normal medical services and to provide free emergency service if and when the Act went into effect. Immediately after this, on June 18, 1962, the Canadian federal election was held and former Premier Douglas (who had resigned to become national leader) and the sixteen other federal CCF-NDP candidates were defeated in the province. The doctors interpreted this result as an expression of public support in their favor.

In the last days of June, meetings between the doctors and the cabinet were called in a last attempt to reach a settlement. The talks ended on June 25 with the announcement that the government, without abandoning the Act, had offered the doctors the right to practice privately if they wished, and that the College had turned down the offer as unrealistic. On July 1 the Act went into effect and the strike was on.

At that time of year, the vacation season for many doctors, the usual number actively practicing in Saskatchewan was roughly between 430 and 470. When the strike was called, 200 of these doctors remained available for emergency service, as the College promised. Saskatchewan's medical needs were additionally provided for by some 20 to 40 doctors who opposed the strike and were willing to practice under the Act, and by about 80 doctors imported by the government for the emergency, as well as by an unknown but significant number of doctors who practiced sub rosa. The strike closed all but 34 of Saskatchewan's 148 hospitals, but the doctors' voluntary emergency service kept about 70 per cent of the province's hospital beds available for patients who needed them. The doctors' strike, then, never entirely cut off medical service.

The imported doctors were recruited by the Medical Care Insurance Commission mostly from England, to serve for between two weeks and a month at a guaranteed pay of from $900 to $1800, plus expenses. Of the 102 doctors recruited by the Commission, 87 were reluctantly registered for practice in Saskatchewan by the College of Physicians and Surgeons. The College regarded these imported doctors as strikebreakers, but was compelled by its reciprocal agreements with the British Medical Association to grant registration to qualified British doctors.

The government supplied these imported doctors to communities that requested their services. In some cases a town council made such a request, only to have the doctor who came to them refused hospital privileges by a local hospital board sympathetic to the striking doctors. But neither the College's refusal to register some "immigrants," nor the antagonism of some hospital boards, could stem the tide. The wages offered were so attractive that applications continued to arrive. The new doctors agreed by contract to practice under the Medical Care Insurance Act. Many of them staffed the cooperative clinics that cropped up in numerous communities to provide medical services during the strike. The striking doctors and the Keep Our Doctors Committee regarded them as "scabs, strikebreakers, and undesirable economic competitors."

When the strike began on July 1, the doctors refused even to negotiate unless the Act was suspended or repealed. But by July 18, the leaders of the profession recognized that the emergency service could not be operated satisfactorily for an indefinite period, that many doctors yearned to get back to work, and that the government with its imported doctors was undermining their position. They agreed to negotiate. The government had brought in a special mediator from England, Lord Taylor, to help find a settlement. Lord Taylor was a doctor, a Labour Party parliamentarian, and one of the architects of Britain's national health plan.

Lord Taylor arrived in Saskatchewan on July 16 at the invitation of Premier Lloyd. On July 23 a settlement, called the Saskatoon Agreement, was signed by the government and the College. The government agreed to amend the Act to provide the doctors with several options as to how they could practice. These included: (1) practicing under the Act as initially planned, whereby the doctors received payment directly from the Medical Care Insurance Commission; (2) billing patients directly, with patients then sending the bill on to the Commission for reimbursement; (3) traditional private practice, "outside the Act"; and (4) participation in any of several approved private insurance plans. Premier Lloyd was reported as saying, after the Saskatoon Agreement, that "all but one of the major concessions by the government—eligibility of private plans as reimbursement agents—had been offered by the government before the strike started."[7] The basic nature of the Act—that it was compulsory, comprehensive, and government-run—remained unchanged. The doctors accepted it.

The parties to the dispute, in the immediate aftermath, had different opinions of the settlement. From interviews with several government officials, the impression given was that the government did not feel too put out by the concessions it had made. The doctors preferred to think of it as a truce—many of them called it an "uneasy truce"—and looked for new trouble spots to appear among the loose ends left by the agreement. Many of the doctors were reportedly far from satisfied, feeling that their gains were not significant.[8]

From the beginning, the effectiveness of the emergency service and the relative lack of solidarity among the doctors weakened the College's position. During the strike many physicians worried about how long and how effectively their emergency service could be continued before serious consequences to patients could be laid at the doctors' feet. Most hospitals reported that they were able to handle the volume of emergency cases adequately during the strike. There were relatively few publicized instances of death that could be blamed on lapses in the emergency network. At the same time, the boycott was expensive, and although official College statements reported that the doctors were managing all right economically, some young doctors privately admitted that they were having financial problems and did not know how long they could hold out.[9] One doctor stated that many rural doctors or doctors in individual practice, who depended on a week-by-week income, would be "obliged by financial pressure to cooperate with the Commission on government terms." He felt that the College was not negotiating for these men.[10]

There was greater loyalty to the College and its position among urban than rural doctors. One spokesman for the College, a Regina doctor, stated that the College had experienced difficulty in maintaining solidarity among its rural members.[11] Adding that there had been attempts to "divide the medical profession" during the strike, he mentioned not only the rural doctors, but also the divisions between the specialists and the general practitioners. It is interesting that the College's problems with its own members came largely from those marginally located within the power structure of the profession—the young, the rural, and the general practitioners.

The government gained heavily in legitimating its socialist programs generally by its success in recruiting doctors who would work under its medical-care plan. The government's show of strength reinforced faith in the party and reasserted to all concerned the CCF's position as the basic power center in the Saskatchewan social order. This position did not need as strong an assertion within the province as it did on the national level. As far as national politics was concerned, it was of the utmost importance that the government provide ample evidence of its strength and effectiveness in dealing with this crisis, since the political future of the CCF-NDP, as a new labor-left party making a bid for federal power, required that the CCF handle the medicare dispute and handle it well.

By supplying doctors upon request, the government assured medical care to communities that might otherwise have suffered badly. This assurance removed the probability of the medicare issue becoming a personal crisis for many voters, and hence diminished the chances of the electorate turning against the government on other, broader issues than medicare per se. The inability of the doctors and those who sympathized with them to involve large numbers in anti-CCF and anti-socialist causes seriously crippled the effectiveness of the protest.

The plan has now been in effect for several years. It is clearly a success, even in the opinion of most doctors. A survey, designed to find out how Saskatchewan doctors felt about practicing under the Act, conducted by W. T. Thompson, president emeritus of the University of Saskatchewan, found that most favored it after having practiced under it. The results based on 242 usable returns on a questionnaire sent to all doctors who had submitted claims for payment to the Medical Care Insurance Commission found as follows:

(1) How would you vote on a secret ballot to decide whether to continue or discard the medicare program?

To continue:	160
To discard:	62
No answer:	20

(2) Is the plan a success?

Yes:	149
No:	54
Partially:	11
No answer:	28

(3) Are the medical needs of the citizens being met?

Better:	78
About the same:	94
Not as well:	35
No answer:	35

Source: W. T. Thompson, "Saskatchewan Doctors' Opinions of Medicare: A Questionnaire Study," *The Canadian Medical Association Journal*, 93 (October 1965), pp. 972–74.

In June 1962, a conservative newsmagazine reported that the number of doctors practicing in Saskatchewan had increased 5 per cent since the strike. The profession was busier and better paid than ever before.[12] The College remains publicly committed to an opposition stance. Condemning "state medicine" has become part of its fixed ideology. The College protested vehemently and sent letters to all the doctors in the province objecting to the Thompson questionnaire. But the members of the College are engaged, not in ideological combat, but in practicing medicine; they have found that they can work with the Act, that their rewards—financial and professional—are more than they had expected.

NOTES

1. Quoted by William Stevenson in the Toronto *Globe & Mail*, March 23, 1962.

2. Everett E. Hagen, *On the Theory of Social Change: How Economic Growth Begins* (Homewood, Ill.: The Dorsey Press, Inc., 1962).

3. Arthur Peart, "The Saskatchewan Story," mimeo (1962), p. 2.

4. Robert Badgley, "The Public and Medical Care in Saskatchewan," mimeo (1962), p. 2.

5. Murray S. Acker, "Saskatchewan's Health Services in Perspective," mimeo (1962), p. 5.

6. *Ibid.,* p. 5.

7. Toronto *Star*, August 3, 1962.

8. Interviews with government spokesmen and doctors, Summer 1962.

9. Regina *Leader-Post*, July 19, 1962.

10. *Ibid.,* July 17, 1962.

11. Interview with Dr. Neville Smith, Saskatchewan, Summer 1962.

12. *U.S. News and World Report*, June 1964.

4

PRAIRIE PROTEST: THE MEDICARE CONFLICT IN SASKATCHEWAN

BY

CYNTHIA KRUEGER

Brooklyn College
of
The City University of New York

INTRODUCTION

THE POSSIBILITY of inaugurating comprehensive medical insurance, medicare, has been seriously considered by governments at all levels on the North American continent for at least four decades. This should not be surprising, since the rising expectations that accompany the industrialization of societies invariably include the desire for good health, and both the United States and Canada have attained the level of social and economic development that is conducive to basic public-welfare reforms. These reforms are often held to be necessary to equilibrate the relationships between technological changes and existing social institutions. In the field of medicine, for example, the financial difficulty of securing medical treatment has increased with advances in medical technology, and the specter of chronic illness or a lingering death is an economic fear for all but the most wealthy. Thus private insurance plans have developed and operate on a huge scale, even though the coverage they provide is notoriously limited and literally millions of individuals cannot afford the premiums. Within this framework, the question of governments' responsibility to secure medical care for their citizens has been raised time and again.

There is little doubt that debate on this issue would have been long since ended—in favor of government action in the sphere of medicine—in Canada and the United States, were it not for the lobbying activities and propaganda efforts of a most powerful and politically energetic interest group, the doctors. Although political effectiveness is increasingly recognized as a hallmark of both the American Medical Association and (to a lesser extent) the Canadian Medical Association, it is far from being an exclusive possession of these organizations. Groups in the United States ranging from the influential Farm Bureau to the Veterans of Foreign Wars and the National Rifle Association literally mold legislation and effectively block proposed legislation that pertains to their interests. One need not subscribe to the "power elite" theory advanced by the late C. Wright Mills[1] to conclude that the operation of the democratic system is in many respects the result of the machinations of interest groups, which in turn may be interpreted as constituting a type of invisible government, beyond the purview of elections.

The importance of interest groups in the operations of democratic governments has been emphasized by various political scientists, including A. Holtzman, who has stated:

Political action by organized interest groups is a fundamental phenomenon of modern democratic societies. Such is the case whether the governmental system is federal or unitary, parliamentary or separation of powers, laissez faire or welfare. In conjunction with political parties, interest groups constitute the principal avenue outside of official public government through which political power is marshaled and applied.[2]

Although sociologists tend to focus on political parties rather than interest groups, Ralf Dahrendorf has given considerable attention to the latter in his book, *Class and Class Conflict in Industrial Society*. As Dahrendorf conceptualizes interest groups, "They have a structure, a form of organization, a program or goal, and a personnel of members."[3] In terms of the influence of interest groups upon legislative bodies, it should be added that their tactics tend to be restricted to lobbying activities in an attempt to influence legislators directly.

In Saskatchewan, however, the activities of the doctors as an interest group were ultimately combined with an emergent, spontaneous protest group, the Keep Our Doctors Committee. Although one probably could dissect the protest group into components of established interest groups, more might be lost than gained in the reduction. For the fact remains that the social effects as well as the character of a group are altered when it openly and actively asserts itself in the public-opinion arena. For example, it is one thing for the public to be able to predict that the National Rifle Association, perhaps incognito, will oppose more than token gun legislation in this country; it would be quite another matter should the NRA begin to picket the White House, organize mass meetings and sponsor public demonstrations to further its legislative aims via marshaling public opinion. This distinction between interest groups and protest groups appears to have been generally ignored by sociologists. Indeed, even the existence of protest groups and protest activities in a democratic society are left largely unexamined.

One traditional view of protest movements interprets them as evidence of a malfunctioning social system or, minimally, proof of tensions within it. Some authors also point out that expressions of social protest are often functional for individuals in various ways, and may in fact culminate in the desired changes of society.[4]

Beyond such insights concerning social protest, little headway has been made in assessing theoretically their locus in a social system or their role in a democratic society. This essay maintains that expressions of protest (and, in addition, fear of such expressions) play a crucial role in a democratic society; they may stimulate equilibrating mechanisms between solutions of the past—including the structure and content of social institutions—and contemporary exigencies. Expressions of protest can raise new issues, or provide more fashionable garb for old ones. Regardless of the fact that one may not agree with their objectives, expressions of protest, whether addressed to a college administration, the conditions of work, or to government foreign policy, are central to our society as factors both influencing the operation of established social structures and providing additional connectors between the individual and his social environment. Although this evaluation of social protest is commonly voiced on an informal level, as individuals acknowledge the NAACP, Viet Nam Teach-Ins, or the emergence of the labor unions as being significant, if not always good, it is exceedingly difficult to find room for such a view in sociological theory.

Indeed, most theories that deal with social movements at all conceptualize them as being partially expressions of protest writ large, and have been primarily restricted to taxonomic classifications of types, or step-by-step delineations of their development. The relative dreariness of theoretical treatment may support the oft repeated claim that sociology does not deal adequately with social change or deviations from a given status quo; it may reflect an as yet unaccounted but central feature of social movements or social protest expressions.[5]

The substantive section of this paper describes one example of democracy in conflict: in this instance, a farmer-controlled political party, which had been in power for seventeen years, not the system of stratification, seemed oppressive to the individuals who protested. On this occasion, the expression of dissent was sharp if not mighty, and was developed (publicly) primarily through the emergence of one activist protest movement, the Keep Our Doctors Committee. The KODC capsulates an instance in which a sizable proportion of the "outs" did not adhere to a decision made by the "ins," and believed that the "ins" had on this occasion, and others before it, given them no consideration. A kind of grass roots ideology, polarization of views and stereotyping of the opponent—in this case, the government and its supporters—developed as a part of the KODC culture.

It is noteworthy that the protagonists of the Saskatchewan conflict were not political parties, but rather individuals who were united and active in reaction to a specific act of the government. To be sure, the vast majority of the members of the KODC were also supporters of parties opposing the governmental party, but their own political parties were not considered adequate means of expressing their discontent. The motivational link between the individuals and their anti-governmental activities was most explicitly loyalty toward the family doctor, not loyalty to Conservative, or Liberal, or Social Credit Parties. In this manner, then, the KODC provides evidence for those who would emphasize that the processes of democracy extend far beyond the structure of political parties and elections. From this perspective, sensitive public opinion, occasions of widespread dissent, and extra-party expressions of conflict constitute significant ingredients of a viable democratic system and must be included in theories concerned with democracy.

Mirroring the government-doctor conflict, the province of Saskatchewan became a divided, hostile land as a result of the reactions to the dispute; the emotional scars it left on friendships and family relations will take some time to disappear. How could such a dispute, between a professional group and the democratically if not majority-elected government, have this impact on a populace? What factors contributed to the active involvement of a part of the population in a conflict with which it, theoretically, need not have been so concerned? This essay is, in part, an attempt to answer those questions. As such, its focus will not be on the actual points of contention between the government and the doctors, but upon the protest movement that arose in defense of the doctors and their anti-government position, the Keep Our Doctors Committee.

This committee constituted the most viable and spontaneous expression of protest in the province since the classic farmer movements documented by Lipset fifteen years earlier. In his study, Lipset observed that the farmers had felt themselves abused by the eastern interests and frustrated by the political impotence of their own economic segment. One of the most important outcomes of the effect of the depression on the farmers was their adoption of a specific political party (the CCF) to represent them on the provincial government level. After seventeen years of provincial rule by that party, other segments of the population, the doctors and the KODC, rose in bitter protest against the medicare legislation as sponsored by the CCF, and in most cases openly registered sentiments of moral outrage against the CCF party itself.

Specific and long-established grievances, such as railroad and elevator services, wheat and consumer-product prices, had spawned organized, persistent action by the farmers. The doctors' strike, which represented the profession's organized revolt against the CCF medicare legislation, was the occasion that stimulated the KODC, if not the reason for its emergence. The grievances, then, of these two examples of protest—the farmers earlier and the supporters of the KODC in this decade—and the sources held accountable for those grievances were different. The feelings of exploitation, rage and frustration of the two groups, however, were of the same stock.

Lipset described the strong grass roots consensus of the farmers concerning some specific desires for reform, as well as depicting the sectional and at times left-wing appeals of the farmers' movement. The KODC, also essentially a grass roots development, was, if anything, right wing politically. Like their earlier farmer counterparts, the members of the KODC represented efforts to organize interests into political effectiveness; unlike the farmers, however, the KODC lacked firm consensus as to their motives for becoming organized and the priority of their goals. And, unlike the farmers, the KODC failed to endure beyond a limited period of crisis.

In spite of the brevity of its career, the KODC capsulates another development in the political history of Saskatchewan; that alone would make it of importance to political sociologists. Thus a chapter is added to Lipset's earlier observations of the machinations of the many and varied local democratic processes. In addition, the KODC is representative of perhaps the most singularly ignored recurrent sociological phenomenon: a spontaneous and relatively widespread expression of protest that lives only a little while, then disappears from the listings of active social groups.

Throughout the entire medicare controversy, the people of Saskatchewan were bombarded with propaganda from both sides. Before, during, and after the 1958 and 1960 elections, the public was encouraged to be aware of the implications of the deadlock for the quality of its medical services. Immediately before and in most stages of the twenty-three-day doctors' strike, the newspapers and other mass media of the provinces were filled with medicare news. Editorials, letters to the editors, news releases from both within and outside the province, and paid advertisements from both pro- and con-medicare groups (including the government of Saskatchewan) dominated the communications media of the province.

Advertisements were extremely numerous during the controversy, and serve as good indices of the propaganda efforts of both sides. For example, the July 6 issue of the Regina *Leader-Post* included the following messages sponsored by the Citizens for Medical Care: (1) "Doctors go back to work; we weren't happy when the government said 'no' to trading stamps, but we didn't leave the province," (2) "Withdrawal of physicians' services unethical and unwise," (3) "Who's kidding who? Does the *Leader-Post* really care about the freedom of the press?" Again, in the July 3, 1962, Regina *Leader-Post,* the Keep Our Doctors Committee purchased space for the following advertisements: "The voice of the people has gone unheard; freedom for all," and "Saskatchewan citizens, let your voice be heard; freedom of choice is being challenged. Your family doctor is meeting that challenge." The Saskatoon *Star-Phoenix,* on the eve of the doctors' strike, exhibited this full-page message from the Saskatoon KODC: "THE ONUS WILL BE ON THE GOVERNMENT. THINK—LIVES DEPEND ON IT."

Public opinion, as well as the propaganda, became characterized by intense emotionalism. What had begun as a conflict between the government and the doctors was now a crisis for the public at large. In personal conversations, each side developed a dogmatic line. People tended to think and communicate in terms of slogans. These were one-or-two-word clichés expressing broad values; for example, "Health For All," on the one hand, and "Freedom For All," on the other. Entire conversations consisted of aggressive exchanges of these basically incontestable values. Communication in terms of such expressions transformed potential debate into grass roots ideological confrontations and had the effect of stifling the normal communication processes of give and take. Thus the pros and cons of medicare—in reality, an administrative and

economic alteration of traditional medical payment procedures—became obscured.

For much of the public, the issue of medicare was translated into the motives and the historical actions—real and/or
imputed—of the individuals and groups for or against the government's plan. For those opposing the government, medicare
was, above all, the occasion for remembering past grievances
against the seemingly invincible and often patently hated CCF
party.

In part, then, medicare was a catalyst for the activation
of value schisms—focused on political-economic interests—already existing in the province. These value conflicts now rose
to conscious awareness and attained great immediate importance for the individuals of the area. Expression—or at least
cognizance—of the schisms became a temporary part of the
culture. These historical grievances, in turn, legitimated and
stimulated a more extreme position with regard to the contemporary issue of medicare.

It was largely by this process that the individual's position
with respect to medicare achieved astounding importance. The
positions of "for or against medicare" became symbolic advertisements of one's stand on many of the province's historic bitter conflicts of interest. In this way, the revisitation
of historical antipathies, rather than the current dispute, constituted much of the medicare conflict for the public. For
many people medicare provided the occasion, the symbol,
and the slogans for pent-up hatreds to be expressed.

It has been mentioned that the government-doctor conflict
brought into focus the frustrations of the two major opposition
parties, which had been beaten in the provincial contests by
the CCF party for seventeen years. Each opposition party
reacted in somewhat the same way: the CCF government had
finally gone too far. This time they had attempted to push
legislation onto an organized group, the doctors. At last the
government's right to force legislation was being effectively
challenged. This agreement among opposition parties caused
them to hope that this issue could lead to the ousting of the
CCF government. Hoping to discredit the CCF in the eyes of
the voters, politicians of all shades of opinion were publicly
active during the conflict.

The tacit agreement that the CCF government had over-extended its legislative rights existed among the general population as well, and many rank and file Conservatives and Liberals were joined in a mobilized consensus against the CCF government. This consensus, which occurred during an off-election year, was unique, because it was not formally inhibited by the customary election rivalry between the supporters of the two old parties.

The political agreement among activated individuals opposing the government was an intensified agreement because (1) such firm consensus was new and unusual and had no established means of expression; (2) it was stimulated by fear and resentment of the possible effects of the legislated social change; (3) there were historical grievances toward the source of that change and loyalty toward its previous "victims"; and (4) existentially, the unprecedented revolt of one of the most highly respected economic sectors—the doctors —provided a model for questioning the legitimacy of all historical, disliked legislation.

For many individuals, then, medicare did not so much constitute a legitimate outcome of respected legislative processes, as it represented yet another despicable shenanigan of the long-hated farmer party.

Thus a new theater for consensus and unique bases of consensus among groups and individuals opposing the government contributed to the public medicare conflict. No mechanisms for the expression of this intensified political agreement of the extreme opposition to the CCF's handling of medicare existed in the established sociopolitical structure. It required a new structure, which emerged in the form of the Keep Our Doctors Committee. Although other organizations also came into being, both for and against the medicare plan, the KODC was the most significant group that developed in the medicare conflict environment.[6]

Although the small town of Carlyle had earlier lodged a formal complaint with the government of Saskatchewan, urging it to postpone implementation of the medicare plan, the direct parent of the KODC protest movement occurred in Regina, the capital of the province, seemingly through the activities of four housewives. One of them described its origins:

It all started on Good Friday. The night before, the four of us were having one of our coffee klatches. We had read that our pediatricians were leaving the province because of medicare, and, naturally, we were concerned. Actually, we were more just plain *worried* than angry, at that point, and we felt that we didn't really know what it was all about. Mrs. X called her doctor to try and find out what was going on. He came out that same evening and explained the issue to us. After he left, we visited some more, and tried to figure out what we could do. We finally decided to circulate a petition, asking the government to delay medicare and try and work something out with the doctors.

The next day, Good Friday, around noon, I called up [Premier] Lloyd, and had a fight with him. I asked for a vote on medicare, and he said that we'd *had* a vote, in the 1960 provincial elections. Finally, I told him that we were going to start a petition, and hung up. Just to make sure, we called our doctors and asked them if they would practice under medicare, and they all said no.

Around three o'clock that afternoon, we started taking petitions to other people in this neighborhood. Almost everyone, except some CCF'ers, signed. Even government employees, although they were afraid to sign, said they agreed with us. We were really encouraged by the number of signers. Almost all the people with young children wanted to sign and a lot of them wanted to help. You'd be surprised how many older people were with us, too.

The same afternoon, radio and TV picked it up, and from then on it just spread. Other women in Regina called for advice, and wanted to do something, too. A gas company offered to duplicate the petitions, and a lawyer living nearby wrote the petitions for the newspapers. People from all over called us up to congratulate us on what we were doing. We were really busy. I didn't have time to do laundry, or anything. We got some more Regina women to help, and we divided up the town into districts for door-to-door campaigns, and got a lot of names from downtown. A few days later, a newspaper editor from X (a small town) called and said they'd cover little towns if we could cover Regina.

We had our first organization meeting on April 27, at Grenfell, and we all got offices. Even then, when we were at Grenfell to organize on a provincial basis, we wanted to keep neutral, but later we weren't treated too nicely by Premier Lloyd; we weren't granted a further hearing. That showed us what the doctors had been up against, and made us come out and fully support the doctors.

There was another formal organizational meeting of the KODC on May 28, 1962, this time at Regina. The editor mentioned above had suggested the meeting and was elected president of the group. At that point, the provincial organization of the protest group consisted of six men and six women.

The first Cavalcade to Regina, on May 30, 1962, involved over four hundred cars (and over nine hundred people). The major delegations were from Saskatoon, Carlyle, Estevan, Moose Jaw, and the Gravelbourg areas. The crowd of KODC'ers waited outside the meeting chambers and called for Premier Lloyd to appear. He did not do so, and the otherwise peaceful summer afternoon of conversations about crops, weather, business and family became punctuated by such remarks as: "How blind can he be?"; "Don't 46,000 names mean anything to this government?"; "They just don't *care*, do they?" The Premier did meet with one hundred members of the group within the legislative buildings. At that time, Premier Lloyd received the petitions, which had first been circulated by the four housewives, and which, by May 30, had 46,000 signatures. Following this meeting, the provincial KODC president urged the KODC to continue its work to "keep doctors in Saskatchewan."[7]

Throughout the controversy, the Premier urged the KODC groups to work through their local representatives, rather than to appeal to him directly. To that end, Premier Lloyd did not meet with subsequent KODC groups that came from different parts of the province to protest the medicare legislation. At the same time, the KODC felt that working through local government representatives was an ineffective approach. It also believed that it represented a force of public opinion that should not and could not be ignored by the provincial center. When the government proceeded to deny it further hearings, it felt unjustifiably snubbed; predictably, participants stated that it was this "callousness" on the part of the government that led to the KODC decision to support the doctors fully and retire from "our mediating role." Whether or not this was actually the case, the militancy and strong propagandistic approach of the KODC increased as tensions mounted with the approach of the doctors' strike.

On July 1, 1962, the government did implement the plan, the doctors did strike, and the Keep Our Doctors Committee movement went into high gear. They sponsored town meetings, TV and radio presentations, and direct advertisements of their cause. The population's fear at the early stages of the doctors' strike provided a fertile field for the KODC charges of "government tyranny," "Who's next to be taken over by the government?" and the group's cries for "freedom." According to both newspaper reports and interviews, the KODC movement caught fire particularly in those rural areas where individuals faced the situation of having to drive miles to get medical attention. Every KODC leader stated that KODC strength depended upon the doctors' cause and rural support, regardless of the leadership's attempts to centralize the organizational power of the group in the two major cities of the province, Regina and Saskatoon.

Just prior to the final Regina Cavalcade of the KODC, for example, there were three separate rural-area meetings, held almost simultaneously. One, in Weyburn, attracted about 250 persons; another, in Melville, involved approximately 150 people; and the third, which occurred in Melfort, was attended by 2500–3000 individuals. It was at such meetings that the public influence of the political opposition parties was particularly felt; opposition representatives offered advice to the KODC meeting organizers on how the events should be scheduled, and gave speeches at those gatherings. They also provided a drawing card for attendance, if they had the reputation of being good speakers. The most popular (and most fiery) speaker during this period was a Catholic priest; when he suddenly became unavailable for speaking engagements, the KODC argued this was "another example of the iron curtain being lowered upon free speech."

Although the agenda for these various meetings varied considerably, depending on the size of the group expected to attend, anthems such as "O Canada" and "God Save the Queen" were customarily part of the program. Occasionally, a local clergyman would provide a prayer, and, if possible, a former CCF supporter—hopefully, a prominent community member—would be invited to express dissatisfaction with his former political party. On all occasions, the audiences were reminded that the government had not kept its promise of "coming up with a program which would be acceptable to the doctors." On all occasions, too, the audiences were told that the medicare act was another instance of "creeping Communism" by the CCF-NDP. An additional event at these meetings was an announcement of the telegrams KODC workers had received—often from individuals in the United States —congratulating the group on its activities to preserve freedom.

As early as July 4, the provincial KODC organization exhibited signs of change. In the minutes of that meeting, the chairman of the provincial organization expressed concern: "It is time to make a definite change in plans. The aim why we were first organized has been successful; now new plans have to be made." The Prince Albert representative then explained how his committee was organized and that it felt it was time for the provincial group to adopt a new name, such as Save Our Saskatchewan. The group decided, however, that to change the name at this point would show "a sign of weakness." The Central Committee, which was set up to provide for "a select few handling the press releases," was instructed to "explain the situation from the people's standpoint instead of stressing the doctors' view too much." The provincial chairman expressed his desire to resign because of outside matters, but was requested by the group to refrain from doing so, because "to have him resign at this time would literally crumple the whole organization."[8]

The final Cavalcade to Regina was to be held on July 11, 1962. All efforts were expended, all stops pulled in an attempt to insure its success. The primary aim was to impress the government with the size of its enemy (the KODC) by the immensity of the crowd assembled. In private discussions, even the possibilities of a fortuitous riot were not ruled out. At least some KODC leaders—at times of high emotion and in private to be sure—were prepared to welcome violence, if they could avoid condemnation for it. In their own eyes, the striking doctors had become martyrs, the hardworking KODC members, saints, and the CCF government, totally bad. Government horror stories—describing government take-over of business, and underhanded dealings—were told to the researcher on every occasion.

In the cities, staunch KODC members put pressure on businesses to close for the day, to allow their employees to attend the event and to reduce the customary provincial economic transactions to minimal proportions. At least one KODC enthusiast was reported to have included threats of sustained and extensive boycotts in her attempts to solicit financial support and the cooperation of store owners.

When the Regina Cavalcade finally took place, the results were disappointing. The KODC expected over thirty thousand individuals to attend (and one member claimed that over thirty thousand were present); Premier Lloyd fixed the actual number at twenty-five hundred, and general consensus —based on news reporters' estimates—established that between four and five thousand people were involved.

In addition to the small turnout, the Regina demonstration was decidedly peaceful. The protesters were careful to use the trash receptacles provided for them by the government, and regardless of how angry the placards were, the people who carried them were often jovial and always polite. The warm July sun, the appetizing lunches, and the greetings called to friends from other towns gave the event a picnic atmosphere. Newspaper reporters had flocked to the city from all parts of Canada and many major cities of the United States, only to find there was no exciting news.

After the Regina Cavalcade, the KODC faced different circumstances; on July 14, the College of Physicians and Surgeons reopened communication with the government, in a less rigid spirit.[9] Communications between the government and doctors were still sporadic, but more positive in the days that followed. Then, on July 16, Lord Taylor—himself a physician —arrived from London at the government's request. Taylor functioned as an arbitrator between the two groups and piloted the Saskatoon Agreement, which ended the deadlock on July 23, 1962.[10]

With the signing of the Saskatoon Agreement, the KODC entered a phase of reexamination to determine what, if anything, it should do. The usual instructions to workers from the main office were to "lay low for a couple of weeks, cool off—relax—and then we'll see what happens to the Committee." By July 24, the chairman of the powerful Saskatoon group and a vice-president of the provincial body resigned from KODC activities. At the executive meeting on July 25, however, the provincial officers decided to continue the group's Strategies Committee. At the same meeting, the motion was made (but not acted upon) to reorganize the KODC as the Keep Our Democracy Committee.

A meeting explicitly intended to reorganize the KODC was held on Sunday afternoon, August 12, at Regina. A trend that had intensified as the KODC grew became strikingly clear: the mature (or dying) KODC was run by men, rather than women. As one of the four Regina housewives responsible for the emergence of KODC expressed it: "Now as far as we're concerned it's all businessmen; now we haven't anything to do with it because it's more than we can handle . . . it's more than the average person can handle. We haven't the money to help with that." According to her, two of the other three women were "disgusted with it, too. All the businessmen want is publicity, so we won't work. We still have coffee together every day, but we don't even talk about it anymore."

At the August 12 meeting, the sizable Saskatoon contingent was temporarily back in the fold, and it was largely due to the Saskatoon leader's insistence that the group decided to retain the name of Keep Our Doctors, rather than change it to Keep Our Democracy. The revived organization (with the same name) was ultimately to have fifteen directors, with the original Strategies Committee instrumental in choosing the remainder. Immediately prior to and after the meeting, the KODC Central Committee (in charge of publicity) actively attacked the government and the co-op clinics being established throughout the province (and under the medicare plan). The KODC claimed that pressure was put on rural doctors to work under the plan; that the government was still advertising in the *Lancet,* a British medical journal, attempting to encourage more British doctors to come to Saskatchewan and "work for the government"; and that the government and its officials were instrumental in establishing the co-op clinics.[11] All these acts, the KODC asserted, were in clear violation of the terms and spirit of the Sakatoon Agreement. In addition, the KODC charged, no provision had been made for radiologists and pathologists in the Medical Care Act, and these professionals wanted to be included in the plan. Finally, the KODC pointed out that none of the doctors nominated by the College of Physicians and Surgeons for posts on the Medical Care Insurance Commission had been approved by the government, and no private insurance carriers (Group Medical Services or Medical Services Incorporated) had received legal status. The evidence, the KODC claimed, indicated that the government was breaking its word (implicit and explicit) in the Saskatoon Agreement.

This was small thunder compared with previous KODC charges, but the conflict atmosphere of the province had diminished even more. Top KODC provincial officials complained that the doctors were no longer "fighting hard enough," and that the private insurance companies were reluctant to "wage a war" with the government. Whether as a corollary or in part a cause of the emotional changes of the public, the newspapers were less sensitized to the KODC efforts; the KODC acting chairman claimed in early August that no editorial of any strength had appeared in the Regina *Leader-Post* since July 23.[12]

A rural community in the northern part of the province may serve as example of the drastic reduction of tensions at the grass roots level by early August. This community was notorious for the animosities the doctor-government deadlock had stimulated. A provincial KODC leader from that area reported several items of past conflict that had occurred there, including: "One man, who was for the government, and his wife, who was pro-doctor, only spoke to each other in order to get the meals served. I know of a brother who told his brother-in-law—they were on opposite sides, too—that if he came into the house again, he'd shoot him. One time, an old friend of a KODC petitioner threw a chair at him.

"Now, though, things have changed. It's all back to normal. We have our four doctors back, and for three fourths of the people, that's what they wanted. People have settled back down to life; there's nothing too radical, now. The clinic's *there* [a co-op clinic working under the plan], but so what? The people who want to go to it go to it, but we have our four doctors."

Although often with regret, provincial KODC leaders noted that the fight had ended. And without an enemy and the cause of the doctors to support, the KODC seemed somewhat irrelevant.

It attempted to extend its functions by reorganizing as an educational association. To that end, it sponsored a speaker imported from Britain the following autumn, to give stirring expositions of democracy and freedom. The fact remained, however, that the public was saturated with not only the issue of medicare, but the tensions it had raised as well. Grim comments, such as "Well, people know where Saskatchewan is, *now*," and "Now we can get back to normal," were frequent. Accordingly, the once-ambitious KODC, which had commanded headlines and crowds, retired from the public spotlight; in the future, only rare and innocent notices of KODC "social gatherings" were to dot the news.

KODC PROFILE

The provincial KODC records showed thirty-three local KODC groups scattered throughout the province. Information was obtained from eighteen of those organizations, and although the data are far from complete, several central characteristics of the movement were obtained.

TABLE 1
KODC GROUPS' WORK FORCE

# Regular Active Workers	Number of Groups
19–	8
20–26	6
26+	4

N = 18, Total Workers = 515

The numbers of regular active workers in KODC groups ranged from 4 in one group to 129 in another. In all, the total number of active workers in this sample was 515. Granting that the data reflect approximately 50 per cent of the local KODC groups, some indication is available concerning the relatively small size of the active KODC organization. Some idea of the strength of the movement requires recognition of additional categories of KODC supporters. To the organizational nucleus should be added (1) those who attended public meetings (and Cavalcades) but were not active workers; (2) those who signed petitions in support of the KODC cause, the doctors; and (3) those who were outside the KODC but nonetheless informally expressed sympathy for the difficulties of the doctors, thus enabling the charges of the KODC to be newsworthy and to achieve some measure of public acceptability.

These same nineteen local KODC groups reported that the highest number of active workers in their organizations totaled 805. Generally, this figure was reached on and just before the final Regina Cavalcade on July 11, 1962. The absolute number of workers is less important, however, than the fact that a relatively (indeed, surprisingly) small group of people were able to command public attention for over two months. This underlines the central feature of the movement: it existed primarily as a loosely knit expression of dissent, rather than as an extensive, viable organization. The spirit of dissent, not the machinations of organization, was its strength.

TABLE 2

KODC: AVERAGE AGE OF GROUPS' WORKERS

Groups' Average Age	Number of Groups
Under 35 Years	1
35–45 Years	16
46–55 Years	2
	N = 19

The appeal and the drive of the KODC were aimed basically at people with children, and those individuals were reported (in the majority of my interviews) as being the core segment of the population that favored the doctors' position. The above table shows the extent to which the KODC organization was buttressed by early middle-aged individuals. We could reasonably expect these individuals to have children still in the home.

TABLE 3

Sex Ratio of Groups' Workers

Males and Females	Number of Groups
More Males than Females	1
Equal Males and Females	7
1 Male per 2 Females	8

$$N = 16$$

The local groups relied heavily on the work investments of women; again, the reactions of many individuals at the prospect of losing the family doctor, or being without one, appear to have mobilized not only a particular age group, but also to have effectively stimulated the wrath of women. Regardless of the increasing tendency of men to direct the organization's activities, the strength of the KODC with respect to workers continued to be in women's hands.

KODC work took time; telephoning, canvassing both in town centers and by means of house-to-house calls add up to a day's work. Not only did most men lack the time to become so involved, but most women could not afford to be that involved indefinitely either. Young mothers, many stirred by feelings of responsibility for the health of their families, were nonetheless limited in the length of time they could devote to a cause. They might be very concerned, but particularly with the fall school term approaching, the mother's role itself became more demanding. Once the legitimations for deviating from this strongly institutionalized role were removed, all values impinged upon women's returning to traditional "mother" activities. And, as the rural community mentioned previously shows, once they had their doctors back, the center of the formal contemporary conflict was removed.

Both the work and the coordination of activities were easier in small towns than in the country, according to KODC

TABLE 4

RESIDENCE OF GROUPS' WORKERS

Town or Country	Number of Groups
Town	16
Country	1
Equal, town and country	2

leaders. Especially during the busy summer months on the farms, we would expect more opportunity for activity in KODC groups among small-town rather than rural dwellers. In addition, in small towns located in rural areas, individuals of any type of service or professional occupation often feel a great deal of alignment among themselves. Under such conditions, the stage is set for empathetic reactions to occur, if the proper symbol is threatened.

The medical doctor could fulfill that role for several reasons. First, doctors are important to the community. In addition to the security and convenience one feels in having medical assistance readily available, doctors are also regarded as assets to the community's business life, by drawing the trade of rural patients. Correspondingly, doctors function as a status symbol for the community as a whole, by providing evidence that the particular community is a good, thriving place in which to live.

Doctors are also often the prestige leaders of any small community, and Saskatchewan is largely a province of small, rural trading communities. In these centers, too, medical doctors are not numerous enough to form a subculture of their own; instead, they comprise a part of the entire local business group of bankers, lawyers, merchants, druggists, etc. In short, the unique situation of small-town doctors is one of close ties of identification with other professionals.

The limitations of the data in Table 5 are obvious; nonetheless, its information is valuable: twelve of the respondents were presidents of their groups; the remainder were secretaries. Two in the secretary category are women, and reported the occupations of their husbands.[13] This occupational profile is representative only of the executive officers who responded to the questionnaire mailed to them. It cannot be interpreted

TABLE 5

OCCUPATION OF RESPONDING EXECUTIVE OFFICER

Occupation	Number of Groups
(Mgrs. of firms or departments)	4
Pharmacists	3
Insurance or Accountants	3
Merchants or Contractors	3
Printers	2
Dental Surgeon	1
Lawyer	1

N = 17

to provide a profile of the KODC groups themselves. We can say, however, that significant leadership for the local groups of KODC came primarily from the white-collar, professional or semi-professional economic segments. Interviews with KODC leaders suggested that the movement, in its organizational structure, was primarily a middle- to upper middle-class activity. This conclusion is partially corroborated and extended by R. F. Badgley, who states: "Groups such as Councils of Women, Boards of Trade, opposition political parties and Chambers of Commerce whose membership included 'merchants, manufacturers, insurance agents, financial interests, farmers and the members of the various professions' were against the medical care legislation proposed by the government." And, more directly to our interest: "The Keep Our Doctors Committee drew support from 'opposition politicians, druggists, dentists, conservative businessmen'. . . ."[14]

Table 6, which shows the number of groups that ranked each reason for organizing groups, makes it apparent that the KODC was a multi-motivated movement. Most KODC members, for example, in interviews emphatically supported the medicare plan itself. "We aren't against the plan . . . just the way it was introduced. The government promised us that the plan would be acceptable to the doctors. Obviously, it isn't. What good is a medicare plan if we don't have any doctors?" queried a provincial KODC leader. The local KODC groups were responses to intense local situations; loyalty to an esteemed doctor appears to be the strongest motivating force.

TABLE 6

REASONS FOR ORGANIZING GROUPS

Primary Reason	Number of Groups
Fear of losing family doctor	10
Creeping Communism	4
Anti-socialism	2
Fear of being without a doctor	2
Dissatisfaction with CCF on this issue	1

N = 19

Leaving aside probable individual members' deviations from the group respondents' assessment of motivations to join KODC, we find that even on the "reasons for joining KODC" level, there is much intergroup variation. This absence of consensus concerning "why KODC emerged" took its toll later in the life of the movement when decisions of a less reacting—to the government—nature were necessary. It is small wonder, considering this basic intergroup variation, that the KODC provincial structure had difficulties in its attempts to fuse together a provincewide organization out of the sporadic, spontaneous local uprisings.

TABLE 7

FUTURE OF YOUR KODC GROUP

Do You Think You Have More Work To Do?	Number of Groups
Yes	10
Possibly (with restrictions)	4
No	5

N = 19

The questionnaire was mailed shortly after the Saskatoon Agreement of July 23, 1962; therefore it might seem surprising that in answer to the question "Do you feel there is any additional work for your KODC to do?" there was no unanimous or even near-unanimous agreement.

As the figures in Table 7 show, five respondents indicated there was no additional work for the KODC to accomplish, and ten indicated that there was. There was an even division (two each) among those answering no but including stipulations, and those responding yes with reservations or stipulations. Collapsing these responses into yes and no categories, the total becomes twelve advocating further KODC work and seven asserting that KODC efforts were finished.

Dealing with these totals and comparing the responses with those assessing the most important reason for local KODC membership, the associations show that 75 per cent (or three out of four) that listed creeping Communism as the number one impetus for their group's emergence felt that further KODC work was in order.

From the negative vector, all those listing either dissatisfaction with the CCF-NDP on this issue, fear of being without a doctor, or anti-socialism as the number one reason for their local KODC emergence and activity (a total of five), gave "no" responses to the question as to whether or not they felt the KODC had more work to do.

An interesting pattern develops when we examine the responses of those listing fear of losing the family doctor as the reason of first importance for those who became active in the KODC movement: seven indicated that there was more work for their KODC to do, and three asserted that there was not. The three that returned negative answers concerning future work listed creeping Communism in last place of five possible positions as a reason for involvement in KODC. But of the seven returning "yes" answers concerning future KODC activity, three placed creeping Communism second in importance, and three placed it third as a motivating force.[15] The combination of those two motivations—fear of losing the family doctor, and the charge of creeping Communism against the CCF government—appears to have been the strongest single combination leading to KODC involvement, and the latter was the strongest single factor leading to the opinion that there was future work for a local KODC group after the Saskatoon Agreement.

Wherever the KODC respondents indicated that there was active rural working support, from part-time assistance to country dominance of the organization, the local group respondent also thought there was further work to do, or possibly further work to be done.[16]

Combining these last two observations—the position of creeping Communism as the perceived reason for becoming involved in KODC work, and the participation of country dwellers—the data indicate that both have a high association with whether or not the groups felt the KODC should close up shop or remain active. Both questions are conceived of as indicating the dimensions of the base of the support of the group, regardless of size.

Size itself, however, also appears to be an independent factor in determining whether or not the group wished to continue. Although size is not correlated with any of the previously mentioned variables, there was a positive relationship between the size of the group and the probability that the group would desire to continue. In general, the larger the group, the less its members conceived of the organization as being a temporary thing. Both the perceptions of the power of the group and the importance of rising in the group's internal structure were viewed as being positively related to the group's size. Relating size to desire to continue the group, I found that of the eight groups with memberships of under twenty, five felt there was no further work for the KODC to accomplish. Of the six groups with memberships of between twenty and twenty-six, only one felt that the KODC activities were over, and in the category including four groups with over twenty-six members, again, only one replied that there was no further work for the local KODC group to do.

It should be noted, too, that the deviant in this last category had neither of the significant factors previously mentioned: fear of creeping Communism was listed in fourth place as the reason for the group's emergence, and it was a town group.

The most distinctive characteristic of the KODC support was its middle-class nature. The organization did not suffer from the lack of financial support. Its leadership dipped heavily into the business and industrial sectors of the population, as well as professional groups. Meetings were always orderly, and even the fiery speeches of discontent generally stayed well within the limits of acceptable, barbed oratory. If the KODC movement could be called an urban middle-class revolt against the farmer-worker party, that revolt must surely be described as a respectable one.

Paradoxically, the very respectability of the KODC was significant to both the emergence and the demise of the movement. With the exception of riots, the expression of protest requires time, some organizational ability, and money. Being primarily middle-class individuals (with upper-class support), the KODC workers had all three to some extent. The advantages accruing from class membership, however, also limited the activities of the KODC to class-appropriate behavior. KODC members generally had no anonymity—the friend of violence—and the KODC refused to participate openly in the game of politics. On most levels, the KODC perceived that this was a moral, rather than a political battle: "Politics has caused this mess; the CCF has used medicare as a political football." Thus most KODC leaders listed the primary reason for the organization's emergence as fear of losing the family doctor. "The way medicare was introduced, not the act itself," was the enemy. Although the list of historical grievances against the CCF-NDP was a long one, the specific stimulus for protest was limited in both time and scope. In short, the KODC did not wish for radical changes in the social system; the broadest of its goals was to "get this government out." Having limited objectives, the means employed were correspondingly uncontroversial for the most part, and, having fought the respectable fight, KODC workers could return to their normal positions in a society that had also gone back to normal.

The KODC movement, by publicly presenting itself as being an apolitical organization (in terms of party, not effect), did not address itself to the possibilities of forming an alternative to the existing multi-party political division. Rather, the KODC presented itself as a novel public spokesman for specific popular sentiment. When the issues changed and the intensity of sentiment directed toward the particular issue diminished, normal channels of political expression—established political parties—were sufficient. Attempts to broaden the base of the movement—as illustrated by the two major moves to change the name of the organization (first to Save Our Saskatchewan, and then to Keep Our Democracy)—were unsuccessful.

Thus individuals within the movement could return with

no difficulty to the political parties they had always favored. Typically they had good jobs, satisfactory incomes, and perhaps "good" children. In short, society without crisis held no dire threats for them and elicited no hatred from them, save for the well-controlled vengeance toward the farmer-socialistic party: "For seventeen years, that CCF government has been telling me what to do; I'm sick and tired of it." "They've [the CCF-NDP] finally gone too far; even the farmers are getting their eyes opened." If nothing else, KODC members had made themselves heard; although their economic and social positions were acceptable to them, the fact of their historical alienation from the powers of provincial legislation was not. In sum, the marginality of the KODC, both as an organization and for the individual members, was perceived to be a political one; for seventeen years they had suffered the disjunction between relatively high economic and social status and political impotence in the face of a farmer-controlled victorious party.

Conclusion

It is difficult to evaluate the long-term effect of the medicare controversy on the life of Saskatchewan. In 1964, it was estimated that approximately 20 per cent of the doctors of Saskatchewan were practicing "under the plan." Tension among pro- and con-medicare doctors with respect to community clinics and hospital privileges continues to exist, and medical journals of the United States continue to essay the difficulties of a medical care program. Meanwhile, the CCF-NDP government lost legislative dominance in the provincial elections held in 1964. It is significant that medicare was not an issue in that campaign. Clearly, political parties of all labels realized that no more political fodder could be made from medicare, pro or con, and the victorious Liberal Party has taken no steps to remove medicare legislation from the books.

Yet these facts do not mean that the struggle over medicare did not contribute to the narrow defeat suffered by the CCF for the first time in twenty years. Many CCF'ers have argued that their defeat stemmed largely from the fact that they had been in office for so long that enough voters were won to the notion of "time for a change" to defeat them. Some even state that it is probably a good thing for the party to spend some time in opposition, so that it can formulate a new program without the need to react to the day-to-day pressure placed on a governing party. Yet one may point to the fact that the Social Credit government of Alberta has remained in office from 1935 to the present. The Liberal Party controlled the provincial government in Saskatchewan for thirty-nine of the forty-four years preceding the CCF's first victory in 1944. Canadian prairie voters are seemingly not a fickle lot. They do not easily throw out their provincial governments.

It may be suggested, therefore, that the fight over medicare did contribute to the defeat of the CCF by providing an issue around which many normally politically inactive opponents of the party could organize. From all reports, the majority of the KODC supporters were not active Liberal or Conservative Party members. One would guess that many who took part in this losing struggle moved from it to participation in the election campaign. The medicare fight also cut across opposition party lines: Liberals, Conservatives, and Social Crediters cooperated in the KODC. And two years later, the election results indicate that many who normally voted Conservative or Social Credit backed Liberal candidates in a successful effort to concentrate the anti-CCF vote. Hence both logic and scanty evidence sustain the conclusions reached by two students of the medicare scene: "The doctors lost, but the strike mobilized majority interest groups antagonistic to the government which previously had been unrelated or only loosely aligned. This temporary coalition of interests may have subsequently contributed to the narrow defeat of the Cooperative Commonwealth Federation (CCF) government."[17]

Ironically then, the CCF's greatest victory over an entrenched center of power, the medical profession, may have been the event that brought it down. But this is a price active politicians must be prepared to pay in democratic society. By upsetting the status quo, they contribute, in the short run at least, to the pool of active oppositionists. In the long run, of course, they must believe that those changes that improve the lot of the population will return them to office. This has certainly been the recent history of the British Labour Party. Whether the Saskatchewan CCF will be equally fortunate remains to be seen.

Regardless of the electoral future of the Saskatchewan CCF, however, the effects of the other public medicare protagonist, the KODC, are impressive. If only for a short while, many individuals who previously did little more than vote for candidates of established parties formed a powerful organization of protest. They effectively challenged the fine line of acceptability dividing the content of legislation and the manner (and sponsor) of legislation. Most importantly, it may be generally true that whether or not the outcome of protest groups is that of party turnover, expressions of protest can shed new light on what voting for a particular party—or failing to vote for a particular party—means. If the classic notion of an enlightened citizenry is still regarded as being central to the philosophy of a democracy, that function of protest groups should in itself assure them a central role in the theories as well as operations of democratic systems.

NOTES

1. C. Wright Mills, *The Power Elite* (New York: Galaxy Books, 1959).

2. A. Holtzman, *Interest Groups and Lobbying* (New York: The Macmillan Co., 1966), p. 1.

3. (Stanford: Stanford University Press, 1959), p. 180. Indeed, Dahrendorf conceives of political parties themselves as being a special case of interest groups. It should be made explicit that Dahrendorf's work is not taken as the point of departure for this discussion. It is, rather, the fact that Dahrendorf is one of the few sociologists to use the term "interest group" that causes me to acknowledge his contribution, even though his use of the term is unique to his theoretical framework. In this essay, the term interest group refers to specific groups such as those mentioned, and goes beyond Dahrendorf's formal definition only in the common-sense dimensions of tactics used, and initial target of influence.

4. A classic treatment of social movements is found in Rudolf Heberle, *Social Movements: An Introduction to Political Sociology* (New York: Appleton-Century-Crofts, 1951), pp. 93–128. The point of view of the individual is stressed in Hans Toch, *The*

Social Psychology of Social Movements (Indianapolis: Bobbs-Merrill Company, Inc., 1965), pp. 157–229. To avoid unnecessary confusion, I use the term "protest movement" rather than "social movement" to describe the phenomena dealt with in this chapter, although the two conceptualizations are closely related. Essentially, a protest movement is a more limited expression of discontent (in terms of time, program or numbers), and may be regarded as a second-order social movement.

5. A separate issue, but one that must be mentioned, is whether or not the lack of an all-encompassing theory of social movements is desirable or undesirable: social movements may vary among themselves as much as do, for example, forms of individual deviance, which often have little in common. Much more insight might be screened out than gained in attempting to put all social movements under the same theoretical umbrella. At least some students of deviant behavior would maintain this mono-theory approach has not been particularly beneficial in that area.

6. A. D. Kelly, at that time secretary of the Canadian Medical Association, has described the KODC as a "popular organization" that "arose spontaneously among people who could clearly foresee that the doctors would not willingly stay in an atmosphere they found distasteful and that, as a consequence of the departure of good men, the medical services would suffer." According to Kelly, the Save Our Saskatchewan organization did "valuable behind-the-scenes work in endeavouring to promote liaison between government and profession as did the leaders of the clergy, the officers of the Saskatchewan Association, the Pharmaceutical Association, the organizations of Rural and Urban Municipalities, and many other community groups." Quite literally, everyone was in the act. See A. D. Kelly, "The Saskatchewan Situation: One Man's View," *Canadian Medical Association Journal*, 87 (November 24, 1962), pp. 1113–18.

7. Regina *Leader-Post*, June 16, 1962.

8. He did eventually retire from active chairmanship of the movement, because of ill health. The press liaison officer, who later encouraged another name change for the organization, became acting chairman as well as retaining his former office. By July 11, the Save Our Saskatchewan organization mentioned previously was formed by a group of Regina businessmen and professionals. The group was described (in that issue of the Regina *Leader-Post*) as being "closely aligned in objective with the KODC," and called "for an end to medicare propaganda." That group disbanded on July 25.

9. Various factors leading the doctors to renew attempts to negotiate with the government included the government's promise to recall the legislature to make necessary revisions of the original act, the fact that some doctors continued working, thus demonstrating that one could "work outside the Act," the increasing

importation of British doctors and the establishment of cooperative clinics, and the mounting evidence that the government was not going to alter its position drastically. See C. W. Baugh, "The Saskatchewan Story," *Journal of the Iowa Medical Society,* 53 (1963), pp. 535–43.

10. Positive appraisals of Lord Taylor's mediating abilities have come from several quarters, including the doctors themselves. See Kelly, *op. cit.*

11. The relationships between the cooperative clinics and the medical profession are delineated by Samuel Wolfe in "Saskatchewan's Community Clinics," *Canadian Medical Association Journal,* 91 (August 1, 1964), pp. 225–29.

12. Most observers agree that public opinion had shifted away from support of the doctors. See E. A. Tollefson, *Bitter Medicine: The Saskatchewan Medicare Feud* (Saskatoon: Modern Press, 1963), p. 111. Both Tollefson and Kelly (*op. cit.*) note the influence of critical press *outside* the province.

13. One president, the only female president in our sample, was the widow of an RCAF pilot. Another individual listed his identification as commissioner on the Chamber of Commerce for his community.

14. R. F. Badgley, "The Public and Medical Care in Saskatchewan," mimeo, presented at the 90th annual meeting of the American Public Health Association, Miami, Florida, October 17, 1962.

15. The seventh "yes" respondent in this category added fear of losing personal freedom in second place.

16. These groups also are included in the "fear of creeping Communism" factor mentioned earlier. Whether one of these two factors encouraged the emergence of the other is impossible to determine with the data available; thus, they are treated as being independent variables with respect to whether or not the group feels it should continue activities.

17. R. F. Badgley and S. Wolfe, "Medical Care and Conflict in Saskatchewan," *The Milbank Memorial Fund Quarterly,* 43 (1965), p. 464.

5

OCCUPATIONAL CLASS AND VOTING BEHAVIOR: ELECTORAL SUPPORT OF A LEFT-WING PROTEST MOVEMENT IN A PERIOD OF PROSPERITY

BY

SANFORD SILVERSTEIN
Bowling Green State University

INTRODUCTION

THE Cooperative Commonwealth Federation (CCF), first elected as the government of the province of Saskatchewan in 1944, won four more successive provincial elections before its defeat in 1964. It was the only North American socialist party to govern a political unit larger than a municipality.

The voters of Saskatchewan elected the socialists after all other attempts at achieving a solution to unbearable economic problems failed. In electing the CCF, they chose the "natural opposition" party to the Liberals. The party was rising in strength and appeared to have a chance to beat the Liberals. It meshed grass roots sentiments with locally respectable, aggressive, provincial political leadership that represented the farmers. The people of Saskatchewan, though they elected an ideologically distinct party, paralleled the earlier electoral responses of farm voters in Alberta to their west and Manitoba to their east. While the socialists in Saskatchewan were elected as a reaction to the deprivations of the great depression, they were retained in the most extended period of prosperity the province had ever known. During this time there was a steady rise in income enjoyed by all occupational sectors. Annual personal income nearly tripled from $632 million in 1944 to $1800 million in 1963, yet was shared by a population increased by only 11 per cent from 1946 to 1961.[1]

The CCF received the bulk of its support from farmers and unionized urban workers whose interests differed on wages, ideology, and other points. A strongly anti-CCF political cartoon with the hopeful title, "Riding for a Fall," was published in a leading provincial newspaper during the 1952 election campaign.[2] The cartoon depicts then premier T. C. Douglas, symbolizing the CCF party in Saskatchewan, doing a circus balancing act on the backs of two circus horses named "farmers" and "labor," to the billing of a sign proclaiming "Thrills —Spills—The CCF Double Riding Act." The horses are depicted as heading in opposite directions. In the 1952 election, more than ever before or since, the two horses proved to be going in the same direction. Since 1952 the support of the CCF, which depended on the two occupational classes, or horses, has declined. To see the way in which different groups of voters have reacted to the CCF in power, the election data from 1948–64 have been analyzed.

TABLE 1

SASKATCHEWAN PROVINCIAL ELECTIONS, 1948–64*

PROVINCEWIDE RETURNS: PERCENTAGE OF VOTE BY PARTY

Party	1948	1952	1956	1960	1964
CCF	47.6%	54.0%	45.2%	40.8%	40.3%
Liberal	31.2	39.3	30.3	32.7	40.4
Progressive-Conservative	7.6	2.3	2.0	14.0	18.9
Social Credit	8.1	3.9	21.5	12.3	.4
Other	5.5	.5	1.0	.2	0 (.01)

* Numbers on which percentages are based were compiled from official election returns furnished by Chief Electoral Officer, Province of Saskatchewan.

TABLE 1: (*continued*)

RURAL FARM: PERCENTAGE OF VOTE BY PARTY

Party	1948	1952	1956	1960	1964
CCF	45.9%	52.1%	42.0%	39.6%	39.9%
Liberal	34.9	41.0	34.2	35.4	42.1
Progressive-Conservative	2.1	1.4	1.0	11.9	6.5
Social Credit	11.5	4.9	22.8	13.1	0
Other	5.6	.5	0	0	.7

URBAN CENTERS:* PERCENTAGE OF VOTE BY PARTY

Party	1948	1952	1956	1960	1964	
CCF	57.2%	59.0%	49.3%	43.5%	41.8%	
Liberal	26.6	34.8	25.7	32.0	38.8	
Progressive-Conservative	8.3	2.7	2.6	15.1	19.4	
Social Credit	14.2	2.7	20.6	9.0	0	(.03)
Other	3.7	.8	1.8	.4	0	(.01)

* Incorporated areas with populations of 1000 and over.

SMALL TOWNS AND VILLAGES:* PERCENTAGE OF VOTE BY PARTY

Party	1948	1952	1956	1960	1964
CCF	40.7%	47.6%	39.2%	36.0%	38.8%
Liberal	38.0	45.0	36.8	36.8	44.7
Progressive-Conservative	2.9	1.1	1.3	13.7	14.9
Social Credit	11.1	5.1	22.8	13.5	1.6
Other	7.4	1.1	0	0	0

* Incorporated areas with populations under 1000.

As Lipset has shown, the farmers and urban workers, who both were relatively worse off than the middle class, were the main categories of voters who contributed their share of the "oversupport" that swept the CCF into office in 1944. Since occupational class was a crucial determinant of original CCF support and this variable has been found to be strongly related to voting elsewhere, the major emphasis here will be on the relationship between class, in the sense of occupation and income, and voting. Since Saskatchewan's economy is still divided into fairly distinct rural and urban sectors, the analytic section reflects this pattern and considers rural and urban change and patterns of support of rural and urban socioeconomic groups.

Along with unprecedented prolonged prosperity and increased urbanization, the occupational structure of the province has undergone considerable change in the direction of more closely approximating that of an industrial social system. These developments may have affected political interests and produced a realignment between occupation and voting.

Much sociological theory stemming from Marx and Weber[3] and empirical voting research agree that occupational differences are important determinants of political behavior for most people, because occupation is the major source of differential rewards, the most important of which is income. Within the urban social system it seems clear that everywhere workers tend to support left parties and the middle class is more likely to support conservative parties.

The emergence of the CCF as an agrarian party can be understood only in the light of provincial social and economic conditions in the 1930's. Although the independent farmers were small capitalists, their relationship to the wheat market paralleled that posited in Marxist theory between workers and capitalists. Due largely to a four-decade history of booms and busts in the wheat market, the control of income was out of the farmers' hands and economically based insecurity was severe and widespread.[4] Many farmers lost their farms in the depression, and most were on relief at one time or another; in fact, Saskatchewan had a higher percentage of its people on relief than any other Canadian province. Similar problems had led the wheat producers in adjoining Alberta and Manitoba to engage in political action on their behalf and to elect provincial governments favorable to their cause.[5] In Saskatchewan, the CCF, with its culturally acceptable socialist leadership, represented a last-ditch attempt on the part of one-crop wheat farmers to gain control over the intolerable grain market situation.[6]

In the years preceding the Second World War, Saskatchewan's population consisted of a large rural sector, a small-town and village sector made up of settlements of less than 1000 population, and a growing urban sector composed mainly of workers and the middle class.[7] In rural areas, where cooperatives and other forms of farmer self-help had existed for years, those farmers who had been high participators in existing voluntary associations were most politically current and exceeded the non-participators in CCF support. High participators were likely to be those farmers who enjoyed above-average incomes. Thus it was the relatively well-off farmers, not the poor ones, who first rallied to support the socialists.[8]

Poor farmers were reluctant to support the CCF in the 1930's. Their unwillingness to vote for the socialists has been explained in terms of social isolation and low levels of social participation, which permitted fear of change to persist and hindered the development of an economically rational (*Zweck*) orientation to politics. In 1944, however, large numbers of poor farmers swung to the CCF column, cancelling out, according to Lipset, the differences in party voting linked to economic position.

Urban blue-collar workers, who also suffered greatly in the depression, were relatively low in support for the CCF in the 1930's, possibly because of their ties to older parties and because the CCF did not offer any promise of a labor platform until 1944.[9] The fact that poorer farmers and lower-level urban blue-collar workers did support the CCF in the mid-1940's points up an interesting time-lag process in which the poorest groups turn to a radical party only after the more well-to-do and secure of their strata provide the initial mass base.

Members of the professions and businessmen were inclined to oppose the CCF largely because of their fear of and opposition to socialization. People in these categories gave below-average support to the new party before it came to power.

The small-town vote for the CCF in the 1930's and 1944 was also below the levels of support in rural farm and urban areas. Saskatchewan's towns and villages of less than 1000 serve the rural countryside as trading and service centers. The small-town occupational structure was composed predominantly of small businessmen and their employees. There were very few industries, and none important enough to employ large numbers of workers. The middle class in villages and

TABLE 2

CORRELATES OF DIFFERENTIAL SUPPORT FOR THE CCF PARTY IN SASKATCHEWAN, 1934-44*

	HIGH CCF SUPPORT		LOW CCF SUPPORT
(A) 1	Farmers, prosperous (1934, 1938) Explanation: Economic deprivation leading to hope for reform of the system in the direction of controlled markets. High political participation brings awareness of CCF's benefits and economically rational (*Zweck*) politics.	1	Farmers, less prosperous (1934, 1938) Explanation: Fear of economic loss due to change in political system. Low participation limits political currency.
(B) 1	Farmers, all levels, especially less prosperous (1944) Explanation: Same desires. Greater participation and awareness that CCF was prime political hope of farmer.		
2	Blue-collar workers (1944) Explanation: CCF adopts pro-labor stance and promises a pro-union program designed by union leaders; trade-union leaders support CCF.	2	Blue-collar workers (1934, 1938) Explanation: Traditional political loyalties, lack of backing by new party of union demands, lack of labor program.
3	Protestant religion (1934, 1938, 1944) Explanation: Correlates highly with social acceptability and high participation as functions of majority-group status.	3	Catholic religion (1934, 1938, 1944) Explanation: Opposition of the hierarchy to socialism so strong that excommunication was threatened.

| 4 | "Acceptable" ethnic identity, British Isles, German, Scandinavian (1934, 1938, 1944)
Explanation: Correlates with social acceptability and thus with high rates of participation. | 4 | French and other less acceptable ethnic identities (1934, 1938, 1944)
Explanation: Correlates with low participation and social discrimination alienating people from common action with majority-group members. |
| 5 | (A) Rural residence (1934, 1938, 1944)
Explanation: High economic importance of wheat and farming.
(B) Urban residence (1944)
Explanation: High percentage of blue collar, and CCF was clearly rising party. | 5 | (A) Small-town residence (1934, 1938, 1944)
Explanation: Middle-class resistance to socialism and lack of organization of labor in 1944.
(B) Urban residence (1934, 1938)
Explanation: White-collar resistance to socialism; blue-collar non-acceptance because of lack of labor plank. |

* Summarized from Seymour Martin Lipset, *Agrarian Socialism*, Ch. 8, pp. 198–208.

towns stood as symbols of the private profit system among cooperative stores and Wheat-Pool elevators, and they were disinclined to support the socialists.

The ecological correlates of differential CCF support in the elections of 1934, 1938, and 1944 is summarized in Table 2.

One current interest in political behavior is particularly relevant to the study of voting in Saskatchewan. This is the attempt to isolate correlates of left and right voting on a cross-national basis. Such surveys have yielded fairly consistent results. Though the unidimensionality of the left-right distinction may break down in detailed analyses, there is often enough similarity in the pattern of opinions and voting on various issues to permit classification of some groups as tending toward conservatism and others as tending toward liberalism. Since the CCF socialists were to the left of all other significant provincial parties on many issues, a left-right distinction is appropriate in Saskatchewan.[10]

TABLE 3

CORRELATES OF LEFT- AND RIGHT-WING VOTING*

Left Voting	Right Voting
Blue-collar occupations, especially non-skilled and semi-skilled categories	White-collar occupations—managers and professionals
Relatively low incomes	High incomes
Ethnic minority status	Majority-group status
Minority religious status	Majority religious status
Urban residence, especially in large cities	Rural or small-town residence

* The table summarizes the results of comparative and intranational voting studies contained in, among others, Seymour Martin Lipset, *Political Man* (Garden City, N.Y.: Anchor Books, 1963), Ch. 7; Robert E. Lane, *Political Life* (Glencoe, Ill.: The Free Press, 1959); Angus Campbell, Gerald Gurin and Warren E. Miller, *The Voter Decides* (Evanston, Ill.: Row, Peterson & Company, 1954); Paul F. Lazarsfeld, Bernard Berelson and Hazel Gaudet, *The People's Choice* (New York: Duell, Sloan & Pearce, 1944); Robert Alford, *Party and Society* (Chicago: Rand McNally & Company, 1963); and Gabriel Almond and Sidney Verba, *The Civic Culture* (Princeton: Princeton University Press, 1963).

A comparison of Tables 2 and 3 indicates that the correlates of high and low levels of support for the left wing in Saskatchewan in the 1930's and 1940's were in several respects similar to those elsewhere.[11] With the exception of relatively well-off farmers, who voted for socialists for economically rational reasons during a serious depression, and particular religious associations, the weight of the evidence supports the same relationship between class and political behavior proposed by classical "sociologists."[12]

The relationships presented in Table 2 hold true both for the prosperous postwar years and for the depression years of the 1930's and early 1940's. Robert Alford has attacked the problem of the persistence of class voting in the post-World War II prosperity in the Anglo-American nations—Great Britain, Australia, the United States, and Canada.[13] He finds that not only does the relationship between class and voting persist, but the relationship holds consistently from the midst of the depression to the prosperous years. In spite of significant, if not always even, increases in prosperity in the four Anglo-American democracies, the often predicted decline in the influence of income and occupation on politics did not materialize. "Although fluctuations in the level of class voting have occurred in the period 1936 to 1960, there is some evidence that no consistent decline has taken place."[14]

Since occupational class was a crucial determinant of original CCF support, and is found to be highly related to voting elsewhere, the major emphasis in this analysis is on the linkage between occupation strata and party support.

Rural Voting Patterns: Land Values and Crop Concentrations

The data in *Agrarian Socialism* indicate that during the rather unusual and prolonged economic deprivations of the great depression the more well-to-do farmers in Saskatchewan tended to reverse the usual tendency of the more prosperous to undersupport socialists. Class, in the sense of differences in levels of income and property, was an extremely important predictor of voting behavior on the prairies; the poorer farmers were disproportionately anti-CCF until 1944. Since some significant economic improvements have lasted over an extended period, it seems reasonable to inquire whether the past relationship between economic factors and voting continues to persist.

Logically, the possible alternative relationships between rural stratification and left-right voting seem to be reducible to three. All of the alternatives involve the assumption that voting for the CCF has continued to be an indication of left-wing support in Saskatchewan elections.[15] First, it is possible that the established relationship between high farm income and CCF support continued. This prediction assumes the tendency for voters to persist in supporting parties that have previously advanced their interests and helped them achieve tangible rewards.

On the basis of an alternative set of assumptions it is reasonable to make the exact opposite prediction. The positive relationship between income and left-wing voting in rural Saskatchewan in the 1930's is a reversal of the negative correlation found elsewhere. The conditions under which CCF support among prosperous and usually conservative farmers developed were unusual in that during the depression the moderate and right-wing parties offered no realistic policy alternatives which would benefit wheat farmers. Developments over recent years have shown this situation to be a temporary one. Given the fact that the improved market conditions of the fifties and sixties resulted only in slight part from the efforts of the CCF, and that the economic uncertainties that underlay the earlier protest were considerably relieved, it might be expected that the wealthier farmers would revert to their "normal" conservative pattern.

Both lines of argument are predicated on the assumption that political action is often viewed by segments of the electorate as a major means to achieve economic ends.

A third approach based on different assumptions is also plausible. Given that the past two decades have witnessed considerable improvement in the economic position of almost all farmers, it is possible that the relationship between income and voting preference has decreased greatly. If economic insecurities have been reduced significantly, economic-based differentiation might now be less significant in predisposing rural voters to support one party as opposed to others. Under such conditions, non-economic variables such as ethnicity and religion would remain as the primary sources of significant correlates of voting preference among the wheat farmers.

To test the plausibility of each of these approaches, the voting data for farm areas have been analyzed for four sources of difference—economic position, ethnicity, religion, and type of agricultural production. The index of economic position is the average total value of farms per farm operator, calculated for all provincial rural municipal units from census data. Data on religious preference, ethnicity, and crop differences employ the same units and come from the same source.

Since the dollar value of a farm reflects wealth in the agricultural economy in a very direct manner, and census data on total farm values available for rural municipalities are more accurate than those for most other indicators, this variable has been selected as the index of agricultural prosperity. In order to make the data comparable from one rural municipality to another, in spite of the fact that the number of farms within them differed, the total value of farms for each rural unit was divided by number of farm operators. Originally tables using 10 per cent breaking points reporting the party vote per category were tabulated, but there was so little internal variation within the upper and lower halves of the distribution that it was decided to collapse the rows and to report data only for two categories, the most and the least prosperous farm operators.

The most obvious conclusion to be drawn from Table 4 is that the positive relationship between farm prosperity and CCF support that was established before 1944 continued in 1948 only to disappear in every other election since that time. The significance of the persistence of CCF support by prosperous farmers into the late forties can be understood if one realizes that though economic conditions improved greatly by that time, relatively few felt certain that good times would continue. Fears of a postwar recession such as occurred after the First World War had not yet subsided, and in these circumstances the CCF's program still appealed to many of the more well-to-do farmers for the reasons discussed by Lipset.

The 1952 elections formed both the high point of CCF support on the farms and a turning point. Never again in the two decades following was the party to come within 10 per

TABLE 4

FARM PROSPERITY AND PARTY VOTE, 1948-64

	Economic Condition	CCF	Liberal	Progressive-Conservative	Social Credit	Other	Total Votes Cast
1948 Vote (1946 Census)	Lower half ↕ Upper half	40.0% 45.0%	30.6 31.9	.3 .6	28.1 22.5	Not Running Not Running	97411 61781
1952 Vote (1951 Census)	Lower half ↕ Upper half	52.0% 52.2%	41.4 40.7	.4 2.5	5.6 4.2	.6 .4	90938 86130
1956 Vote (1951 Census)	Lower half ↕ Upper half	41.5% 42.6%	35.2 33.2	.3 1.8	23.0 22.4	Not Running Not Running	83406 77308
1960 Vote (1961 Census)	Lower half ↕ Upper half	39.4% 40.0%	34.9 36.4	11.9 11.9	13.8 11.6	(0) .1	94416 49577
1964 Vote (1961 Census)	Lower half ↕ Upper half	39.9% 40.1%	41.2 43.8	18.1 15.7	Not Running Not Running	.8 .4	91754 44858

cent of the rural vote, which it carried in 1952. Though the long-term shift away from the CCF was clearly to the advantage of the Liberals, losses sustained in 1956 and 1960 seemed to go largely to the Social Credit Party in 1956, and to Social Credit and the Conservatives in 1960.

Comparing levels of support for the CCF in 1952 with those in 1948 sheds further light on the relationship between farm wealth and voting behavior. In 1952 farmers both rich and poor gave about the same amount of support to the government. This meant that the CCF gained disproportionately among the less well-to-do (12 per cent among the lower half as compared to 7 per cent among the upper). This dramatic increase in support among the less prosperous farmers is consistent with the tendency discussed by Lipset of the poor to respond favorably to good times, as seemed to have occurred in the 1944 election.

Three types of responses on the part of the farm segment of the provincial electorate are discernible, making it possible to distinguish three types of election since the CCF came to power in 1944. First, there is the 1952 pattern, characterized by very low levels of third-party voting. In a more or less straight two-party race, the CCF won decisively over the Liberals. Second, in 1948, 1956, and 1960, the Social Credit Party ran effective campaigns and received a large vote. Under such conditions also the CCF remained the strongest party in the rural areas. In 1964, the Social Crediters withdrew from contention, and their vote was seemingly largely distributed to the two old parties, the Conservatives and Liberals. Since by the fifties it was clear that Social Credit was the most right-wing of the four parties, it is not surprising that the Conservatives appeared to have absorbed about 70 per cent of the Social Credit support, while the Liberals seemingly captured the rest. Disregarding individual shifts to and from the CCF, it appears from Table 1 that the CCF farm support remained almost constant between 1956 and 1964, i.e., they secured about 40 per cent in the three elections, after dropping over 10 per cent between 1952 and 1956. The Liberal growth to the position of first party in rural Saskatchewan was largely a result of absorbing part of the Social Credit backing. If CCF support continues to remain constant, it may be aided in regaining its leadership position if Social Credit should again take an active political role in Saskatchewan.

The most important sociologically relevant finding reported thus far is that the positive relationship between farm prosperity and CCF support diminished significantly after 1948. Since CCF rural support prior to 1948 also correlated with crop area—predominantly wheat districts were more radical than cattle regions or those growing other crops—it seems important to analyze the effect of varying forms of agriculture on voting patterns as well. In the two decades since the midforties the rural economy of the "wheat province" has become more diversified than ever before. Greater diversification means that a higher proportion of all agriculturalists are engaged in producing crops other than wheat. One obvious question suggested by this development is whether or not the drop in CCF rural support reflected these economic changes.

The data presented in Table 5 contrast party vote for predominantly wheat-producing areas with those devoted to other crops. The index of predominance of wheat over other crops selected is the proportion of acreage in crops in each rural municipality devoted to wheat or other crops. The cutting point of 65 per cent between the wheat and non-wheat areas reflects the fact that this figure is almost exactly the mean average actually planted in wheat over the twenty-year period covered in this study.

Comparison of the wheat areas with the non-wheat areas clearly indicates that concentration on wheat continued to correlate with support for the CCF. The findings hold for every election! Wheat production has remained predictive of CCF preference long after the most serious problems of wheat producers were well on the way to being ameliorated or solved. Non-wheat districts show a relatively consistent preference for voting Conservative whenever that party secured a significant vote. With the exception of one election, 1956, Social Credit also has been disproportionately strong in districts where wheat is less significant.

The Liberal vote is the only one that seems to have changed much over the years. From 1948 to 1956, the Liberals did much better in non-wheat areas. In 1960 and 1964, however, the party gained heavily among wheat farmers.

TABLE 5

AGRICULTURAL PRODUCT AND PARTY VOTE, 1948–64

	CCF	Liberal	Progressive-Conservative	Social Credit	Other	Number Casting Ballots
1948 ELECTION						
Total Votes Cast by Party, Rural-Farm Areas	45.8%	34.9	2.1	11.5	5.7	192994
Wheat over .65	48.3%	28.6	3.8	10.7	8.6	102535
Wheat under .65	43.1%	42.0	0.2	12.4	2.3	90459
1952 ELECTION						
Total Votes Cast by Party, Rural-Farm Areas	52.1%	42.0	1.4	4.9	.5	177068
Wheat over .65	54.1%	39.3	1.8	4.0	.8	132370
Wheat under .65	46.1%	46.1	.1	7.8	Not Running	44698
1956 ELECTION						
Total Votes Cast by Party, Rural-Farm Areas	42.0%	34.3	1.0	22.7	Not Running	159193

TABLE 5 (continued)

	CCF	Liberal	Progressive-Conservative	Social Credit	Other	Number Casting Ballots
Wheat over .65	43.6%	31.06	.3	25.02	Not Running	136157
Wheat under .65	32.1%	53.3	5.4	9.2	Not Running	23036
1960 ELECTION						
Total Votes Cast by Party, Rural-Farm Areas	39.5%	35.5	11.9	13.1	.0	143993
Wheat over .65	40.7%	36.7	10.6	12.0	.0	109541
Wheat under .65	36.0%	31.3	16.0	16.6	.1	34452
1964 ELECTION						
Total Votes Cast by Party, Rural-Farm Areas	39.9%	42.0	17.3	Not Running	.7	136612
Wheat over .65	41.3%	43.9	14.1	Not Running	.7	97296
Wheat under .65	36.6%	37.3	25.4	Not Running	.52	39316

Thus far we have seen that CCF rural support varies according to crop ecology much more than according to relative economic position within the agrarian economy. The pattern described in *Agrarian Socialism* for North American rural politics during the nineteenth and twentieth centuries, a strong correlation between wheat growing and agrarian radicalism, has continued under the CCF in Saskatchewan in the 1950's and 1960's. But if other economic factors did not differentiate the rural electorate much, political values linked to ethnic and religious ties did, much as occurred between 1935 and 1944.

Rural Voting Patterns: Ethnicity and Religion

Differentials in CCF rural support by ethnic groups that persisted after the 1944 election strongly resemble those reported by Lipset for the preceding elections. One ethnic group that has consistently given disproportionate support to the CCF has been the Scandinavians.[16] This finding has held up for every provincial election held over the period of this study and the preceding one, although, of course, fluctuations in actual levels of support have occurred from election to election.

Interviews with Saskatchewan farmers of Scandinavian origin suggest that their bias in favor of the CCF derives in part from their identification of the party with the cooperative and social-democratic movements in Scandinavia. Several of them told the author of their pride at Swedish economic and social developments in recent years.[17]

After the Scandinavians, those of British background were more disposed to favor the CCF than voters from central or eastern Europe. The British have also been more disposed to back the Conservatives, another linkage of long standing. It is difficult to explain the relationship with CCF voting in other than negative terms. Most of those classified as British in the Canadian census are also Protestant, either United Church or Anglican. As such they have had an antipathy to the Liberals, who in many areas have been viewed as the party of non-Anglo-Saxons and Catholics. Hence the CCF has com-

TABLE 6

Party Voting by Ethnic Groups Constituting a Majority in at Least One Rural Municipality, 1952–64

Rural Municipalities with more than 50 per cent in one ethnic group	CCF	Liberal	Progressive-Conservative	Social Credit	Other	Total Votes Cast
1952 ELECTION						
British	55.35%	38.17	3.37	2.92	0.17	46319
French	48.36%	47.23	Not Running	3.71	0.68	2636
German	44.63%	41.76	1.14	11.46	0.98	12742
Dutch	40.05%	43.80	1.52	14.61	Not Running	1970
Scandinavian	69.02%	30.03	0.94	Not Running	Not Running	1585
Ukrainian	50.84%	42.78	Not Running	4.73	1.63	11744
Other Europeans	51.86%	44.52	Not Running	3.07	0.52	2273
Native Indians and Eskimos	57.12%	29.67	Not Running	3.56	9.64	674
1956 ELECTION						
British	44.86%	30.76	2.28	22.08	Not Running	43455

French	42.22%	26.98	Not Running	30.78	Not Running	1923
German	34.46%	37.77	0.36	27.39	Not Running	11218
Dutch	24.60%	25.12	0.52	49.76	Not Running	2500
Scandinavian	59.32%	15.63	Not Running	25.03	Not Running	1266
Ukrainian	39.04%	42.74	0.11	18.09	Not Running	11799
Other Europeans	38.07%	43.41	0.59	17.90	Not Running	1854
Native Indians and Eskimos	56.76%	30.16	Not Running	13.06	Not Running	421

1960 ELECTION

British	41.15%	32.01	14.64	12.06	0.12	32390
French	40.05%	43.96	6.49	9.48	Not Running	1540
German	30.24%	46.09	5.34	18.31	Not Running	7558
Dutch	29.18%	37.41	2.74	30.65	Not Running	1021
Scandinavian	56.25%	19.04	11.70	12.99	Not Running	1239
Ukrainian	39.45%	35.58	11.14	13.81	Not Running	8440

TABLE 6 (continued)

Rural Municipalities with more than 50 per cent in one ethnic group	CCF	Liberal	Progressive-Conservative	Social Credit	Other	Total Votes Cast
Other Europeans	36.78%	44.86	8.28	9.92	0.13	2971
Native Indians and Eskimos	36.15%	27.68	16.61	19.54	Not Running	307

	CCF	Liberal	Progressive-Conservative	Other	Total Votes Cast
		1964 ELECTION			
British	40.50%	40.35	18.95	0.18	31067
French	49.16%	46.77	2.39	1.66	1922
German	33.43%	48.82	15.01	2.72	7115
Dutch	23.35%	44.63	14.54	17.45	1203
Scandinavian	62.98%	31.20	5.81	Not Running	1067
Ukrainian	42.18%	39.71	18.09	Not Running	8351
Other Europeans	36.13%	42.16	21.44	0.25	3185
Native Indians and Eskimos	22.91%	59.72	17.36	Not Running	288

peted with the Conservatives for the support of the dominant ethnic group, Anglo-Saxon Protestants, in the rural areas. (The situation, as Lipset points out, is different in urban districts.) Scandinavians have been socially acceptable to the Anglo-Saxon majority because of the relatively small cultural differences between them.

On the lower end of the continuum of CCF support stand those reported of German and Dutch origins. Both groups have consistently undersupported the CCF, though they differed in the support given other parties. The Dutch have not only been consistently low in their support for the CCF, they have been consistently high in favoring right-wing alternatives when these have been available. As contrasted with the larger German group, whose refusal to support the CCF mainly has tended to favor the Liberals, Dutch voters have been the most inclined of all ethnic groups to oversupport the right-wing Social Credit Party.

The relative weakness of the CCF among German voters reflects, as Lipset has suggested, the ties of Catholic and non-Anglo-Saxon voters to the Liberal Party. Although the CCF seemingly could break this linkage in urban areas among working-class voters, it never was able to do so in the countryside.

The explanation of the voting patterns of Saskatchewan's Dutch farmers is that those living in the rural municipality with a Dutch majority are not really Dutch, but are Mennonites who originally left the Netherlands for Russia centuries ago to flee religious persecution. Many of them then migrated to Canada in the late nineteenth and early twentieth centuries. In Russia and Canada they remained an encapsulated, highly traditionalistic, devout minority at odds with the twentieth century. They are very anti-Communist and quite fundamentalist, beliefs that make them receptive to the appeal of the Social Credit Party with its fundamentalist leadership.

French-Canadians constitute only 6.5 per cent of the entire provincial population.[18] They form a numerical majority in only three rural municipalities out of a total of three hundred. The relatively low levels of CCF support of these three districts are to be explained not only by historic ties to the Liberals, but to an even greater extent by the nearly complete allegiance of the French to the Catholic Church. Thus religion has continued to be a major factor in resistance to the CCF for reasons suggested by Lipset for the earlier years.

Ukrainian voting is more difficult to explain. This group is a mixture of members of the Catholic and Orthodox Churches. Historically, they have been divided by their attitude to the Russian Revolution. The most consistently anti-CCF Ukrainians are probably those who most detest the Soviet Union and associate CCF socialism with Communism. It is difficult to differentiate between these groups or to account for fluctuations in support. A number of CCF leaders and members of the legislature have been drawn from the radical wing of the Ukrainians. There are some indications that the effects of Canadian public education and generational replacement have been operating to reduce the differences within the community.

The native Indian and Eskimo population, who live in the north, are generally considered to be relatively apolitical. They have shown a tendency to shift support from party to party in the two decades since the election of the CCF. Their political concerns focus on improvements in earnings and levels of living, which have been quite low. One informant, long familiar with Saskatchewan politics, expressed the opinion that their tendency to favor the CCF in the 1940's and the subsequent decrease in support for the party later reflect first a hopeful optimism about the CCF's promises to improve their living standards, followed by disillusionment over the fact that they have remained in poverty. This interpretation is consistent with the voting data.

The effects of religion on Saskatchewan voting have been discussed in earlier research and must be considered here in the effort to account for ethnic variations during the recent period. The Catholics, as has been noted, form a consistent source of opposition to the CCF. Membership in the Catholic Church has had a depressing effect on CCF support, especially since the order of Cardinal Villenueve forbidding communicants to support socialist and Communist candidates.[19] In the 1940's, anti-CCF pressures were exerted both by provincial parish priests and by administrators of Catholic social-service and educational associations. Although this formal position has changed since the CCF victory in 1944, the antipathy to socialism seemingly continues. The tiny, conservative Mennonite population, as we have seen, has also been opposed to the Socialist Party, but their numbers are so small that they have not posed a very serious threat at election time.

The CCF sought to increase support among Catholics and minority ethnic groups by nominating candidates from these groups. The data reported in Table 7, however, indicate that although the party gained in 1952, its high-point year among Catholics as among others, it never secured a majority among them.

Successive elections were to show that Catholics generally remained loyal to the Liberals and gave very limited support to the Social Credit Party, which has been accused of harboring anti-Catholic sentiments. Such prejudices were expressed by a majority of Social Credit supporters interviewed by me in Swift Current in 1962. The party has often become identified with opposition to governmental aid to church schools.

Of the two major denominations preferred by members of the Anglo-Saxon majority, the Anglican Church tends to be more identified with British culture and with local urban middle-class interests. The United Church of Canada recruits members from a wider social base and resembles the English Nonconformist churches in its emphasis on social-gospel teachings and liberal philosophy. Unfortunately, for the purpose of this analysis, the Anglicans do not form a majority in a single rural municipality.[20]

The same cannot be said of the United Church. It is the largest denomination in the province. By 1961 fully 32 per cent of the provincial population reported themselves to the Canadian census as preferring the United Church.

The voting data clearly indicate that United Church membership has been positively associated with CCF support in every election, although districts characterized by United Church majorities did resemble those dominated by other churches in fluctuating in support for the CCF. Seemingly, the aspects inherent in Nonconformism, which have biased adherents of these churches first toward the Liberal and later

TABLE 7

PARTY VOTING IN RURAL-FARM AREAS OF SASKATCHEWAN FOR
RELIGIONS REPRESENTED AS MAJORITIES IN ONE OR MORE
UNITS IN THE CENSUS, 1952–64

Rural Municipalities with a Majority of One Religious Group	CCF	Liberal	Progressive-Conservative	Social Credit	Other	Votes Cast
1952 PROVINCIAL ELECTION						
Lutheran	51.12%	37.76	Not Running	9.16	1.94	2619
Mennonite	38.24%	44.22	0.86	15.42	1.24	3462
Roman Catholic	45.35%	45.34	0.31	8.69	0.29	21926
Ukrainian Orthodox	45.73%	48.81	Not Running	5.44	Not Running	1561
United Church	55.52%	40.57	2.39	1.18	0.32	18735
1956 PROVINCIAL ELECTION						
Lutheran	39.26%	33.00	0.37	27.35	Not Running	2109
Mennonite	25.09%	27.11	0.34	47.45	Not Running	3806
Roman Catholic	35.13%	41.47	0.40	22.98	Not Running	18537
Ukrainian Orthodox	32.09%	43.46	0.13	24.30	Not Running	1477
United Church	44.74%	33.10	3.28	18.85	Not Running	19271

Rural Municipalities with a Majority of One Religious Group	CCF	Liberal	Progressive Conservative		Other	Votes Cast
Greek Orthodox	37.78%	31.10	15.30	15.70	Not Running	614
Lutheran	37.28%	40.39	8.89	13.41	Not Running	1416
Mennonite	28.81%	31.97	4.60	34.60	Not Running	3127
Roman Catholic	33.18%	47.68	7.26	11.85	Not Running	16816
Ukrainian Orthodox	35.42%	34.00	7.43	23.14	Not Running	1197
United Church	42.60%	31.66	14.77	10.77	0.18	22662

1964 PROVINCIAL ELECTION

Rural Municipalities with a Majority of One Religious Group	CCF	Liberal	Progressive Conservative	Other	Votes Cast
Greek Orthodox	36.24%	44.44	19.30	Not Running	1098
Lutheran	37.71%	39.84	22.44	Not Running	1127
Mennonite	28.99%	46.64	6.57	17.78	2980
Roman Catholic	36.91%	49.76	12.80	0.50	16309
Ukrainian Orthodox	40.90%	36.71	22.38	Not Running	1193
United Church	41.16%	41.47	17.05	0.30	20218

to the Labour Party in Britain, have operated in Saskatchewan as well.

The rural ecological findings bearing on the political behavior of the different religious groups correspond closely to the results of a 1964 questionnaire survey of the electorate of Saskatoon, the second largest city in the province. These data, reported in Table 10 below, suggest that the ecological results are reliable, since one would expect that the political effect of the religious factor would be similar in urban and rural areas.

URBAN SUPPORT OF THE CCF

Urbanization has been a relatively recent process in Saskatchewan. The attrition of economically unsuccessful farmers, consolidation of acreages by successful operators, and improved technical efficiency have created a surplus of rural emigrants seeking jobs. While many have gone to the cities of the province, others have been drawn to higher earnings and more attractive cultural advantages outside the province. As a result, Saskatchewan's population has only increased from 895,992 in 1941 to 925,181 in 1961.[21]

Saskatchewan's urban development has been dominated by the comparatively small but growing centers of Regina and Saskatoon. In 1961, Regina was slightly larger, with a population of 112,141 as compared to Saskatoon's 95,526.[22] Regina, the provincial capital, is located on major rail and highway arteries. Saskatoon, located on the Saskatchewan River, is the seat of the University of Saskatchewan and has many small and middle-sized industries. Moose Jaw and Prince Albert, the third and fourth largest cities, had populations of approximately 33,000 and 24,000 respectively in 1961, and other cities were considerably smaller.[23] Only seven other centers surpassed the 5000 population requisite for designation as a city in 1961. The remainder of the provincial urban population was scattered in numerous smaller trading and service centers.

In 1946 the distribution of Saskatchewan's population was 25.1 per cent urban, 53.3 per cent rural farm, and 21.6 per cent rural non-farm. By 1961 it had changed to 43.0 per cent urban, 32.9 per cent rural farm and 24 per cent rural non-farm.[24] The number of Saskatchewan urban residents has almost doubled since 1946, from 208,872 to 398,091 in 1961.[25] During the 1950's urban population increased at high rates, ranging from 57.2 and 79.3 per cent for Regina and Saskatoon respectively to a high of 96.4 per cent for the relatively small city of Estevan.[26] This growth contrasts sharply with the standstill in towns and villages and the decline in rural farm population.

The intercensal period between 1956 and 1961 witnessed the percentage of urban residents surpassing the percentage of those living on farms for the first time.[27] Wage income replaced farm income as the largest single source of provincial wealth in 1953.

The largest portion of these wages was earned in the urban centers in the southern part of the province, where the bulk of the population resides. Under the CCF, Saskatchewan workers have gained higher income and more fringe benefits, such as paid vacations, than ever before. Data on average weekly earnings provide a view of the extent to which Saskatchewan incomes have increased since 1946, when the average worker earned $32.15 a week. By 1961 the average had grown to $74.19 a week, an increase of almost $15 every five years.[28]

This improvement in income should have enhanced CCF support among the union members, since the CCF government strongly backed trade unions and these in turn tended to endorse the party for reelection. Although the unions sought to organize white-collar workers, they tended to fail in this effort except among government employees. The strong, positive relationship between blue-collar occupations and union membership that occurs elsewhere exists in Saskatchewan as well. In the twenty years since its first election, the CCF continued to make strong appeals to unionized labor in every campaign and won the support of the trade-union leadership each time. Several important party provincial leaders have been recruited from the ranks of trade-union leaders.

TABLE 8

PARTY VOTE PERCENTAGES IN BLUE- AND WHITE-COLLAR SOCIAL AREAS, REGINA AND SASKATOON, 1948–64*

Year	Party Social Area	REGINA					SASKATOON				
		CCF†	Liberal	Progressive-Conservative	Social Credit	Other	CCF	Liberal	Progressive-Conservative	Social Credit	Other
1948	Blue-Collar	(2) 61.7%	(1) 17.5	(1) 18.0	(2) 2.8	(0) —	(2) 60.0%	(1) 15.7	(1) 19.6	(1) 4.7	(0) —
	White-Collar	44.3%	26.4	26.7	2.6	—	45.0%	23.8	27.8	3.4	—
1952	Blue-Collar	(3) 68.3%	(3) 27.1	(1) 1.0	(3) 3.1	(1) .5	(2) 68.3%	(2) 20.6	(2) 8.5	(2) 2.6	(0) —
	White-Collar	50.7%	42.8	1.5	4.6	.4	56.4%	30.8	10.7	2.1	—
1956	Blue-Collar	(3) 56.0%	(3) 21.0	(0) —	(1) 22.7	(1) .3	(2) 60.2%	(2) 16.4	(2) 5.5	(2) 17.4	(1) .5
	White-Collar	44.8%	31.0	—	23.9	.3	52.3%	23.8	11.2	12.6	.1
1960	Blue-Collar	(4) 47.9%	(4) 24.4	(4) 10.8	(4) 16.1	(0) .8	(5) 46.8%	(5) 26.0	(3) 17.5	(3) 9.7	(0) —
	White-Collar	36.1%	34.8	17.3	11.1	.7	40.7%	33.1	19.7	6.5	—
1964	Regina East Blue-Collar	(2) 47.9%	(2) 39.5	(2) 12.6	(0) —	(0) —	(5) 41.9%	(5) 27.8	(5) 30.3	(0) —	(0) —
	White-Collar	42.8%	46.3	10.9	—	—	32.8%	46.4	21.0	—	—

Regina West				
Blue-Collar	(2) 53.7%	(2) 37.1	(1) 10	(0) —
White-Collar	42.2%	45.7	12.1	—
Regina North				
Blue-Collar	(1) 54.6%	(1) 44.6	(0) —	(1) .8
White-Collar	—	—	—	—
Regina South				
Blue-Collar	(1) —	(1) —	(0) —	(0) —
White-Collar	30.6%	69.4	—	—

* SOURCE: Raw data from Chief Electoral Officer, Province of Saskatchewan, Official Election Returns. Percentages are based on total numbers of assigned votes only. Absentee, declared, and unlocated ballots are omitted. Blue- and white-collar tracts were so labeled according to which occupational category constituted over 50 per cent of the labor force residing in the tract. The four-way occupational split in Table 7, based on clusters of tracts, yields slightly different percentages.

† Percentages are for total party vote. The number of candidates per party is shown in parentheses.

To analyze the vote of the different urban strata, the social characteristics of different census tracts in the two largest cities have been correlated with the election returns. These cities were not divided into tracts before the CCF was elected, so Lipset necessarily used a different method.

Social areas (tracts) are dichotomized according to which category of workers (blue-collar or white-collar) are in the majority (over 50 per cent) of the labor force for the appropriate census year.

The CCF had more consistent support in cities than in any other part of Saskatchewan in the 1948–64 period. Blue-collar workers gave much more support to the CCF than white-collar workers or the farm population in each of the five general elections since 1948. The blue-collar workers' districts also have supported Social Credit more than have white-collar areas. In a real sense, the CCF in Saskatchewan, as in the rest of Canada, has had its greatest appeal among manual workers.

The census data permit a greater specification of the relationship between occupational class and voting beyond the simple blue-collar-white-collar dichotomy.[29] Though laborers and related workers may wear blue collars on the job and belong to unions as do skilled craftsmen and operatives, there are important differences between the former and latter subgroups in social prestige, interest in work, and income. The upper blue-collar worker has more social prestige and economic advantages than the lower blue-collar workers and consequently may be less disposed to support the CCF.

Although skilled workers are often better paid and may even have higher prestige than the lower levels of the white-collar labor force, the former seemingly remain more disposed to back leftist politics. They are more likely to be union members than white-collar workers, and therefore are more politically subject to the unions' influence. They may also be more likely than white-collar workers to socialize with other blue-collar workers who have pro-CCF attitudes. Furthermore, skilled blue-collar workers are more often likely to have risen from the ranks of the lower blue-collar group than are white-collar workers. For these reasons, one would expect that upper blue-collar tracts will continue to cast more

TABLE 9

PARTY VOTE IN PERCENTAGES BY OCCUPATIONAL LEVEL, REGINA AND SASKATOON, 1948–64*

Year	Party	REGINA				
		CCF	Liberal	Progressive-Conservative	Social Credit	Other
	Occupational Level					
1948		(2)	(1)	(1)	(2)	(0)
	Low Blue-Collar	61.9%	17.4	18.0	2.7	—
	High Blue-Collar	47.9%	19.4	19.6	3.1	—
	Low White-Collar	43.9%	26.7	27.3	2.1	—
	High White-Collar	—	—	—	—	—
1952		(3)	(3)	(1)	(3)	(1)
	Low Blue-Collar	66.9%	28.0	.5	3.9	.5
	High Blue-Collar	64.8%	30.2	1.3	3.2	.5
	Low White-Collar	47.6%	44.8	1.6	5.6	.4
	High White-Collar	44.1%	51.3	2.0	2.3	.3
1956		(3)	(3)	(0)	(1)	(1)
	Low Blue-Collar	55.7%	19.4	—	24.5	.4
	High Blue-Collar	52.4%	24.3	—	23.0	.3
	Low White-Collar	45.1%	32.2	—	22.4	.3
	High White-Collar	40.6%	34.2	—	25.1	.1
1960		(4)	(4)	(4)	(4)	(3)
	Low Blue-Collar	48.9%	23.1	10.0	18.0	—
	High Blue-Collar	47.7%	25.9	11.7	14.7	—
	Low White-Collar	35.6%	35.5	17.8	11.1	—

TABLE 9 (continued)

Year	Party / Occupational Level	CCF	Liberal	Progressive-Conservative	Social Credit	Other
	High White-Collar	39.1%	33.6	16.0	11.3	—
1964	*Regina East*					
	Low Blue-Collar	(2) 45.6%	(2) 42.7	(2) 11.7	(0)	(0)
	High Blue-Collar	50.7%	35.8	13.5	—	—
	Low White-Collar	48.9%	38.6	12.5	—	—
	High White-Collar	—	—	—	—	—
	Regina West					
	Low Blue-Collar	(2) 54.4%	(2) 32.7	(1) 12.9	(0)	(0)
	High Blue-Collar	49.3%	38.1	12.6	—	—
	Low White-Collar	41.5%	46.5	12.0	—	—
	High White-Collar	44.1%	43.8	12.1	—	—
	Regina North					
	Low Blue-Collar	(1) 54.4%	(1) 44.8	(0) —	(0)	(1)
	High Blue-Collar	55.5%	44.0	—	—	.8
	Low White-Collar	—	—	—	—	.5
	High White-Collar	—	—	—	—	—
	Regina South					
	Low Blue-Collar	(1) —	(1) —	(0) —	(0)	(0)
	High Blue-Collar	—	—	—	—	—
	Low White-Collar	—	—	—	—	—
	High White-Collar	30.6%	69.4	—	—	—

SASKATOON

Year		(2)	(1)	(1)	(1)	(0)
1948	Low Blue-Collar	61.4%	16.3	17.2	5.1	—
	High Blue-Collar	60.5%	14.5	21.1	3.9	—
	Low White-Collar	51.8%	19.3	22.7	6.2	—
	High White-Collar	30.0%	31.8	33.7	4.5	—

Year		(2)	(2)	(2)	(2)	(0)
1952	Low Blue-Collar	67.1%	21.6	8.7	2.6	—
	High Blue-Collar	69.0%	19.6	8.3	3.1	—
	Low White-Collar	56.8%	30.4	11.2	1.5	—
	High White-Collar	55.0%	32.0	10.6	2.4	—

Year		(2)	(2)	(2)	(2)	(1)
1956	Low Blue-Collar	60.9%	16.2	4.4	18.5	—
	High Blue-Collar	59.0%	18.0	7.8	15.2	—
	Low White-Collar	54.7%	22.0	11.7	11.5	—
	High White-Collar	48.7%	25.1	13.4	12.8	—

Year		(3)	(3)	(3)	(3)	(0)
1960	Low Blue-Collar	55.0%	18.3	15.9	10.8	—
	High Blue-Collar	41.9%	29.0	12.5	11.5	—
	Low White-Collar	45.0%	29.1	18.8	7.1	—
	High White-Collar	36.6%	37.8	19.4	6.2	—

Year		(5)	(5)	(5)	(0)	(0)
1964	Low Blue-Collar	49.3%	18.6	32.1	—	—
	High Blue-Collar	41.3%	27.0	31.7	—	—
	Low White-Collar	36.1%	37.4	26.5	—	—
	High White-Collar	33.0%	46.4	20.6	—	—

* SOURCE: Raw data from Chief Electoral Officer, Province of Saskatchewan, Official Election Returns, and Dominion Bureau of Statistics, Census of Canada, Regina, Saskatoon, 1946, 1951, 1961, Ottawa.

CCF votes than lower white-collar tracts. The logic of a class-status analysis would clearly lead us to expect that the order of support for the CCF should be lower blue-collar, upper blue-collar, lower white-collar, and upper white-collar tracts.[30]

With a few exceptions, the data clearly support the expected rank order of preference for the CCF. Most reversals of anticipated rank order involve very small differences. These results indicate that class factors are of major importance in affecting the votes of urban Saskatchewan.

The behavior of upper white-collar voters in Regina is particularly noteworthy in this respect. The upper white-collar group supported the CCF to a somewhat greater extent than might be expected, particularly in Regina West in 1964, where over 40 per cent voted CCF, as contrasted to 30 per cent in Regina South. The explanation for the exceptional pattern in Regina West may lie in part in the concentration of civil servants in the district. Presumably, by the sixties many of these were pro-CCF and remained loyal to the government. Thus it would appear that the CCF retained a strong lead among blue-collar workers, but got less than a third of the white-collar vote.

The findings based on ecological data are reinforced by the results of a questionnaire survey of the Saskatoon electorate in the 1964 provincial and federal elections. The study indicates that CCF provincial supporters there were disproportionately to be found among males; older people (sixty-five plus); transportation, unskilled, skilled, and service workers (in that order); Presbyterians, United Church and Lutheran church members. Conversely, the CCF was very weak among those employed in managerial and sales occupations. Catholics, Mennonites, and Anglicans were the religious denominations most opposed to the party.

These results, presented in Table 10, are very similar to findings based on ecological data. Other data in the survey indicate that CCF provincial voters who defect from the party

SOURCE: Adapted from John C. Courtney and David E. Smith, "Voting in a Provincial General Election and a Federal By-Election: A Constituency Study of Saskatoon City," *Canadian Journal of Economics and Political Science,* 32 (1966), pp. 348–49.

TABLE 10

The Social Basis of Party Choice, City of Saskatoon—
1964 Provincial Election Vote Preference

	CCF-NDP	Liberal	Progressive-Conservative	N
Sex				
Male	41.6%	41.5	16.9	(526)
Female	35.6%	40.8	23.6	(549)
Age				
21–24	35.8%	48.5	15.7	(95)
25–34	34.5%	42.4	23.1	(242)
35–44	35.3%	43.7	21.0	(230)
45–54	39.0%	41.1	19.9	(198)
55–64	43.3%	39.3	17.4	(128)
65 plus	45.4%	34.3	20.3	(182)
Occupation				
Managerial	16.9%	63.0	20.1	(65)
Professional	35.3%	50.8	13.9	(130)
Clerical	45.0%	38.1	16.9	(89)
Sales	23.3%	55.0	21.7	(60)
Craftsman	52.2%	25.0	22.8	(44)
Transportation	68.2%	13.6	18.2	(22)
Laborer	58.4%	20.0	21.6	(60)
Servile	49.1%	33.4	17.5	(63)
Farmer	40.0%	46.7	13.3	(15)
Retired	45.8%	31.3	22.9	(96)
Homemaker	33.2%	42.9	23.9	(365)
Religion				
United Church	44.0%	40.6	15.4	(332)
Presbyterian	57.0%	21.5	21.5	(28)
Lutheran	47.3%	28.5	26.2	(42)
Mennonite	23.0%	42.4	34.6	(26)
Baptist	20.0%	40.0	40.0	(15)
Pentecostal	0.0%	80.0	20.0	(5)
Anglican	30.5%	39.7	29.8	(121)
Greek Orthodox	28.5%	42.9	28.6	(14)
Ukrainian Orthodox	40.0%	30.0	30.0	(10)
Roman Catholic	27.1%	58.6	14.3	(203)
Jewish	11.1%	88.9	0.0	(9)
Education				
Elementary 1–4	50.1%	24.9	25.0	(16)
Elementary 5–8	45.8%	27.4	26.8	(205)
H.S. 9–10	41.3%	31.1	27.6	(196)
H.S. 11–12	36.3%	45.9	17.8	(342)
Univ. 13–14	28.3%	56.8	14.9	(67)
Univ. 15–16	36.0%	60.0	4.0	(100)
Postgrad. 16+	39.4%	51.5	9.1	(33)

federally tend to shift to the Conservatives. As the ecological data suggest, both are disproportionately based on Protestants of British ancestry.

VOTING IN SMALL TOWNS AND VILLAGES

In the 1930's and 1940's CCF support was lower in small towns and villages than in the rural farm areas or urban centers.[31] In 1944 for instance, small towns gave only 38.8 per cent of their votes to the CCF, while rural farm areas gave 58.1 per cent and large cities ranged upward from 50 per cent.[32] The conservatism of the small towns presumably reflected the domination of these communities by merchants and independent professionals.

During the two post-World War II decades, Saskatchewan's small-town and village population remained relatively stable compared to the changing rural farm areas and large urban centers. While the population of farm areas decreased dramatically from 1941 to 1961 and large urban centers grew rapidly, the proportion of residents in small towns and villages increased only slightly, from 21.7 per cent of the 1941 provincial population to 24.0 per cent in 1961.[33]

The Canadian census does not report occupational data for towns and villages under 1000, so it is not possible for us to analyze electoral returns according to an occupational breakdown. It is clear, however, that these communities contain a limited occupational structure—small-town businessmen and professionals, blue-collar and lower white-collar workers, and resident farmers living near their acreages.[34] The major change since 1944 appears to have been an increase in the proportion of resident farmers. Since industrialization has not had a significant impact on most small towns and villages, occupational changes among non-farming residents have not been dramatic.

A comparative historical treatment of small-town voting patterns is difficult, since increasing numbers of non-resident farmers have been casting their votes in the towns near their farms because of the consolidation of rural polls. As a result, the number of votes cast in small centers has often been in rather obvious disproportion to, and in some cases in excess of, their adult census population.

Small-town party voting proportions are reported in Table 1 for 1948–64. The peaks and declines in CCF support in small towns coincide with those in urban and rural areas.

Comparison of the small-town vote with rural and urban returns reveals that the former have continued to lag behind both other sectors with respect to CCF support. At the CCF's peak of popularity, in 1952, when the party drew over 52 per cent of farmers' votes and almost 60 per cent in large urban centers, small-town voters gave the party 47.6 per cent of their votes. Small towns have ranked last in CCF support and first in Liberal support in every election. In 1960, the Liberals actually won a slightly higher percentage of votes in towns and villages than did the CCF, the first time that party achieved a lead in one of the three sectors since the depression. In 1964, the Liberals led the CCF by 5 per cent in the small towns.

Small-town support for the Conservatives from 1948 through 1956 paralleled that in rural farm areas. The party was very weak in both. In the campaigns of 1960 and 1964, Conservatives attempted to redefine their role in the provincial political struggle. They hoped, in the event of a CCF defeat, to replace that party as the "natural opposition" to the Liberals. They have been more successful in rebuilding their provincial strength in the cities and small towns than in the farm districts. Social Credit support in small towns has closely resembled their farm voting pattern in the twenty-year period.

Conclusions

This detailed look at the variations among different groups of Saskatchewan voters since 1948 points up a number of similarities, as well as important differences, with the pattern of CCF support reported by Lipset for the period during which the party was rising to power. The linkage between the wheat economy and agrarian radicalism clearly continues. Although CCF support has declined in all rural sectors, particularly as compared with its zenith in 1952, those districts that have continued to concentrate on raising wheat have given the party a higher vote than those in which other forms of agriculture play a significant role. Except for the 1948 election, however, the pattern of the more well-to-do farm districts voting more heavily for the CCF no longer holds true.

Differences in voting behavior associated with ethnic and religious variations have persisted in Saskatchewan during the 1950's and 1960's in more or less the same fashion as reported for the earlier period. Seemingly, the ties between Liberalism and Catholicism are still meaningful, as are those between United Church affiliation and CCF support. Although the absence of geographical concentrations of Anglicans prevents a detailed ecological analysis of their voting behavior, a variety of impressionistic evidence, as well as scattered statistical data, indicates that the Conservatives have continued to draw disproportionately from the Saskatchewan members of the Church of England.

Seemingly, the most consistent source of opposition to the CCF has been the business and professional strata of the small towns and the cities. The CCF's greatest loss in 1964 was in the Regina South constituency, where its candidate was defeated in a two-party race by a margin of seven to three. Census-tract data reveal that the tract in which the constituency is located (tract 8) is unique in respect to two variables, which seem to account for its voting response. The tract has the highest concentration of managers, professionals, and technical workers of either city. Forty-three per cent of its labor force is included in the upper white-collar category, which is almost precisely double the city average of 22 per cent. Furthermore, residents of the tract enjoyed the highest average income of the two cities. The tract average of $5640 exceeded the second highest tract by more than $1350.[35] To the extent that this result can be generalized, high-level occupation and income probably are most effective in precipitating adverse voting reaction to measures held to be socialistic where these characteristics are highly concentrated and mutually reinforcing.

Although white-collar employees have consistently cast a smaller proportion of the vote for the CCF than have blue-collar workers, it is important to note that the party has consistently retained a large following among non-manual workers. To some extent, this support may be linked to the strength of the United Church within this stratum. It may also reflect the appeal to the white collars as employees of welfare-state measures, such as the various hospitalization plans, medicare, compulsory government automobile insurance, and increased financial support for higher levels of public education. Many younger white-collar workers are the children of farmers and blue-collar workers with traditional family ties to the CCF. Seemingly, the struggles over medicare did not alienate any considerable body of white-collar support.

The most reliable body of CCF supporters in Saskatchewan are clearly the manual workers, many of whom belong to trade unions. In a real sense, the trends in Saskatchewan parallel those in Canada generally, as far as the CCF-NDP is concerned. In general, the national party has lost its ability to elect members of the Canadian House of Commons from rural districts. Almost all the CCF seats across Canada are in urban or mining districts. The party in eastern Canada, as well as in British Columbia, has in large measure taken on the coloration of a labor party, drawing considerable support from the trade-union movement. Although it continues to draw substantial farm backing in provincial elections in Saskatchewan, it no longer can elect federal M.P.'s there either.

The CCF experience in postwar Saskatchewan is an example of the adaption of democratic socialism to society and of society to democratic socialism. The party gained political power as the long-hoped-for means to a solution of serious economic problems. In 1944, the CCF appeared to offer the Saskatchewan voters their best hope for new prosperity in the postwar world. Since the replacement of the Liberals was achieved in an orderly and legal manner, the CCF's election clearly was not a revolution in any sociologically or politically meaningful sense of the term. The CCF story in Saskatchewan is an example of the ability of Canadian (Anglo-American) democracy to absorb, sustain, and utilize dissonant ideologies once they have been adapted to social and economic realities.

The political goals and eventual party channeling of this unrest reflected democratic realities, norms, and values, as well as social and economic realities. Unlike North American workers, Saskatchewan's farmers had the opportunity to organize a political party of their own at the grass roots level and did so, and then succeeded, despite several successive electoral defeats in the 1930's, to elect their own party. Eventually, Saskatchewan's urban workers joined to obtain economic benefits through legislation by a party favorable to their interests.

In spite of crucial differences on an abstract level, some parallels can be perceived between the wheat farmers and Marx's workers. These parallels of social process and collective behavior occurred in spite of differences in occupation, ownership of property, and the acceptance of democratic institutions that provided possible access to the power structure. Wheat farmers produced a product, but on their own land and with their own (or borrowed) capital. They were often subject to severe economic crises and deprivation. As a result of their situation, communication among farmers in search of a solution increased, they were aroused by their leaders, and political group consciousness did develop.

The CCF experience reveals a set of conditions under which a socialist party has been able to succeed in a large political unit in North America. In spite of the shift from economic deprivation to prosperity, culturally acceptable forms of socialism have been able to fill a political vacuum and retain considerable public popularity. The possibility has been maximized in Saskatchewan by a government that has been effective and has not transcended the political norms. Given the decline in agrarian radicalism as the economic insecurities in the position of farmers are reduced with federal-government guaranteed prices and other forms of assistance, the chances for a viable socialism in Saskatchewan and Canada as a whole depend increasingly on the extent to which it can appeal to urban employees, both blue-collar and white-collar. The potential for agrarian radicalism as a base for mass political action has also declined steadily with the drastic reduction in the proportion of farmers among the electorate.

In the mid-1960's, a strong fear of all forms of socialism exists in many quarters in the United States and in parts of Canada. For many people, this fear may have been generalized from their anxiety about and aversion to Communism, with which different types of socialism are often confused. Given this generalized fear, it is understandable that "creeping socialism" has become a meaningful political symbol, one that is used to oppose big and expanding centralized government. Interestingly, for a movement with Populist roots such as the CCF, current forms of anti-socialism reflect some of the same fears of centralized control that formed one important basis of the earlier Populist movement.

Recognition that the very term socialism has negative connotations to many North Americans who favor centralized planning, government guarantees of farm prices, state medicine, and other welfare-state measures, led the CCF leaders nationally to reorganize their party in 1961, and change its name to the New Democratic Party. This change is, perhaps, the culmination of the process described by Lipset in which the CCF has come to terms with its society.

Although the CCF-NDP has lost power in Saskatchewan, it has clearly not been eliminated as a political force, either in the province or nationally. Provincially, it remains the official opposition, and has, in fact, not lost popular support as compared to its vote in the 1960 elections. The main cause of its defeat in 1964 was not increased opposition to the government, but rather a regrouping of anti-CCF votes behind the Liberal Party. This increased unification of opposition voting may have been an outcome of the medicare fight, which brought together Liberals, Conservatives, and Social Crediters in a common cause. If this is so, the reign of the Saskatchewan Liberals may be short-lived, since the pressures of competitive politics find the other opposition parties in strong resistance to the Liberals.

In the long run, however, the principal allies of the CCF are the allied processes of industrialization and urbanization. As these develop in the future, the number of potential working-class supporters of the CCF-NDP may increase. Whether or not this potential is converted into actual figures in the party column depends partly on economic conditions, partly on the labor policies of other parties, and partly on factors difficult to predict at present. On the known side are the continued allegiance of trade-union leaders to the party and their ability to convince members that the CCF-NDP is their most reasonable political choice.

Both of these conditions are rather recent experiences in the Canadian prairies, although they have been relatively well developed in parts of eastern Canada and in British Columbia. The crucial point in the future of class politics in the prairie provinces will come when the contest for the support of the increasing labor stratum is resolved.

NOTES

1. Saskatchewan Economic Advisory and Planning Board, *Saskatchewan Economic Review,* 12 (March 1958), p. 4, and 18 (March 1964), p. 5.

2. Regina *Leader-Post*, May 23, 1952. Cartoon by Charles E. Bell.

3. Karl Marx and Friedrich Engels, "Manifesto of the Communist Party," *Marx and Engels: Basic Writings in Politics and Philosophy* ed. Lewis Feuer (Garden City, N.Y.: Anchor Books, 1959), pp. 1–41. Max Weber, "Class, Status, and Party," *Max Weber: Essays in Sociology* trans. and ed. Hans H. Gerth and C. Wright Mills (New York: Oxford University Press, 1946), pp. 180–95.

4. Paul F. Sharp, *The Agrarian Revolt in Western Canada* (Minneapolis: University of Minnesota Press, 1948).

5. For Alberta see John A. Irving, *The Social Credit Movement in Alberta* (Toronto: University of Toronto Press, 1959). For Manitoba see M. S. Donnelly, *The Government of Manitoba* (Toronto: University of Toronto Press, 1963).

6. Seymour Martin Lipset, *Agrarian Socialism.*

7. Technically, villages may be erected to towns when a 500 population is reached. Towns become cities when they reach 5000. All places of 1000 or more population are categorized as urban. These categories are used both by the Canadian census and the provincial government.

8. Lipset, *op. cit.,* pp. 201–4.

9. *Ibid.,* Ch. 8.

10. Robert Alford, *Party and Society* (Chicago: Rand McNally & Company, 1963), classified the CCF-NDP (New Democratic Party) as a social-democratic-left party in Table 1–1.

11. The relatively consistent cross-national trends in the relationship between social variables and vote have important implications for the cultural, relativistic approach to comparative social structure. These findings and those summarized by Inkeles and Rossi, "National Comparisons of Occupational Prestige," *American Journal of Sociology,* 65 (1956), pp. 329–39, indicating that occupational prestige hierarchies are very similar from one industrialized nation to another, lead away from a relativistic view of industrial societies. An explanation emphasizing the effects of the characteristic social structure of industrialism rather than culturally unique values as determinants is suggested. The exact reason this is so remains an intriguing problem for future research. Undoubtedly certain structural regularities and opportunity structures create pressures on the family and hence on the socialization process. Perhaps meaningful research might develop along the lines established by David McClelland in *The Achieving Society* (Princeton: D. Van Nostrand Company, Inc., 1961).

12. The quotation marks indicate the author's unwillingness to claim for sociology important thinkers who did not identify themselves with such.

13. Alford, *op. cit.,* Chs. 9 and 10. The study involves the secondary analysis of political surveys.

14. *Ibid.,* p. 225. This finding, that class persists as a correlate of right-left voting, may be interpreted by Marxians as supporting the strength of economic differences, since they hold up as predictors of political behavior even when the radical differences of which Marx spoke have diminished. On the other hand, this raises the question of whether economic differences should still predict political behavior when blue-collar workers (the proletariat) are relatively well-off. In these circumstances, what are they protesting? Marxists may have answered that they are protesting alienating conditions of life and work. Those lower white-collar and certainly blue-collar workers who would, for example, vote Republican in the United States, are considered to exemplify false consciousness from this point of view. Whether or not the latter argument is correct, it is difficult to convincingly explain why economic conditions make no more difference in depressions than in prosperity.

15. It may be claimed that the support for the Communists was the "true" left-wing response, but the party's proportion of the total vote has been so small as to be infinitesimal.

16. We have eliminated ethnic groups so small as to constitute less than 2 per cent of the entire provincial population, and those with no majorities in any rural municipalities. The term ethnic

group is defined in terms of national origin by the Canadian census, except for Jews, and native Indians and Eskimos.

17. Interviews conducted in Swift Current, Saskatchewan, July 1962.

18. Dominion Bureau of Statistics, *1961 Census of Canada, Bulletin SP-2*, inside front cover (no pagination).

19. Lipset, *Agrarian Socialism*, pp. 208–11.

20. Anglican membership in Saskatchewan was 95,476 or 11.5 per cent in 1951 and 94,593 or 10.2 per cent in 1961. Dominion Bureau of Statistics, *1951 Census of Canada*, Table 41, p. 65, and *1961 Census of Canada, Bulletin SP-3*, p. 11.

21. *Saskatchewan Economic Review*, 18 (March 1964), Table 1, p. 3.

22. *Ibid.*, Table 5, p. 4.

23. *Ibid.*

24. *Ibid.*, Table 4, p. 3. Calculated from table.

25. *Saskatchewan Economic Review*, 12 (March 1958), Table 4, p. 3. Note to Table 4: "The 1956 definition (of urban places) specified that all cities, towns and villages of 1000 and over, whether incorporated or unincorporated, as well as all parts of census metropolitan areas and other major urban areas are classified as urban. The difference from 1951 is that the fringe parts of other major urban areas were included with the rural. 1946 figures given above are according to the 1951 definition." Cities have 5000 as their lower size limit.

26. *Saskatchewan Economic Review*, 18 (March 1964), Table 5, p. 4. Calculated from table.

27. *Ibid.*, Table 4, p. 3.

28. *Saskatchewan Economic Review*, 12 (March 1958), Table 16, p. 6, and 18 (March 1964), Table 8, p. 4. The data refer to firms with fifteen or more employees.

29. The occupational categories used in the four-way split were as follows:

1946, 1951 categories

Upper Blue-Collar: manufacturing and mechanical, construction, transportation and communication

Lower Blue-Collar: primary, service, laborers

Upper White-Collar: proprietor and managerial, professional and technical

Lower White-Collar: clerical, commercial and financial

(The data on occupations for 1951 were used for 1956 vote analysis since no occupation census was taken in that year.)

1961 categories

Upper Blue-Collar: crafts, transportation and communication

Lower Blue-Collar: laborers, primary, service and recreation

Upper White-Collar: proprietor and managerial, professional and technical

Lower White-Collar: clerical, commercial and financial

30. Survey data were not available to permit precise testing of

the hypothesis of differential support for the CCF in the four-category breakdown. An approach was devised whereby tracts were classified by the percentage distribution of their labor force in each of the four categories in the hope that some insight could be gained into patterns of relationships. In order to be included in the same group, tracts could not have intraclass differences of more than 7 per cent of the cell values in any category. This type of classification produced three of four groups of tracts that differed from each other in their occupational composition.

31. The category of small towns and villages falls within the Canadian census category of rural non-farm and refers to the many towns and villages of less than 1000 that dot the Saskatchewan countryside.

32. Lipset, *Agrarian Socialism,* p. 198 *et passim*. Also, inspection of Official Election Returns, Saskatchewan Provincial Election, 1944.

33. *Saskatchewan Economic Review,* 18 (March 1964), Table 4, p. 3. Calculated from table.

34. I am grateful in this and other matters for the generous assistance of Dr. John W. Bennett, Mr. Charles Thomas, Mrs. Sena Kohl, Mr. Carl Meilicke, Dr. Norman Ward, Dr. Vernon Fowke, and Mr. Stephen Levitas.

35. Dominion Bureau of Statistics, *1961 Census of Canada* (Regina: Census Tracts), p. 7.

INDEX

ANCHOR BOOKS

SOCIOLOGY

Sociology (continued)

Sociology (continued)

ANCHOR BOOKS

GOVERNMENT AND POLITICAL SCIENCE

Government and Political Science (continued)